The American International
Pictures Video Guide

The American International Pictures Video Guide

GARY A. SMITH

Foreword by Mark McGee

McFarland & Company, Inc., Publishers
Jefferson, North Carolina

ALSO BY GARY A. SMITH

Vampire Films of the 1970s: Dracula to Blaculaand Every Fang Between (2017)

Epic Films: Casts, Credits and Commentary on More Than 350 Historical Spectacle Movies, 2d ed. (2004; paperback 2009)

Uneasy Dreams: The Golden Age of British Horror Films, 1956–1976 (2000; paperback 2006)

Frontispiece: Samuel Z. Arkoff and James H. Nicholson

The present work is a reprint of the illustrated case bound edition of The American International Pictures Video Guide, *first published in 2009 by McFarland.*

LIBRARY OF CONGRESS CATALOGUING-IN-PUBLICATION DATA

Smith, Gary A.
The American International Pictures video guide /
Gary A. Smith ; foreword by Mark McGee.
p.   cm.
Includes bibliographical references and index.
ISBN 978-1-4766-8519-9
softcover: 50# alkaline paper ∞

1. American International Pictures (Firm)—Catalogs.
2. Motion pictures—United States—Catalogs.
3. American International Pictures (Firm)—History.
I. Title.
PN1999.A6S65   2021
791.430973—dc22   2008055592

BRITISH LIBRARY CATALOGUING DATA ARE AVAILABLE

© 2021 Gary A. Smith. All rights reserved

No part of this book may be reproduced or transmitted in any form or by any means, electronic or mechanical, including photocopying or recording, or by any information storage and retrieval system, without permission in writing from the publisher.

On the cover: Poster for *Dragstrip Girl* (1957)
Photofest; © American International Pictures

Printed in the United States of America

*McFarland & Company, Inc., Publishers
Box 611, Jefferson, North Carolina 28640
www.mcfarlandpub.com*

Dedicated to the memory of Tippi,
1988–2008

Acknowledgments

Heartfelt thanks to my dear friends Mark McGee,
Lucy Chase Williams, Howard Mandlebaum at Photofest,
and Mike Mariano. And, most important of all,
special thanks to my partner Michael Hirschbein
for his love and encouragement.

Table of Contents

Acknowledgments vi
Foreword by Mark McGee 1
Introduction 3

THE FILMS 9

Appendix 1: American International Television 175
Appendix 2: The Unfilmed AIP 185
Appendix 3: Prepackaged Features 191
Appendix 4: Title Changes 195
Appendix 5: AIP Comic Books and Paperback Novel Tie-Ins 198
Bibliography 201
Index 203

Foreword

I have been waiting for someone to write this book for a long time, and I was delighted that Gary Smith was the one to finally do it. His wonderful *Epic Films* was not only great fun but was most helpful to me when I was writing my own book on American International. That book was a history of the company, and this one is a history of their product. It's a perfect companion piece, written by someone who loves and knows his subject. In other words, he's done his homework. As ridiculous and as impossible as it sounds, he has actually seen each and every film he writes about from start to finish, often more than once! If there's more than one version of the same title, he's seen them both. Night after night, stone cold sober and for months on end he's been watching these pictures and recording his thoughts. And as anyone could have told him (and he was warned many times, so don't feel too sorry for him), it is my unhappy duty to report that it finally took its toll. It was, I believe, either *Dragstrip Girl* or *She-Gods of Shark Reef* that left him in a state of catatonic shock, and Gary is now in a home for the criminally insane. Better him than you, right?

Mark McGee
January 2009
Los Angeles

Mark McGee is the author of *Faster and Furiouser: The Revised and Fattened Fable of American International Pictures* (McFarland, 1996).

Introduction

"Since its shoestring inception in 1954, American International Pictures has brought forth one unforgettable title—*I Was a Teenage Werewolf*—and some 180 forgettable, trivial, mindless and relatively innocent entertainments like *I Was a Teenage Frankenstein*, *House of Usher*, *How to Stuff a Wild Bikini*, *Bikini Beach*, *Muscle Beach Party*, and *Ski Party*. None of these atrocities sounds innocent, but they were" (*Newsweek*, August 1966).

"American International Pictures": for a generation of baby boomers, the frequently changing logo on the front of a film usually elicited one of two responses: a shout of joy in anticipation of the outlandish experience

The American International logo

about to unfold on the screen or a groan of agony at the prospect of yet another cheesy lowbrow production. It all depended on your point of view ... and it still does.

The story of AIP has often been told, most notably in Mark McGee's book *Fast and Furious: The Story of American International Pictures*. In short, AIP was the brainchild of two men: James H. Nicholson and Samuel Z. Arkoff. Nicholson was the general sales manager for Realart Pictures. Arkoff was a lawyer whose client, producer Alex Gordon, wanted to get one of his pictures distributed through Realart. Sam met Jim and, as they say, the rest is history. The two men formed American Releasing Corporation in 1954 with Nicholson as president and Arkoff as vice president. The first film they picked up for distribution was *The Fast and the Furious* (1954), produced by a young man named Roger Corman. The film was successful enough to encourage Nicholson and Arkoff to plan eight features, the first of which, *Five Guns West* (1955), marked Corman's directorial debut. He would continue to work with AIP for the next fifteen years, directing some of their most memorable movies.

On March 20, 1955, Nicholson addressed the members of Northern Central Allied Independent Exhibitors at their annual convention in Pittsburgh. In his speech he discussed the formation of American Releasing Corporation and the success of *The Fast and the Furious*. Their second film, *Five Guns West*, was just about to be released and their third picture, *The Beast with a Million Eyes* was going to start shooting the following week. In May they would begin filming *Apache Woman*. He went on to say: "Later in the year we will release *One Mile Below*, *Jungle Queen*, *Johnny Big Gun*, and *Day the World Ended* ... all pictures which the Exhibitor faction of American Releasing will book with the feeling that they will make a profit at the box office."

Nicholson was the idea man. He came up with a title, commissioned a poster to be made, and sent the artwork out to exhibitors before the filming had even started. This way, if there was no interest, there would be no movie. ARC's first sci-fi-horror movie, *The Beast with a Million Eyes* (1955), was developed using this strategy. Theatre owners may have been disappointed that the many-eyed beast pictured on the poster somehow never made it into the film but the movie earned a respectable amount of money nevertheless. Nicholson and Arkoff soon realized that single features were not going to be as profitable for them as pre-packaged double bills. Their first double feature was to be *Day the World Ended* and *The Phantom from 10,000 Leagues*. The screenplays for both were written by Sam Arkoff's brother-in-law Lou Rusoff. ARC put most of their resources into *Day the World Ended*, directed by Roger Corman in a widescreen process called SuperScope. They had also planned to make the picture in color but the budget wouldn't allow it. With little money left over to finance the co-feature, Nicholson and Arkoff entrusted the making of *The Phantom from 10,000 Leagues* to brothers Jack and Dan Milner. The combo opened in January 1956 to huge box office returns. A month after its opening, ARC had to increase their regular print order by 100 to keep up with the bookings they had contracted.

Producer Herman Cohen at the entrance to Ziv Studios, where an "American International Studios" sign has been temporarily erected for use in scenes in Cohen's *How to Make a Monster*.

In March 1956, Jim and Sam decided to give ARC the more expansive name of American International Pictures. They continued to use the same formula which had become so successful for them. Once again Nicholson addressed the Exhibitors, saying: "Most of us here at American International are former exhibitors ... in fact, some of us still are. We know there has been talk about more product ... but with each announcement less pictures are actually made. We are not talking ... we are *making* pictures ... pictures which we feel have merit at the box office and can produce a profit for the exhibitor. This is our policy."

As it was, most of these films were long on imagination but short on cash and aimed at the movie-going youth market. The first of their teenage horror pictures was *I Was a Teenage Werewolf* in 1957. Herman Cohen came to AIP with the idea of making a werewolf movie and Nicholson provided the title. Shot in seven days with a budget of $125,000, the picture went on to make over $2 million in less than a year. Although vilified by parents' organizations and in the press, *I Was a Teenage Werewolf* showed Hollywood that AIP, the self-proclaimed "Infant of the Industry," was a force to be reckoned with.

Dr. Fredric Wertham, a psychiatrist who successfully engineered the demise of the "Horror Comics" in the early Fifties, now turned his misguided attention to movies. AIP's horror films in particular were accused by Dr. Wertham of making "the average U.S. child indifferent to human suffering" and contributing to "the rise of crime by the young." *New York Times* writer Richard W. Nason voiced similar concerns in his January 30, 1958, review of *I Was a Teenage Frankenstein*: "Such films may aggravate juvenile delinquency. It may be as good a time as any to raise the question of what effect this further indulgence of the cult of teenism ultimately could have." Producer Cohen responded to both by saying, "I'm performing a public service because my horror films provide a healthy way of releasing tension." He went on to explain that "by participating vicariously in on-screen violence, children rid themselves of their own violent and hostile impulses." Who were we to believe?

By 1960, AIP began to realize that their black-and-white double bills were no longer as profitable as they once had been. The "classier" color features from Britain's Hammer Films were now the leaders in the horror market. The solution to this problem came when Nicholson and Arkoff gave Roger Corman a budget of $270,000 and a fifteen-day shooting schedule to make a widescreen color adaptation of Edgar Allan Poe's "The Fall of the House of Usher." For added box office clout, they hired Vincent Price to star. Price had appeared in several horror films since *House of Wax* in 1953 and he was now widely considered Hollywood's "Merchant of Menace." *House of Usher* became AIP's biggest success thus far and launched a lengthy cycle of Poe adaptations. In 1963, AIP tapped into another aspect of the youth market with a series of "Beach Party" movies starring Frankie Avalon and Annette Funicello. In a May 5, 1967, *Time* magazine article entitled "Z as in Zzzz, or Zowie," Sam Arkoff explained the success of AIP's films with teenage audiences: "They don't want message pictures. They want pure escapism, a never-never land without parents, without adults, without authorities. Kids get lectures from their parents all the time. They don't want to hear them from us."

Nicholson and Arkoff declared the 1966–67 motion picture season to be their "Champagne Year." In a promotional booklet sent to exhibitors they said: "We are justifiably a bit high, not on the Champagne, but on our big planned program of 20 feature productions for which we have allocated a record appropriation of $19,000,000. And we know too that you can't support a Champagne appetite on a beer pocket book, so several of our top budget films are being backed up with a multi-million dollar budget." Although some of the "multi-

Vincent Price, left, and Jim Nicholson on the set of *Master of the World*.

million dollar" attempts to compete with the mainstream "big league" studios would fail, AIP continued to be a success.

In 1971, Nicholson left AIP. Publicly, the reason given was that he wanted to become an independent producer. Privately, it was because Nicholson had divorced in 1964, losing much of his financial interest in the company to his ex-wife in the settlement. When Nicholson married actress Susan Hart, the close bond that had existed between Nicholson and Arkoff ended. The Nicholsons and Arkoffs had formerly been like one big family and Sam felt a sense of betrayal. Corman has stated: "Jim Nicholson had become a true—and increasingly conservative—pillar of Hollywood's professional and civic community. Arkoff remained liberal." Nicholson died on December 10, 1972, having produced only one more picture (*The Legend of Hell House* for 20th Century–Fox). It was released the year after his death. Arkoff outlived him by nearly three decades, surviving to see the maverick company that he and Nicholson had founded gain a respectability it had never known in Nicholson's lifetime. In August 1979, New York's Museum of Modern Art opened a 39-picture retrospective of AIP with the statement "Not only are American International's films rich in their depiction of our culture, but indeed they have played a not insignificant part in it." That same year AIP merged with Filmways and Arkoff's final film for the company was Brian De Palma's *Dressed to Kill*.

In 1994, the Showtime cable TV network presented the "Rebel Highway" series which consisted of supposed remakes of the following ten AIP films: *Dragstrip Girl, Jailbreakers, Soror-*

Sam Arkoff and the cast at the launch party for *Wuthering Heights*. The actors, from left: Harry Andrews, Anna Calder-Marshall, Hilary Dwyer, Julian Glover and Judy Cornwell.

ity Girl, Reform School Girl, Runaway Daughters, The Cool and the Crazy, Girls in Prison, Motorcycle Gang, Roadracers and Shake, Rattle and Rock. Other than using the titles, these shows had very little to do with the original movies. Arkoff's son, Lou, was a producer on the series. In 2001, Showtime presented another series of original movies called "Creature Features." Once again old AIP titles were attached to new movies which had little or nothing to do with the originals. These films were She Creature, Teenage Caveman, Earth vs. the Spider, The Day the World Ended and How to Make a Monster. Lou again functioned as a producer and Sam served as executive producer on all but How to Make a Monster, which was dedicated "In Loving Memory" to him. Only She Creature, a story set in Victorian times and featuring a murderous mermaid, had merit.

Hollywood lost the last of the old-style movie moguls when Samuel Arkoff died on September 16, 2001. In Arkoff's *Entertainment Weekly* obituary, Corman recalled: "Hollywood wasn't making films for the youth cultures yet, but AIP knew the only way in was to make movies that appealed to teens. By the time the studios realized what they were missing, Sam already had the jump on them."

The rights to the AIP films are now scattered all over the place. When Nicholson left AIP in 1971, the rights to much of the company's output were divided between him and Arkoff. The rights to some AIP films are now owned by his widow, the former Susan Hart. Some of AIP's movies, mostly the pickup productions, passed into public domain, which is why titles like Dementia 13, The Screaming Skull, Attack of the Giant Leeches and others are available on a variety of budget labels. When Orion Pictures acquired Filmways they also came into possession of many films in the AIP library which were then released on video through Warner, Embassy, and HBO. The Orion library was later taken over by MGM, which released a large number of the AIP titles as part of their outstanding "Midnite Movies" series on VHS and later on DVD. The Orion–AIP films have since passed through the hands of Sony and are now being handled by Fox. RCA/Columbia (later Columbia/TriStar) once had the Sam Arkoff library and released the majority of those titles on video. More recently, some of the Arkoff films have been released as double features on DVD by Lionsgate. Confusing? It certainly is!

The movies included herein are those films which had a theatrical release by American International Pictures or were purchased by AIP for television release. Excluded are the dozens of films which were picked up for distribution by American International Television but had previously been released theatrically by companies other than AIP. *The Phantom Planet* is a good example. It had been released in theatres by Four Crown but later showed up in an AIP TV package. In other cases, such as Terror in the Crypt, the only U.S. release the film had was through American International Television. All movies are listed under the AIP release title with the date being that of the AIP theatrical or television release.

THE FILMS

Abby

"ABBY DOESN'T NEED A MAN ANYMORE ... THE DEVIL IS HER LOVER NOW!"

(December 1974) Color by Movielab. A Mid-America Picture. Produced by William Girdler, Mike Henry, and G. Cornell Layne. Directed by William Girdler. Written by G. Cornell Layne and William Girdler. Starring William Marshall, Terry Carter, Carol Speed, Austin Stoker. DVD: CineFear Releasing (1.33) 92 min.; Extras: Theatrical trailer, Radio spot, Posters, stills, and lobby cards galleries.

While on an archaeological dig in Nigeria, Dr. Williams (William Marshall) accidentally unleashes the spirit of the sex demon Eshu. Back in Louisville, Kentucky, his son, the Rev. Emmet Williams (Terry Carter), and daughter-in-law, Abby (Carol Speed), are moving into their new home. Not long after this, Abby starts to act very strangely. She bellows foul language in a man's voice, kicks her husband in the balls, and scares a neighbor to death. Doctors are unable to diagnose Abby's condition and Emmet begins to suspect that demonic possession is a definite possibility. He calls his father in Nigeria and begs him to come home to help. Abby was released a year after The Exorcist; Warner Bros. threatened to sue AIP and director William Girdler for copyright infringement. A fearful Sam Arkoff quickly withdrew Abby from theatres, despite the fact that it was bringing in big bucks at the box office. The following year Warner Bros. attempted a similar action against the American distributor of the Italian production Beyond the Door. Unlike Arkoff, he refused to succumb. After a court hearing in which the distributor rightly claimed that Warner Bros. did not have a monopoly on demons or exorcism, Warner Bros. dropped the lawsuit. Actually, Abby is less like The Exorcist than one might initially suspect. Instead of a vomit-spewing, head-spinning demon confined to a bed, Abby is out on the streets looking for a good time, and a good man, wherever she can find them. The most surprising aspect of Abby is the presence of Juanita Moore as Abby's "Mama." Ms. Moore had turned in a wonderful performance in Douglas Sirk's Imitation of Life (1959) but was thereafter badly neglected by Hollywood. It's nice to see her again in Abby, although her role is a fairly thankless one. For many years considered the "Unholy Grail" of blaxploitation cinema, Abby has finally been made available to home viewers. Unfortunately, the transfer is taken from a somewhat beat-up print (probably 16mm) with below average results in both sound and picture quality.

The Abominable Dr. Phibes

"DR. PHIBES HAS GREAT VIBES."

(May 1971) Color by Movielab. Produced by Louis M. Heyward and Ronald S. Dunas. Directed by Robert Fuest. Written by James Whiton and William Goldstein. Starring Vincent Price, Joseph Cotten, Virginia North, Hugh Griffith. DVD: MGM (1.85) 93 min.; Extras: Theatrical trailer, Midnite Movies co-feature: Dr. Phibes Rises Again.

Dr. Phibes (Vincent Price, right) is about to subject Alex Scott to the "Plague of Frogs" in *The Abominable Dr. Phibes*.

Diabolical mastermind Dr. Anton Phibes (Vincent Price) is determined to enact a terrible revenge on the members of the medical team who failed to save the life of his wife. To do this, Phibes engineers elaborate deaths in the form of the Ten Plagues of Egypt from the book of Exodus in the Bible. Chief investigator of the murders is Inspector Trout (Peter Jeffrey) who is always one step behind the devilishly elusive perpetrator of the crimes. Although the cast and crew of *The Abominable Dr. Phibes* felt that they had created something special, there was little enthusiasm for the film at the home office back in Hollywood ... until audiences responded in a very big way. The combination of imaginative production design, a delightfully wry script, and a collection of spot-on performances make *The Abominable Dr. Phibes* a class act in every respect. Price pantomimes the title character to perfection (his dialogue is all done in voiceover). Future Hammer glamour girl Caroline Munro is Phibes' dearly departed wife Victoria. She is seen only in photographs and as a corpse.

Review: *Variety* (May 21, 1971), "Anachronistic period horror musical camp fantasy is a fair description."

The Amazing Colossal Man

"A Savage Giant on a Blood-Mad Rampage!"

(September 1957) Black & White. Produced and Directed by Bert I. Gordon. Written by Mark Hanna and Bert I. Gordon. Starring Glenn Langan, Cathy Downs, William Hudson, Larry Thor. VHS: Columbia/TriStar (1.33) 80 min.

In April 1957, Universal-International released *The Incredible Shrinking Man* with enormous success. Five months later, American International offered their answer to this by reversing the idea and coming up with *The Amazing Colossal Man*. This was producer-director Bert I. Gordon's first film for AIP; he had previously explored gigantism in his films *King Dinosaur*, *Beginning of the End*, and *The Cyclops* for other companies. Suggested by a short story called "The Nth Man," the film was originally conceived with Dick Miller in mind for the lead. Once the project was turned over to Gordon, the entire production took a different turn. An original treatment that Charles Griffith had written was scrapped and Mark Hanna was brought in to collaborate with Gordon on a new concept. In the final version, Col. Glenn Manning is caught in the test blast of a plutonium bomb and 95 percent of his body is burned. The doctors have little hope for his recovery but, miraculously, his skin regenerates itself overnight. The tragic side effect is that he is rapidly growing to giant size and, as he continues to grow, his mental stability becomes dangerously unbalanced. The climax occurs when a 60-foot Col. Manning goes on a low-budget rampage through the streets of Las Vegas. The movie benefits greatly from a strong performance by Glenn Langan in the title role. Langan had been a 20th Century-Fox contract player who, during the Forties, had supporting roles in high-profile films such as *Dragonwyck* and *Forever Amber*. After his Fox contract ended, his career took a nose dive. Although he continued to appear in films and television, he is now probably best remembered as the Amazing Colossal Man. In 1951, Langan married Adele Jergens, who appeared in some of AIP's early films. They remained together until his death in 1991. In addition to Langan, Cathy Downs also gives a good performance as Col. Manning's loyal fiancée. Downs started her Hollywood career in John Ford's *My Darling Clementine* but ended up in AIP's *The Phantom from 10,000 Leagues* and *The She-Creature*. Despite some above-average acting and writing, the typically tacky Bert I. Gordon special effects bring the movie down to the level of his other films. Nevertheless, *The Amazing Colossal Man* was a huge moneymaker for AIP and spawned a sequel, *War of the Colossal Beast*, the following year.

Review: *Harrison's Reports* (September 7, 1957), "Although the story is incredible, it is put over by expert special effects work."

The Amazing Transparent Man

"INVISIBLE AND DEADLY!"

(July 1960) Black & White. An MCP Picture. Produced by Lester D. Guthrie. Directed by Edgar G. Ulmer. Written by Jack Lewis. Starring Marguerite Chapman, Douglas Kennedy, James Griffith, Ivan Triesault. VHS: MGM (1.33) 57 min.; Extras: Theatrical trailer.

Given a brief theatrical release in 1960 by Miller-Consolidated Pictures, the independent company that produced it, *The Amazing Transparent Man* was picked up by American International and redistributed in August of the following year. Running under an hour, the movie resembles many of the low-budget black and white AIP films of the fifties. Convict Joey Faust (Douglas Kennedy) is sprung from prison by Laura Matson (Marguerite Chapman) under orders from Major Krenner (James Griffith). Krenner needs Faust's safecracking abilities to help him secure radioactive materials to be used in experiments being conducted by Dr. Ulof (Ivan Triesault). Dr. Ulof has discovered a way of rendering a man invisible and Krenner wants to create an invisible army which he will control. Faust wants to use invisibility to rob banks. The most interesting aspect of this movie is that it was directed by Edgar G. Ulmer, the master of low-budget filmmaking who directed such diverse fantasy fare as *The Black Cat* (1934), *The Man from Planet X* (1951), and *Daughter of Dr. Jekyll*

(1957). The MGM VHS tape of *The Amazing Transparent Man* is an immaculate digital video transfer.

Review: *Harrison's Reports* (April 15, 1961), "Fair. A modest-budgeted science fiction crime adventure. The feature lacks helpful star names, good acting and dialogue."

The Amityville Horror

"For God's Sake ... Get Out!"

(July 1979) Color by Movielab. A Professional Films Inc./Cinema 77 Production. Produced by Ronald Saland and Elliot Geisinger. Directed by Stuart Rosenberg. Written by Sandor Stein. Starring James Brolin, Margot Kidder, Rod Steiger, Don Stroud. DVD: MGM (1.85) 119 min.; Extras: Theatrical trailer, Full-screen version.

Following in the cloven hoofprints of *The Exorcist* (1973) and *The Omen* (1976) came the film version of the best-selling book by Jay Anson. Like its predecessors, *The Amityville Horror* deals with the Catholic Church and Satanic evil. When the big Hollywood studios finally discovered that horror had great box office potential, AIP joined the major leaguers and released this glossy "A" production. James Brolin and Margot Kidder play George and Kathy Lutz, newlyweds who buy a house which was once the scene of a mass murder. They move in with Kathy's three young children from a previous marriage and, soon after, some disturbing incidents take place. Both a priest and a nun become violently ill after entering the house. The youngest child Amy has conversations with an invisible "friend" named Jody, who just happens to be one of the victims of the prior massacre. George becomes increasingly disheveled and surly and in no time at all he is sharpening an ax with evil intent in his bloodshot eyes. Actually ax-wielding George seems to be a direct precursor to ax-wielding Jack Nicholson in *The Shining*,

Director Stuart Rosenberg instructs Margot Kidder and James Brolin to at least try and look scared in *The Amityville Horror*.

which would be released the following year. The problem with *The Amityville Horror* is that it isn't very scary. One "shocking" scene involves toilets which overflow with something that looks like crude oil. You don't know whether they should call a plumber or a priest ... or just build an oil derrick. Also, in an eerie foreshadowing of his future, James Brolin's hairstyle occasionally looks disturbingly like that of Barbra Streisand in *A Star is Born*. Now that's scary! Made at a cost of $4.7 million, *The Amityville Horror* earned $65 million in domestic rentals alone, making it the most successful film in AIP's history. It spawned a number of sequels and was remade in 2005 with mixed results.

Review: *Time* (September 17, 1979), "The movie's creators should have invented something to scare the pants off us. As it is, they have managed to merely bore them off."

Angel Unchained

"THIS IS THE HELL RUN THAT
YOU MAKE ALL ALONE!"

(December 1970) Color by Movielab. Produced and Directed by Lee Madden. Written by Jeffrey Alladin Fiskin and Lee Madden. Starring Don Stroud, Luke Askew, Larry Bishop, Tyne Daly. DVD: MGM (1.85) 86 min.; Extras: Theatrical trailer, Midnite Movies co-feature: *The Cycle Savages*.

After a rumble with a rival gang in a children's amusement park, biker club leader Angel (Don Stroud) realizes he has had enough of the violent life and needs some "peace time." He turns over his "colors" to Pilot (Larry Bishop) and takes off on his own. He comes across a hippie commune in the Arizona desert and decides to join them. The peaceful hippies are terrorized in a dune buggy assault by some local redneck cowboys and Tremaine (Luke Askew), the commune leader, asks Angel to prevail upon his former biker buddies to give them protection. It turns out that the "cure" may be worse than the "illness" when the bikers arrive and turn the commune

Don Stroud (in *Angel Unchained*) was a familiar face in AIP films of the seventies.

upside down with their antisocial antics. A very young Tyne Daly plays the hippie girl Marilee, who becomes the object of Angel's affections ... and a target for rape by one of the marauding bikers. It seems there's no peace time for Angel after all. Aldo Ray appears in one amusing scene as the sheriff of the redneck community.

Review: *New York Times* (December 17, 1970), "*Angel Unchained* just leaves you tired."

The Angry Red Planet

"SPECTACULAR ADVENTURE BEYOND
TIME AND SPACE"

(February 1960) Cinemagic and Eastman Color. A Sino Production. Produced by Sidney Pink and Norman Maurer. Directed by Ib Melchior. Written by Sidney Pink and Ib Melchior. Starring Gerald Mohr, Nora Hayden, Les Tremayne, Jack Kruschen. DVD: MGM (1.33) 83 min.; Extras: Theatrical trailer.

14 *Apache Woman*

An artist's concept of the horrors on *The Angry Red Planet*.

A wacky "space opera" with all the conventions of the genre circa 1960. The first manned rocket to Mars carries a crew of four stereotypical characters: the strong and stoic leader (Gerald Mohr), the pretty lady scientist (Nora Hayden), the older wise professor (Les Tremayne), and the wisecracking goofball (Jack Kruschen). They land on Mars and encounter an enormous carnivorous plant, a 40-foot-tall monster that looks like a winged rat with crab claws, a giant amoeba, and a three-eyed Martian. All of this is accomplished by the miracle of Cinemagic, which is basically bad special effects tinted with a red filter. Whenever the crew goes outside the spaceship to explore, everything is red, *red*, RED! By the time they go back inside and the color returns to normal, you may feel like your eyeballs are about to fall out. Actually *The Angry Red Planet* is good, silly fun. It was the first of several films that Sidney Pink produced for AIP.

Apache Woman

"CALL HER HALF-BREED ... AND ALL HELL BREAKS LOOSE!

(October 1955) Pathécolor. A Golden State Production. Produced and Directed by Roger Corman. Written by Lou Rusoff. Starring Lloyd Bridges, Joan Taylor, Lance Fuller, Morgan Jones. VHS: Columbia/TriStar (1.33) 83 min.

Apache Woman, Roger Corman's second Western for American Releasing Corporation, opens excitingly with a knife fight between Joan Taylor ("Don't call me squaw!") and Jonathan Haze. Seems that Anne Libeau (Taylor) is half Apache and the Apaches have been terrorizing the locals of late ... or have they? Government agent Rex Moffet (Lloyd Bridges) is an expert on Indian affairs so he is brought in to try and get to the bottom of the situation. A possible suspect is Armand Libeau (Lance Fuller), Anne's college-educated crazy brother who is very handy with a bow and arrow. Most of the picture is long on talk and short on action until the final scene which is a typical climactic shootout between the good guys and the bad. The script is decent and the acting is generally good ... with the exception of Fuller, who gives an even worse performance than he usually does. Taylor looks especially lovely in her dusky makeup but her character has to endure such insults as "tramp," "trash," "squaw woman," and "halfbreed" so it's no wonder that she seems testy much of the time. Jonathan Haze and Dick Miller each play both cowboys and Indians during the course of the film, which must have been a challenge for the continuity girl. Talented but underrated composer Ronald Stein contributes his first background score for both ARC and Roger Corman, and it is a very good one. The Columbia/TriStar video release of *Apache Woman* is good quality but, for some unknown reason, it is a black-and-white print (the film was presented theatrically in color).

Review: *Harrison's Reports* (October 22, 1955), "It is handicapped by an inadequate script and by the fact that the action is very slow in the second half."

Joan Taylor and Lloyd Bridges in Roger Corman's *Apache Woman*.

The Astounding She-Monster

"A Creature from Beyond the Stars. Evil ... Beautiful ... Deadly!"

(December 1957) Black & White. A Hollywood International Production. Produced and Directed by Ronnie Ashcroft. Written by Frank Hall and Ronnie Ashcroft. Starring Robert Clarke, Shirley Kilpatrick, Kenne Duncan, Marilyn Harvey. DVD: Image/Wade Williams (1.33) 62 min.; Extras: Theatrical trailer.

Gangsters kidnap an heiress (Marilyn Harvey) and whisk her off to a remote cabin in the mountains where they plan to hold her for ransom. Nothing seems to go right with their plan, not the least of which is the appearance of a mysterious space woman (Shirley Kilpatrick) whose touch causes instant death. This bargain basement offering was the brainchild of former film editor and independent producer Ronnie Ashcroft. Made for about $18,000, the film was picked up by AIP and distributed as half of one of their double feature programs. The spectacular poster art gave no indication of the dire fate which awaited audiences. It is rumored that schlockmeister Ed Wood had a hand in the production and, indeed, it seems very much like one of his films. Need I say more?

Review: *Harrison's Reports* (April 26, 1958), "The story has been handled in imaginative fashion and many of the situations hold one in tense suspense."

At the Earth's Core

"Take the Most Terrifying Journey of Your Life!"

(June 1976) Color by Movielab. A Samuel Z. Arkoff–Amicus Production. Produced by John

Dark. Directed by Kevin Connor. Written by Milton Subotsky. Starring Doug McClure, Peter Cushing, Caroline Munro, Cy Grant. DVD: MGM (1.85) 90 min.; Extras: Theatrical trailer, Midnite Movies co-feature: *War-Gods of the Deep*.

In addition to creating Tarzan and John Carter of Mars, Edgar Rice Burroughs also wrote a fascinating series of novels set in the prehistoric lost world of Pellucidar, which lies deep beneath the Earth's surface. *At the Earth's Core* was the first book in this series of imaginative stories but this British production from Milton Subotsky and Max J. Rosenberg's Amicus Films does little justice to the source material. The adventurous David Innes (Doug McClure) and the brilliant but eccentric Prof. Perry (Peter Cushing) are making a test run in a new burrowing machine called "The Iron Mole" when they lose control and end up in a strange world some 4,000 miles under the surface of the Earth. They discover that this curious place is called Pellucidar and that it is inhabited by terrible monsters (actually men in terrible monster suits) and unfriendly natives. The rulers of this world are reptilian birds called Mahars, and Innes and Perry soon become their captives. The production values are decidedly paltry and in no way approach Burroughs' fantastic visions. The one plus factor is genre icon Caroline Munro, who is shown to good advantage in her revealing costume.

Atragon

"Will It Conquer the World
or ... Destroy It Forever?"

(March 1965) ColorScope (TohoScope and Eastman Color). A Toho Co. Ltd. Production. Produced by Tomoyuki Tanaka. Directed by Ishiro Honda. Written by Shinichi Sekizawa. Starring Tadao Takashima, Yoko Fujiyama, Kenji Sahara, Jun Tazaki. DVD: Media Blasters (2.35) 96 min.; Extras: Theatrical trailer, Audio commentary by Koji Kajita.

The Mu empire, sunk beneath the Pacific Ocean for 10,000 years, decides that it is time for Empress Mu (Tetsuko Kobayashi) to rule the world. They threaten the various governments of the world, demanding total surrender or complete annihilation. The Japanese government seeks out Captain Jinguji (Jun Tazaki) who has been working on a super submarine since the end of World War II. Unfortunately, Jinguji is still incredibly nationalistic and wants only Japan to benefit from his invention. Eventually Jinguji comes to his senses and uses his submarine Atragon to save the world from the Mu empire. Atragon, which flies through the air as easily as it dives under the ocean, proves to be a formidable weapon indeed. *Atragon* includes elements from several genres. At first it appears to be an espionage thriller with sci-fi overtones. Sequences in the Mu empire look like something out of a sword-and-sandal spectacular with a pseudo-ancient Egyptian motif combined with futuristic machinery. Then there is the giant monster Manda, whom the Mu people worship with the inevitable elaborate production number. Manda, a skinny sea serpent who looks like a close relative of Reptilicus, would later put in a guest appearance in *Destroy All Monsters*. The film was released in Japan as *Kaitei Gunkan* in 1964; AIP distributed *Atragon* in the U.S. a year later, cut to 88 minutes. The DVD runs the full 96 minutes and has a different English dub than the AIP theatrical version.

Review: *Variety* (March 17, 1965), "Good acting, fast-paced direction and editing."

Attack of the Giant Leeches

"Crawling Horror ... Rising from the Depths of Hell to Kill and Conquer!"

(October 1959) Black & White. Produced by Gene and Roger Corman. Directed by Bernard L. Kowalski. Written by Leo Gordon. Starring Ken Clark, Yvette Vickers, Jan Shepard, Michael Emmet. DVD: Alpha (1.33) 62 min.

Also known as *The Giant Leeches*, Bernard Kowalski's second film for Gene and Roger Corman is even creepier than his first (which was *Night of the Blood Beast*). A Florida backwoods community is panic-stricken when several people disappear in the local swamp. These poor unfortunates are victims of giant leeches who capture their prey alive, hide them in an underwater cave, and slowly drain them of blood. Hirsute hunk Ken Clark is the wildlife ranger who tries to get to the bottom of the mysterious disappearances. Clark appeared in a number of American movies in the fifties (including *South Pacific*) and later found employment in European genre films throughout the sixties. Despite an extremely low budget, *Attack of the Giant Leeches* is filled with disturbing imagery and manages to deliver a number of shocks. And sexy Yvette Vickers simply has to be seen to be believed.

Attack of the Puppet People

"DOLL DWARFS VERSUS THE CRUSHING GIANT BEASTS!"

(July 1958) Black & White. Produced and Directed by Bert I. Gordon. Written by George Worthing Yates. Starring John Agar, John Hoyt, June Kenny, Michael Mark. DVD: MGM (1.33) 79 min.; Extras: Theatrical trailer, Midnite Movies co-feature: *Village of the Giants*.

Producer Bert I. Gordon had an obsession with size (please note his initials) and most of his movies dealt with gigantism. *Attack of the Puppet People* was an exception, although the miniature cast members do have to deal with an oversized world. A kindly old doll maker, Mr. Franz (John Hoyt), finds a unique

From left, Marlene Willis, Scott Peters, June Kenny, Laurie Mitchell, Kenny Miller, and John Agar in *Attack of the Puppet People*.

The infamous *Baron Blood* attempts to hide from his pursuers.

way of making the people he loves stay with him. Using an apparatus that he has invented, he shrinks them down to doll size. He then stores them in canisters and takes them out only for his own amusement, which includes forcing Marlene Willis to sing an especially insipid song. Filmed under the title *The Fantastic Puppet People*, this was a big hit for AIP as were the other three movies Gordon produced for them in the late fifties. Although the effects in Gordon's films are usually pretty cheesy, the movies are somewhat more endearing because of it. The requisite plug for another Bert I. Gordon film comes when John Agar and June Kenny go to a drive-in showing of *The Amazing Colossal Man*.

Song: "You're My Living Doll"

Review: *Variety* (August 20, 1958), "[Bert] Gordon is a master of special effects and his tricks are ingenious and intriguing."

Baron Blood

"THE ULTIMATE IN HUMAN AGONY ...
WITH INSTRUMENTS OF TORTURE
GHASTLY BEYOND BELIEF!"

(October 1972) Technicolor. A Leone International Film. Produced by Alfredo Leone. Directed by Mario Bava. Written by Vincent G. Fotre. Starring Joseph Cotten, Elke Sommer, Massimo Girotti, Antonio Cantafora. VHS: HBO Video (1.33) 90 min., DVD: Image (1.85) 100 min.; European English-language version, Extras: Theatrical trailer, Photo and poster gallery.

A fairly run-of-the-mill horror story is given the Mario Bava treatment in *Baron Blood*. For some ridiculous reason, a young couple decides to read an ancient incantation which will presumably call forth the spirit of the dread Baron Otto Von Kleist (a.k.a. "Baron

Blood"). Von Kleist was a 16th century sadist who tortured and murdered countless victims in his castle on the hill. When a rich American (Joseph Cotten) subsequently turns up to buy the castle and restore it to its former gory glory, a series of mysterious killings ensues. In the hands of director Bava, this pedestrian collection of horror clichés becomes a memorably stylish thriller with a number of genuine shocks. Bava was a master at taking rather routine material and transforming it into something quite remarkable. AIP cut the film by ten minutes and, predictably, replaced Stelvio Cipriani's score with one by Les Baxter. The AIP theatrical version was available on VHS from HBO Video as *The Torture Chamber of Baron Blood*.

The Bat People

"AFTER THE SUN SETS AND THE NIGHT WIND HAS DIED COMES THE HOUR OF THE BAT PEOPLE!"

(January 1974) Color by DeLuxe. A Lou Shaw Production. Produced and Written by Lou Shaw. Directed by Jerry Jameson. Starring Stewart Moss, Marianne McAndrew, Michael Pataki, Paul Carr. DVD: MGM/Fox (1.85) 95 min.; Midnite Movies co-feature: *The Beast Within*.

American International must have known that had a real turkey on their hands with this film as they released it with two different titles and ad campaigns. The alternate title was *It Lives by Night* ("No matter how hard you pray ... or how loud you scream it's no use!"). And no matter how hard AIP tried ... it was still a major stinker. Dr. John Beck and his wife Cathy (real life husband-and-wife Stewart Moss and Marianne McAndrew) are on their long-delayed honeymoon. On the way to the ski slopes, they take a detour to Carlsbad Caverns where John is bitten by a bat. After undergoing treatment for rabies he begins to experience some very strange side effects. Most of the film's interminable length is spent with John running away from Sergeant Ward (Michael Pataki), a sleazy small-town

Stewart Moss and Marianne McAndrew are perhaps discussing the uncertain future of their careers after making *The Bat People*.

sheriff. When John finally transforms in a "Bat Person" at the end, it is hardly worth the wait, the makeup being one of Stan Winston's early and less successful endeavors. Marianne McAndrew dropped yet another rung on the career ladder with her participation in this film. Previously she played a major role in the big-budget musical *Hello Dolly* (1969) and then appeared in Russ Meyer's *The Seven Minutes* (1971). After *The Bat People* she worked in television.

Battle Beyond the Sun

"THE GIGANTIC BATTLE! WHICH RACE WILL WIN ... AND RULE THE UNIVERSE?"

(April 1963) Color. A Filmgroup Presentation. Produced by Francis Ford Coppola. Directed by Thomas Colchart. Written by Nicholas Colbert and Edwin Palmer. Starring Edd Perry, Arla Powell, Andy Stewart, Bruce Hunter. DVD: RetroMedia (1.33) 75 min.; Extras: Theatrical trailer, Bonus feature: *Star Pilot*.

This AIP release was a product of Roger Corman's Filmgroup company. Having acquired footage from a 1959 Russian space movie, Corman assigned Francis Ford Coppola the task of fashioning a marketable film for U.S. consumption. Coppola retained the basic story of a race to Mars by competing nations but re-edited the movie, Americanized the Russian names in the credits, and dubbed it into English. He also added, at Corman's behest, a new scene featuring two of the most bizarre monsters in sci-fi history, one of which looks like a giant vagina with teeth. Oddly, the monsters are seen far more clearly in the trailer than in the film itself. The title of the original Russian film was *Niebo Zowiet* and it was directed by Aleksander Kozyr.

Beach Blanket Bingo

"It's the Game That Separates the Girls and the Boys ... Into Groups of Two!"

(April 1965) Panavision and Pathécolor. Produced by James H. Nicholson and Samuel Z. Arkoff. Directed by William Asher. Written by William Asher and Leo Townsend. Starring Frankie Avalon, Annette Funicello, Deborah Walley, Linda Evans. DVD: MGM (2.35) 97 min.; Extras: Theatrical trailer, Midnite Movies co-feature: *How to Stuff a Wild Bikini*.

Press agent "Bullets" (Paul Lynde) uses the Beach Party gang to help promote his new singing sensation Sugar Kane (Linda Evans, in a role originally set for Nancy Sinatra). This all leads to Frankie (Avalon) and Dee Dee (Annette Funicello) taking to the skies for some skydiving with a female instructor (Deborah Walley) who has her eye on Frankie. Marta (*Lost in Space*) Kristen is a mermaid with designs on Bonehead (Jody McCrea), who is given far more to do than in any of the other films in the series. No surprise cameo this time, although gossip columnist Earl Wilson appears (uncomfortably) in a few scenes.

Songs: "Beach Blanket Bingo," "It Only Hurts When I Cry," "Follow Your Leader," "I Think You Think," "These Are the Good Times," "He's My New Love," "He's My Fly Boy"

Review: *Variety* (April 7, 1965), "No one can blame Nicholson and Arkoff for continuing a pattern that has made them money, but this is ridiculous."

Jody McCrea falls in love with mermaid Marta Kristen in *Beach Blanket Bingo*.

Beach Party

"Surfin' All Day ... Swingin' All Night ... You Are Invited to a Beach Party Tonight"

(August 1963) Panavision and Pathécolor. Produced by James H. Nicholson and Samuel Z. Arkoff. Directed by William Asher. Written by Lou Rusoff. Starring Bob Cummings, Dorothy Malone, Frankie Avalon, Annette Funicello. DVD: MGM (2.35) 98 min.; Extras: Theatrical trailer, Midnite Movies co-feature: *Bikini Beach*.

This is the first, and arguably the best, of the "Beach Party" series. Bob Cummings plays a stodgy professor who is doing an anthropological study of the sex habits of the American teenager. Dorothy Malone is his long-suffering assistant, who secretly loves him. With these two stars, AIP hoped to attract the adult audience as well as the teenagers. They really needn't have bothered as it was the teenagers who turned out in droves to see Frankie and Annette, making this one of AIP's most successful productions ever. As the series progressed, the films became more absurd but youthful audiences continued to eat them up. At least *Beach Party* does have a semblance of plot and some nice songs by Gary Usher and Roger Christian. Worth noting is "Miss Perpetual Motion" Candy Johnson, a "dancin' fool" if ever there was one. There is also a fun cameo by Vincent Price at the end. William Asher was already an old hand at comedy, having directed episodes of TV's *Bewitched* and *I Love Lucy*. The single release MGM DVD has both fullscreen and widescreen versions.

Songs: "Beach Party," "Don't Stop Now," "Swingin' and Surfin'," "Secret Surfin's Spot," "Promise Me Anything," "Treat Him Nicely"

Review: *Time* (August 16, 1963), "*Beach Party* is an anthropological documentary with songs. As a study of primitive behavior patterns, *Beach Party* is more unoriginal than aboriginal."

The Beast with a Million Eyes

"An Unspeakable Horror ... Destroying ... Terrifying!"

(June 1955) Black & White. A San Mateo Production presented by Palo Alto Productions. Produced and Directed by David Kramarsky. Written by Tom Filer. Starring Paul Birch, Lorna Thayer, Dona Cole, Richard Sargent. DVD: MGM/Fox (1.33) 77 min.; Midnite Movies co-feature: *The Phantom from 10,000 Leagues*.

Carol Kelly (Lorna Thayer) is tired of her life on a date ranch in the California desert. She is bitter toward her husband Allen (Paul Birch) and her daughter Sandy (Dona Cole) because she feels that youth and opportunity have passed her by. The arrival of an invader from outer space eventually makes her grateful for what she does have. Despite the obvious low budget, erratic editing, lapses in continuity, and a particularly awful background score (by John Bickford), the movie does have some imaginative ideas. As the first AIP (then ARC) foray into the sci-fi genre, it also has an important place in the company's history. The title of the film is figurative, although the literal representation on the poster art would lead one to believe otherwise. "The Beast" is able to control the minds of lesser creatures, thereby turning a formerly docile German Shepherd into a ferocious killer and the local bird population into candidates for Alfred Hitchcock's *The Birds*. Several members of the small cast are worth mentioning. Paul Birch acted in four Roger Corman films, most notably as the vampire alien in *Not of This Earth* (1957). Lorna Thayer, who acts her heart out in *The Beast with a Million Eyes*, would later appear as the waitress in the memorable "chicken salad sandwich" scene in *Five Easy Pieces* (1970). Onetime Keystone comedian Chester Conklin does a bit of hokey silent movie shtick before he is trampled to death by a crazed dairy cow. Lastly, Richard (a.k.a. Dick) Sargent went on to become the "second Darren" on the *Bewitched* TV series. Corman backed the production for around $30,000 but took no official credit on the film. Arkoff's often repeated story that he and Nicholson bought an eight dollar tea kettle, poked holes in it and turned it into the title monster is utter nonsense. The special effects were by Paul Blaisdell, who began a long association with AIP with this picture. His effects herein consist of a spaceship and its interplanetary occupant (a briefly glimpsed puppet).

Above and following two pages: *Bikini Beach* babes Mary Hughes, Delores Wells, and Patti Chandler.

Bikini Beach

"It's Where the Boys Meet the Girls ... and Everyone Can See What They're Gonna Be Up Against!"

(July 1964) Panavision and Pathécolor. Produced by James H. Nicholson and Samuel Z. Arkoff. Directed by William Asher. Written by William Asher, Leo Townsend and Robert Dillon. Starring Frankie Avalon, Annette Funi-

cello, Martha Hyer, Don Rickles. DVD: MGM (2.35) 100 min.; Extras: Theatrical trailer, Midnite Movies co-feature: *Beach Party*.

In this installment of the "Beach Party" series, Frankie's (Avalon) rival for Dee Dee (Annette Funicello) is a mop-topped British singer called Potato Bug (also played by Frankie Avalon). Complicating matters is Harvey Honeywagon (Keenan Wynn), who plans to close down Bikini Beach and turn it into the site of an old folks' home. Frankie and

24   *Bikini Beach*

Potato Bug compete in a drag race, with the best man to win Dee Dee as the prize. This ends up in a typically frantic car chase and brawl. Boris Karloff is the "surprise cameo" this time around. Frankie and Annette share a quintessential "Beach Party" moment when they sing the charming duet "Because You're You" written by Guy Hemric and Jerry Styner. Frankie Avalon had one of the longest and most varied affiliations with AIP of any actor. Only Vincent Price would topline more films for the company. Avalon began his association with the company when he voiced the title character for the animated feature *Alakazam the Great* in 1961 and ended it nearly a decade later with *Horror House*. The single release MGM DVD of *Bikini Beach* has both fullscreen and widescreen versions.

Songs: "Bikini Beach," "Love's a Secret Weapon," "Gimme Your Love," "Yeah Yeah Yeah," "How About That," "Because You're You," "This Time It's Love," "Happy Feelin'," "Dance and Shout," "Bikini Drag," "Record Run," "Gotcha Where I Wantcha"

Review: *Variety* (July 8, 1964), "William Asher's nimble direction never lets anything slow the pace."

Black Caesar

"HAIL CAESAR … GODFATHER OF HARLEM!"

(February 1973) Color by DeLuxe. A Larco Production. Produced, Directed and Written by Larry Cohen. Starring Fred Williamson, Art Lund, Gloria Hendry, Martin D'Urville. DVD: MGM (1.85) 94 min.; Extras: Theatrical trailer, Audio commentary by Larry Cohen.

Black Caesar follows the story of Tommy Gibbs (Fred Williamson) beginning with his days as a shoeshine boy in 1953. In 1965 he becomes a hit man for the Italian syndicate and is rewarded with his own turf in Harlem. Tommy's philosophy is simple: "It's a jungle and it takes a jungle bunny to run it." Tommy has bigger aspirations and they eventually lead him to overthrow the Italians and become a gangland czar. Life at the top is lonely after the woman Tommy loves (Gloria Hendry) runs off with his best friend Joe (Philip Roye). A corrupt cop (Art Lund) finally puts a hit on Tommy and the film ends in 1972 with a shot, beaten, and bloody Tommy presumably dying in the ruins of the tenement building where he grew up. Julius W. Harris plays Tommy's traveling salesman father who would return inexplicably as a crime lord in the sequel *Hell Up in Harlem*. The music in *Black Caesar* is composed and performed by none other than the great James Brown.

Black Sabbath

"NOT SINCE *FRANKENSTEIN* HAVE YOU SEEN SUCH HORROR!"

(May 1964) Pathécolor (Eastman Color). A Galatea/Emmepi/Societe Cinematographique Lyre Production. Produced by Paolo Mercuri. Directed by Mario Bava. Written by Marcello Fondato and Alberto Bevilacqua. Starring Boris Karloff, Mark Damon, Michele Mercier, Susy Anderson. VHS: Thorn EMI/HBO (1.33) 99 min., DVD: Image (1.78) 92 min.; Italian-language version with English subtitles, Extras: Italian theatrical trailer.

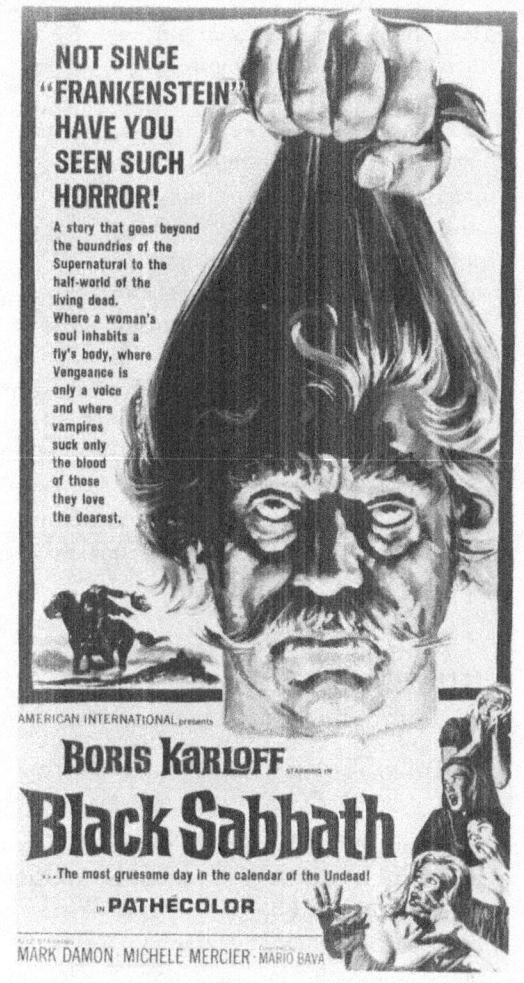

Artwork for *Black Sabbath*.

Filmed in 1963 by Mario Bava, this horror masterpiece, (originally titled *I tre volti della paura/The Three Faces of Fear*) features three stories with linking narration by Boris Karloff. The first story is "The Telephone," in which Michele Mercier is stalked by the lover she has betrayed. The second and most elaborate tale is "The Wurdulak," featuring Boris Karloff as a Russian vampire who preys on members of his own family. The final story, "The Drop of Water," is the most frightening. It concerns a nurse (Jacqueline Pierreux) who steals a valuable ring off the finger of a dead medium. The medium returns to take her terrible revenge. For the 1964 AIP release of *Black Sabbath*, the order of the stories was changed, Les Baxter replaced the original Roberto Nicolosi score, and the content of "The Telephone" was drastically altered to add supernatural overtones and eliminate any hints of lesbianism. The distinctive voice of Karloff is sorely missed on the DVD which features only the Italian-language version. The AIP version was available on VHS from Thorn EMI/HBO.

Barbara Steele and John Richardson in Mario Bava's *Black Sunday*.

Review: *Time* (May 15, 1964), "Silly stuff, of course, but it's nice to know that a monster emeritus [Boris Karloff] can somehow manage to eeeeeeek out a living."

Black Sunday

"ONCE EVERY 100 YEARS ... THE UNDEAD DEMONS OF HELL TERRORIZE THE WORLD IN AN ORGY OF STARK TERROR!"

(February 1961) Black & White. A Galatea-Jolly Film Production. Produced by Massimo De Rita. Directed by Mario Bava. Written by Ennio De Concini, Marcello Coscia and Mario Serandrei. Starring Barbara Steele, John Richardson, Ivo Garrani, Andrea Checchi. DVD: Image (1.66) 87 min.; English-language European version, Extras: Theatrical trailer, Audio commentary by Tim Lucas.

Filmed in Italy in 1960, *Black Sunday* (a.k.a. *La maschera del demonio/The Mask of Satan*) is Mario Bava's first solo directorial credit (he had co-directed several features prior to this). It is also a landmark film in the horror genre. Based on Nikolai Gogol's story "The Vij," *Black Sunday* tells of the vampire-witch Asa (Barbara Steele) who is condemned to death along with her lover Javutich (Arturo Dominici). Two hundred years later they are accidentally brought back to life and Asa proceeds to take over the body of her lookalike descendant Princess Katia. Barbara Steele plays both Asa and Katia and her performance assured her a place in the pantheon of horror movie icons. For the AIP release, about four minutes were trimmed, the film was redubbed, and Les Baxter replaced the original score by

Roberto Nicolosi. The AIP cut was available on laser disc from Image Entertainment, double-billed with the AIP version of *Black Sabbath*.

Review: *Time* (September 1, 1961), "A piece of fine Italian handiwork that atones for its ludicrous lapses with brilliant intuitions of the spectral."

Blacula

"The Most Terrifying Film of the Decade"

(August 1972) Color by Movielab. Produced by Joseph T. Naar. Directed by William Crain. Written by Joan Torres and Raymond Koenig. Starring William Marshall, Vonetta McGee, Denise Nicholas, Thalmus Rasulala. DVD: MGM (1.85) 93 min.; Extras: Theatrical trailer.

Blacula begins in the year 1780 at Dracula's castle in Transylvania. An African prince, Mamuwalde (William Marshall), and his bride have come to Europe to try and convince a delegation of noblemen to stop the slave trade.

William Marshall as *Blacula*.

Mamuwalde and Dracula (Charles Macaulay) quarrel and the evil count inflicts the curse of vampirism on his guest, renaming him "Blacula." Hundreds of years later, "two faggot interior decorators" (the scripts words, not mine) come to Castle Dracula and purchase all of the furnishings ... including a padlocked coffin. They transport their acquisitions back to Los Angeles where they inadvertently let loose Blacula into the modern world. Vonetta McGee plays Tina, the beautiful girl who is a double for Blacula's African princess. It is a sad irony that such a fine Shakespearean actor as Marshall will probably be best remembered for playing Blacula and the King of Cartoons on *Pee-Wee's Playhouse*, although his 2003 *Variety* obituary said that the role of Blacula was his own invention.

Blast-Off

"The Most Fabulous Entertainment Event of the Year!"

(June 1967) Panavision and Eastman Color. Produced by Harry Alan Towers. Directed by Don Sharp. Written by Dave Freeman and Peter Welbeck (a.k.a. Harry Alan Towers). Starring Burl Ives, Troy Donahue, Daliah Lavi, Gert Frobe. VHS: HBO/Cannon Video (1.33) 95 min.; DVD: Momentum (as *Jules Verne's Rocket to the Moon*) (2.35) 101 min., Region 2 DVD from the United Kingdom.

This is one of those films which appeared under a variety of different titles, all with different running times. Made in England and released there as *Jules Verne's Rocket to the Moon*, the title was changed for the U.S. release to *Those Fantastic Flying Fools*. AIP hoped to capitalize on the success of *Those Magnificent Men in Their Flying Machines* (20th Century–Fox, 1965) a big-budget comedy with a period setting and a large cast. Released in the U.S. with an original running time of 119 minutes, *Those Fantastic Flying Fools* simply failed to take off. The movie was quickly withdrawn, cut to 95 minutes and re-released under the title *Blast-Off*. This was all for naught as the film still failed to make much of an impact at the box office. The plot is vaguely suggested by Jules Verne's novel *From the Earth to the Moon* but Verne's name is primarily evoked for commercial reasons on the part of producer Harry Alan Towers. A down-on-his-luck P.T. Barnum (Burl Ives, in a role originally intended for Bing Crosby) goes to England where he becomes involved in a scheme to send a rocket to the moon. The rocket's designer Gaylord Sullivan (Troy Donahue) is prevailed upon to become the first astronaut. But his girlfriend Madelaine (Daliah Lavi) must foil a plot she has discovered which will sabotage the experiment and put Gaylord's life in danger. Participating in the crazy antics are such famed character actors as Dennis Price, Lionel Jeffries, Terry-Thomas, Gert Frobe, Graham Stark, and Hermione Gingold. The part of a Russian spy was originally to have been played by Klaus Kinski but he was replaced shortly after filming began by Joachim Teege. Although it is by no stretch of the imagination a great movie, the wholesale butchering of *Blast-Off* prevents it from being an even mediocre one. With nearly half an hour cut from the running time, much of the relationship between characters and the motivation for their actions is entirely missing. The 95-minute version is so irritating you might wonder how having to endure more could make it better ... but it does. The British cut runs 101 minutes but eliminates several scenes involving Graham Stark. It also shortens an amusing sequence in which Terry-Thomas attempts to seduce Daliah Lavi. It's a real pity that the DVD isn't complete as it is a beautiful widescreen transfer. Although the U.S. VHS tape and the U.K. DVD are cut versions, *Those Fantastic Flying Fools* has surfaced in cable TV showings in its uncut 119 minute form which is a vast improvement.

Review: (Reviewed as *Those Fantastic Flying Fools*), *Time* (June 16, 1967), "The detailed sight gags and the cast's irrepressible energy provide a variety of lunatic fringe benefits."

Blood from the Mummy's Tomb

"A Severed Hand Beckons from an Open Grave!"

(May 1972) Color by DeLuxe. A Hammer Film for EMI Film Productions Ltd. Produced by Howard Brandy. Directed by Seth Holt. Written by Christopher Wicking. Starring Andrew Keir, Valerie Leon, James Villiers, Hugh Burden. DVD: Anchor Bay (1.85) 94 min.; Extras: Theatrical trailer, Interviews with Valerie Leon and Christopher Wicking, TV and radio spots, Still gallery, Bonus Disc: Hammer trailer collection.

This film was based on *The Jewel of Seven Stars*, a lesser-known work by *Dracula* author Bram Stoker. *Blood from the Mummy's Tomb* is a modern-gothic horror which tells of Tera, an ancient Egyptian sorceress who attempts to reincarnate herself in a contemporary woman. She takes possession of Margaret Fuchs, daughter of the man who discovered her tomb in Egypt. Tera forces Margaret to kill anyone who might thwart her evil purpose. Valerie Leon plays the dual role of Tera and Margaret to great effect, alternately sympathetic and frightening but never anything less than stunningly beautiful. Director Seth Holt died during the final weeks of shooting and the movie was finished by Michael Carreras. Holt's death created a major problem in the editing of the film and, although great efforts were made to preserve his original vision, the movie sometimes has a patched-together feel to it. When AIP picked up the U.S. distribution rights, they cut out some brief nudity and most of the gore to ensure a PG rating. It was released on a double bill with the even more heavily edited *Night of the Blood Monster* (a.k.a. *The Bloody Judge*); the ads proclaimed: "More Gore Than Ever Before!" ... but most of the gore ended up on the cutting room floor. The Anchor Bay DVD is the uncut British version.

Review: *Variety* (October 8, 1971), "Polished and well-acted but rather tame Hammer horror entry."

Sandra Harrison, left, confronts her new roommates in *Blood of Dracula*.

Blood of Dracula

"IN HER EYES ... DESIRE! IN HER VEINS ... THE BLOOD OF A MONSTER!"

(November 1957) Black & White. Produced by Herman Cohen. Directed by Herbert L. Strock. Written by Ralph Thornton. Starring Sandra Harrison, Louise Lewis, Gail Ganley, Jerry Blaine. DVD: Lionsgate (1.33) 78 min.; DVD co-feature: *How to Make a Monster*.

Troubled teen Nancy Perkins (Sandra Harrison), enrolled at the Sherwood School for Girls, meets a deranged science teacher (Louise Lewis) who is in possession of a powerful amulet from the Carpathian Mountains. The teacher uses this amulet to turn Nancy into a ferocious vampire. *Blood of Dracula* is basically a distaff variation on *I Was a Teenage Werewolf*. It might better have been called "I Was a Teenage Vampire" as the story has nothing to do with Dracula other than a police detective conjecturing that the murders might have been committed by "a Dracula" (huh?). Harrison's vampire makeup is uniquely creepy and the acting, with the exception of Gail Ganley, isn't bad at all. Jerry Blaine performs a musical number accompanied by some especially goofy choreography. Harrison is very effective as the heroine-monster but this was her only feature film role.

Song: "Puppy Love"

Review: *Variety* (January 8, 1958), "Slow in takeoff, film nevertheless packs enough interest to salve its intended audience and holds to logical climax."

Bloody Mama

"YOU GOTTA BELIEVE ... YOU GOTTA HAVE FAITH ... BUT FIRST YOU GOTTA GET RID OF THE WITNESSES!"

Bloody Mama

At first young Robert De Niro doesn't seem so bad to Pamela Dunlap but she soon finds out otherwise in *Bloody Mama*.

(March 1970) Color by Movielab. Produced and Directed by Roger Corman. Written by Robert Thom and Donald Peters. Starring Shelley Winters, Pat Hingle, Don Stroud, Diane Varsi. DVD: MGM/Fox Roger Corman box set (1.85) 91 min.

The success of *Bonnie and Clyde* (1967) inspired AIP to film a gangster picture of their own. AIP sent the script of *Bloody Mama* to Roger Corman and he agreed to direct it. They had wanted him to shoot the movie in Hollywood but Corman decided to make it entirely on location in Arkansas to take advantage of the rural local color. Kate Barker's four sons are accused of raping a local girl so Ma (Shelley Winters) leaves her husband (Alex Nicol) and takes her boys away so the law can't prosecute them. The boys are a strange brood. Eldest son Herman (Don Stroud) is a psychopath, Lloyd (Robert De Niro) is a dope addict, Fred (Robert Walden) is a homosexual masochist, and Arthur (Clint Kimbrough) is an introverted bookworm. The boys continue their antisocial behavior and when it lands two of them in jail, Ma picks up a machine gun herself to help them out. When Ma eventually comes up with a plan to kidnap a wealthy man (Pat Hingle) to extort money from his family, it proves to be the Barkers' undoing. Also in the strong cast are Diane Varsi as a prostitute named Mona and Bruce Dern as Fred's sadistic lover Kevin. *Bloody Mama* has rape, incest, sadism, robbery, murder, drugs, sodomy ... and Shelley Winters. Ms. Winters' career was filled with excessive performances and her Ma Barker may be the most over-the-top of them all. Corman's attempts to direct her Method performance reportedly left him baffled and exhausted. At the end, Shelley really goes out of control. For the final shootout she suddenly looks as if she has aged ten years and gained twenty pounds. She shrieks, she whines, she drools ... and eventually she dies. *Bloody Mama* is a very well made film, as are the majority of Corman's movies, but it is also unrelentingly brutal which often makes it very unpleasant and difficult to watch. But then there is always Shelley to make sure you don't look away for too long.

Review: *Time* (May 11, 1970), "*Bloody Mama* is a lurid little number featuring Shelley Winters doing her smothering-mother thing as the nefarious Ma Barker."

The Bonnie Parker Story

"CIGAR SMOKING HELLCAT OF THE ROARING THIRTIES!"

(May 1958) Superama and Black & White. Produced and Written by Stan Shpetner. Directed by William Witney. Starring Dorothy Provine, Jack Hogan, Richard Bakalyan, Douglas Kennedy. DVD: Direct Video Distribution (1.33) 79 min.; Region-Free DVD from United Kingdom, Extras: Audio interview with Samuel Z. Arkoff, Trailers.

Dorothy Provine and Richard Bakalyan in the early AIP gangster movie *The Bonnie Parker Story*.

The Bonnie Parker Story stars Dorothy Provine in the title role nearly a decade before Faye Dunaway forever became identified with the character. Some of the facts about the real Bonnie and Clyde manage to find their way into the script but they are few and far between. In real life, Clyde Barrow (herein renamed "Guy Darrow") was the brains of the outfit and Bonnie was, by all accounts, totally enamored of him. In *The Bonnie Parker Story*, Bonnie definitely wears the pants and calls all the shots. When the film opens, Bonnie is a waitress with a husband in jail and no prospects for her future (all factual). Enter Guy Darrow (Jack Hogan) who soon teaches her the thrills of robbing gas stations. Not satisfied with such penny ante endeavors, Bonnie decides to spring her husband Duke (Richard Bakalyan) from prison and step their operation up to bank robbing. Both Guy and Duke are hot for Bonnie but she treats them like the brainless fools they are. When she meets a handsome architecture student, Bonnie has a brief glimpse of what her life might have been with the right kind of man. Duke is killed in a botched attempt to rob an armored truck. Bonnie and Guy soon meet their ends in a trap set by a determined law enforcement officer (Douglas Kennedy) who has doggedly followed their trail. The ending is definitely anti-climactic, particularly when compared to the slow-motion slaughter in the 1967 film version of the same event. In *The Bonnie Parker Story* the officers open fire on their car, which runs off the road and overturns. End of picture.

Review: *Variety* (July 9, 1958), "Obviously an exploitation item, but it is capably constructed and intelligently carried out."

The Born Losers

"WHICH ONE OF YOU CATS IS FIRST?"

(September 1967) Color. An Otis Productions Picture. Produced by Don Henderson. Directed by T.C. Frank. Written by James Lloyd. Starring Tom Laughlin, Elizabeth James, Jeremy Slate, William Wellman Jr. DVD: Ventura (1.33) 112 min.; Audio commentary by Tom Laughlin and Delores Taylor.

"The Born Losers" are a particularly vile motorcycle gang led by Danny Carmody (Jeremy Slate) and members with names like Speechless, Cueball, Gangrene and Crabs ("'cause he's got 'em"). When vacationing college student Vicky Barrington (Elizabeth James) goes riding on her motorcycle dressed in a white bikini with matching go-go boots, she is definitely asking for trouble. The gang takes her back to their beach pad where all manner of depravity ensues. It's up to a "part–Injun" and former Green Beret, Billy Jack (Tom Laughlin), to save Vicky with his own brand of vigilante justice. *The Born Losers* is one of those "special" movies that is so bad it's good. Most of the acting is truly abysmal. Even Jane Russell, in a guest star cameo, has to be seen to be believed ... and even then you won't. Worst of the lot is leading lady Elizabeth James, who looks like Liza Minnelli as Pookie Adams in *The Sterile Cuckoo* ... but with the body of a Playboy Playmate. Most of her lines consist of wisecracks that she can't deliver to save her soul. Why would they have chosen her, you may ask? Well, she wrote those lines under the name "James Lloyd." Ms. James isn't the only one using a pseudonym. Star Tom Laughlin produced the film (with his wife Delores Taylor) as "Don Henderson" and directed it as "T.C. Frank." Jeremy Slate, who often appears as the protagonist in AIP biker films, switches gears here and turns in a good performance as the main villain ... and dig those crazy sunglasses! *The Born Losers* was successful enough to encourage Laughlin and Taylor to make a sequel called *Billy Jack* (1971). This film became a huge box office success and generated two sequels, *The Trial of Billy Jack* (1974) and *Billy Jack Goes to Washington* (1977). AIP was not involved in any of the sequels but in order to capitalize on them, they reissued *The Born Losers* in 1974: "Back by Popular Demand! The original screen appearance of TOM LAUGHLIN as BILLY JACK!" *The Born Losers* was once available from Ventura on a single DVD, which is long out of print and difficult to find. Now the only way to get the film on DVD is in the "Billy Jack 35th Anniversary Ultimate Collection" which also includes the three sequels.

Boxcar Bertha

"AMERICA IN THE 30'S WAS A FREE COUNTRY. BERTHA WAS JES' A BIT FREE'ER THAN MOST."

(June 1972) Color by Movielab. Produced by Roger Corman. Directed by Martin Scorsese. Written by Joyce H. Corrington and John William Corrington. Starring Barbara Hershey, David Carradine, Barry Premis, Bernie Casey. DVD: MGM (1.85) 88 min.; Extras: Theatrical trailer.

Based on *Sister of the Road*, the autobiography of Bertha Thompson, *Boxcar Bertha* is another entry in the genre of AIP gangster movies. In the South during the Great Depression, a young Bertha (Barbara Hershey) meets devout Union supporter Big Bill Shelly (David Carradine). After Bill leads a strike against the railroad, he and his friends are forced to take to the rails to escape an anti-union faction. Bertha happens to be riding the rails herself and the two become reacquainted and fall in love. Bill and Bertha join forces with a card shark named Rake Brown (Barry Primus) and

Jane Russell suffering the indignity of appearing in *The Born Losers*.

Bill's black buddy Von Horton (Bernie Casey) to form a gang which specializes in holding up trains. This way Bill can get even with railroad boss Mr. Sartoris (John Carradine) and get rich too. Over the next few years Bertha goes from a boxcar-riding hobo to gangster, to prostitute, and back to gangster. The movie ends in the kind of typical Hollywood gangster bloodbath that became the norm after *Bonnie and Clyde*. Although he had made a few films prior to *Boxcar Bertha*, this was the breakout movie for director Martin Scorsese. There is, however, little indication of his directorial style and the major influence on the movie seems to be producer Roger Corman. In both tone and execution, *Boxcar Bertha* greatly resembles Corman's *Bloody Mama*.

The following year Scorsese would come into his own with *Mean Streets*. Watch for Scorsese in a cameo as one of Bertha's clients during the brothel montage.

The Brain Eaters

"Crawling, Slimy Things Terror-Bent on Destroying the World!"

(October 1958) Black & White. Produced by Edwin Nelson. Directed by Bruno VeSota. Written by Gordon Urquhart. Starring Edwin Nelson, Joanna Lee, Alan Frost, Jack Hill. VHS: Columbia/TriStar (1.33) 60 min.; DVD: Direct Video Distribution (1.33) 60 min., Region-Free DVD from United Kingdom, Extras: Audio interview with Samuel Z. Arkoff, Trailers.

The Brain Eaters is a perfect example of the type of movie that was the bane of kiddie matinee moviegoers in the fifties. Lured in by a titillating title and exciting poster art, pre-adolescent audiences were then subjected to an excruciating hour of boredom. "Where are the monsters?" we would scream as we threw our popcorn boxes at the screen. Instead we were given fuzz balls with pipe cleaner antennae. AIP had duped us again! A cone-shaped structure mysteriously appears in Riverdale, Illinois, and shortly thereafter some of the inhabitants of the city begin to act oddly. They walk as if in a trance and carry around what look like glowing fishbowls. Inside the fishbowls are the abovementioned fuzz balls which are actually parasites that attach themselves to humans, taking over their minds and bodies. In one particularly misguided scene, a parasite attaches itself to scientist Edwin Nelson's arm and his lab assistant–girlfriend tries to beat it to death with a clipboard! *The Brain Eaters* went through more than its share of title changes before reaching the screen: *The Keepers*, *The Keepers of the Earth*, *Attack of the Blood Leeches*, and *Battle of the Brain Eaters*. "A rose by any other name would smell as sweet" applies here in reverse. Bruno VeSota provides his usual uninspired direction and the cast, except for Nelson, give desultory performances. One of the players is Leonard Nimoy, unrecognizable in "Father Time"–type makeup. An overwrought background score by Tom Jonson doesn't help. *The Brain Eaters* is an uncredited adaptation of Robert Heinlein's novel *The Puppet Masters*, which was made into a 1994 film of that title starring Donald Sutherland.

Review: *Variety* (November 5, 1958), "Routine. Within its drawbacks, it is competently done."

The Brain That Wouldn't Die

"Alive ... Without a Body ... Fed by an Unspeakable Horror from Hell!"

(August 1962) Black & White. A Sterling Production. Produced by Rex Carlton. Written and Directed by Joseph Green. Starring Herb (a.k.a. Jason) Evers, Virginia Leith, Adele Lamont, Bruce Brighton. VHS: MGM (1.33) 70 min.; DVD: Alpha (1.33) 82 min.

Dr. Bill Cortner (Herb Evers) causes a traffic accident in which his fiancée Jan (Virginia Leith) is decapitated. He "rescues" her head and keeps it alive while he goes in search of a new body. Filmed independently in 1959 under the title *The Head That Wouldn't Die*, the movie was eventually picked up by AIP and released in 1962 on a double bill with *Invasion of the Star Creatures*. Although many sources claim the film was cut for television, the edits were actually made by AIP for the theatrical release. Both Warner and MGM released this 70-minute cut version on video. The Alpha DVD release is a good-quality uncut print which restores the excessive gore and extends the scenes in the strip club where Cortner goes in search of a new body for Jan. *The Brain That Wouldn't Die* is one of the most deliriously bizarre movies of all time. At times it has the look, feel, and sleazy qualities of an early John Waters film. This is intended as an enthusiastic recommendation.

The Brute and the Beast

"WHAT KIND OF MEN LIVE ONLY TO KILL?"

(December 1968) ColorScope by Perfect (Cromoscope and Eastman Color). A Mega Film Colt/I.F. Produzioni Cinematografiche Production. Produced by Livio Maffei. Directed by Lucio Fulci. Written by Fernando Di Leo. Starring Franco Nero, George Hilton, Nino Castelnuovo, John M. Douglas. DVD: Substance (as *Massacre Time*) (2.35) 92 min., Extras: U.S. and European trailers, Poster and still gallery.

Although AIP seemed to take full advantage of every cinematic trend, the Spaghetti Western was one genre that they barely tapped. It is odd, considering the vast number of Spaghetti Westerns, that AIP imported only two for release: *The Brute and the Beast* and *God Forgives ... I Don't!* The former started off as the 1966 film *Tempo di massacaro/Massacre Time* and, after undergoing a title change, was released in the U.S. by AIP two years later. It is an outstanding example of the genre, filled with all the weird quirks one has come to expect from these movies. *The Brute and the Beast* stars two icons of the genre, Franco Nero and George Hilton. Tom Corbett (Nero) is busy panning for gold when he receives an urgent message pleading for him to return to his home in Laramie Town. When he arrives there he discovers that Mr. Scott (John M. Douglas) has taken over the town, including his father's property which had been left to Tom's brother Jeff (Hilton). Jeff is now a drunkard, living in a shack with the former family servant. Tom is determined to get his brother's land back, which means dealing with the Scott family. While Mr. Scott may be unscrupulous, his son Junior (Nino Castelnuovo) is a total psychopath who is far more trouble than Tom bargained for. When things seem most hopeless, it turns out that brother Jeff is as fast-shootin' as he is hard-drinkin.' *The Brute and the Beast* is expertly directed by Lucio Fulci, who would later achieve his greatest fame with a series of excessively gruesome horror movies. The film also benefits greatly from Riccardo Pallonttini's widescreen cinematography and a typically over-the-top Spaghetti Western score by Lallo Gori, complete with title song ("A Man Alone" sung by Sergio Endrigo).

A Bucket of Blood

"YOU'LL BE SICK, SICK, SICK—FROM LAUGHING!"

(October 1959) Black & White. Produced and Directed by Roger Corman. Written by Charles B. Griffith. Starring Dick Miller, Barboura Morris, Anthony Carbone, Ed Nelson. DVD: MGM (1.33) 66 min.

Poor Walter Paisley (Dick Miller) is a busboy at The Yellow Door, a beatnik coffee house where artistic types gather every night. Walter is a bit of a dim bulb and after he mistakenly kills his landlady's cat, he covers the corpse in clay and presents it as a statue to the coffee house crowd. His "work of art" is a tremendous success so when he is threatened by an undercover police officer for drug possession, Walter kills the cop and makes a statue out of him as well. Walter soon discovers that the price of fame is sometimes too high. This ultra-black comedy, concocted by Roger Corman and writer Charles Griffith, paved the way for 1960's *The Little Shop of Horrors* which

Barboura Morris in Roger Corman's horror comedy *A Bucket of Blood*.

has the same tone but a greater cult following. Dick Miller has the best role of his career and brings it off marvelously.

Even though he is a murderer, Miller's tragic Walter never loses audience sympathy. Barboura Morris was a member of Corman's stock company of actors and always gave a noteworthy performance whether in a bit part (*The Trip*) or a lead (*Atlas*). Tragically, she died of cancer in 1975 at the age of 43. *A Bucket of Blood* is available from many sources but the MGM DVD is by far the best quality presentation. In 1995, Showtime aired the series "Roger Corman Presents"; one episode was a remake of *A Bucket of Blood* starring Anthony Michael Hall as Walter Paisley and directed by Michael McDonald. While not bad, it does not live up to the original.

Review: *Variety* (October 28, 1959), "A 66-minute joke compounded of beatniks and gore."

Bucktown

"WHATEVER YOU WANT THEY'VE GOT ... AND BUCKTOWN IS WHERE YOU'LL FIND IT!"

(July 1975) Color by Movielab. Produced by Bernard Schwartz. Directed by Arthur Marks. Written by Bob Ellison. Starring Fred Williamson, Pam Grier, Thalmus Rasulala, Art Lund. DVD: MGM (1.85) 94 min., Extras: Theatrical trailer.

When Duke Johnson (Fred Williamson) checks into the sleazy Dixie Hotel in Bucktown, the pretty desk clerk asks him: "What's a fine black thang like you doin' in town?" Well, Duke has come to bury his brother and reopen the bar that he left him in his will. Unfortunately, Duke didn't know beforehand that Bucktown is the most scummy and corrupt city since Gomorrah. Most corrupt of all is the redneck police chief (Art Lund) whose philosophy is "We're the law ... God is on our side." When Duke gets roughed up by the local police, he contacts his buddy Roy (Thalmus Rasulala) in the Big City and calls in a few favors. Roy shows up in town with his black posse and in no time at all the white cracker

Fred Williamson (in *Bucktown*) was the King of AIP blaxploitation films.

cops are pushing up daisies. And everybody in Bucktown lived happily ever after. Not quite. Roy decides that he and his gang are going to stay and take over Bucktown and it turns out they are even more greedy and ruthless than the rednecks were. Duke kindly asks Roy to leave town but as long as "the dice keep rollin', the hos keep hoin', and the money keeps flowin'" Roy ain't goin' anywhere. When one of Roy's men tries to rape Duke's girl Aretha (Pam Grier), Duke sets his lantern jaw and decides that he has had enough. He is going to rid Bucktown of these dudes even if it means "borrowing" a tank from the nearby Army base. This pairing of the king and queen of AIP blaxploitation should have been more memorable than it is. Pam Grier has little to do other than look beautiful (which she does effortlessly) and Fred Williamson isn't given an opportunity to rise to the level of his famous "Black Caesar" character. Still both stars are always worth watching and the action in *Bucktown* seldom lets up.

Burn Witch, Burn

"Do the Undead Demons of Hell Still Arise to Terrorize the World?"

(April 1962) Black & White. A Julian Wintle–Leslie Parkyn Production. Produced by Albert Fennell. Directed by Sidney Hayers. Written by Richard Matheson, Charles Beaumont and George Baxt. Starring Janet Blair, Peter Wyngarde, Margaret Johnston, Anthony Nicholls. VHS: MGM (1.33) 87 min.; DVD: Optimum (as *Night of the Eagle*) (1.78) 87 min., Region 2 DVD from United Kingdom.

In *Burn, Witch, Burn*, Peter Wyngarde is a skeptic who learns that black magic is real and very close to home.

Successful college professor Norman Taylor (Peter Wyngarde) teaches his students to reject superstition and accept only the cold hard facts of reality. Therefore, it comes as a great shock to him to discover that his wife Tansy (Janet Blair) is a confirmed believer in witchcraft and that she has been using her powers to try to further his academic career. When Norman forces Tansy to destroy her magic talismans, his life takes a definite turn for the worst. It seems that Tansy isn't the only one practicing black magic at the college and now those forces are working to destroy Norman. Based on Fritz Leiber's novel *Conjure Wife* (previously filmed in 1944 as *Weird Woman*), this English-made movie's original title was *Night of the Eagle*. The title change is taken from a line of dialogue in the film and actually suits it better ... in addition to being more exploitative for AIP purposes. Whatever the title, this is a fine horror film. It is one of a triumvirate of outstanding black magic movies which also includes *Night of the Demon* (1958) and *The Devil Rides Out* (1968). Although each was made in England by a different company, they all share a similar high level of intelligent filmmaking, in addition to being formidable thrillers guaranteed to chill your blood. Although George Baxt is listed as a writer in the British credits, he is uncredited in the U.S. version.

Review: *New York Herald Tribune* (July 5, 1962), "*Burn Witch, Burn* is an exceptionally well turned exercise in the occult. Direction and acting are excellent."

Cat Girl

"SCREAMING TERROR! ...
TO CARESS ME IS TO TEMPT DEATH!"

(September 1957) Black & White. An Insignia Films Ltd. Production. Produced by Lou Rusoff and Herbert Smith. Directed by Alfred Shaughnessy. Written by Lou Rusoff. Starring Barbara Shelley, Robert Ayers, Kay Callard, Ernest Milton. VHS: Columbia/TriStar (1.33) 69 min.

At the request of her uncle, Leonora Brandt (Barbara Shelley) returns to the family mansion to collect her inheritance, which includes a large sum of money ... and a family curse. It seems the Brandt family suffers from a generations-old affliction which links their minds with that of a leopard. Not long after their arrival at Brandt Manor, Leonora's greedy, philandering husband becomes the first victim. A local psychiatrist (Robert Ayres), with whom Leonora has always been in love, is convinced the curse is all in her disturbed mind. *Cat Girl* was the first AIP British co-production and started as a Lou Rusoff script entitled *Wolf-Girl*. The plot definitely owes more to *Cat People* than *The Wolf Man* although in one scene they refer to the family curse as "lycanthropy" and say that Leonora's uncle turned into a "werewolf" when clearly the animal in question was a leopard. The best reason for watching this film is Barbara Shelley in the first of her many horror roles. To this rather unremarkable offering she brings the same level of intensity to her acting that she would display in such Hammer films as *The Gorgon* (1964), *Dracula–Prince of Darkness* and *Rasputin the Mad Monk* (both 1966). For the U.S. release of *Cat Girl*, a very brief sequence of Ms. Shelley transforming into a cat-like creature was inserted with makeup designed by Paul Blaisdell. Better it had been left to audiences' imagination as it looks more cuddly than frightening. According to the AIP publicity for *Cat Girl*, the leopard was played by a four-year-old Bengal leopard named "Big Chief Horrible Noise" or "Chiefy" for short. It was his first film role.

Review: *Harrison's Reports* (September 7, 1957), "[A] rather weak picture of its kind and leaves much to be desired."

Chastity

"SHE'S NOT A GIRL ... SHE'S AN EXPERIENCE!
PICK HER UP IF YOU DARE!"

(June 1969) Color by DeLuxe. A Progress Motion Pictures Presentation. Produced and Written by Sonny Bono. Directed by Alessio de Paola. Starring Cher, Barbara London, Stephen Whittaker, Richard Armstrong. DVD: MGM (1.85) 82 min., Extras: Teaser trailer, Fullscreen version.

Many years before the succession of highly acclaimed performances which began with *Come Back to the Five and Dime, Jimmy Dean, Jimmy Dean* in 1982, Cher made her dramatic debut in this movie written for her by then-husband Sonny Bono. Sonny obviously conceived of *Chastity* as a worshipful showcase for Cher and she is featured in every scene. Chastity (Cher) is a young woman on the run who talks to herself a lot. She hitchhikes to Arizona where she meet a decent young man but, after an unfortunate experience in a church confessional, she steals a car and drives south of the border. In a Mexican border town she buys a couple of tacos and decides to try her hand at being a prostitute ... sort of. At the local bordello she attracts the adoring attention of the lesbian madam (Barbara London) and they enter into a relationship ... sort of. At this point the film veers perilously close to becoming total camp as the madam is dressed like Tippi Hedren in *The Birds* and acts like Barbara Stanwyck in *Walk on the Wild Side*. After a lesbian montage sequence ("Be careful, Chas, this is a new scene. Here you are, rubbing noses with a dyke"), Chastity has had enough and tearfully flees the bordello to hitchhike back to Arizona. She returns to the decent young man but happiness is not in the cards for our Chastity. She runs away again and in the end we find out why she is on the run ... sort of. Although Cher plays most of her part using the deadpan, cynical persona of her *Sonny and Cher Show* days, she does have a few moments to dramatically shine and has no trouble carrying the weight of the picture.

She also has two brief nude scenes. One seems to be a body double but the other does not. Needless to say, *Chastity* is a must for Cher's legion of fans. Sonny Bono also wrote the background score and the song Cher sings over the opening credits.

Chrome and Hot Leather

"DON'T MUCK AROUND WITH A GREEN BERET'S MAMA!"

(August 1971) Color by Movielab. A Wes Bishop-Lee Frost Production. Produced by Wes Bishop. Directed by Lee Frost. Written by Michael Allen Haynes, David Neibel, and Don Tait. Starring William Smith, Tony Young, Michael Haynes, Peter Brown. DVD: MGM (1.85) 92 min., Extras: Theatrical trailer, Midnite Movies co-feature: *The Mini-Skirt Mob*.

Stone-faced Green Beret Mitch (Tony Young) finds out that his fiancée Kathy (Cherie Moor a.k.a. Cheryl Ladd) has been killed in an automobile accident caused by a group of bikers. He and three of his Green Beret buddies (Peter Brown, Michael Sterns, and Marvin Gaye) pose as bikers in order to find out who was responsible for the accident. Their search leads them to "The Wizards," a gang of tough thugs lead by T.J. (William Smith). When T.J. realizes what's up, he moves his gang into hiding in the Superstition Mountains (actually good ol' Bronson Caves in Griffith Park, Los Angeles). Using their military expertise, Mitch and his friends launch a full-scale assault on the bikers. Although *Chrome and Hot Leather* is one of the more interesting AIP biker films and moves along at a fairly brisk pace, the most fascinating thing about this movie is the cast. Film veteran and weightlifting champion William Smith looks like a cross between a young Jack Palance and a Tom of Finland drawing. Not your typical-looking AIP movie biker by any means. Since he did his own motorcycle stunts, he ended up starring in several of these films, most notably Joe Solomon's *Run, Angel, Run* (1969). Also in the cast are singers Marvin Gaye and Bobby "Boris" Pickett, the latter of "Monster Mash" fame. Sundry uncredited bikers include Dan Haggerty (*Grizzly Adams*) and Erik Estrada (*CHiPs*).

Vanda Hudson comes to a gruesome end in *Circus of Horrors*.

Circus of Horrors

"Spectacular Towering Terror!"

(May 1960) Specta-Color (Eastman Color). Produced by Julian Wintle and Leslie Parkyn. Directed by Sidney Hayers. Written by George Baxt. Starring Anton Diffring, Erika Remberg, Yvonne Monlaur, Donald Pleasence. DVD: Anchor Bay (1.77) 91 min., Extras: Theatrical trailer, TV spots, Poster, still and advertising galleries.

Following the impressive box office take of *Horrors of the Black Museum*, Britain's Anglo Amalgamated and AIP were eager to duplicate its success. They found a likely property in the Julian Wintle-Leslie Parkyn production *Circus of Horrors*. The formula was similar to that of the previous film in which a crazed journalist commits bizarre murders with buxom women as the victims. This time around, a crazed plastic surgeon commits bizarre murders with buxom circus performers as the victims. The similarity ends there and *Circus of Horrors* stands on its own perverse merits and not merely as a retread of the earlier film. A coldly handsome Anton Diffring stars as Dr. Rossiter, a plastic surgeon forced to flee England because of a botched operation. Assuming the name Bernard Schuler, he continues to practice his medical skills while hiding behind the guise of a traveling circus owner. His beautiful star performers are disfigured prostitutes, thieves, and murderers whose beauty has been restored through his brilliant surgery. When they attempt to leave him, Schuler sees to it that they meet with untimely ends. For the U.S. release of *Circus of Horrors*, AIP designed new main titles and cut about three minutes from the film. The Anchor Bay DVD is an uncut version. The song "Look for a Star," which is featured prominently throughout the movie, was a popular hit on both sides of the Atlantic and had a number of different recordings at the time.

Review: *New York Herald Tribune* (September 1, 1960), "*Circus of Horrors* is horrible. Not spine-chilling horrible. Just horrible, horrible."

Coffy

"SHE'S THE GODMOTHER OF THEM ALL ...
THE BADDEST ONE-CHICK HIT-SQUAD
THAT EVER HIT TOWN!"

(May 1973) Color by Movielab. Produced by Robert A. Papazian. Directed and Written by Jack Hill. Starring Pam Grier, Booker Bradshaw, Robert Doqui, William Elliott. DVD: MGM (1.85) 90 min., Extras: Theatrical trailer, Audio Commentary by Jack Hill.

Pam Grier made her AIP debut in the 1972 film *Black Mama, White Mama*. The following year she starred in *Coffy*, the role she would become most identified with and which would confirm her position as "Queen of Blaxploitation." Eleven-year-old LuBelle gets hooked on drugs and her big sister Coffy intends to do something about it. Coffy becomes a one-woman revenge machine and vows to take out the black drug pushers and white gangsters behind them. To get closer to the top man she poses as a Jamaican call girl named Mistique. When the white scumbags catch on, there is no end of trouble for Coffy. This prime example of blaxploitation has nudity, Afros, car chases, blood, and every racial slur you can imagine ... plus a few you can't. It also has one of the best girl fights ever put on film. Grier is stunning in the title role and, as usual, gives it her all and then some. Writer-director Jack Hill would recycle most of the ideas in *Coffy* for *Foxy Brown*, with even more outrageous results.

The Comedy of Terrors

"WHERE THE GHOULS ARE ...
IS WHERE THE FUN IS!"

(December 1963) Panavision and Pathécolor. Produced by James H. Nicholson and Samuel Z. Arkoff. Directed by Jacques Tourneur. Written by Richard Matheson. Starring Vincent Price, Peter Lorre, Boris Karloff, Basil Rathbone. DVD: MGM (2.35) 88 min., Extras: Theatrical trailer, Richard Matheson featurette, Midnite Movies co-feature: *The Raven*.

In the wake of the box office success of Roger Corman's *The Raven*, AIP decided that another exercise in comedy and horror was seriously to be considered. Jim Nicholson came up with the title "The Graveside Story" and Richard Matheson was hired to write a screenplay which would reunite the three stars of *The Raven*, Vincent Price, Peter Lorre, and Boris Karloff. For added horror star power, Basil Rathbone was also added to the cast.

The advertising art for *The Comedy of Terrors*.

In 1890 New England, the Hinchley and Trumbull Funeral Home has fallen on hard times, with only one coffin in stock and a woeful lack of prospective clients to fill it. Waldo Trumbull (Price) decides to take matters into his own hands and, with the help of his reluctant assistant Felix Gillie (Lorre), goes out to drum up some much-needed business. Unfortunately his intended victim, John F. Black (Rathbone), a Shakespeare-spouting skinflint, refuses to stay dead. Also on hand for the mayhem is 92-year-old Amos Hinchley (Karloff) and his unhappily married daughter Amaryllis Trumbull (Joyce Jameson), the constant target of husband Waldo's cruel insults. The original intent had been for Karloff to portray Black but his lack of mobility prevented it so he switched parts with Rathbone. Although the jokes are sometimes a bit labored, it is wonderful to see the leads in a film which allows them to utilize their comedic talents. Everyone seems to be having a terrific time. The production values are in the same league as the Corman Poe films, not too surprising since Daniel Haller was responsible for the production design and art direction with Floyd Crosby as cinematographer. The only negative factor is the background score by Les Baxter which accompanies each gag and pratfall with a whiz, bang, or pop. Matheson came up with the final title and, in retrospect, he believes that using the word "comedy" in the title lessened the movie's chances for duplicating the success of The Raven.

Review: *Time* (May 15, 1964), "*Comedy of Terrors* is a lushly produced little parody of Hollywood scream fare, hopefully labeled a 'horroromp.'"

Conqueror Worm

"LEAVE THE CHILDREN HOME ...
AND IF YOU ARE SQUEAMISH ...
STAY HOME WITH THEM!"

(May 1968) Color by Perfect (Eastman Color). A Tigon British/American International Production. Produced by Louis M. Heyward, Philip Waddilove, and Arnold L. Miller. Directed by Michael Reeves. Written by Michael Reeves, Tom Baker and Louis M. Heyward. Starring Vincent Price, Ian Ogilvy, Hilary Dwyer, Rupert Davies. VHS: MGM (1.33) 87 min., Extras: Theatrical trailer; DVD: MGM/Fox (as *Witchfinder General*) (1.85) 87 min., Extras: Audio commentary by Philip Waddilove and Ian Ogilvy, *Witchfinder General: Michael Reeves' Horror Classic*.

This "historical horror film" was produced in England under the title *Witchfinder General* and tells the violent and unsettling story of real-life personage Matthew Hopkins who, during the British Civil War, went from village to village seeking out witches. When he found someone who was suspected of being a witch, he had that individual tortured and put to death. Hopkins (Vincent Price) makes the mistake of "interfering" with the fiancée of soldier Richard Marshall (Ian Ogilvy), who vows to take revenge on the Witchfinder. *Witchfinder General* is an outstanding film in every respect. Director Michael Reeves showed great promise with this, his third picture, but he died at age 25 just months after the release of what would be his masterwork. Price gives one of his finest performances as the despicable Hopkins and the rest of the cast is exemplary. Hilary Dwyer, in particular, is especially good in her AIP debut. Vilified by many at the time of its release, *Witchfinder General* is now widely considered a masterpiece. Unfortunately, the treatment given the film in the U.S. has not always reflected such exalted cinematic status. When AIP released *Witchfinder General* in the U.S. they decided to make it part of their Edgar Allan Poe series by changing the title to *Conqueror Worm* and having Price recite some lines from Poe's poem at the beginning and end. Used for the original video release by HBO was an alternate print which featured some nudity which had not been in the U.S. theatrical release. Because of a dispute over the music rights, this video replaced Paul Ferris' original score with a synthesized one by Kendall Schmidt. Since Ferris' haunting music was a key element, this damaged the movie considerably. Several years later, when it was

Paul Ferris (lower center) composed the score and also appears in *Conqueror Worm*.

announced that *Conqueror Worm* was going to be reissued on video as part of the MGM Midnite Movie series, fans hopes ran high. These hopes were dashed with the release of the video. Although it was a new digital transfer, the MGM release still featured the Kendall Schmidt score. Even worse, whoever worked on the video failed to notice that one of the reels was out of order, making for unforgivable lapses in the story's continuity. No movie deserves this kind of treatment, particularly one as good as this. Fortunately, all of this has been corrected with the 2007 MGM Midnite Movie DVD edition of *Witchfinder General*. This is Michael Reeves' original cut of the film; all violence intact, no topless tavern wenches, and the Paul Ferris score restored. The picture quality is superb and the color breathtaking. At last there is a definitive version available of this seminal horror movie.

Review: *Variety* (May 6, 1968), "Substitutes gore for suspense and action."

The Cool and the Crazy

"Seven Savage Punks on a Weekend Binge of Violence!"

(March 1958) Black & White. An Imperial Productions Presentation. Produced by E. C. Rhoden Jr. Directed by William Witney. Written by Richard C. Sarafian. Starring Scott Marlowe, Gigi Perreau, Dick Bakalyan, Dick Jones. DVD: Direct Video Distribution (1.33) 78 min., Region-Free DVD from United Kingdom, Extras: Audio interview with Samuel Z. Arkoff, Trailers.

Reefer Madness AIP style. Bennie (Scott Marlowe) is the new kid in high school, fresh from a stint in reform school. Bennie is also working for the local drug dealer whose motto is "Get 'em on the smoke and then the other stuff." He ingratiates himself with a group of high school bad boys (none of whom looks under twenty-five years old). One wild Saturday night Bennie gives the gang some reefers and the next thing you know they are banging their heads on tables, clutching their throats and, in raspy voices, begging him for more "M." As the local cop says, "M don't stand for Mother." It must be some pretty strong stuff because one smoke and they are *hooked*. Jackie (Dick Bakalyan) is the only one of the bunch who stays clean but he does steal a precious antique knick-knack from his girlfriend's house to get enough money to help out a drug-crazed buddy. When Bennie murders the dealer and turns to "the needle," he really goes bonkers. A cautionary tale with a lesson to be learned by all of us. If you could change the locale from Kansas City to Baltimore and substitute Scott Marlowe with Divine, you would have one hell of a John Waters movie.

Song: "Cool and Crazy"

Review: *Harrison's Reports* (May 10, 1958), "The direction and acting are fairly skillful, but what is shown is decidedly unpleasant and unwholesome."

Count Yorga, Vampire

"A Tale of Unspeakable Cravings ... the Most Terrifying Experience of Your Life!"

(June 1970) Color by Movielab. Produced by Michael Macready. Written and Directed by Bob Kelljan. Starring Robert Quarry, Roger Perry, Donna Anderson, Michael Murphy. DVD: MGM (1.85) 93 min., Extras: Theatrical trailer, Midnite Movies co-feature: *The Return of Count Yorga*.

Roger Perry attempts to ward off Count Yorga (Robert Quarry) using the tried-and-true weapons.

Although by 1970 Hammer was the preeminent purveyors of vampire cinema, thus far all of their films had a period setting. *Count Yorga, Vampire* brought the vampire into contemporary times. A wooden crate arrives at the Port of Los Angeles and is taken to a mansion on the outskirts of the city. Shortly thereafter, a Bulgarian "count" enters into the lives of Donna (Donna Anderson) and a group of her friends, with fatal results. This was originally conceived as a softcore porn movie, but its creators soon realized that had something with far more widespread potential on their hands and shifted gears. The end result was a surprising box office success when it was picked up and released by American International. Made for less than $200,000, the film went on to make millions. Robert Quarry, who plays the rather effete Count Yorga, erroneously fancied himself as the successor to Vincent Price. He did manage to get himself a contract with AIP and eventually appeared in five more of their releases. The original title of the film was *The Loves of Count Iorga* and that is what appears on the DVD release, which also includes more gore than the 91-minute theatrical version.

The Crimson Cult

"COME FACE TO FACE WITH NAKED FEAR ON THE ALTAR OF EVIL!"

(May 1970) Color by Movielab. A Tigon British Film Production. Produced by Louis M. Heyward. Directed by Vernon Sewell. Written by Mervyn Haisman and Henry Lincoln. Starring Boris Karloff, Christopher Lee, Mark Eden, Barbara Steele. VHS: HBO Video (1.33) 89 min.; DVD: D D Home Entertainment (as *Curse of the Crimson Altar*); (1.85) 87 min.; Region-Free DVD from United Kingdom; Extras: Interview with Christopher Lee; Trailer; Photo gallery.

When his brother Peter goes missing, antiques dealer Robert Manning (Mark Eden) goes to the village of Greymarsh to look for him. The Manning brothers are the last descendants of villagers who, 300 years before, burned to death the Black Witch of Greymarsh, Lavinia Morley (Barbara Steele). Robert soon discovers that there is much more going on in the sleepy village than one would surmise. The film features a powerhouse lineup of horror performers, but none of them makes much of an impression, with the notable exception of Boris Karloff. Christopher Lee walks through his role like a somnambulist. Barbara Steele's part is limited to green body paint and a ridiculous costume. Michael Gough is uncharacteristically subdued as an addled servant. But Karloff, with his usual degree of professionalism, turns in an alternately menacing and witty performance despite being wheelchair-bound for the duration. The film introduces the lovely Virginia Wetherell who went on to appear in several Hammer films. She married Hammer leading man Ralph Bates after meeting him on *Dr. Jekyll and Sister Hyde*. The HBO tape is listed on the box as *The Crimson Cult* with an 87 minute running time. Actually the video is a completely uncut version of the film with an onscreen title of *Curse of the Crimson Altar* and a running time of 89 minutes. The two minutes of restored footage consists mainly of nudity and some shots of a girl being whipped by a scantily clad woman in S&M leather gear. Unfortunately this is yet another instance where the original score (by Peter Knight) was replaced on the video version by Kendall Schmidt. The British DVD does have a couple of brief shots of the "leather lady" which were not in the U.S. theatrical release but the whipping scene is missing. Fortunately the Peter Knight score is intact on the DVD. Music and whipping aside, this is quite simply not a very good film. Loosely based on H.P. Lovecraft's story "Dreams in the Witch House," *The Crimson Cult* is indifferently directed and rather shoddily put together. Karloff, nearing the end of his illustrious career, deserved a better showcase for his talents than this. Apparently screenwriters Mervyn Haisman and Henry Lincoln felt the same way as they requested, without success, that their names be removed from the film which they had originally scripted under the title *The Reincarnation.*

Cry of the Banshee

"EDGAR ALLAN POE PROBES NEW DEPTHS OF TERROR!"

(July 1970) Color by Movielab. Produced and Directed by Gordon Hessler. Written by Tim Kelly and Christopher Wicking. Starring Vincent Price, Essy Persson, Patrick Mower, Elisabeth Bergner. VHS: HBO/Cannon Video (1.33) 87 min.; DVD: MGM (1.85) 91 min., Extras: Featurette: "A Devilish Tale of Poe," Theatrical trailer, Midnite Movies co-feature: *Murders in the Rue Morgue.*

When a director turned his finished film in to AIP there was always the possibility that it wasn't really "finished" at all. Tampering with a director's final cut became part and parcel of AIP's way of operating, particularly in the seventies. Because of this, some directors refused to work for the company ever again. In AIP's defense, sometimes their tampering improved the movie. *Cry of the Banshee* is an example of this, although it still isn't a very good film. According to director Gordon Hessler, *Cry of the Banshee* was a script that had been pre-sold to exhibitors. It was sent to Louis M. Heyward at American International's British offices to be produced in the United Kingdom. Gordon Hessler was hired to direct the film and he brought on screenwriter Christopher Wicking to help improve the script.

Although the original screenplay was rewritten extensively by Hessler and Wicking, they were informed that only 10 percent of their changes could be used. The story, set in 16th century England, tells of the harsh magistrate Lord Edward Whitman (Vincent Price) and his attempts to eradicate the practice of witchcraft in the village under his jurisdiction. Oona (Elisabeth Bergner) is the leader of the witches and she summons a demonic "Sidhe" (Patrick Mower) to exact her revenge against Whitman and his family. Although presented as yet another Poe film, only a quote at the

Beautiful Hilary Dwyer (in *Cry of the Banshee*) appeared in four of AIP's British productions.

beginning provides any link with the author. Gordon Hessler's original cut of *Cry of the Banshee* was shown in England without alteration, but the movie underwent many changes before appearing in U.S. theatres. A sequence involving Whitman's massacre of a coven of witches and Oona's subsequent curse on him and his family originally occurred 30 minutes into the movie. AIP took this scene and made it a pre-credits prologue for the U.S. version. This sets up the story far more effectively ... and quickly. Other changes include a red tinting on some of the witchcraft sequences, toning down the gore, and eliminating all the nudity. In regard to the latter, the original version has so much random bodice-ripping that it becomes ridiculous. Nearly every actress in the film has her blouse ripped open and her breasts exposed. Also excised from the U.S. prints is an unpleasant sequence in which Lady Patricia Whitman (Essy Persson) is raped by her stepson (Stephen Chase). The soundtrack of *Cry of the Banshee* also went through some alterations. The original score by Wilfred Josephs was replaced by a new one composed by Les Baxter. Baxter's score does provide some much-needed punch and includes a particularly beautiful theme to accompany a love scene between Patrick Mower and Hilary Dwyer. The "cry of the banshee" in the British version is merely the sound of a dog howling but it is given a much more eerie quality for the U.S. release. One change that is definitely not for the better is the substitution of Terry Gilliam's brilliant credits with a more mundane version by Cinefx. The positive factors that both versions of *Cry of the Banshee* have in common are an interesting cast, outstanding location photography by John Coquillon, and sumptuous costuming (courtesy *Anne of the Thousand Days*). Academy Award winner Hugh Griffith is given prominent billing but his part as a drunken gravedigger has little to do with the proceedings. The AIP U.S. version of *Cry of the Banshee* was available on the original HBO/Cannon VHS release but subsequent VHS and DVD releases are the British version.

Review: *Variety* (July 29, 1970), "One wishes that the script were better developed to take full advantage of the film's physical values."

The Cycle Savages

"Hot Steel Between Their Legs ...
The Wildest Bunch of the 70s!"

(April 1970) Color by Movielab. A Trans-American Films Release. Produced by Maurice Smith. Written and Directed by Bill Brame. Starring Bruce Dern, Melody Patterson, Chris Robinson, Linda Banks. DVD: MGM (1.85) 85 min., Extras: Theatrical trailer; Midnite Movies co-feature: *Angel Unchained*.

The sketches of a young artist (Chris Robinson) incur the wrath of Keeg (Bruce Dern), the leader of a biker gang. Keeg decides to "hurt the man's hands" to stop him from drawing and enlists the aid of Lea (Melody Patterson), an innocent girl whose sister was forced into prostitution by Keeg. In recent interviews, Bruce Dern has mentioned that drug use was not unusual when making these films, although he never participated. It's hard to believe he wasn't stoned out of his mind when he was making this because his performance is absolutely crazed. He rants, raves, foams at the mouth, seemingly ad libs dialogue, and carries on like a maniac ... very scary! The movie also includes a particularly graphic (for the time) gang rape scene, among other varied atrocities. This is definitely one of the more hard-hitting biker films in AIP's canon. *The Cycle Savages* was released by Trans American Films, a division of American International Pictures which was created to distribute some of their more questionable product.

Daddy-"O"

"Meet the 'Beat'! Daring to Live ...
Daring to Love!"

(March 1959) Black & White. An Imperial Production. Produced by Elmer Rhoden Jr. Directed by Lou Place. Written by David Moessinger. Starring Dick Contino, Sandra Giles, Bruno VeSota, Gloria Victor. VHS: Columbia/TriStar (1.33) 74 min.; DVD: Direct Video Distribution (1.33) 74 min.; Region-Free DVD from United Kingdom; Extras: Audio interview with Samuel Z. Arkoff, Trailers.

Paul Sandifer (Dick Contino) is a fast-drivin' cool cat who sings at the local juke joint. After he is nearly run off the road by blonde bombshell Jana Ryan (Lizabeth Scott lookalike Sandra Giles), she goads him into a drag race to prove who is the better driver. During the race, Paul gets nabbed by the cops who accuse him of causing a hit-and-run accident in which the other driver was killed. Turns out that the victim in the accident was Paul's best friend Sonny Di Marco (Bob Banas). At first Paul thinks that Jana caused the accident but he soon finds a clue which leads him to believe that slimy nightclub owner Sidney Chillas (Bruno VeSota) may be the real culprit. Paul takes a job at Chillas' Hi-Note Club, singing under the name of "Daddy-O" to see if he can find proof of his suspicions. According to AIP publicity, Contino was a "famed accordionist" prior to being cast as the lead in this picture. *Daddy-"O"* is the first credited film score for Academy Award–winning composer John Williams.

Songs: "Rock Candy Baby," "Angel Eyes," "Wait'll I Get You Home"

Sandra Giles threatens Dick Contino in *Daddy-"O."*

Day the World Ended

"THE SCREEN'S NEW HIGH IN NAKED SHRIEKING TERROR!"

(January 1956) SuperScope and Black & White. A Golden State Production. Produced and Directed by Roger Corman. Written by Lou Rusoff. Starring Richard Denning, Lori Nelson, Adele Jergens, Touch Connors. DVD: Lionsgate (2.35) 82 min. DVD cofeature: *The She-Creature.*

This was one of the features on American Releasing Corporation's first double bill.

It was also Roger Corman's first experience directing a science fiction–horror film, although he had uncredited involvement in the production of *The Beast with a Million Eyes* the year before. After a nuclear holocaust, most of the Earth's population has been killed. Seven survivors end up together at the home of Jim Maddison (Paul Birch) and his daughter Louise (Lori Nelson). Maddison had been anticipating this disaster but has prepared survival rations for just three people. To further complicate an already dire situation, radiation has turned another faction of survivors into carnivorous mutants. *Day the World Ended* has a thoughtful script which is well-acted by the cast. Adele Jergens is especially memorable as an ex-stripper named Ruby. Monster maker Paul Blaisdell designed the bizarre three-eyed mutant and also played the part. Mike "Touch" Connors appeared in several AIP pro-

Paul Blaisdell created and played the mutant in *Day the World Ended.*

ductions prior to finding fame as *Mannix* on television. In an interview years later he said of his experiences at AIP: "I liked Nicholson. I think he was the real brains behind the actual picture-making. Arkoff was the businessman. As far as I was concerned, he didn't have a lot of integrity. You never knew what he was gonna do." For *Day the World Ended*, Corman utilized widescreen to interesting effect, particularly in his use of close-ups. Fortunately this can once again be appreciated as the Lionsgate DVD restores the film to its original SuperScope format. The following year Corman directed *Attack of the Crab Monsters* for Allied Artists release; another story of post–A-bomb mutated monsters, it is similar in tone to *Day the World Ended*, with both films sharing a bleak and serious approach to the deadly subject at hand. The Columbia/TriStar VHS of *Day the World Ended* was fullscreen as is the U.K. DVD from Direct Video Distribution.

Review: *Harrison's Reports* (January 21, 1956), "A moderately interesting science-fiction melodrama. The direction is adequate and so is the acting."

Deathmaster

"Eyes Like Hot Coals ... Fangs Like Razors!"

(August 1972) Color by Movielab. World Entertainment Productions. Produced by Fred Sadoff. Directed by Ray Danton. Written by R.L. Grove. Starring Robert Quarry, Bill Ewing, John Fiedler, Brenda Dickson. DVD: RetroMedia (1.85) 88 min. Extras: Theatrical trailer; Audio commentary by Robert Quarry.

A coffin washes ashore on the beach at Malibu. Soon after, a mysterious stranger named Korda (Robert Quarry) becomes guru to members of a Topanga Canyon hippie community. Only Pico (Bill Ewing) is immune to Korda's hypnotic influence and discovers that the guru is actually a vampire. After the success of the Count Yorga films, Quarry associate-produced this independent production which was then released by AIP. Basically it's the same formula as the two previous movies, with Quarry giving a similar performance. Only this time he sports shoulder-length hair and wears a Kaftan instead of a cape. A novel idea, but the pacing is slow and the thrills are few and far between. The transfer (from the original camera negative) is excellent, making this one of the best-looking DVDs that Retro-Media has released thus far.

Dementia 13

"A Brand New Concept in Motion Picture Shock!"

(September 1963) Black & White. A Filmgroup Production. Produced by Roger Corman. Written and Directed by Francis Coppola. Starring William Campbell, Luana Anders, Bart Patton, Patrick Magee. DVD: Movie Classics (1.33) 81 min.

While in Europe working with Roger Corman on *The Young Racers*, Francis Coppola convinced his boss to give him the money to shoot another picture in Dublin. According to Coppola, Corman wanted a "low-budget psychological thriller." Coppola wrote a script and Corman gave him $22,000 to shoot it. When Corman viewed the finished film he felt that another murder was needed and had Jack Hill script and shoot some additional footage in the U.S. *Dementia 13* owes much to *Psycho* (1960), which is obviously the intention. The audience is led to believe that Louise Haloran (Luana Anders) is the main character but she is bloodily dispatched about a third of the way into the story, just like Janet Leigh's character was in the Hitchcock film. Atmospherically photographed, directed with some style, and providing a number of effective shocks, the movie almost makes you fail to notice that the plot makes almost no sense at all. Dr. William Joseph Bryan was hired as technical advisor and, to help promote the film, he was asked to concoct the "D-13" test which audience members would take before viewing the movie. Presumably, if you didn't pass the test, your mental state was such that you shouldn't be

Roberts Blossom and Cossette Lee in a scene from *Deranged*, a fictionalized version of the story of real-life serial killer Ed Gein.

allowed to see it at all. Luana Anders often played the "good girl" parts in such films as *Night Tide* and *Pit and the Pendulum*. She is cast against that type in *Dementia 13* and gives a wonderful performance as the greedy and conniving Louise. After years of inferior transfers on both VHS and DVD, a surprisingly good print of *Dementia 13* has been shown on Turner Movie Classics, although at 1.85 it seemed overly matted.

Review: (Reviewed under the British title *The Haunted and the Hunted*) *Films and Filming* (March 1965), "The director, Francis Coppola, has confidently assembled the film and given it a sharp sense of atmosphere. It lacks polish but its ideas are right."

Deranged

"PRETTY SALLY MAE DIED A VERY UNNATURAL DEATH! ... BUT THE WORST HASN'T HAPPENED TO HER YET!"

(February 1974) Color by Movielab. Produced by Tom Karr. Directed by Jeff Gillen and Alan Ormsby. Written by Alan Ormsby. Starring Roberts Blossom, Cosette Lee, Robert Warner, Pat Orr. DVD: MGM (1.85) 82 min.; Extras: Theatrical trailer; Midnite Movies co-feature: *Motel Hell*.

Deranged is a fictionalized account of the murderous exploits of Ed Gein, the real-life killer who inspired the character of Norman Bates in *Psycho*. Herein he is called "Ezra Cobb" and the basic facts of his macabre life are presented as a docudrama complete with onscreen narrator. Although it is both ghoulish and horrifying, what could have been an exercise in bad taste comes across as a fascinating account of a man's descent into madness. Roberts Blossom is excellent as Cobb, giving a performance which is alternately chilling and pitiable, no small feat given the extent of the ghastly crimes which are depicted.

De Sade

"HE MADE EVIL AN ART, VIRTUE A VICE, AND PAIN A PLEASURE!"

(August 1969) Color by Berkey Pathé. An American International-CCC Film-Trans Continental Production. Produced by Samuel Z. Arkoff and James H. Nicholson. Directed by Cy Endfield. Written by Richard Matheson. Starring Keir Dullea, Senta Berger, Lilli Palmer, John Huston. DVD: MGM (1.85) 104 min.; Extras: Theatrical trailer; Richard Matheson interview.

De Sade was one of the most expensive productions in AIP's history and also one of their biggest box office flops. Nicholson and Arkoff were normally astute in predicting the type of film the audience of the moment wanted. How they went so wrong with De Sade is anybody's guess. In his autobiography, Arkoff says that Variety thought the film would "bridge the generation gap" by attracting "the turned-on hip and the dirty old men."

As it turned out, nobody wanted to see it. The movie did have a tremendous amount of encouraging elements going for it. Keir Dullea, fresh from his success in 2001: A Space Odyssey, in the lead. Cy Endfield, who had directed the highly successful Zulu. A screen-

Left to right, John Huston, Sam Arkoff, and Keir Dullea on the set of De Sade.

play by Richard Matheson, a longtime favorite at AIP who had written some of their most popular films. Plus an interesting supporting cast of talented performers. The decision was made to shoot *De Sade* in Germany to take advantage of additional German financing. According to executive producer Louis M. Heyward, Gordon Hessler was set to produce the film but Endfield didn't get along with him and asked that he be removed from the picture, which he was. Endfield also shied away from directing any of the more sexually explicit sequences called for in the script and shot around them. By the time there was nothing left to shoot but these scenes, Endfield had himself hospitalized for exhaustion. Suddenly left without a director, Sam Arkoff flew to Germany and asked John Huston, who was playing a supporting role, to finish the picture. Huston declined and Arkoff and Louis Heyward eventually convinced a reluctant Roger Corman to step in and complete *De Sade*. In addition to the gamier sequences, Corman also directed the deathbed scene which features one of his "regulars," Barboura Morris, as a nun listening to the final words of the dying De Sade. In the surrealistic, non-linear storyline, Louis Alphonse Donatien Marquis de Sade (Dullea) is forced to marry the frigid sister (Anna Massey) of the woman he truly loves (Senta Berger). He spends the rest of his life indulging in "vile excesses" which eventually lead to his imprisonment in an asylum.

Keir Dullea as *De Sade* pays for a life of depravity by being put into an insane asylum.

One of the great failings of the film is its depiction of these "vile excesses," which are more silly than titillating. These sequences are tinted red so we will know when the "vile excesses" are being shown. The movie is done a further disservice by composer Billy Strange, who contributes a schizophrenic and sometimes wildly inappropriate score. Although AIP had planned to "roadshow" *De Sade*, these plans were curtailed when the MPAA gave the film an "X" rating and it was condemned by the Catholic Legion of Decency. From its original running time of 120 minutes, *De Sade* was edited to 114 minutes with the hope it would appease both the MPPA and the Catholic Church. It didn't and both ratings were upheld for the initial release. Later it was further cut to 92 minutes and given an "R" rating for the general release. Curiously, the DVD release is an unrated 104-minute version. *De Sade* is a visually magnificent but dramatically wanting misfire ... one of the very few major miscalculations in the history of AIP.

Review: *Time* (October 24, 1969), "The orgies are only slightly more titillating than a Playboy centerfold, and a good deal less polished."

Destroy All Monsters

"THE MONSTERS ARE IN REVOLT ... AND THE WORLD IS ON THE BRINK OF DESTRUCTION!"

(May 1969) Widescreen and Color by Berkey-Pathé. (TohoScope and Eastman Color). A Toho Co. Ltd. Production. Produced by Tomoyuki Tanaka. Directed by Ishiro Honda. Written by Ishiro Honda and Kaoru Mabuchi. Starring Akira Kubo, Yukiko Kobayshi, Kyoko Ai, Kenji Sahara. DVD: A.D.V. Films (2.35) 90 min.

All the monsters on Earth have been confined to Monsterland, an island near Japan. They are held in check there by an underground control center where scientists work round the clock to keep track of them. Says one enlightened scientist: "The monsters look cute from this angle." The control system is destroyed when aliens from the planet Kilaak use the monsters to demolish several of the Earth's major cities. Then the monsters are all sent to converge on Japan. This is a ruse to divert the military while the aliens construct a Kilaak base near Mount Fuji. Earth science eventually frees the monsters, who all turn their destructive forces on the aliens. The aliens summon Ghidorah the Space Monster to battle the Earth monsters but he is defeated and the Kilaak stronghold is destroyed. Released in Japan in 1968 as *Kaiji Soshingeki/Monster Invasion*, it was released the following year in the U.S. with advertising which proclaimed "Starring Mothra, Godzilla, Rodan, Manda." How did Mothra get top billing? In addition to these four stars, this monster free-for-all also features Gorosaurus, Ghidorah, Anguirus, Kumonga, Minilla, Baragon, and Varan. In other words, every monster suit laying around Toho studios was put to use for this movie. The early part of *Destroy All Monsters* has very little screen time devoted to the monsters and most of the action is saved for the final quarter of the movie. The A.D.V. DVD annoyingly has no chapters or menu.

The Devil Within Her

"PRAY FOR THE DEVIL WITHIN HER
BEFORE IT PREYS ON YOU!"

(February 1976) Color by Movielab (Eastman Color). A Unicapital Production. Produced by Nato De Angeles and Norma Corney. Directed by Peter Sasdy. Written by Stanley Price and Nato De Angeles. Starring Joan Collins, Eileen Atkins, Ralph Bates, Donald Pleasence. VHS: Axon Video (1.33) 95 min. DVD: New Star/Jef Films (as *I Don't Want to Be Born*) (1.33) 95 min.

After directing three fine films for Hammer (*Taste the Blood of Dracula*, *Countess Dracula*, and *Hands of the Ripper*), Peter Sasdy helmed this utterly worthless piece of trash. Filmed in England in 1975 as *I Don't Want to Be Born*, this is a rip-off of ideas from *Rosemary's Baby* and *The Exorcist*. Prior to her marriage, Lucy Carlesi (Joan Collins) had been a dancer in a sleazy London strip club. After rebuffing the advances of Hercules (George Claydon), a dwarf who appeared with her in the show, he puts a curse on the issue of her womb. True to Hercules' prediction, Lucy's baby boy is a monster possessed of the devil. An impressive cast of normally fine performers is totally wasted here. In addition to the principals, Hammer girls Caroline Munro and Janet Key are also on view with little or nothing to do. The solemn-looking baby is never even slightly menacing and the hysterics of the cast members when reacting to him merely look silly. The AIP theatrical cut of the film ran 90 minutes but the VHS and DVD versions are uncut. The Axon VHS tape is better quality than the U.S. DVD but a good quality Region 2 DVD is available in the United Kingdom from Carlton under the title *The Monster*.

The Devil's Widow

"THE STORY OF THE KIND OF WOMAN
FEW PEOPLE EVEN KNOW EXISTS"

(November 1971) Panavision and Technicolor. A Commonwealth United Presentation. Produced by Alan Ladd Jr. and Stanley Mann. Directed by Roddy McDowall. Written by William Spier. Starring Ava Gardner, Ian McShane, Stephanie Beacham, Richard Wattis. VHS: Republic (as *The Ballad of Tam Lin*) (2.35) 106 min.

"The Ballad of Tam Lin" has its origins in Scottish folklore. It relates the tale of Tam Lin, a handsome youth who is held captive by a powerful fairy queen. In the end he is saved by the love and unyielding devotion of a young girl named Janet. *The Devil's Widow* is a modern allegory of this story set in England during the swinging late sixties. Mrs. Michaela Cazaret (Ava Gardner), known to her intimates as Mickie, is a gorgeous and immensely wealthy middle-aged woman who surrounds herself with a collection of young hangers-on ("What a torpid group," Mickie exclaims at

Ava Gardner threatens Ian McShane in Roddy McDowall's underappreciated film *The Devil's Widow*.

one point in obvious disgust). She also takes beautiful young men as lovers and then discards them when they no longer amuse her. Her current lover is Tom Lynn (Ian McShane), who is just as dissolute as the rest of the gang until he meets the local vicar's daughter Janet (Stephanie Beacham). Tom falls deeply in love with Janet but when he attempts to leave Mickie she warns him, "I never give in and I never let go." Tom soon discovers that several of the previous men who attempted to leave Mickie met with untimely deaths. *The Ballad of Tam Lin*, Roddy McDowall's only film as a director, went through a series of unfortunate circumstances on its way to the screen. It was filmed in 1969; the original production company went bankrupt; after being shelved for two years, the movie eventually ended up in the hands of AIP, who changed the title and then gave it only the most minimal release. The movie would have been consigned to complete oblivion had Martin Scorsese not intervened and provided the means for a complete restoration. The 1998 Republic video release is hosted by Roddy McDowall, who is obviously delighted that his film is finally being presented to the public. He provides many interesting comments on Ava Gardner (whom he clearly adored) and the movie's troubled production history. *The Ballad of Tam Lin* certainly deserves to be seen by a wider audience. It is a complex and fascinating film and it also supplied Ava Gardner with one last great showcase for her beauty and talent. Although she did appear in other films afterwards, none of them provided a role as good as the one she has here. Both Ian McShane and Stephanie Beacham are outstanding as well, a fact happily acknowledged by McDowall in his introduction. In the supporting cast are three future Hammer glamour girls: Joanna Lumley, Jenny Hanley, and Madeline Smith. Beacham would go on to appear in Hammer's *Dracula A.D. 1972*.

Diary of a High School Bride

"THE BOLD MOTION PICTURE THAT DARES TO SPEAK FOR TEENAGE LOVERS!"

(July 1959) Black & White. Produced and Directed by Burt Topper. Written by Burt Topper, Mark & Jan Lowell. Starring Anita Sands, Ronald Foster, Chris Robinson, Wendy Wilde. VHS: MGM/Amazon (1.33) 80 min.

This cautionary tale provided as a "public service" by American International opens with this statement: "Teenage marriage is one of today's most controversial subjects. The producers of the picture you are about to see do not attempt to present a solution or take sides. It is a composite of several actual case histories ... a story of a teenage girl who could be your daughter, your sister ... or *you*...!" Thank you, AIP. Steve Redding and his new bride Judy ("I'm almost eighteen!") return to their hometown after a quickie Las Vegas wedding. They are met with opposition on every side. Judy's parents want to have the marriage annulled. Judy's classmates, convinced that she "had" to get married, ridicule her. Worst of all, Judy's psycho ex-boyfriend Chuck ("I dig married women") is determined to cause trouble between her and Steve. Judy certainly doesn't seem cut out for marriage. When she isn't busy clutching her stuffed animal, she is burning the dinner, being overwhelmed by laundry, and obsessing over having to mop the kitchen floor. She actually seems to be emotionally retarded. The climax of the film takes place on the sound stages of "Harco Studios located at Sunset and La Brea" where they manage to get in a not-too-subtle plug for *The Screaming Skull*. As Chuck, Chris Robinson plays his part like a crazed James Dean. Also on hand is American International Records recording star Tony Casanova singing the title song plus another little ditty. Although there were some LPs released by AIP Records, the 45rpm singles plugged in their films never seem to have existed commercially. The pressbook for *Diary of a High School Bride* has the following blurb: "American International Records ... has had success with its early records in the modern beat. Contact your local AIP exchange for promotional records at special discount prices on *Diary of a High School Bride*. Other American International records now in release are: *Girls, Girls, Girls-Campus Raid, Roadracers-Leadfoot, Charge-Geronimo, Horrors of the Black Museum—The Headless Ghost*." Has anybody actually ever seen any of these records?

Songs: "Diary of a High School Bride," "When I Say Bye Bye"

Review: *Variety* (August 12, 1959), "The story follows the tried-and-true pattern of 'true confession' romance magazines."

Die, Monster, Die!

"CAN YOU FACE THE ULTIMATE IN DIABOLISM ... CAN YOU STAND PURE TERROR?"

(November 1965) ColorScope (Pathéscope and Pathécolor). Produced by Pat Green. Directed by Daniel Haller. Written by Jerry Sohl. Starring Boris Karloff, Nick Adams, Suzan Farmer, Freda Jackson. DVD: MGM (2.35) 79 min.; Extras: Theatrical trailer. Midnite Movies co-feature: *The Dunwich Horror*.

Based on H. P. Lovecraft's story "The Colour Out of Space," this English-made film was the first to be directed by longtime Roger Corman associate Daniel Haller. Steve Reinhart (Nick Adams) arrives at the village of Arkham (relocated from Lovecraft's New England to the British countryside) to see Susan Witley (Suzan Farmer), a girl he met in America and fell in love with. He soon realizes that the Witley family, particularly Susan's father Nahum (Boris Karloff), has its share of skeletons in the closet. A maidservant disappears, the butler dies mysteriously, Mrs. Witley

(Freda Jackson) suffers from a strange malady, and an unearthly glow emanates from the greenhouse where eerie animal cries are heard. Wheelchair-bound Karloff gives a typically excellent performance in one of the better roles of his later career. Although Suzan Farmer is "introduced" in this film, she had already played a featured part in Hammer's *Devil-Ship Pirates* the previous year. The British title of this movie was the far less evocative *Monster of Terror*.

Dillinger

"HE WAS THE BEST DAMN BANK ROBBER IN THE WHOLE WIDE WORLD!"

(June 1973) Color by Movielab. Produced by Buzz Feitshans. Written and Directed by John Milius. Starring Warren Oates, Ben Johnson, Michelle Phillips, Cloris Leachman. DVD: MGM (1.85) 109 min.; Extras: Theatrical trailer.

John Dillinger (Warren Oates) and his girlfriend Billie (Michelle Phillips) in AIP's gangster movie *Dillinger*.

During the early Thirties, gangster John Dillinger (Warren Oates) robs and murders his way to becoming Public Enemy Number One. As he and his gang go on a bank robbing spree, they are hotly pursued by G-Man Melvin Purvis (Ben Johnson). The last in AIP's series of gangster films is also the best. Like its predecessors *Bloody Mama* and *Boxcar Bertha*, there is a great deal of rural location work but it is a far more glossy production and can stand up favorably against any of the "A" pictures of the time. Although *Dillinger* is certainly a violent and bloody affair, it never reaches the repugnant level of *Bloody Mama*. *Dillinger* boasts lively direction, an excellent sense of period detail, and a cast which features a large number of notable performers. Oates is given one of the only leading roles of his all-too-brief career and, from the opening scene, he makes his John Dillinger a complex and fascinating character. Former "Mamas and Papas" singer Michelle Phillips makes her acting debut as Dillinger's girlfriend Billie Franchette. Her performance earned her a Golden Globe Award nomination as "Most Promising Newcomer." Johnson, who had just won a Best Supporting Actor Oscar for *The Last Picture Show*, gives a rather sinister interpretation of FBI agent Melvin Purvis. Quite often, he seems more like the villain of the piece than a force for good. Dillinger's gang members include Harry Dean Stanton and Richard Dreyfuss (as Baby Face Nelson). Cloris Leachman plays Anna Sage, the infamous "Lady in Red" who betrays Dillinger in the end. Although she appears in only two scenes, Ms. Leachman's performance is a standout. *Dillinger* was the directing debut of John Milius who had previously written the screenplays for the high profile movies *Jeremiah Johnson* and *The Life and Times of Judge Roy Bean*. He had also co-written *The Devil's 8* for AIP in 1969. *Dillinger* was not Milius' final word on Depression era gangsters. The following year he wrote the script for the TV movie *Melvin Purvis G-Man*, starring Dale Robertson in the title role. This was the unsold pilot film for a proposed series produced by Dan Curtis of *Dark Shadows* fame. Milius' next feature film assignment

56 Dr. Goldfoot and the Bikini Machine

Dwayne Hickman meets a beautiful robot (Susan Hart) in *Dr. Goldfoot and the Bikini Machine.*

would be writing and directing *The Wind and the Lion*, a big-budget picture for MGM and quite a step up from AIP. The critical consensus on *Dillinger* was extremely mixed and it never managed to achieve anything close to the elevated reputation of the inferior *Boxcar Bertha*. Be sure to sit through the end credits of *Dillinger* so you can hear the "uplifting" words of J. Edgar Hoover.

Review: *Time* (September 1973), "Instead of the brash and abrasive effort that might have been expected, *Dillinger* is slack and derivative."

Dr. Goldfoot and the Bikini Machine

"It Has a KISS-BUTTON and a KILL-BUTTON. You Have to Know Which Button to Push!"

(November 1965) Panavision and Pathécolor. Produced by James H. Nicholson and Samuel Z. Arkoff. Directed by Norman Taurog. Written by Elwood Ullman and Robert Kaufman. Starring Vincent Price, Frankie Avalon, Dwayne Hickman, Susan Hart. DVD: MGM (2.35) 89 min.; Extras: Theatrical trailer.

Dr. Goldfoot and the Bikini Machine was AIP's first production to have a million dollar budget, due in part to the film's extensive location photography in San Francisco. The plot consists of little more than a series of silly gags, very much in the mode of the "Beach Party" series. What sets it apart from these films is the welcome presence of Vincent Price as Dr. Goldfoot and a surprisingly delightful comedic performance by Susan Hart as a robot named Diane. Leading men Frankie Avalon and Dwayne Hickman don't fare nearly so well. The film also features cameos by "Beach Party" regulars Aron Kincaid, Deborah Walley, Harvey Lembeck, and a very clever bit by Annette Funicello. Typical of AIP's penchant for self-promotion, during one scene a theatre marquee can be seen featuring *The Girl in the Glass Bikini* (which came out the following year as *The Ghost in the Invisible Bikini*). Title changes were commonplace for AIP product. *Dr. Goldfoot and the Bikini Machine* was originally called *Dr. Goldfoot and the Sex Machine*. Shortly prior to the film's release in November 1965, the ABC television teen music show *Shindig* aired a half-hour original program, *The Wild Weird World of Dr. Goldfoot*, promoting the movie. The show featured the songs "It Works" and "What's a Boy Supposed to Do?" which were written for the film but not used.

Song: "Dr. Goldfoot and the Bikini Machine"

Review: *Variety* (November 2, 1965), "The expensive looking production runs the comedy gamut from high to low."

Dr. Goldfoot and the Girl Bombs

"MEET THE GIRLS WITH THE THERMO-NUCLEAR NAVELS!"

(November 1966) Technicolor. Produced by Fulvio Lucisano and Louis M. Heyward. Directed by Mario Bava. Written by Louis M. Heyward, Robert Kaufman, and James Hartford [James H. Nicholson]. Starring Vincent Price, Fabian, Franco & Ciccio, Laura Antonelli. VHS: Orion (1.33) 79 min.

In 1965, *Dr. Goldfoot and the Bikini Machine* had been a big success which, of course, called for a sequel. Exactly one year later, AIP released the much inferior *Dr. Goldfoot and the Girl Bombs*. Made in Italy under the title *Dr. Goldfoot and the Love Bomb*, the film was directed by, of all people, the great Italian horror maestro Mario Bava. The "Bomb" in the title proved to be all too prophetic. Bava had a great track record of five films for AIP which had all been successful but little in those movies would indicate that he

Vincent Price is trapped behind bars and in the terrible movie *Dr. Goldfoot and the Girl Bombs*.

was a suitable director for a comedy. As it turned out, he wasn't. This time Dr. Goldfoot (Vincent Price) attempts to start a war between the U.S. and the U.S.S.R. using explosive babes as his weapons. Secret agent Bill Dexter (Fabian) must find a way to stop the buxom, beauteous bombs and save the world from certain destruction. This may not sound all that awful but the inclusion of the dreadful Italian comedy team of Franco and Ciccio makes the film all but unwatchable. Even the usually reliable Price can't save it. The same year AIP again teamed with producer Fulvio Lucisano for *War Italian Style*, which stars the great Buster Keaton but, shockingly, again features Franco and Ciccio! The end result is even worse than *Dr. Goldfoot and the Girl Bombs*, which hardly seems possible.

Review: *Variety* (November 14, 1966), "This belabored spy spoof reprise suffers by comparison with earlier and much funnier original."

Dr. Jekyll and Sister Hyde

"WARNING! THE SEXUAL TRANSFORMATION OF A MAN INTO A WOMAN WILL ACTUALLY TAKE PLACE BEFORE YOUR VERY EYES!"

(April 1972) Technicolor. A Hammer Film for EMI Film Productions Ltd. Produced by Albert Fennell and Brian Clemens. Directed by

Roy Ward Baker. Written by Brian Clemens. Starring Ralph Bates, Martine Beswick, Gerald Sim, Susan Brodrick. DVD: Anchor Bay (1.85) 97 min.; Extras: Theatrical trailer; Audio commentary by Martine Beswick, Roy Ward Baker, and Brian Clemens; Radio spots; Poster and still gallery.

Promoted by AIP in the U.S. with an incredibly unappealing advertising campaign, *Dr. Jekyll and Sister Hyde* is one of the best films from Hammer's later period. Considering the potential sleaze factor of the subject, it is also surprisingly restrained. This fact was not lost on many of the contemporary reviewers, who were quick to point out that this was a cut above the average horror fare of the time. The adroit script by Brian Clemens combines the Jekyll/Hyde story with Jack the Ripper and throws in Burke and Hare for good measure. In this version, an altruistic Dr. Jekyll gets sidetracked in his search to develop a vaccine which will cure all illness. He accidentally transforms himself into a lethal but beautiful Mrs. Hyde, who fights to take permanent possession of his body. When Jekyll is forced to murder some prostitutes in the Whitechapel area of London in order to continue his research, he becomes the criminal known as Jack the Ripper. Ralph Bates and Martine Beswick are excellent in the title roles and Roy Ward Baker's direction is top-notch. In order to get a PG rating for the film, AIP cut it by about three minutes, eliminating all the nudity and much of the more graphic violence. This did not deter them from emphasizing these elements in their advertising and providing the following advisory: "PARENTS: Be sure your children are sufficiently mature to witness the intimate details of this frank and revealing film." The DVD is the original British cut of the film.

Review: *Los Angeles Times* (April 1972), "This elegant period picture is actually a satisfactory horror entertainment, stylish rather than simply campy."

Dr. Phibes Rises Again

"DEATH! TORTURE! MURDER MOST FOUL! DR. PHIBES IS AMUSING HIMSELF."

(July 1972) Color by DeLuxe. Produced by Louis M. Heyward. Directed by Robert Fuest. Written by Robert Fuest and Robert Blees. Starring Vincent Price, Robert Quarry, Fiona Lewis, Valli Kemp. DVD: MGM (1.85) 89 min.; Extras: Theatrical trailer. Midnite Movies co-feature: *The Abominable Dr. Phibes*.

Although it is basically a rehash of ideas from the previous film, *Dr. Phibes Rises Again* still manages to be entertaining in its own right. Three years after he was presumably interred forever with his beloved wife Victoria (Caroline Munro), demented genius Dr. Anton Phibes (Vincent Price) is back among the living with a new agenda. While the motivation in the original movie was revenge, this time it's the search for an ancient Egyptian

Valli Kemp and Vincent Price are determined to win the race to find the Egyptian "River of Life" in *Dr. Phibes Rises Again*.

"River of Life" which legend says can restore and prolong life indefinitely. Phibes' rival is Darius Biederbeck (Robert Quarry), who has a most urgent reason of his own for wanting to locate the mystical river. Peter Jeffrey and John Cater reprise their characters (a pair of confused Scotland Yard inspectors on the trail of Phibes) from the first film. For the sake of marquee value, Hugh Griffith and Terry-Thomas also return (but in new roles) while Peter Cushing and Beryl Reid have one-scene cameos. The rest of the cast is made up of a roster of familiar British character actors (Gerald Sim, Lewis Fiander, Milton Reid, etc.). This time around, Phibes' assistant Vulnavia is played by beautiful Valli Kemp, who replaced a pregnant Virginia North.

Review: *New York Times* (January 11, 1973), "Mysteriously, a lot of it works, probably because Robert Fuest, the director, knows just how long to hold an effect before it wilts."

"River of Life" seekers Robert Quarry and Fiona Lewis in *Dr. Phibes Rises Again*.

Dorian Gray

"ETERNAL YOUTH IS THE ULTIMATE PERVERSION"

(November 1970) Color by Movielab. A Towers of London Production. A Commonwealth United Presentation. Produced by Harry Alan Towers. Directed by Massimo Dallamano. Written by Marcello Coscia and Massimo Dallamano. Starring Helmut Berger, Richard Todd, Herbert Lom, Marie Liljedahl. VHS: NTA/Republic (1.33) 93 min.

Filmed primarily in England with an Italian director and a German star, *Dorian Gray* (a.k.a. *The Secret of Dorian Gray*) is, according to the credits, "A modern allegory inspired by the works of Oscar Wilde." Having previously watched this film and written about it negatively, I was surprised to discover on a second viewing that it really isn't bad at all ... other than the costumes and decor, which are mostly hideous. Certainly at the time it was made, there were few actors as handsome as star Helmut Berger. As Dorian he possesses a somewhat androgynous beauty which makes the attraction felt toward him by both sexes perfectly understandable. The camera dwells on him like an adoring lover. The basic Oscar Wilde plot is here with Dorian's portrait being painted by his friend Basil (Richard Todd). The subject becomes so enamored of his own youthful beauty that he offers to trade his soul if he can look like his image in the picture forever. Eternal youth soon leads to indulgence in every excess that will bring him pleasure with no thought of the consequences to the others involved. Along the way Dorian manages to bed most of the characters and is responsible for the deaths of at least three of them. He even becomes a porn star with his picture appearing on the cover of *Cinema X* magazine. The cast delivers some good performances, particularly Todd as the painter, Herbert Lom as a cynical homosexual, and Isa Miranda as a wealthy, lecherous socialite. Berger simply needs to look gorgeous, which he does admirably. Margaret Lee and Maria Rohm, regulars in many of Harry Alan Towers' productions, are also in the cast. Most film versions of this story seem

Sybil Vane (Marie Liljedahl) and Dorian Gray (Helmut Berger) share a brief moment of happiness before tragedy intrudes.

to suffer from the same problem: There is little indication of the passage of time. The MGM version seems trapped in an eternal Victorian era London while this one is set in a never-ending "swinging London" of the late sixties and early seventies. The British prints of *Dorian Gray* run 101 minutes with even more sex on view than the version shown in the United States.

Dragstrip Girl

"Car Crazy! ... Speed Crazy! ... Boy Crazy!"

(April 1957) Black & White. A Golden State Production. Produced by Alex Gordon. Directed by Edward L. Cahn. Written by Lou Rusoff. Starring Fay Spain, Steve Terrell, John Ashley, Frank Gorshin. VHS: Columbia/Tri-Star (1.33) 69 min. DVD: Direct Video Distribution (1.33) 69 min.; Region-Free DVD from United Kingdom; Extras: Audio interview with Samuel Z. Arkoff; Trailers.

When fast-driving chick Louise Banks (Fay Spain) moves to town, she catches the eyes of hot-rodders Jim Donaldson (Steve Terrell) and Fred Armstrong (John Ashley). For awhile she plays them against each other for kicks but she soon realizes that Jim is the guy for her. Although Fred comes from a wealthy family, he has always been in the shadow of Jim. Now his resentment reaches a boiling point and he declares an all-out war for Louise's affections. Ashley, making his AIP debut, won his role when he did an impromptu Elvis Presley impersonation for screenwriter Lou Rusoff. Rusoff was so impressed he wrote a scene into

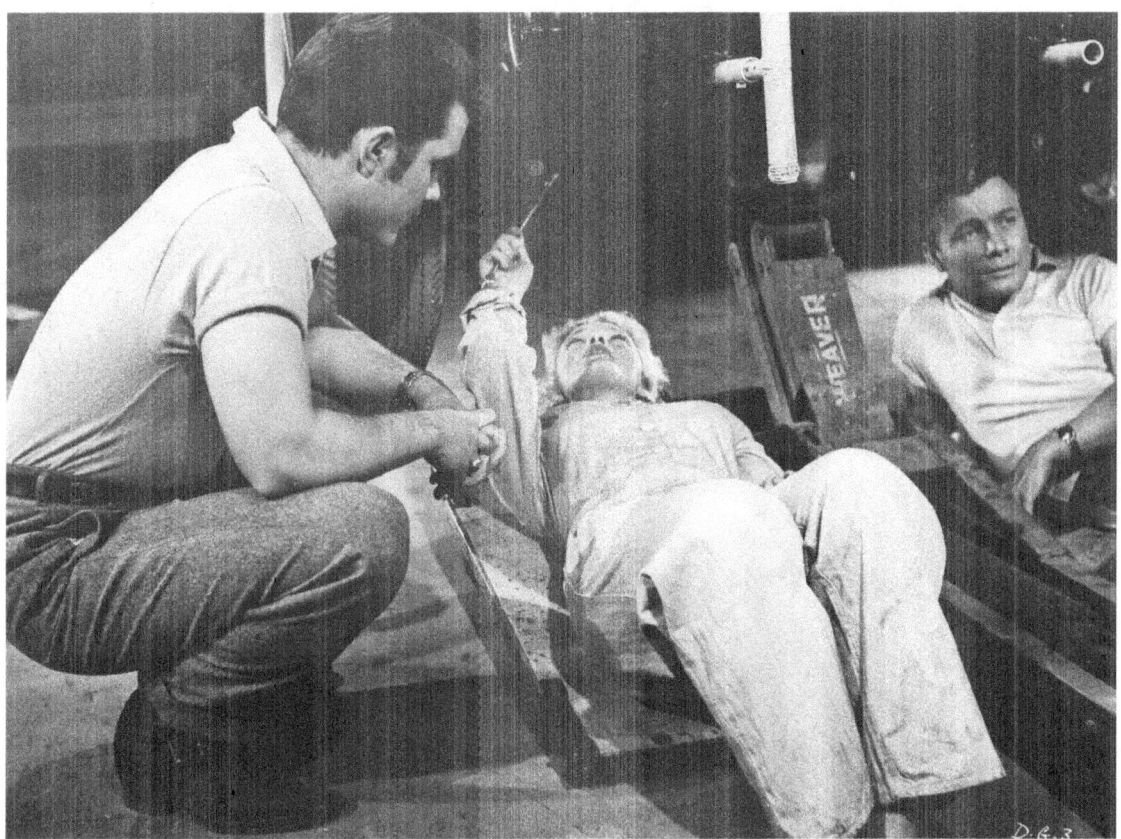

John Ashley (left) and Steve Terrell take it easy while Fay Spain tunes up her hot rod in *Dragstrip Girl*.

the script to allow Ashley to repeat his Elvis routine onscreen. *Dragstrip Girl* is "memorable" for having some of the most unconvincing rear screen projection ever. A few months later, producer Alex Gordon recycled the script with the same director and two male leads for *Motorcycle Gang*, which is actually a marginally better film ... but only just.

Review: *Harrison's Reports* (May 4, 1957), "The action moves along at a fast pace and there are plentiful chills and thrills."

Dressed to Kill

"BRIAN DE PALMA, MASTER OF THE MACABRE, INVITES YOU TO A SHOWING OF THE LATEST FASHION ... IN MURDER."

(July 1980) Panavision and Technicolor. A Samuel Z. Arkoff Presentation of a George Litto Production. A Cinema 77/Film Group/Filmways Picture. Produced by George Litto. Directed and Written by Brian De Palma. Starring Michael Caine, Angie Dickinson, Nancy Allen, Keith Gordon. DVD: MGM (2.35) 105 min.; Extras: Theatrical and unrated versions; 3 "Making of" featurettes; Theatrical trailer; Animated photo gallery.

In early 1979, Sam Arkoff, with his usual sense of economy, entered into an agreement with producer George Litto and director Brian De Palma for AIP to finance their new movie *Dressed to Kill*, provided the budget did not exceed $6 million. AIP had released De Palma's breakthrough picture *Sisters* so Arkoff and De Palma had a mutual success behind them. The new picture ran over-budget and De Palma and Litto had to put up $250,000 to cover their share of the costs but the film

62 *Dressed to Kill*

Nancy Allen is unaware that danger lurks nearby in *Dressed to Kill*.

went on to become a tremendous financial success for all involved. Although *Dressed to Kill* was dismissed in some critical circles as nothing more than a pastiche of elements stolen from Hitchcock and in others as an unpleasant exercise in misogyny, audiences responded enthusiastically. *Dressed to Kill* is actually closer in spirit to an Italian Giallo than Hitchcock. All the Giallo elements are there: the black-gloved, razor-wielding killer; twisted sexuality; an innocent bystander who must prove her innocence by solving the crime. Stylishly directed by De Palma, the film is filled with memorable set pieces. The best of these is a lengthy art museum sequence without dialogue. The stunning visuals here are beautifully complemented by Pino Donaggio's outstanding score. In his autobiography, Sam Arkoff said: "*Dressed to Kill* was a picture I was proud of, a truly brilliant film, full of unexpected plot twists and more thrills and heart-stopping moments than the roller coaster at Coney Island."

It was to be the swan song for American International Pictures. In July 1979, Arkoff agreed to a financial merger with Filmways Pictures, and AIP was absorbed by that company. By the time *Dressed to Kill* was released it had become a Filmways Picture and AIP was a thing of the past. Arkoff soon had reason to regret his decision to merge with Filmways. He and Richard Bloch, the head of Filmways, were diametrically opposed in their approaches to filmmaking. Five months after the merger, Arkoff resigned from the company. At least *Dressed to Kill* allowed him to go out on a high note.

Review: *Time* (July 28, 1980), "Moviegoers may not [respond] especially those who hoped that [Brian] De Palma would become the heir to Hitchcock's throne rather than the scavenger of his vaults."

Left to right, Sam Jaffe, Ed Begley, Dean Stockwell, Sandra Dee, and Donna Baccala discuss the strange goings-on in *The Dunwich Horror*.

The Dunwich Horror

"A FEW YEARS AGO IN DUNWICH A HALF-WITTED GIRL BORE ILLEGITIMATE TWINS. ONE OF THEM WAS ALMOST HUMAN!"

(January 1970) Color by Movielab. Produced by James H. Nicholson and Samuel Z. Arkoff. Directed by Daniel Haller. Written by Curtis Lee Hanson, Henry Rosenbaum, and Ronald Silkosky. Starring Sandra Dee, Dean Stockwell, Ed Begley, Sam Jaffe. DVD: MGM (1.85) 88 min.; Extras: Theatrical trailer; Midnite Movies co-feature: *Die, Monster, Die!*

Roger Corman served as executive producer on his former art director's second directorial foray into H.P. Lovecraft territory. Weird Wilbur Whately, played by an even weirder Dean Stockwell, attempts to view the infamous book *The Necronomicon* which is housed in the library at Miskatonic University (actually UCLA). Student Nancy Walker (Sandra Dee) becomes infatuated with Wilbur and goes with him to his home in Dunwich (apparently transported from New England to the California coastline). Once she arrives there, she is troubled by psychedelic dreams in which she is pursued by what looks like a band of demented flower children. Wilbur is actually drugging Nancy and plans to use her in his attempts to bring the "Old Ones," evil beings from another dimension, back into our world. In the tepid climax, Wilbur's monstrous twin brother, a spawn of the "Old Ones," goes on a rampage until he is vanquished after Wilbur is hit by a bolt of lightning. Lovecraft's classic story is given a lackluster presentation herein. Not much really happens and what does isn't all that exciting or interesting. At the time of the release of *The Dunwich Horror* there was much publicity about Sandra Dee's nude scene: ("Police stationed at stage doors were instructed not only to verify who gained admittance but to make certain that no personal cameras were brought in for secret snapshots.") They really needn't have bothered as the scene seems to have been shot using a body double. Other nudity was trimmed to get the film an MPAA M rating. The MGM Midnite Movie DVD is an R-rated version with all nudity restored. It also boasts, as do many of the other MGM DVDs of AIP releases, much more vibrant color than the theatrical release ever had. Look for Corman regulars Beach Dickerson and Barboura Morris in small roles as a farmer and his wife.

Review: *New York Times* (July 9, 1970), "The picture is nothing more than standard, old-fashioned haunted-house spookery."

Earth vs the Spider

"BULLETS WON'T KILL IT! FLAMES WON'T HURT IT! NOTHING CAN STOP IT!"

(October 1958) Black & White. Produced and Directed by Bert I. Gordon. Written by Laszlo Gorog and George Worthing Yates. Starring Edward Kemmer, June Kenny, Gene Persson, Sally Fraser. DVD: Lionsgate (1.33) 73 min. DVD co-feature: *War of the Colossal Beast*.

AIP's entry in the "giant bug" boom of the fifties was *Earth vs the Spider* (a.k.a. *The Spider*). Produced and directed by Bert I. Gordon, AIP's resident "giant monster" maven, this is one of his most entertaining efforts. Two teenagers exploring a cave near their hometown encounter a giant spider. The authorities (presumably) kill the monster with a massive dose of DDT. The dead spider is put on display in the local high school gymnasium where it is revived by the loud playing of a rock 'n' roll band (don't ask!). After trashing the town, the creature goes back to its cave, where the same teenage couple who discovered it have returned to search for a lost bracelet. In a typical AIP plug for their product, the town theatre is playing *The Amazing Colossal Man* and *Attack of the Puppet People*. Unfortunately Gordon and AIP would temporarily part company when he hit them with a lawsuit claiming that they had not given him the due profits on his pictures. Gordon did not make another film for American International until *Food of the Gods* in 1976.

Review: *Variety* (November 5, 1958), "Good exploitationer characterized by well done special effects and a reasonably credible plot."

Empire of the Ants

"FOR THEY SHALL INHERIT THE EARTH ... SOONER THAN YOU THINK!"

(July 1977) Color by Movielab. A Cinema 77 Film. Produced and Directed by Bert I. Gordon. Written by Jack Turley and Bert I. Gordon. Starring Joan Collins, Robert Lansing, John David Carson, Albert Salmi. DVD: MGM (1.85) 90 min.; Extras: Theatrical trailer. Midnite Movies co-feature: *Tentacles*.

Bert I. Gordon's final film for AIP is arguably his worst for the company. Bitchy real estate agent Marilyn Fryser (Joan Collins) takes a boatload of losers to view the Dreamland Shores land development. Radioactive waste dumped offshore nearby has washed up on the beach and the local ants have been having a picnic on it. Consequently, Dreamland Shores is now the home to vast numbers of giant ants. Once again Gordon attempts to pass off one of his lame efforts using poor H.G. Wells' work as the basis. *Empire of the Ants* has little to do with Wells other than the idea of ants becoming the dominant species on Earth. The early part of the movie is basically a "nature gone wild" scenario with people running from and being killed by the enlarged insects. The second half becomes slightly reminiscent of *Invasion of the Body Snatchers* when the characters stumble upon a town where the inhabitants have been brainwashed and subjugated by the ants. The effects are a throwback to Gordon's 1957 giant grasshopper movie *Beginning of the End* ... and that is no compliment. In the slump between her days as a 20th Century–Fox contract player and *Dynasty*, Joan Collins hits the low point in her career with *Empire of the Ants*. Even *The Bitch* and *The Stud* are more entertaining movies.

Erik the Conqueror

"HE LIVED ONLY FOR THE FLESH AND THE SWORD!"

(September 1963) ColorScope (Dyaliscope and Technicolor). A Galatea-Lyre-Criterion Production. Produced by Massimo De Rita. Directed by Mario Bava. Written by Oreste Biancoli, Piero Pierotti, Mario Bava. Starring Cameron Mitchell, Giorgio Ardisson, Alice and Ellen Kessler. DVD: Starz/Anchor Bay (2.35) 90 min.; Extras: Audio commentary by Tim Lucas; Audio interview with Cameron Mitchell; U.S. and German trailers; Poster and still gallery; Mario Bava bio.

Obviously inspired by Richard Fleischer's *The Vikings* (1958), *Gli invasori/The Invaders* often surpasses its source of inspiration in terms of imagination and vision. Once again Mario Bava is able to take material which is derivative and transform it into something unique. The plot concerns two Viking brothers who are separated as youngsters. Eron (Cameron Mitchell) becomes the Viking king and the other, Erik (Giorgio Ardisson), is adopted by Alice (Francoise Christophe), the widowed queen of England, and brought up as her son. As fate would have it, each of the brothers falls in love with a Viking priestess (twin sisters Alice and Ellen Kessler). The movie is filled with exciting set pieces and has lavish production values. Typically for a Bava film, there is wonderfully atmospheric cinematography and kaleidoscopic color schemes. Although Mitchell is top-billed, the main focus of the story is handsome French actor Ardisson, who previously appeared in Bava's *Hercules in the Haunted World*. The movie was originally released in Europe in 1962; AIP bought the rights, changed the title to *Erik the Conqueror*, and cut the film to 81 minutes. For once they did not replace the original score (by Roberto Nicolosi) with one by Les Baxter. The DVD is the full-length version derived from a European source. The otherwise excellent DVD presentation is slightly marred by a duped-looking end title taken from the AIP release which has all too obviously been tacked on. Despite the claim on the box that the DVD "includes footage never before seen in America," the content is the same as the Panther Video VHS tape, although that was a pan-and-scan transfer.

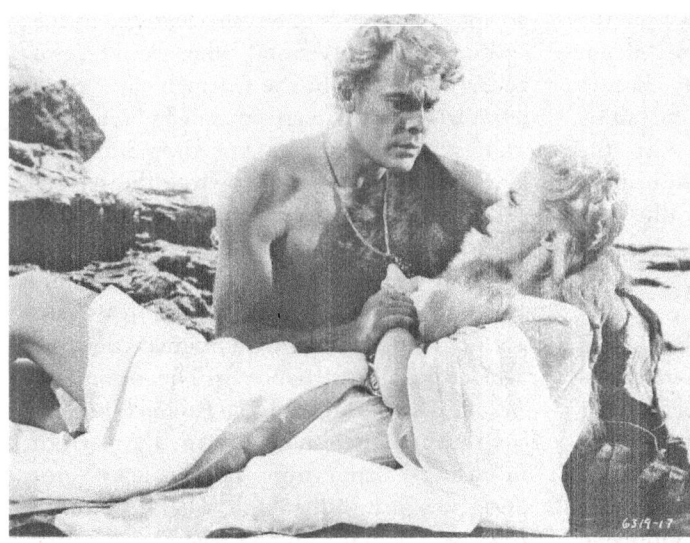

Erik the Conqueror (Giorgio Ardisson) falls in love with a Viking priestess (Ellen Kessler).

The Evil Eye

"WHAT DOES IT WANT? ... WHAT WILL SATISFY ITS CRAVINGS? ... ONLY THE DEAD KNOW AND THOSE THEY CHOOSE TO TELL!"

(May 1964) Black & White. A Galatea-Coronet Production.

Produced by Massimo De Rita. Directed by Mario Bava. Written by Ennio De Concini, Eliana De Sabata, Franco Prosperi, Enzo Corbucci, Mino Guerrini, Mario Bava. Starring Leticia Roman, John Saxon, Valentina Cortesa, Dante Di Paolo. DVD: Image (as *The Girl Who Knew Too Much*) (1.66) 86 min.; Italian-language version with English subtitles; Extras: Italian theatrical trailer; Photo and poster gallery.

The beginnings of the entire Giallo film genre can be traced to Mario Bava's *La regazza che sapeva troppo/The Girl Who Knew Too Much*, filmed in Italy in 1962. All the elements which would come to embody the Gialli are here: women in peril, gruesome murders, red herrings, and a complicated plot with a surprise ending. Nora Davis (Leticia Roman) has come to Rome to visit her aged aunt, Ethel. During Nora's first night in the Eternal City, Aunt Ethel dies and Nora attempts to go to the hospital for help. On the way, she is mugged and then witnesses the bloody murder of a young woman. The police assume she is distraught over the death of her aunt and give little credence to her story. It takes Nora, assisted by handsome young doctor Marcello Bassi (John Saxon), to learn the identity of the killer. The version of Bava's film which was released in the U.S. by AIP in 1964 differs greatly from the Italian one. Retitled *The Evil Eye*, the AIP cut runs 92 minutes and includes several scenes that are not in the Italian version, including a different beginning and ending. Also, the tone of the AIP version is far more light-hearted than its Italian counterpart. Typically, they also replaced the original score by Roberto Nicolosi with one by Les Baxter.

One thing the two versions have in common is some stunning atmospheric black-and-white cinematography by director Mario Bava. Through his camera's eye, Rome at night is transformed into a frighteningly sinister place. Leticia Roman, daughter of Italian costume designer Vittorio Nino Novarese, is both pretty and appealing as the heroine. Oddly, in the U.S. version, her character's name was changed from Nora Davis to Nora Dralston.

The Fast and the Furious

"High Speed Excitement ... As a Wanted Man ... Meets a Wanting Woman!"

(November 1954) Black & White. A Palo Alto Production. Produced by Roger Corman. Directed by Edwards Samson and John Ireland. Written by Jerome Odium, Jean Howell, and Roger Corman. Starring John Ireland, Dorothy Malone, Bruce Carlisle, Marshall Bradford. DVD: DigiView (1.33) 65 min.

Escaped convict Frank Webster (John Ireland) kidnaps lady race car driver Connie Adair (Dorothy Malone) and her white Jaguar. His plan is to drive in the Pebble Beach International sports car race which will give him an opportunity to escape to Mexico. After much bickering and hard-boiled patter between them, Frank and Connie fall in love. She begs him to turn himself in to the authorities but he is still bent on crossing the border. Using most of his $66,000 profit from *Monster from the Ocean Floor* (Lippert, 1954), Roger Corman produced *The Fast and the Furious* without the benefit of a prearranged distribution deal. Originally John Ireland turned down Corman's request to star in the low-budget production. But when Ireland was also given the chance to co-direct the picture, he accepted Corman's offer. Also featured in the cast are Bruno VeSota, who would soon become a regular in the Corman stock company, Iris Adrian, in an amusing bit as a diner waitress, and silent film comedian Snub Pollard. Jean Howell, who co-wrote the screenplay, appears in a clever scene as another lady race car driver. When filming was completed, Corman was approached by both Republic and Columbia with distribution deals but, wanting a quicker return on his investment, he decided to take a chance on Nicholson and Arkoff, who distributed *The Fast and the Furious* through their newly formed American Releasing Corporation. The associate producer was Jack Milner who, with his brother Dan, would soon produce *The Phantom from 10,000 Leagues* for ARC. The movie is available on DVD through several P.D. companies;

the DigiView edition is as good as any and can usually be had for $1.00.

Review: *Hollywood Reporter* (Oct. 28, 1954), "During the first couple of reels it looks as if it is going to pay off in a top-flight, low budget production. But unfortunately the script fails to deliver a concentrated love story."

Female Jungle

"EXCITEMENT SCREAMS LIKE A SIREN IN THE NIGHT!"

(June 1956) Black & White. A Burt Kaiser Production. Produced by Burt Kaiser. Directed by Bruno VeSota. Written by Burt Kaiser and Bruno VeSota. Starring Lawrence Tierney, Kathleen Crowley, John Carradine, Jayne Mansfield. VHS: RCA/Columbia (1.33) 71 min.; DVD: Direct Video Distribution (1.33) 71 min.; Region-Free DVD from United Kingdom; Extras: Audio interview with Samuel Z. Arkoff; Trailers.

Movie star Monica Madison is murdered in a disreputable part of town and a cop with a drinking problem (Lawrence Tierney) is determined to solve the case. This *film noir* is filled with eccentric characters who behave very strangely most of the time. Although Bruno VeSota was a reliable, rotund character actor in many films, his efforts for AIP as a director are fairly hopeless endeavors ... and *Female Jungle* is no exception. Excessive performances abound and there seems to have been no attempt by VeSota to rein them in a bit. The confused story unfolds in what is basically "real time." At the end, one character even says that the murder was solved in slightly over an hour. The movie does have its place in cinema history for "introducing" Jayne Mansfield in her first major role. Her character Candy Price is a blonde sexpot (what else?) and Jayne does her best Marilyn Monroe impersonation in playing the part. John Carradine turns in the most credible performance as the prime suspect in the killing. Producer-writer Burt Kaiser plays an important role in the movie and VeSota is featured in a small part as well. The print quality on the DVD is definitely a bit too *noir*.

Fireball 500

"THEY LIVE FROM SPINOUT TO CRACK UP ... AND THEY LOVE AS FAST AS THEY CAN GET IT!"

(June 1966) Panavision and Pathécolor. Produced by James H. Nicholson, Samuel Z. Arkoff, and Burt Topper. Directed by William Asher. Written by William Asher and Leo Townsend. Starring Frankie Avalon, Annette Funicello, Fabian, Julie Parrish. DVD: MGM (2.35) 92 min.; Extras: Theatrical trailer. Midnite Movies co-feature: *Thunder Alley*.

With the "Beach Party" franchise played out but Frankie and Annette still under contract, AIP looked to put them in more serious roles. *Fireball 500* is an attempt to do this. William Asher, who had directed most

Kathleen Crowley enjoys a large drink and John Carradine's company in Female Jungle.

of the "Beach Party" series, was brought on board to help them make the transition. Also on hand were "Beach Party" alums Harvey Lembeck and, in a slightly larger role than usual, Mike Nader. In *Fireball 500*, Avalon turns in his surfboard for a race car: His character Dave Owen is a Southern California champion slotcar racer who wants to compete at Daytona. On his way to Florida he becomes mixed up with an illegal moonshine running operation run by Charlie Bigg (Harvey Lembeck). He also gets involved with carny hotdog seller Jane (Annette) and heiress Martha (Julie Parrish). Dave's rival for both Jane and winning car races is Sonny Leander Fox (Fabian). Annette's role isn't all that different from Dee Dee in the "Beach Party" movies but she does come to the conclusion that sometimes a hearth and home isn't everything. This is something that Dee Dee would never have admitted. Although Frankie plays a tough guy here, AIP still wasn't quite ready to have him entirely shed his clean-cut persona. He pours himself a glass of whiskey, thinks about it and then pours it back in the bottle. Also, a scene in which he spends the night with Julie Parrish (she brings him breakfast in bed the next morning) was cut from the final film. A few musical numbers are thrown in for good measure but they seem wildly out of place given the mostly serious tone of the story. Although the end credits lists six songs, two of them ("A Chance Like That" and "Country Carnival") were cut before release. *Fireball 500* opens and closes with some brief Claymation sequences courtesy of the people who gave the world "Gumby."

Songs: "Fireball 500," "Step Right Up," "My Way," "Turn Around"

Five Guns West

"Kiss for Kiss! Bullet for Bullet!"

(April 1955) Pathécolor. Produced and Directed by Roger Corman. Written by R. Wright Campbell. Starring John Lund, Dorothy Malone, Touch Connors, Paul Birch. DVD: MGM (1.33) 78 min.; Extras: Theatrical trailer.

Toward the end of the Civil War, the South begins to pardon convicts in order to enlist them for the Confederate cause. Five such convicts (John Lund, Touch Connors, Paul Birch, Jonathan Haze, and Bob Campbell) are pardoned on condition that they agree to go through Indian territory and waylay a Yankee stagecoach transporting a Confederate traitor and a fortune in gold. They end up at a stage stop run by Shalee (Dorothy Malone) and her drunken uncle (James Stone). *Five Guns West* was the first of four Westerns that Roger Corman directed for ARC, the others being *Apache Woman*, *The Oklahoma Woman*, and *Gunslinger*. After the encouraging success of *The Fast and the Furious*, Nicholson and Arkoff were anxious to get another picture in the can as quickly as possible. They gave Corman a $60,000 budget and nine days to make a movie. With some trepidation, Corman decided to direct as well as produce. He soon regretted his decision as the first day's location shoot was delayed because of a rainstorm. Behind schedule before he even started, Corman made up for this by learning to set up his shots very quickly, a trait he continued throughout his career. Before *Five Guns West* was released, Corman was already at work on his next Western. As in *The Fast and the Furious*, Dorothy Malone gives a noteworthy performance. The following year she would win a Best Supporting Actress Oscar for her work at Universal in Douglas Sirk's *Written on the Wind*. The ever reliable Jonathan Haze is memorable in the type of quirky character role that would become his trademark in Corman films. Floyd Crosby's color photography gives *Five Guns West* a polished look that helps conceal its modest budget. His outstanding contributions as a cinematographer would continue to be a significant asset for both Corman and AIP in the years to come.

Review: *Harrison's Reports* (April 30, 1955), "This program western should prove acceptable to those who like pictures of this type, particularly because of the fine Pathécolor photography."

Five Guns West was Roger Corman's directorial debut.

The Food of the Gods

" ... FOR A TASTE OF HELL! H.G. WELLS' MASTERPIECE OF SCIENCE FICTION!"

(June 1976) Color by Movielab. Produced, Directed and Written by Bert I. Gordon. Starring Marjoe Gortner, Pamela Franklin, Ralph Meeker, Ida Lupino. DVD: MGM/Fox (1.85) 88 min.

Bert I. Gordon returned to AIP for the first time since *Earth vs the Spider* (1958) with *The Food of the Gods*. Gordon had already adapted H.G. Wells' novel for his dreadful *Village of the Giants* (Embassy, 1965) and this film, though not particularly good, is definitely an improvement over the former. Very little of the original story is in evidence and basically all Gordon has done is use Wells' concept of a substance that causes gigantism. Pro football player Morgan (an unlikely and unlikable Marjoe Gortner) and two of his teammates go for a vacation to an island in the Pacific Northwest. Shortly after they arrive, one of the men is stung to death by giant wasps. While attempting to get help at a remote farmhouse, Morgan is attacked by a giant chicken. He is told by the farm's owner Mrs. Skinner (Ida Lupino) that she and her husband have been feeding their chickens with a substance they found oozing from the ground not far from their house. Unfortunately wasps, rats, and some particularly nasty-looking worms have also dined on the mysterious substance and grown to gigantic proportions. Greedy businessman Jack Bensington (Ralph Meeker) and his assistant Lorna Scott (Pamela Franklin) show up to buy the rights to the Skinners' dis-

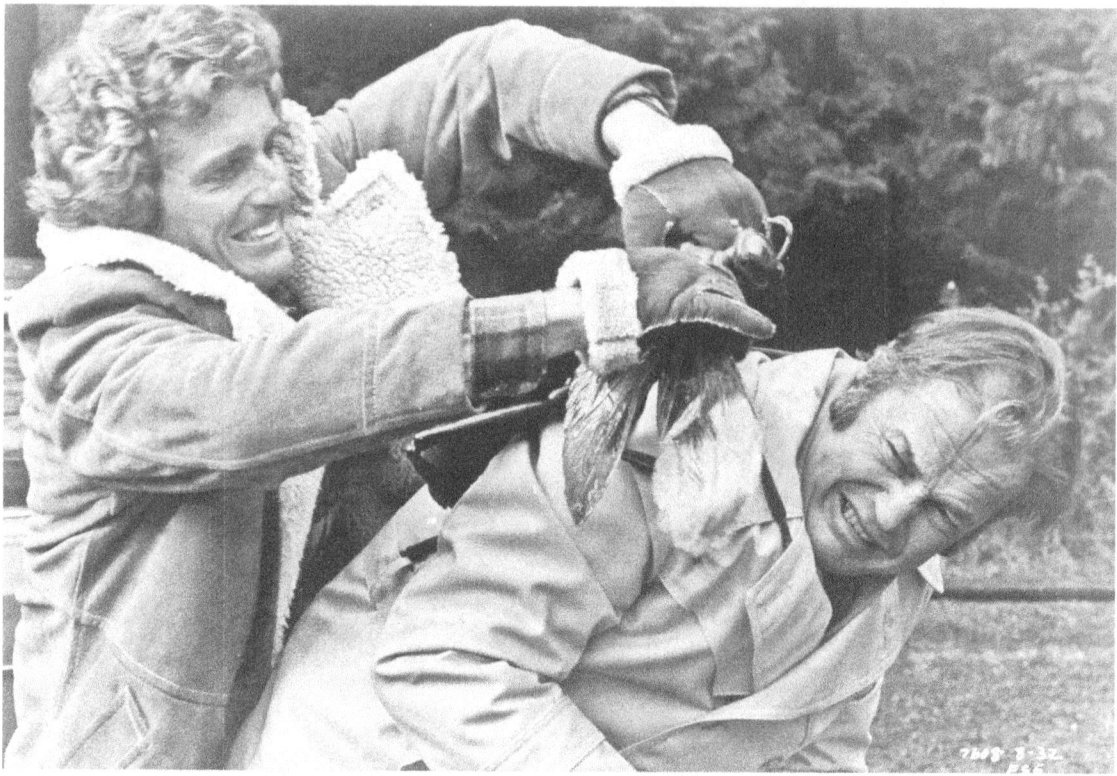

Marjoe Gortner pulls an oversize wasp off Ralph Meeker in *The Food of the Gods*.

covery and get far more than they bargained for when giant rats attack the farmhouse. It's up to Morgan to save the day. *The Food of the Gods* substitutes the naive charm of Gordon's fifties monster movies with an excess of blood and gore. As usual, Gordon did the special effects. Some aren't bad (the giant rats) but others are awful (the giant wasps). Full-size mockups of the enlarged wildlife which were executed by Tom Burman and associates are far more effective. There isn't a disclaimer on the film saying that "No animals were harmed in the making of this motion picture" and it is distressingly apparent that hordes of real rats were actually shot, blown up and drown. The intervention of the ASPCA was desperately needed on this film.

Foxy Brown

"DON'T MESS AROUN' WITH FOXY BROWN ... SHE'S THE MEANEST CHICK IN TOWN!"

(April 1974) Color by Movielab. Produced by Buzz Feitshans. Directed and Written by Jack Hill. Starring Pam Grier, Peter Brown, Terry Carter, Katherine Loder. DVD: MGM (1.85) 91 min.; Extras: Theatrical trailer; Audio commentary by Jack Hill.

Once in a while you run across a movie that causes your jaw to drop and makes you wonder why people aren't talking about it all of the time. For me, *Foxy Brown* is just that sort of movie. The blaxploitation genre flourished in the wake of the Black Power Movement and American International jumped on this particular bandwagon with both feet ... to the continual consternation of the Coalition Against Blaxploitation. No other company released as many "baadasss" pictures as AIP did and the biggest, baddest baadassss mama of them all was the incredible Pam Grier. *Foxy Brown* is definitely one of her signature roles right beside *Coffy*, *Friday Foster*, and *Sheba, Baby*. Her Afro is big and her attitude is even bigger. And don't even get me started on her bust! Foxy's man is a former narc who is killed by the local drug syndicate. Foxy swears to get even. She discovers that a high-class call girl operation is the front for the drug dealers. She goes to them using the name Misty Cotton and asks for a job. Since she is a total knockout, they immediately hire her. To say more would be to give away all the "fun" which includes a brawl in a dyke bar (sorry, but that's the only way to describe it) and a penis in a pickle jar. Willie Hutch, of Motown Records fame, composed the score and sings the background songs. Great psychedelic opening credits too!

Frankenstein Conquers the World

"HE ROLLED THE SEVEN WONDERS OF THE WORLD INTO ONE!"

(July 1966) ColorScope (TohoScope and Pathé Color). A Toho Co. Ltd./Henry G. Saperstein Enterprises Production. Produced by Tomoyuki Tanaka. Directed by Ishiro Honda. Written by Kaoru Mabuchi, Jerry Sohl, Reuben Bercovitch. Starring Nick Adams, Tadao Takashima, Kumi Mizuno, Yoshio Tsuchiya. DVD: Media Blasters (2.35) 87 min.; Extras: Japanese version; International version; Trailers; Deleted scenes; Photo gallery; Audio commentary by Sadamasa Arikawa.

Frankenstein Conquers the World has a history dating back to a project conceived by stop-motion animator Willis O'Brien ("King Kong vs. Frankenstein") in which Kong was to be pitted against a giant Frankenstein Monster. This concept eventually evolved into the Japanese film *King Kong vs. Godzilla* (1962) which was made without the participation of O'Brien ... or Frankenstein. The idea of the giant Frankenstein Monster was then developed by Henry G. Saperstein, who co-produced *Furankenshutain Tai Baragon/Frankenstein vs. Baragon* (1965) with Japan's Toho Company. At the end of World War II, the living heart of the Frankenstein Monster is taken by the Nazis and given to the Japanese (the reasons for this are rather vague). Almost immediately after the heart arrives in Hiroshima, the fatal bomb is dropped and the city is destroyed. Fifteen years later a mysterious boy is discovered behaving like a wild animal and growing at an alarming rate. Scientists suspect that the boy has evolved from the heart of Frankenstein combined with large doses of radioactivity. "Franken-boy" escapes from captivity and is considered to be a menace by the military, who are anxious to blow him to bits with their artillery. A great deal of death and destruction occurs following the sudden appearance of an enormous prehistoric monster called Baragon. The blame falls on Frankenstein until the existence of Baragon is finally discovered. Frankenstein and Baragon meet in another of those interminable fight scenes which are so dear to Japanese moviemakers. The Japanese version of this film runs 95 minutes, the major difference being a completely different ending. In the U.S. version, Frankenstein defeats Baragon and is then swallowed up by an earthquake. In the Japanese version, Frankenstein defeats Baragon but is immediately attacked by a giant octopus which drags him down into the water, presumably to his death. Whatever the ending, this is definitely one of the oddest movies of the Japanese monster genre. A year after *Furankenshutain Tai Baragon* was filmed, Toho made the inevitable sequel *Furankenshutain No Kaiju-Sanda Tai Gailah* in which the severed hand of the monster from the previous movie grows a new body. When it was released in the U.S. as *War of the Gargantuas* in 1970, all references to the former film had been deleted. The *Frankenstein Conquers the World* DVD from Media Blasters has three different versions, including the U.S. version, complete with AIP opening credits and the AIP dubbing.

Friday Foster

"WHAM! BAM! HERE COMES PAM!!!"

(December 1975) Color by Movielab. Produced and Directed by Arthur Marks. Written by Orville Hampton and Arthur Marks. Starring Pam Grier, Yaphet Kotto, Godfrey Cambridge, Thalmus Rasulala. DVD: MGM (1.85) 89 min.; Extras: Theatrical trailer.

Friday Foster was the last of Pam Grier's signature roles for AIP. The movie is tamer than *Coffy* and *Foxy Brown* and, although it is a slick production, it is a bit slight on action. Friday Foster (Grier) is a fashion model turned photographer. When she attempts to photograph multi-millionaire Blake Tarr (Thalmus Rasulala) she inadvertently discovers an assassination plot. With the help of her sidekick, private investigator Colt Hawkins (Yaphet Kotto), Friday sets out to protect Tarr and foil a plan to destroy the black political power structure. The cast also includes Eartha Kitt as fashion designer Madame Rena, Scatman Crothers as a minister, and Godfrey Cambridge enacting one of the worst gay stereotypes ever.

Frogs

"Cold Green Skin Against Soft Warm Flesh!"

(March 1972) Color by Movielab. An American International-Peter Thomas-George Edwards Production. Produced by George Edwards and Peter Thomas. Directed by George McCowan. Written by Robert Hutchison and Robert Blees. Starring Ray Milland, Sam Elliott, Joan Van Ark, Adam Roarke. DVD: MGM (1.85) 90 min.; Extras: Theatrical trailer; Fullscreen version.

Nature strikes back at a young Sam Elliott in *Frogs*.

Nature strikes back in this surprisingly sober AIP thriller. Environmentalist Pickett Smith (Sam Elliott) is documenting the pollution in a Florida swamp when his canoe is accidentally overturned by a speedboat. He is taken to the plantation-style home of cranky millionaire Jason Crockett (Ray Milland), who is hosting a family gathering to celebrate his birthday. Smith and the Crockett family soon realize that something is not quite right as hordes of creepy crawlies begin to invade the mansion and grounds. One by one, members of the Crockett clan are picked off by all manner of slimy fauna. The frogs (and toads) just croak and hop around, leaving the real mayhem to snakes, spiders, alligators, and even snapping turtles. A very young and handsome Sam Elliott (*sans* mustache and wearing the tightest jeans you've ever seen) is the sole voice of reason as he tries to convince curmudgeonly Milland to flee for his life. *Frogs* has actually improved with age and seems a much better film now than when it was originally released.

Gas-s-s! or It Became Necessary to Destroy the World in Order to Save It

"Invite a few friends over to watch the end of the world!"

(March 1971) Color by Movielab. Produced and Directed by Roger Corman. Written by George Armitage. Starring Robert Corff, Elaine Giftos, Bud Cort, Ben Vereen. DVD: MGM (1.85) 78 min.; Extras: Theatrical trailer. Midnite Movies co-feature: *Wild in the Streets*.

The U.S. military accidentally releases an experimental drug into the atmosphere which kills anyone over the age of twenty-five. This results in total anarchy so a group of hippies set off from Texas to join a peaceful commune located at a New Mexico pueblo. *Gas!* (or *Gas-s-s-s* if you prefer the way it was advertised) was Roger Corman's final film for AIP. Corman seems to be trying for the kind of wild comedy typified by Richard Lester's *Help!* (1965) but his film never comes close to achieving that level of inspired lunacy. Of course, Lester had The Beatles for inspiration. Corman has Robert Corff and Elaine Giftos in the leads. In supporting roles are Ben Vereen, Bud Cort, Talia Shire (herein billed as Tally Coppola), and Cindy Williams, all of whom went on the bigger things. Williams deserves special mention for giving a performance so awful that her work in *Laverne and Shirley* seems like Shakespeare by comparison. Screenwriter George Armitage, who reportedly rewrote the script on a daily basis, plays the car-rustling "Billy the Kid." Country Joe and the Fish provide the songs and appear on screen during a concert sequence in a drive-in theatre. In a nod to his previous films, Corman has Edgar Allan Poe (Bruce Katcher) appear in a couple of scenes riding a motorcycle. When Corman finished shooting on *Gas!* he turned in his final cut to AIP and immediately left for Ireland to begin filming *Von Richthofen and Brown*. In his autobiography Corman says: "AIP was losing their nerve, maybe shaken by the controversy around the biker and acid movies." When Corman saw *Gas!* at the Edinburgh Film Festival, the content had been altered considerably without his knowledge. Said Corman: "Jim [Nicholson] had grown conservative and it was his objections to my work that led to the cuts." After directing 30 films for AIP, Corman had enough and severed his ties with the company.

Poster art for Roger Corman's last AIP film *Gas-s-s-s*.

The Ghost in the Invisible Bikini

"THERE'S SOMETHING BLOOD CURDLING FOR EVERYONE!"

(April 1966) Panavision and Pathécolor. Produced by James H. Nicholson and Samuel Z. Arkoff. Directed by Don Weis. Written by Louis M. Heyward and Elwood Ullman. Starring Tommy Kirk, Deborah Walley, Susan Hart, Boris Karloff. DVD: MGM (2.35) 83 min.; Extras: Theatrical trailer. Midnite Movies co-feature: *Ghost of Dragstrip Hollow*.

Recently deceased Hiram Stokley (Boris Karloff) is told by the ghost of the title (Susan Hart) that if he wants to spend eternity "up there" with her, he must perform one good deed. The good deed is to make sure that his heirs (Tommy Kirk, Deborah Walley, and Patsy Kelly) are not cheated of their inheritance by an unscrupulous lawyer (Basil Rathbone). The ghost goes along to make sure that things work out for the good guys. When the heirs converge at Stokley Mansion for the reading of the will, all manner of strange occurrences take place. Not the least of these is the arrival of Aron Kincaid and an entire busload of bathing suit–clad, gyrating teenagers including Nancy Sinatra and diminutive Italian songstress Piccola Pupa. Also on hand are Harvey Lembeck and his Rat Pack plus oldtimer Francis X. Bushman as a butler who gets bumped off early on by Rathbone. There is also an escaped gorilla, a knockoff of the Aztec Mummy, and Jesse White wearing one of the creature costumes from Larry Buchanan's *The Eye Creatures*. As the catchline says, "There's Something BLOOD CURDLING for Everyone!" For me it was Piccola Pupa.

Songs: "Geronimo," "Swing A-Ma-Thing," "Don't Try and Fight It Baby," "Stand Up and Fight," "Make the Music Pretty"

Ghost of Dragstrip Hollow

"The Hot-Rod Gang meets the Ghost!"

(July 1959) Black & White. Produced and Written by Lou Rusoff. Directed by William Hole. Starring Jody Fair, Russ Bender, Henry McCann, Dorothy Neumann. DVD: MGM (1.33) 65 min. Midnite Movies co-feature: *The Ghost in the Invisible Bikini*.

If this isn't the worst movie AIP ever made, it certainly is a leading contender. This lame comedy, a precursor to the "Beach Party" movies, is filled with the same type of puerile humor. The all but nonexistent storyline has a drag racing club throwing a costume party in a supposedly haunted house owned by Anastasia Abernathy (Dorothy Neumann doing a reprise of her character from *Hot Rod Gang* the previous year). Turns out the house is "haunted" by AIP monster maker Paul Blaisdell dressed in a modified "She-Creature" costume. When his hoax is exposed, Blaisdell confesses in a squeaky voice that he's upset because after appearing in *Day the World Ended* and *The She-Creature*, they didn't cast him in *Horrors of the Black Museum*. Was there no end to the self-promotion this company would resort to? As if this wasn't enough, one of the partygoers wears an alien costume from *Invasion of the Saucer Men*. They also manage to get in a very unsubtle plug for American International Records. A very long 65 minutes indeed!

Songs: "Charge," "Geronimo," "Ghost Train," "Tongue Tied," "He's My Guy," "I Promise You"

Review: *Variety* (August 12, 1959), "It's virtually impossible to assess individual actors since the script is so poor and the directing so perfunctory."

Girls in Prison

"The Shocking Story of One Man Against 1000 Women!"

(July 1956) Black & White. A Golden State Production. Produced by Alex Gordon. Directed by Edward L. Cahn. Written by Lou Rusoff. Starring Joan Taylor, Richard Denning, Adele Jergens, Lance Fuller. VHS: Columbia/TriStar (1.33) 87 min.; DVD: Direct Video Distribution (1.33) 87 min.; Region-Free DVD from United Kingdom; Extras: Audio interview with Samuel Z. Arkoff; Trailers.

A respectable entry in the "Women in Prison" genre. A new "fish" in the tank, Anne Carson (Joan Taylor) has been found guilty of assisting in the "sensational Modesto bank robbery" and making off with $38,000 which she has apparently hidden. Kind-hearted prison clergyman the Rev. Fulton (Richard Denning) believes she is innocent. Anne's cellmates are sociopath Melanee (Helen Gilbert), delusional loony Dorothy (Phyllis Coates), and Queen Bee of the Hive Jennie (Adele Jergens). Anne rejects Melanee's amorous advances and they become bitter enemies. Jennie decides to take Anne under her wing with the hope that

Left to right: Helen Gilbert, Joan Taylor, and Adele Jergens are *Girls in Prison*.

she will learn where the money has been hidden. When Jennie and Melanee decide to make a break for freedom and force Anne to go with them, a timely earthquake (think *The Last Days of Pompeii* caliber) provides an easy means of escape. On the outside, Anne's sleazy accomplice Paul (the ever scummy Lance Fuller) is waiting for her with a gun and the intent to get all the money for himself. Despite the typical campy elements inherent in the genre, *Girls in Prison* has some very good performances and decent writing. Joan Taylor is probably best remembered for her leading lady roles in the Ray Harryhausen classics *Earth vs. the Flying Saucers* (1956) and *20 Million Miles to Earth* (1957). Adele Jergens is always a tough broad worth watching. Also in the cast are oldtimers Jane Darwell as the kindly prison matron Mrs. Jamison and silent film star Mae Marsh as inmate Grandma Edwards, an old biddy who is on the side of anybody who will cough up ten bucks. Marsh had been in pictures since 1910 and often appeared in films directed by the great D.W. Griffith, including *Birth of a Nation* (1915) and *Intolerance* (1916).

Song: "Tom's Beat"

Review: *Variety* (Sept. 12, 1956), "An overlength jail yarn with telegraphic situations which reduce the movement to a walk."

The Glory Stompers

"The DEADLIEST CYCLE WAR EVER WAGED!"

(November 1967) ColorScope by Pathé. A Norman T. Herman Production. Produced by John Lawrence. Directed by Anthony N.

Lanza. Written by James Gordon White and John Lawrence. Starring Dennis Hopper, Jody McCrea, Chris Noel, Jock Mahoney. VHS: MGM/Amazon (1.33) 85 min.

Darryl, a.k.a. "Cowboy" (Jody McCrea), is a member of the relatively clean-cut Glory Stompers biker gang. Clean-cut or not, his girlfriend Chris (Chris Noel) wants him to quit the club. While they are discussing this, Cowboy and Chris are set upon by the considerably more uncouth Black Souls gang. They beat up Cowboy and leave him for dead. The Black Souls' leader Chino (Dennis Hopper) decides that they should kidnap Chris and sell her as a prostitute in Mexico. The film chiefly consists of the Black Souls on their way to Mexico with a remarkably well-recovered Cowboy in hot pursuit. Along the way, Cowboy is joined by Smiley (Jock Mahoney), a former Glory Stomper who quit the gang when he realized he was on a trip to nowhere. There is, of course, an extended biker party scene (no biker movie would be complete without it). This one includes lots of dancing, beer- and wine-guzzling, girls riding around on motorcycles in their bras, a biker chick fight, and that ultimate expression of depravity in any AIP party sequence ... body painting! The cast is an interesting one. Jody McCrea, in his last AIP picture, finally is able to discard his dopey "Beach Party" persona and Dennis Hopper gives a performance so depraved that even Bruce Dern would be envious. Unfortunately, Jock Mahoney is wasted. Even his good looks are hidden behind huge dark glasses and a phony mustache. Also on hand as one of the Black Souls is deejay Casey Kasem, who served as an executive producer on the film as well. Kasem, John Lawrence, and Anthony N. Lanza would return to AIP a few years later for *The Incredible 2-Headed Transplant*.

Godzilla vs. the Smog Monster

"POLLUTION'S HIDEOUS SPAWN DOOMS THE EARTH TO CHOKING HORROR!"

(February 1972) ColorScope (TohoScope and Eastman Color). A Toho Co. Ltd. Production. Produced by Tomoyuki Tanaka. Directed by Yoshimitsu Banno. Written by Kaoru Mabuchi and Yoshimitsu Banno. Starring Akira Yamauchi, Hiroyuki Kawase, Toshie Kimura, Toshio Shibamoto. VHS: Orion (1.33) 86 min.; DVD: Sony (as *Godzilla vs. Hedorah*) (2.35) 86 min.

As the original Godzilla series continued, the plots got sillier, Godzilla looked more goofy, and the movies became increasingly "kid friendly." This entry is one of the oddest of all: a Godzilla movie with an anti-pollution message. Growing pollution of the oceans surrounding Japan brings about the creation of a sludge-like creature which comes to be known as Hedorah. Hedorah actually looks like an ambulatory pile of oily rags with big red eyeballs. Very annoyed at having his natural habitat befouled, Godzilla takes on Hedorah in one of those endless battles which were part and parcel of this series. What saves this from being standard Japanese monster fare are some inventive cinematic touches by director Yoshimitsu Banno. These include psychedelic lighting effects, cartoon sequences, and multi-images filling the screen. The Orion Video VHS release had the AIP credits and the Japanese songs dubbed into English, which the Sony DVD does not.

Godzilla vs. the Thing

"NOTHING LIKE IT EVER ON THE SCREEN!"

(October 1964) ColorScope (TohoScope and Eastman Color). A Toho Co. Ltd. Production. Produced by Tomoyuki Tanaka. Directed by Ishiro Honda. Written by Shinichi Arikawa. Starring Akira Takarada, Yuriko Hoshi, Hiroshi Koizumi, Yu Fujiki. . DVD: Simitar (as *Godzilla vs. Mothra*) (2.35) 87 min.; Extras: Godzilla trailer collection; Interactive trivia game; Fullscreen version.

A violent storm washes an enormous egg up onto a Japanese beach and greedy businessmen want to make it a tourist attraction. Two tiny twin sisters appear and beg for the egg to be returned to the island from which they have come, explaining that it is the egg of Mothra. When a land excavation inadvertently unearths Godzilla, the fire-breathing beast goes on a rampage throughout Japan. The only hope of saving mankind is Mothra but, after a battle with Godzilla, the giant moth dies. The twins "sing" the egg into hatching and it reveals two giant larvae. When Godzilla attacks an island where schoolchildren have gone on an excursion, the larvae come to the rescue. They spin a silk cocoon around Godzilla and he falls off a cliff, disappearing into the ocean (until the next sequel). In this film, Godzilla is still the "bad guy" but shortly thereafter the behemoth would become a kid-friendly hero. When AIP distributed *Godzilla vs. Mothra*, they decided to change the title to *Godzilla vs. the Thing* and keep the true identity of "the Thing" hidden in the publicity campaign. In the dubbed AIP version, Mothra is occasionally referred to as "the Thing" to justify the title. Although many of the Toho productions on DVD (such as *Atragon* and *Destroy All Monsters*) do not have the AIP dub, the Simitar release of *Godzilla vs. the Thing* does. The widescreen version also has the original AIP credits.

Review: *Variety* (September 30, 1964), "An orgy of special effects that should satisfy devotees of the fare."

Goliath and the Barbarians

"A THOUSAND AND ONE WOMEN DREAM OF HIS EMBRACE!"

(December 1959) ColorScope (Totalscope and Eastman Color). A Standard Production. Produced by Emimmo Salvi. Directed by Carlo Campogalliani. Written by Emimmo Salvi, Gino Mangini, Nino Stresa, Giuseppe Tafarel and Carlo Campogalliani. Starring Steve Reeves, Chelo Alonso, Bruce Cabot, Livio Lorenzon. DVD: Wild East (2.35) 88 min.; Extras: Theatrical trailer; Photo gallery; DVD co-feature: *Goliath and the Vampires*.

American International scored quite a coup when they obtained the U.S. distribution rights to the Italian production *Il terrore dei barbari/The Terror of the Barbarians*. The recent release of *Hercules* had made a star of muscular leading man Steve Reeves. *Il terrore dei barbari* was the movie he had filmed immediately after his stint as Hercules in two back-to-back productions for director Pietro Francisci. American promoter Joseph E. Levine had parlayed *Hercules* into a tremendous box office success with an avalanche of publicity. AIP took their cue from him and, after changing the title of their acquisition to *Goliath and the Barbarians*, they devised an elaborate advertising campaign to promote its release. The effort paid off handsomely and the result was a big take at the box office for AIP ("Gigantic GOLIATH Grosses Everywhere!"). They also managed to get their film into theatres long before *Hercules Unchained* was released in the U.S. The action-filled story of *Goliath and the Barbarians* begins in A.D. 568 as barbarians, led by Alboino (Bruce Cabot), are sweeping through northern Italy. When his village is raided and his father murdered, Emiliano (Steve Reeves) is determined to get revenge. In the guise of a terrible monster, which the barbarians dub "Goliath," Emiliano gives them a taste of their own medicine. Cuban beauty Chelo Alonso plays the daughter of a barbarian chieftain. As such, the former Folies Bergere star is called upon to perform two exotic dance numbers. In the first of many such assignments, composer Les Baxter was hired by AIP to replace the original score by Carlo Innocenzi. The Wild East transfer is apparently taken from the same source as the good quality Spanish Cine Epico DVD which has an optional English-language track. This version opens with the Italian credits backed by the original score. Immediately afterwards, the soundtrack changes to the AIP English-language version with the Les Baxter music.

Review: *New York Herald Tribune* (January 7, 1960), "The acting throughout is reminiscent of a serious High School dramatic effort."

78 *Goliath and the Barbarians*

The spectacular poster art for *Goliath and the Barbarians* features Steve Reeves and Chelo Alonso.

Goliath and the Dragon

"THE MIGHTIEST ADVENTURE OF THEM ALL!"

(November 1960) ColorScope (Totalscope and Eastman Color). A Piazzi Produzione, Rome-Comptoir Francais, Paris Production. Produced By Achille Piazzi and Gianni Fuchs. Directed by Vittorio Cottafavi. Written by Marco Piccolo and Archibald Zounds Jr. Starring Mark Forest, Broderick Crawford, Eleonora Ruffo, Gaby Andre. DVD: Something Weird (2.35) 87 min.; Extras: Sword-and-Sandal trailer collection; 3 Sword-and-Sandal short subjects; Poster and still gallery; Bonus Feature: *The Conqueror of Atlantis.*

When Steve Reeves decided not to appear as Hercules again, Italian producers began to consider other musclemen for a replacement. The first of these was Lou Degni, a Brooklyn bodybuilder who, using the name Mark Forest, subsequently starred in a dozen sword-and-sandal spectaculars. The European title of this film was *La vendetta di Ercole/The Vengeance of Hercules* but AIP, having already scored a big success with *Goliath and the Barbarians* (1959), decided to change the name of the title character to Goliath. The name Goliath became a mainstay for AIP and *Goliath and the Vampires* and *Goliath and the Sins of Babylon* followed. Feeling the original movie lacked a dynamic finale, AIP ordered new scenes featuring a dragon, which also enabled them to justify a title change to *Goliath and the Dragon.* The brief long shots of the dragon were done by stop-motion animation expert Jim Danforth. Although there have been many complaints about the tampering Jim Nicholson and Sam Arkoff did with films, their sense of exploitation possibilities was usually concise. The AIP version of this film is an improvement over the original European cut in many respects. As with most of their imports, AIP replaced the original score (by Alexandre Derevitsky) with one by their resident composer Les Baxter, who reuses many of his themes from *Goliath and the Barbarians.*

Review: *Harrison's Reports* (December 24, 1960), "Italian-made, badly dubbed ColorScope vehicle. Brooklyn-born Mark Forest is a worthy, muscle-rippling Goliath. Special effects are excellent."

Goliath and the Sins of Babylon

"SEE THE THOUSAND AND ONE ORGIES OF TORTURE!"

(February 1964) Techniscope and Technicolor. A Leone Film Production. Produced by Elio Scardamaglia. Directed by Michele Lupo. Written by Roberto Gianviti, Francesco Scardamaglia, Francesco Ardamaglia. and Lionello De Felice. Starring Mark Forest, Eleanora Bianchi, Giuliano Gemma, Jose Greci. DVD: Retromedia (2.35) 80 min.; DVD co-feature: *Colossus and the Amazon Queen.*

AIP imported *Maciste, l'eroe piu grande del mondo/Maciste, the Greatest Hero in the World* and turned it into *Goliath and the Sins of Babylon.* The city of Nefer is suffering under the tyranny of Babylon, whose king demands that local virgins be offered up periodically for sacrifice. Maciste (Mark Forest) and a band of ex-gladiators (in Babylon?) do what they can to fight this oppression with the aid of Resia (Eleanora Bianchi), the princess of Nefer. The production values in this sword-and-sandal entry are of a higher quality than usual, particularly in respect to the sets and costumes. The film's major set pieces are a sea battle, a chariot race and the burning of Babylon ... all of which are accomplished using stock footage from *Carthage in Flames* (1960) and *Theodora, Slave Empress* (1954). It is obvious that much care was taken to seamlessly incorporate that footage into this film and the results are surprisingly successful. In addition to Peplum star Forest as Goliath, the cast also includes frequent sword-and-sandal performers Mimmo Palmara, Livio Lorenzon and Giuliano Gemma, who later became the Spaghetti Western star Montgomery Wood. Although the AIP credits list Les Baxter as the composer, his standard "Goliath" theme is heard only briefly. Most of the music is the original score by

Goliath (Gordon Scott) unmasks the monster Kobrak in *Goliath and the Vampires*.

Francesco De Masi. The widescreen DVD of *Goliath and the Sins of Babylon* from Retromedia proves once again how spectacular these often maligned movies can look when given a proper presentation.

Goliath and the Vampires

"MONSTER vs. GOLIATH ... ALL NEW ... THE MIGHTIEST BATTLE OF THEM ALL!"

(May 1964) ColorScope (Totalscope and Technicolor). A Dino De Laurentiis Presentation. An Ambrosiana Cinematographica Production. Produced by Paolo Moffa. Directed by Giacomo Gentilomo. Written by Sergio Corbucci and Duccio Tessari. Starring Gordon Scott, Gianna Maria Canale, Jacques Sernas, Eleonora Ruffo. DVD: Wild East (2.35) 92 min.; Extras: Theatrical trailer; Photo gallery; DVD co-feature: *Goliath and the Barbarians*.

Released in Europe in 1961 as *Maciste contro il vampiro/Maciste Against the Vampire*, this sword-and-sandal movie has more than its share of fantasy-horror elements. Although the vampire connection is somewhat cursory, there is a great amount of blood imagery. The mighty strongman Goliath (Gordon Scott) goes to the kingdom of Salmanak which has been taken over by the evil Kobrak, a mysterious entity who drinks the blood of maidens. Aided by the rebel Kurtik (Jacques Sernas), leader of the "Blue Men," Goliath strives to use his tremendous strength to overthrow the monster. Unfortunately Kobrak is able to assume Goliath's form and engage him in mortal combat ... with himself! With enough plot devices for a dozen Peplum films, *Goliath and the Vampires* is often engaging and imaginative. Also, the "Arabian Nights"–style scenery is a welcome change from the usual Greek, Roman or Egyptian settings. When AIP released the film to television, it was titled simply *The Vampires*. The DVD from Wild East is a disappointment. Although the picture is correctly letterboxed at 2.35, the image is grainy and the color faded. Adding insult to injury, the trailer has the vibrant color that the feature should have.

Review: *Time* (May 15, 1964), "*Goliath and the Vampires* improbably combines a routine fang film with a beefcake B."

Gunslinger

"Hired to kill the woman he loved..."

(June 1956) Pathécolor. Produced and Directed by Roger Corman. Written by Charles B. Griffith and Mark Hanna. Starring John Ireland, Beverly Garland, Allison Hayes, Martin Kingsley. VHS: Dura Vision (1.33) 83 min.

Roger Corman's finale Western for ARC is also his most interesting, primarily because of the strong performances given by two female B-movie icons. In 1878, the marshall of Oracle, Texas, is gunned down and his widow Rose (Beverly Garland) puts on his badge. Her first official duty is to impose a curfew on the Red Dog Saloon, an act which is not appreciated by owner Erica Page (Allison Hayes). Erica, who has plans to take over the town when the railroad comes through, hires gunslinger Cane Miro (John Ireland) to kill Rose. Miro falls for Rose in a big way. Most of the people who were involved in the filming of *Gunslinger* have said that shooting it was an arduous experience with more than its share of mishaps. Despite this, the end result is above average in writing, direction and acting. If the production values had been of a higher caliber, this could have been a truly memorable Western in every respect. Jonathan Haze, Dick Miller and Bruno VeSota are featured in supporting parts. The bulk of the acting honors go to Garland and Hayes, who play off each other to great effect. And for those of you partial to "girl fights," they engage in a full-on barroom brawl. *Gunslinger* is available on DVD in "The Mystery Science Theater 3000 Collection Vol. 6" but the less said about that particular aberration, the better.

Review: *Variety* (August 1, 1956), "Since the material isn't very believable, the star performances are on the same level."

The Hand

"From War-Torn Burma to the Asphalt Jungles of the Big City—His Revenge Was The Crime of the Century!"

(April 1961) Black & White. Produced by Bill Luckwell. Directed by Henry Cass. Written by Ray Cooney and Tony Hilton. Starring Derek Bond, Ronald Leigh Hunt, Reed de Rouen, Ray Cooney. DVD: Alpha (1.33) 61 min.

This obscure British mystery was filmed in 1960 and released in the U.S. by AIP the following year. It is a somewhat inexplicable choice as a pickup item for them as the exploitation possibilities are rather limited. From the AIP ad campaign you can't really tell much of anything. It could be a horror movie or a gangster film. Turns out that it is neither. The story opens in 1946 Burma where three British soldiers have been captured by the Japanese. This opening scene looks like something from Hammer's *The Camp on Blood Island*. The story then moves to present-day (circa 1960) England. A man is found unconscious in an alley with £500 in his pocket and missing his right hand. A short while later, he is abducted from the hospital and murdered. The focus of the rest of the film is on the police search to find the killer. The denouement is fairly routine and it should be easy for anyone in the audience to solve the mystery long before the police in the movie do. The cast is made up of unfamiliar faces. Director Henry Cass previously helmed *Blood of the Vampire* (1958), the first British movie which attempted to copy the style of Hammer's gothic horror films.

The Haunted Palace

"WHAT WAS THE TERRIFYING THING IN THE PIT THAT WANTED WOMEN?"

(August 1963) Panavision and Pathécolor. Produced and Directed by Roger Corman. Written by Charles Beaumont. Starring Vincent Price, Debra Paget, Lon Chaney, Frank Maxwell. DVD: MGM (2.35) 87 min.; Extras: Theatrical trailer; Interview with Roger Corman—"A Change of Poe." Midnite Movies co-feature: *Tower of London*.

In an attempt to take a break from the Poe series, Roger Corman convinced AIP to let him adapt H. P. Lovecraft's story "The Case of Charles Dexter Ward" for the screen. It was first announced as *The Haunted Village*; by the time the picture reached theatres some, quotes from Poe's poem (intoned by Vincent Price at the beginning and end) turned it into Edgar Allan Poe's *The Haunted Palace*. Charles Dexter Ward (Price) and his wife (Debra Paget) arrive in the village of Arkham to claim the palace he has inherited. They are met with hostility from the townspeople because Ward is the descendant of Joseph Curwen, a warlock who placed a curse on Arkham over a hundred years before. Curwen's evil spirit soon takes over Ward and he begins his reign of terror anew. Price is outstanding in the dual role, with a skillful change of expression and tone of voice to denote his transformation from Curwen to Ward. Boris Karloff had originally been suggested by AIP for the part of sinister caretaker Simon Orne, but Corman felt that Lon Chaney was better suited for the role. This was the final movie of Debra Paget's career. After filming finished, she married millionaire Louis Kung and retired from the screen. Ronald Stein contributes one of his finest scores ever, with a particularly haunting main theme.

Review: *San Diego Evening Tribune* (August 1963), "Enough witches, warlocks and evil curses to give the kiddies nightmares for a full week. They'll love it."

The cast assembles on an impressive set for *The Haunted Palace*.

The Headless Ghost

"HEAD-HUNTING TEENAGERS LOST IN THE HAUNTED CASTLE!"

(April 1959) Dyaliscope and Black & White. Produced by Jack Greenwood and Herman Cohen. Directed by Peter Graham Scott. Written by Kenneth Langtry and Herman Cohen. Starring Richard Lyon, Liliane Sottane, David Rose, Clive Revill. DVD: Cheezy Flicks (2.35) 63 min.; Extras: Trailers.

Silly shenanigans in a haunted English castle. Three students on a tour of Ambrose Castle decide to hide away and spend the night to see if they encounter any ghosts. They do indeed and end up helping the ghost of the title recover his head. This quickie was made in England to accompany *Horrors of the Black Museum* on a double bill. *The Headless Ghost* was a light-hearted reprieve from the grim horrors of the main feature. Despite the rather dubious moniker of Cheezy Flicks, this is an okay transfer of the film. It is also widescreen, a fact which is not mentioned anywhere on the box. Even the Cheezy Flicks website says it's fullscreen. Both this and the quality of the image came as a very pleasant surprise. This isn't a great film by any stretch of the imagination but there are worse ways to spend an hour and seeing it in the original widescreen aspect ratio is a treat.

Review: *New York Times* (April 22, 1959), "Pretty dismal. A pale and protracted bit of miscast whimsy."

Hell Squad

"HITS LIKE STEEL! THE GUTS AND GORE OF DESERT WAR!"

(July 1958) Black & White. A Rhonda Production. Produced, Directed and Written by Burt Topper. Starring Wally Campo, Brandon Carroll, Fredric Gavlin, Gregg Stewart. VHS: Columbia/TriStar (1.33) 64 min.; VHS co-feature: *Suicide Battalion*.

In 1943 a small group of American foot soldiers are separated from their unit and become lost in the Tunisian desert. They encounter a troop of Nazis and after a bloody battle only two men are left alive. It then becomes a contest of wills between the remaining American (Wally Campo) and a Nazi (Brandon Carroll). *Hell Squad* benefits from being completely shot on location in the California desert. This gives it a grittier atmosphere than other AIP war movies which were filmed in the confines of a studio (the unconvincing jungle sets of *Suicide Battalion* come to mind). The acting is suitably earnest and director Burt Topper manages to generate a substantial amount of suspense, particularly in the final scenes between the soldier and the Nazi. Burt Topper was a former actor who got fed up with acting and decided to make his own movie. He shot *Hell Squad* on weekends and eventually sold it to American International. This began a long association with AIP in which he functioned in the various capacities of producer, director, writer, and even narrator on a couple of AIP "Mondo" films.

Review: *Variety* (October 29, 1958), "Somewhat novel plot but too much footage is wasted leading up to it."

Brandon Carroll is a Nazi soldier in *Hell Squad*.

Hell Up in Harlem

"BLACK GODFATHER'S MAD ... AND THAT'S REAL BAD!"

(January 1974) Color by Movielab. A Larco Production. Produced, Directed and Written by Larry Cohen. Starring Fred Williamson, Julius W. Harris, Gloria Hendry, Margaret Avery. DVD: MGM (1.85) 94 min.; Extras: Theatrical and teaser trailers; Audio commentary by Larry Cohen.

Before creating the *It's Alive* trilogy and *Q, the Winged Serpent*, Larry

84   Hell's Angels on Wheels

In *Hell Up in Harlem*, Fred Williamson reprises his role of "Black Caesar" Tommy Gibbs.

Cohen directed a pair of blaxploitation films featuring Fred Williamson as Tommy Gibbs, the "Black Caesar of Harlem." AIP released a myriad of blaxploitation films during the seventies and *Hell Up in Harlem* is one of the most entertaining of the lot. Tommy Gibbs takes it upon himself to clean up Harlem by getting rid of the corrupt police, politicians, and drug lords. When Gibbs' former girlfriend (Gloria Hendry) is murdered, he blames her death on his father (Julius W. Harris). Disgusted, he turns over his gang to dear old dad and moves to Beverly Hills. But even in sunny California, Tommy cannot escape from his bloody past. Ultra-violent and frantically paced, *Hell Up in Harlem* benefits greatly from the larger-than-life presence of former football star Fred "The Hammer" Williamson.

Hell's Angels on Wheels

"Now! For the First Time! The Shattering Story of the Hell's Angels!"

(June 1967) Eastman Color. A Fanfare Film Production. Produced by Joe Solomon. Directed by Richard Rush. Written by R. Wright Campbell. Starring Adam Roarke, Jack Nicholson, Sabrina Scharf, Richard Anders. DVD: Image (1.85) 95 min.; Extras: Theatrical trailer.

Joe Solomon was an AIP distributor who decided to form his own production company and make pictures. Initially *Hell's Angels on Wheels* was released by U.S. Films but it was later picked up by AIP and shown as part of their "Cycle Rider Spectacular." The movie opens in San Francisco with a gathering of the "clans." More precisely the Hell's Angels of Oakland, San Francisco, Daly City, and Richmond. A small troop of Angels, led by Buddy (Adam Roarke), breaks away from the rest of the group to raise cain in a small town. They terrorize motorists and pedestrians alike and, along the way, pick up a fledgling member for their gang named Poet (Jack Nicholson). Poet soon falls for Buddy's "righteous old lady" Shill (Sabrina Scharf), but she can't seem to make up her mind as to who she wants to be with. The plot consists of brawls, a wild party, more brawls, a biker wedding, another brawl, a run-in with the local fuzz, and a final brawl between Buddy and Poet over Shill. *Hell's Angels on Wheels* is one of the best of the biker movies. The photography of Lazlo Kovacs' (billed in the credits as "Leslie Kovacs") is top-notch and the story, what there is of it, moves briskly along. Adam Roarke is top-billed in this, the first of his three AIP biker flicks. He basically plays the same part in all of them with only a change of name to differentiate one from another. Jack Nicholson, young and good-looking as the idealistic Poet, turns in a decent performance as well. Originally John Ashley had been offered the role of Poet but turned it down because he felt he was too old for the part. Also in the cast is future AIP director Bob Kelljan as a "body painter" during the biker party scene. Hell's Angels president Sonny Barger puts in a cameo appearance in the opening credits sequence where he plants a big kiss on Adam Roarke's lips to everyone's apparent surprise. Barger also served as a technical advisor on the film. What that entailed is anybody's guess. If you are looking for a fast-paced and mindless bit of fun, you could do a lot worse than *Hell's Angels on Wheels*.

Sabrina Scharf and Jack Nicholson in *Hell's Angels on Wheels*.

Hell's Angels '69

"THIS WAS THE RUMBLE THAT ROCKED LAS VEGAS!"

(1969) Color by Berkey-Pathé. A Tracom Production. Produced by Tom Stern. Directed by Lee Madden. Written by Don Tait. Starring Tom Stern, Jeremy Slate, Conny Van Dyke, Steve Sandor. DVD: Media Blasters (1.33) 93 min.; Extras: Theatrical trailer; Audio commentary by Joe Bob Briggs; Conny Van Dyke "Message to her fans."

Tom Stern and Jeremy Slate play brothers who decide to rob Caesar's Palace in Las Vegas just for kicks. In order to do this, they concoct a plan in which they will join the Hell's Angels motorcycle gang and then use them as unknowing decoys. When the Angels realize they have been duped, the two brothers have hell to pay. Singer Conny Van Dyke is the "biker mama" whom Tom Stern "buys" for a pack of cigarettes. *Hell's Angels '69* is especially intriguing because the on-screen Hell's Angels are actually played by members of the gang's Okland chapter, including leader Sonny Barger. The most incredible performance comes from real-life Angel "Terry the Tramp" who is downright frightening. This was his one big chance in the spotlight as he died shortly after the film was released. Jeremy Slate was a regular fixture in AIP biker movies. He had already appeared in *Born Losers* (1967) and *Mini Skirt Mob* (1968) and followed *Hell's Angels '69* with *Hell's Belles* (1969). One noticeable gaffe in continuity occurs when Stern and Slate arrive at Caesar's Palace. The billboard prominently features "Celeste Holm as Mame" but when the Angels arrive later the same evening, Milton Berle is the headliner.

Hell's Belles

"MEET THE DEBUTANTE IN A LEATHER SKIRT"

(April 1969) Color by Berkey-Pathé. A Maury Dexter Production. Produced and Directed by Maury Dexter. Written by James Gordon White and R. G. McMullen. Starring Jeremy Slate, Adam Roarke, Jocelyn Lane, Angelique Pettyjohn. DVD: MGM (1.85) 96 min.; Extras: Theatrical trailer; Midnite Movies co-feature: *The Wild Angels*.

When cowboy Dan (Jeremy Slate) gets his new motorcycle stolen by a gang of thugs, he takes off into the desert after them, determined to get it back. The head of the gang, Tampa (Adam Roarke), is just as determined to keep the bike and leaves "biker belle" Nancy (Jocelyn Lane) for Dan in exchange. Dan definitely does not think this is a fair trade. Switch horses for motorcycles and transport the story to the Old West via Italy and you'd have the makings for a decent Spaghetti Western. As it is, this is one of the lesser entries in AIP's series of biker films. Not all that bad, but not terribly exciting either. And the *Hell's Belles* of the title actually look more like "Carnaby Street Cuties" than biker babes.

Joyce (Yvonne Lime) listens to a lecture from her well-meaning teacher Miss Davis (Rhoda Williams) in *High School Hellcats*.

High School Hellcats

"What Must a Good Girl Say to 'Belong'?"

(July 1959) Black & White. Produced by Charles "Buddy" Rogers. Directed by Edward Bernds. Written by Mark and Jan Lowell. Starring Yvonne Lime, Brett Halsey, Jana Lund, Suzanne Sidney. VHS: MGM (1.33) 69 min.

When the opening scene has three "bad girls" smoking cigs in the school bathroom, you know you're in for a delirious camp treat ... and *High School Hellcats* certainly doesn't disappoint in that respect. New girl in school Joyce (Yvonne Lime) is told by her classmates that everybody is wearing slacks the following day despite it being against the school dress code. When she shows up in her slacks, she is the only girl to do so. Her refusal to admit to her teacher that she was tricked into wearing them by her classmates passes her initiation test into the girl gang known as the "Hellcats." Joyce, who is tired of the attitude of her busy and neglectful parents, joins the "Hellcats" mostly out of a desire to belong. Connie (Jana Lund) is the leader and her "henchman" is Dolly (Suzanne Sidney), a psychotic girl who resembles Mickey Rooney in drag. Although her new boyfriend Mike (Brett Halsey) endlessly nags her to drop out of the gang, Joyce continues to meet with the other girls in a deserted theatre. When a wild party ends in tragedy, the local police become involved and Dolly really loses her marbles, placing Joyce in real danger. In addition to all the teenage hijinks, there is an honest-to-goodness message here about parental neglect and lack of understanding. When Joyce innocently runs around the house in her slip and her overreacting father slaps her, it is a jarring and disturbing moment which makes you wonder if there is more to Dad (and the film) than meets the eye.

Review: *Harrison's Reports* (September 6, 1958), "A fairly good program picture. Several of the situations are suspenseful. The direction and acting are good."

Horror House

"Terror Waits Behind Its Forbidden Doors!"

(May 1970) Color by Movielab. A Tigon British Film Production. Produced by Tony Tenser. Directed by Michael Armstrong. Written by Michael Armstrong and Peter Marcus. Starring Frankie Avalon, Jill Haworth, Dennis Price, Mark Wynter. DVD: Anchor Bay UK/Starz Tigon Box Set (as *The Haunted House of Horror*); (1.66) 92 min.; Region 2 DVD from United Kingdom; Extras: Audio commentary by Michael Armstrong; Theatrical trailer and radio spots; Poster and stills gallery; Biographies of cast and crew.

At age 22, Michael Armstrong directed a 14-minute short film called *The Image* (1967) which starred David Bowie. This film was brought to the attention of Tigon Films exec Tony Tenser who invited Armstrong to direct a film for the company. Armstrong wrote a haunted house thriller called *The Dark* and it was decided that this would be a co-production between Tigon and American International. Original plans for casting included Ian Ogilvy, Jane Merrow, and David Bowie, who would also compose the score. AIP's man in charge of British productions Louis "Deke" Heyward insisted that Ogilvy be replaced by either Frankie Avalon or Fabian and suggested Carol Lynley (who eventually proved unavailable) for the female lead. Also he did not want David Bowie in any capacity. In addition to this, Heyward was not pleased with Armstrong's script. He created the part of a police inspector with the idea of casting Boris Karloff in the role and brought in Gerry Levy to write additional material (using the name Peter Marcus). Karloff was in such ill health, as a result of poor working conditions on the previous Tigon–American International co-production *The Curse of the Crimson Altar*, that he was unable to appear in the film and the part went to Dennis Price. Armstrong and Heyward were continually at odds during the filming and eventually Levy was engaged to direct two weeks' worth of additional footage. For kicks, a group of swinging mod–Londoners ... and Frankie Avalon ... go to a deserted country house where several brutal murders had occurred twenty years before. Of course, once they arrive, they all wander off by themselves. One of the young men is bloodily slashed to death by an unknown assailant. When his body is discovered by the rest of the group, they unwisely decide not to call the police. Instead they hide the body and pretend as if it all never happened. Needless to say, this is not the last of it for any of them and a return visit to the house results in further horror. Armstrong was understandably unhappy with the tampering done to his feature film debut. The final blow came when Tenser retitled it *The Haunted House of Horror*. However, this was not the end of the tampering. When the film was released in the United States, AIP cut it to 79 minutes (eliminating most of a subplot involving Gina Warwick and George Sewell) and retitled it *Horror House*. The full-length version has since surfaced under its original British title on cable TV in the U.S. Armstrong would go on to direct *Mark of the Devil* (1970) and *House of the Long Shadows* (1982).

Horrors of the Black Museum

"Modern Science Has Perfected an Ancient Art to Put You in the Picture!"

(April 1959) CinemaScope and Eastman Color. Produced by Jack Greenwood and Herman Cohen. Directed by Arthur Crabtree. Written by Aben Kandel and Herman Cohen. Starring Michael Gough, Graham Curnow, June Cunningham, Shirley Anne Field. DVD: VCI (2.35) 94 min.; Extras: HypnoVista prologue; Trailers; Herman Cohen video tribute; Audio commentary by Herman Cohen, Gerard Schurmann and David Del Valle.

American International had a successful relationship with Nat Cohen, the managing director of Britain's Anglo Amalgamated Pictures, dating back to early 1956. AIP supplied Anglo with product which they then distributed to U.K. cinemas. When the British horror boom took off, AIP sent Herman Cohen to England to produce a script he had co-written with Aben Kandel. Kandel had written all of Cohen's previous AIP films using pseudonyms: *Blood of Dracula* and *I Was a Teenage Werewolf* as "Ralph Thornton," *I Was a Teenage Frankenstein* and *How to Make a Monster* as "Kenneth Langtry." AIP wanted to upgrade their pictures to compete with Hammer Films which, although made cheaply, looked far more expensive than they actually were. Nicholson and Arkoff entered into a deal with Anglo in which that company would pay for half the cost of the picture and reap half the profits in return. This additional funding enabled them to film this picture in CinemaScope and color, a first for AIP. A total exercise in Grand Guignol, *Horrors of the Black Museum* had some of the most violent content of any horror film up to that time. Michael Gough plays a crime writer who commits sensational murders which he can then write about. His weapons of choice include a portable guillotine, ice tongs, a vat of acid, and a particularly gruesome "death by binoculars," which anyone who has seen the film will never forget. As with several previous Cohen films, the theme of a dominating older man forcing his will on a younger male is a major plot point. Made for about $250,000, the picture grossed over a million dollars. For the U.S. release, the extreme violence was apparently not draw enough and AIP added a thirteen-minute prologue in which Dr. Emil Franchel explains a new screen gimmick known as HypnoVista ... "You Can't Resist It!"

Review: *New York Herald Tribune* (April 30, 1959), "Has a way of making its points as a spine-chiller."

Hot Rod Girl

"Youth on the Loose! Teen-age Terrorists Burning Up the Streets!"

(July 1956) Black & White. A Nacirema Production. Produced by Norman Herman. Directed by Leslie Martinson. Written by John McGreevey. Starring Lori Nelson, Chuck Connors, John Smith, Frank Gorshin. DVD: Alpha (1.33) 75 min.

The City Council and the chief of police are determined to enact a ban on hot rodders but good cop Chuck Connors believes he can solve the problem by getting the kids to restrict their driving to a dragstrip. When tough guy Mark Andrews comes to town, the situation starts to get out of hand. It's up to twenty-something "teenagers" Lori Nelson and John Smith to get the gang back on track. But when a child is killed in a hit-and-run accident involving one of the hot rodders, things get com-

Michael Gough, a frequent performer in British horror films, starred in AIP's *Horrors of the Black Museum* and *Konga*.

John Smith and Lori Nelson are "long of tooth" teens in *Hot Rod Girl*.

plicated. Pretty dull stuff but still notable as the first of AIP's "youth" movies.

Review: *Los Angeles Examiner* (July 1956), "As a thriller, it holds up fine. This is a pretty slick little package."

House of Fright

"ROBERT LOUIS STEVENSON'S STUDY IN TERRIFYING EVIL!"

(May 1961) MegaScope and Technicolor. A Hammer Film Production. Produced by Michael Carreras. Directed by Terence Fisher. Written by Wolf Mankowitz. Starring Paul Massie, Christopher Lee, Dawn Addams, David Kossoff. DVD: Sony (as *The Two Faces of Dr. Jekyll*) (2.35) 88 mins. Hammer: Icons of Horror box set.

In this revisionist take on the classic story, Dr. Jekyll is an unattractive middle-aged man who, after injecting himself with an experimental drug of his own invention, becomes the young, handsome, and totally amoral Mr. Hyde. It was originally conceived by screenwriter Wolf Mankowitz to star Laurence Harvey; the actor proved unavailable and Hammer signed Paul Massie for the lead. Massie was a Canadian actor who had made a considerable impression in the British films *Sapphire* and *Libel* (both 1959). Directed with style by Hammer veteran Terence Fisher, *The Two Faces of Dr. Jekyll* was to have been released in the U.S. as part of a long-standing association between Hammer and Columbia Pictures. Columbia, who had already gone so far as to print the advertising material for the film, took a look at the picture and decided that it was definitely not their cup of tea. Instead of a "monster movie," they had been delivered a complex study in good and evil with a considerable amount of depravity thrown into the mix. At first Columbia considered distributing the film through one of their subsidiary companies but finally they decided to sell the U.S. theatrical rights to American International. AIP cut the film to 80 minutes and retitled it *Jekyll's Inferno*. Before it was released, AIP changed the title from *Jekyll's Inferno* to *House of Fright* when their film *House of Usher* proved to be a huge moneymaker. Columbia retained the television rights to the movie and, because of this, it turned up on video in a censored television print with dreadful color. In June 2006 the American Cinematheque in Los Angeles showed a beautifully remastered widescreen uncut print of *The Two Faces of Dr. Jekyll* which had been provided by Sony/Columbia. This was released on DVD as part of a Hammer box set from Sony in October 2008.

Review: *New York Herald Tribune* (August 24, 1961), "A colorful, ingenious remake of the Stevenson story."

House of 1000 Dolls

"Missing! ... Just one of thousands of young girls who disappear each year—victims of a tragic traffic in beauty and human flesh!"

(October 1967) ColorScope. Produced by Harry Alan Towers. Directed by Jeremy Summers. Written by Peter Welbeck (a.k.a. Harry Alan Towers). Starring Vincent Price, Martha Hyer, George Nader, Ann Smyrner. VHS: HBO Video (1.33) 78 min.

Even Vincent Price can't save this typically sleazy Harry Alan Towers German-Spanish co-production. *House of 1000 Dolls* was planned as a sort of follow-up to Towers' *The Million Eyes of Su-Muru*, which was released by AIP earlier the same year and also starred George Nader. Towers, who produced several films starring Christopher Lee as Fu Manchu, originally scripted this as *Sax Rohmer's House of Dolls*. Stage magician Felix Manderville (Vincent Price) and his assistant Rebecca (Martha Hyer) are actually fronts for a white slavery syndicate. Manderville and Rebecca use their nightclub act to abduct beautiful young women who are conscripted to be prostitutes in a Tangiers brothel called "The House of Dolls." When the best friend of visiting tourist Stephen Armstrong (George Nader) is found murdered, Armstrong is determined to find the killer. This almost gets him killed and his wife Maria (Ann Smyrner) recruited as the latest "doll." Much of the story seems merely an excuse to show sexy babes lounging around in flimsy lingerie or, in an especially scummy sequence, manacled and whipped while wearing only bra and panties. There is also some female mud wrestling thrown in for good measure. In the supporting cast are lovely Towers' regular Maria Rohm and Wolfgang Kieling, best remembered as "Gromek" in Alfred Hitchcock's *Torn Curtain*. Nude scenes were filmed for a 90-minute West German version, apparently without the foreknowledge of Price and Hyer.

Review: *Variety* (November 3, 1967), "Plottage, while routine, has the melodramatic ingredients to carry it."

House of Usher

"Edgar Allan Poe's Classic Tale of the Ungodly ... the Evil"

(July 1960) CinemaScope and Eastman Color. Produced and Directed by Roger Corman. Written by Richard Matheson. Starring Vincent Price, Mark Damon, Myrna Fahey, Harry Ellerbe. DVD: MGM (as *The Fall of the House of Usher*) (2.35) 80 min.; Extras: Theatrical trailer; Audio commentary by Roger Corman. Midnite Movies co-feature: *Pit and the Pendulum*.

House of Usher was a major milestone in the history of American International Pictures. Realizing that their inexpensive black-and-white double features could no longer compete with the more elaborate color productions being turned out by Britain's Hammer Films, Nicholson and Arkoff decided to put all their eggs in one basket ... a widescreen color adaptation of Edgar Allan Poe's classic story "The Fall of the House of Usher." If the film had failed, it could have ruined the company but, fortunately, the risk paid off big time! Poe was the perfect literary source as all his stories were in public domain. Roger Corman was an equally perfect choice for director as he could be counted on to bring a picture in on budget as well as infuse it with a considerable amount of style. The single biggest expenditure in the $270,000 budget was the $35,000 salary of star Vincent Price, who was well worth the investment. The combination of Price, Corman, art director Daniel Haller, and cinematographer Floyd Crosby worked to create a whole new type of American horror film. This team would work together again on four subsequent Poe films and Price would become AIP's greatest asset. In January 2006, *House of Usher* was the first AIP film to be inducted into the Library of Congress' National Film Registry, an honor Nicholson and Arkoff probably never could have foreseen. Seeing the Poe films beautifully restored on DVD is a revelation after decades of watching washed-out pan-and-scan television and video presentations. At last they are being seen as they were always meant to be and the results are often stunning.

Mark Damon and Myrna Fahey are ill-fated lovers in *House of Usher*.

Review: *Variety* (June 17, 1960), "All things considered, pro and con, the fall of the *House of Usher* seems to herald the rise of the House of AIP."

House of Whipcord

"THE STORY OF A STRANGE HOBBY AND ITS VICTIMS, WHOSE ONLY CRIME WAS TO BE YOUNG AND BEAUTIFUL!"

(March 1975) Color by Movielab (Eastman Color). A Pete Walker Production. Produced and Directed by Pete Walker. Written by David McGillivray and Pete Walker. Starring Barbara Markham, Patrick Barr, Ray Brooks, Ann Michelle. DVD: Shriek Show/Media Blasters (1.85) 102 min.; Extras: Audio commentary by Peter Walker; Still gallery; Trailers.

Beginning with *Die Screaming, Marianne* (1971), former softcore porn filmmaker Pete Walker embarked on a series of horror movies which were the antithesis of those being produced by other British studios at the time. While Hammer and Amicus were turning out films with traditional horror themes, Walker was pushing the limit of the newly permissive cinema with his exercises in contemporary sadism. One of the best of his movies is *House of Whipcord*. Crazed conservatives Mrs. Wakehurst (Barbara Markham) and Justice Bailey (Patrick Barr) use their illegitimate son Mark E. Desade (Robert Tayman) to lure young and potentially sinful girls to their personal "house of correction." Once there, the girls are subjected to all manner of torments by prison guards Walker (Sheila Keith) and Bates (Dorothy Gordon). The main focus of the story is a beautiful but dumb French model named Ann-Marie (Penny Irving) who disappears after a date with Desade. Ann-Marie's concerned roommate Julia (Ann Michelle) tracks her friend to the isolated country estate where she also becomes an inmate. Despite the lurid premise, *House of Whipcord* is a surprisingly well-made movie and has some truly unexpected twists. Made in 1974, the film was released in the U.S. the following year by AIP, who cut it to 94 minutes to insure an R rating instead of an X.

The House That Screamed

"One By One They Will Die!"

(January 1971) Panavision and Color by Movielab (Eastman Color). An Anabel Films Production. Produced by Arturo Gonzalez. Directed by Narciso Ibanez Serrador. Written by Luis Verna Penafiel. Starring Lilli Palmer, Cristina Galbo, John Moulder Brown, Mary Maude. DVD: Shout Factory (2.35) 98 min. Elvira's Movie Macabre co-feature: *Maneater of Hydra*.

Theresa (Cristina Galbo) is enrolled in a school for girls run by Madame Fourneau (Lilli Palmer), a formidable headmistress with a penchant for punishment. Theresa also has to contend with a trio of mean-spirited L.U.G.s (Lesbians Until Graduation) who torment her whenever possible. Theresa's one respite is the time she spends with Madame Fourneau's young son Luis (John Moulder Brown). Three-quarters of the way into the picture, events take a completely unexpected turn. Sometimes dismissed as mere sexploitation, *The House That Screamed* is actually a very well-directed exercise in suspense with some wonderfully effective cross-cutting sequences. The students say their bedtime prayers as one student is whipped for insubordination; the girls shower, unaware that Luis is trapped in a small crawl-space nearby and desperately trying to escape; frustrated students in a sewing class work at their needlepoint envious of another lucky girl getting banged by the local woodcutter. All of this is accompanied by an outstanding background score by Waldo de los Rios. Filmed in Spain in 1969 as *La Residencia*, this excellent Euro-horror film was retitled and released two years later in the U.S. by AIP with a 94-minute running time. The announcement that *The House That Screamed* would be available on DVD as one of "Elvira's Movie Macabre" double features was disheartening. Previous releases in this series would lead one to believe that Shout Factory actually tries to find the worst elements available for transfer. Surprisingly *The House That Screamed* is taken from a very good widescreen Spanish print (with English-language dialogue) which does have some minor cuts but still runs longer than the AIP theatrical version. Apparently this good-quality transfer is an aberration in the series as the companion feature *Maneater of Hydra* is all but unwatchable. Both movies have options available which allow you to watch the films with or without interruptions by Elvira, Mistress of the Dark.

How to Make a Monster

"It Will SCARE the Living Yell Out of You!"

(July 1958) Black & White. Produced by Herman Cohen. Directed by Herbert L. Strock. Written by Kenneth Langtry and Herman Cohen. Starring Robert H. Harris, Paul Brinegar, Gary Conway, Gary Clarke. DVD: Lionsgate (1.33) 74 min.; DVD co-feature: *Blood of Dracula*.

When movies about behind-the-scenes Hollywood are discussed, *How to Make a Monster* is always sadly neglected. But it is a "Hollywood Story" that definitely deserves attention. The new executives at American International Pictures have decided that monster movies are out and musicals are what the public wants. Because of this, monster makeup artist Pete Dumond (Robert H. Harris) is given his walking papers. To get even with the executives, Dumond makes up two young actors as Teenage Frankenstein (Gary Conway) and Teenage Werewolf (Gary Clarke) and orders them to commit murders while under his hypnotic influence. John Ashley guest stars as himself in a musical number. In the movie, AIP plugs *I Was a Teenage Werewolf*, *I Was a Teenage Frankenstein*, and even the yet-to-be-filmed *Horrors of the Black Museum*. The last ten minutes of the movie are in color, a feature which was missing from the original RCA/Columbia video release but is restored on the DVD.

Song: "You've Got to Have EE-OOO"

Gary Conway, left, and Robert H. Harris in *How to Make a Monster*.

Review: *Variety* (September 17, 1958), "More a mystery-suspense picture than a horror item, and the horror effects are rather mild."

How to Stuff a Wild Bikini

"IT'S THE BARE OUTLINE ... OF A BEGINNER'S COURSE IN BOY-GIRLSMANSHIP WITH A SPECIAL EMPHASIS ON FIGURES!"

(July 1965) Panavision and Pathécolor. Produced by James H. Nicholson and Samuel Z. Arkoff. Directed by William Asher. Written by William Asher and Leo Townsend. Starring Annette Funicello, Dwayne Hickman, Beverly Adams, John Ashley. DVD: MGM (2.35) 93 min.; Extras: Theatrical trailer. Midnite Movies co-feature: *Beach Blanket Bingo*.

When Frankie (Avalon) finds himself stationed on a tropical island with the Naval Reserves, he begins to worry about Dee Dee (Annette Funicello), his girl back home. Turns out he has something to worry about as Dee Dee is being romanced by a guy named Ricky (Dwayne Hickman). Frankie hires a local witch doctor to send sexy Beverly Adams as a decoy to lure Ricky away from Dee Dee. This time the beach shenanigans take a back seat to a cross-country motorcycle race. Oldtimers Brian Donlevy, Buster Keaton, and Mickey Rooney join the youngsters in all the foolishness. Annette, who was several months pregnant during the filming, is conspicuously overdressed throughout. Avalon's part is little more than an extended bit, with a big plug for his upcoming movie *Sergeant Deadhead* (1965). Elizabeth Montgomery (then-wife of director William Asher) has a "bewitching" cameo at the end. Beware: The single release disc of this

Annette Funicello (with Dwayne Hickman) may know *How to Stuff a Wild Bikini* but she never wears one in the film.

film features both widescreen and fullscreen versions. The Midnite Movies double feature has only the fullscreen version of *How to Stuff a Wild Bikini* although the packaging says it is widescreen.

Songs: "Give Her Lovin'," "How About Us," "I Am My Ideal," "Better Be Ready," "The Boy Next Door," "The Perfect Boy," "If It Had to Be," "After the Party," "Stuff a Wild Bikini"

I Was a Teenage Frankenstein

"BODY OF A BOY ... MIND OF A MONSTER ... SOUL OF AN UNEARTHLY THING!"

(November 1957) Black & White. Produced by Herman Cohen. Directed by Herbert L. Strock. Written by Kenneth Langtry. Starring Whit Bissell, Phyllis Coates, Robert Burton, Gary Conway. VHS: RCA/Columbia (as *Teenage Frankenstein*) (1.33) 72 min.

In May 1957, Warner Bros. released Hammer's *The Curse of Frankenstein* and the movie was a tremendous box office success. Six months later AIP had their Frankenstein film in theatres. Professor Frankenstein (Whit Bissell) comes to America to lecture on organ transplants. A convenient car crash involving teenagers occurs in front of his house, providing him with a means for testing his theories. Like his illustrious ancestor, he pieces together a man from various body parts. The result is a teenager (Gary Conway) with a knockout body but a grotesque face. Frankenstein attempts to keep his creation under wraps but the monster longs to be free of his basement prison. He escapes one night and kills a beautiful blonde babe. Frankenstein realizes that

Gary Conway strangles Whit Bissell in *I Was a Teenage Frankenstein*.

now he must think about giving his creature a new face to avoid detection. Although taking place in contemporary times as opposed to Hammer's ornate gothic settings, *I Was a Teenage Frankenstein* owes some obvious debts to *The Curse of Frankenstein*. Bloody amputated body parts are shown in grisly detail, albeit in black and white as opposed to Hammer's brilliant colors. A scene in which Frankenstein's prying fiancée becomes a victim of the monster is very close to a similar scene in the Hammer film. One thing Hammer certainly didn't think of was an alligator hidden behind a panel in Frankenstein's laboratory; it is used to dispose of unwanted body parts ... and unwanted bodies. *I Was a Teenage Frankenstein* has a color sequence at the end when the unfortunate creation throws himself against a panel in the laboratory and is electrocuted. As Frankenstein's assistant recalls the monster's once hideous countenance, we are treated to a close-up of it in full color. We also get a color shot of the alligator munching on the bloody remains of Professor Frankenstein. The RCA/Columbia video was taken from a British print which has the title *Teenage Frankenstein* and opens with the British "X" Certificate rating followed by the Anglo Amalgamated logo. It is also missing a brief shot of Gary Conway's decapitated head which was in the U.S. theatrical version but censored in England.

Review: *Time* (March 10, 1958), "As a sequel to *I Was a Teenage Werewolf, IWATF* will probably rank as one of the year's biggest horrors."

I Was a Teenage Werewolf

"EXPLOSIVE! AMAZING! TERRIFYING! YOU WON'T BELIEVE YOUR EYES!"

(June 1957) Black & White. Produced by Herman Cohen. Directed by Gene Fowler Jr. Written by Ralph Thornton. Starring Michael

Landon, Yvonne Lime, Whit Bissell, Tony Marshall. VHS: RCA/Columbia (1.33) 75 min.

Without doubt, the most famous title in the history of American International Pictures is *I Was a Teenage Werewolf*. Producer Herman Cohen and writer Aben Kandel had co-written a script using the pseudonym Ralph Thornton. Cohen took the script to Nicholson and Arkoff who agreed to let him produce the picture for them. This deft combination of teen angst and horror tells the tragic story of Tony (Michael Landon), an adolescent powder keg about to explode. The student has been involved in a number of violent confrontations at Rockdale High. At the behest of the local police and his girlfriend Arlene (Yvonne Lime), Tony goes to see Dr. Brandon (Whit Bissell) for some much-needed mental therapy. Brandon has been conducting an experiment to release the primitive animal instincts in man and, in Tony, he has found the perfect guinea pig. Using a combination of hypnosis and drugs, Brandon turns Tony into a bloodthirsty werewolf. Before *I Was a Teenage Werewolf* was even in theatres, concerned parental groups, school authorities, politicians, and film critics were condemning the film, without having seen it, on the basis of the title alone. Senators Paul Douglas and Estes Kefauver were especially aghast at the supposed connection between motion pictures and juvenile delinquency, although no such connection had been established. Of course, all this publicity fueled public curiosity and the movie went on to make millions. *I Was a Teenage Werewolf* is a surprisingly good film. Editor–first-time director Gene Fowler Jr. handles his cast with assurance and comes up with a number of effective performances. Not the least of these is that given by Michael Landon. Landon won the part over actors Jack Nicholson and Scott Marlowe and, although he was later embarrassed to admit he had been in the film, he certainly had nothing to be ashamed of. AIP wasn't going to let him forget it either. Shortly after the 1959 debut of the TV series *Bonanza*, which featured Landon in one of the lead roles, AIP reissued *I Was a Teenage Werewolf* on a "Twin Teen Terror-Bill" with *I Was a Teenage Frankenstein*. "Michael Landon ... star of *Bonanza*" was prominently featured in the publicity campaign.

Song: "Eeny, Meeny, Miney, Mo"

Review: *Time* (September 9, 1958), "The next step in low, lowbrow cinema was a marriage of the undead and the underdone: *I Was a Teenage Werewolf*."

The Incredible Melting Man

"THE FIRST NEW HORROR CREATURE ... COME PREPARED!"

(December 1977) Color by Movielab. A Max J. Rosenberg Presentation of a Rosenberg-Gelfman Production. Produced by Samuel W. Gelfman. Directed and Written by William Sachs. Starring Alex Rebar, Burr DeBenning, Michael Allredge, Myron Healey. VHS: MGM (1.33) 86 min.; Extras: Theatrical trailer. DVD: Vipco (1.85) 86 min.; Region-Free DVD from United Kingdom.

Three astronauts pass through the Rings of Saturn with disastrous results. Two of them are killed and the third (Alex Rebar) returns

Michael Landon and Yvonne Lime are the stars of the box office hit *I Was a Teenage Werewolf*.

Myron Healey meets *The Incredible Melting Man* (Alex Rebar).

to Earth with his flesh literally melting off his bones. Attempts to study his condition are thwarted when the "melting man" escapes from a top secret medical facility. He spends the rest of the movie wandering around and killing anyone he comes into contact with while a doctor (Burr DeBenning) and a military general (Myron Healey) pursue him. The gooey special effects makeup was created by Rick Baker, who helped usher in a new era of gore horror with this film. The makeup is the only memorable thing about *The Incredible Melting Man*, other than some of the names connected with it. Max J. Rosenberg was half of the Amicus team that created some fine anthology films during the Golden Age of British horror. Future director Jonathan Demme appears briefly as one of the melting man's victims. Rainbeaux Smith is on hand for some gratuitous nudity. Vaguely reminiscent of *First Man Into Space* (1959), *The Incredible Melting Man* even fails to attain that film's minor level of impact. Acting, direction, writing, musical score, and production values are all on a Poverty Row level.

Review: *Cinefantastique* (Vol. 7, No. 2, 1978), "Poorly written and directed by [William] Sachs, the film is almost totally implausible on a narrative level."

The Incredible 2-Headed Transplant

"ONE BRAIN WANTS TO LOVE ... ONE BRAIN WANTS TO KILL!" (APRIL 1971) COLOR BY DELUXE

A John Lawrence-Mutual General Production. Produced by John Lawrence. Directed by Anthony N. Lanza. Written by James Gordon White and John Lawrence. Starring Bruce Dern, Pat Priest, Casey Kasem, Albert Cole. DVD: MGM (1.85) 88 min.; Extras: Theatrical trailer. Midnite Movies co-feature: *The Thing with Two Heads*.

It's medical madness galore when Dr. Roger Gerard (Bruce Dern) transplants the head of a homicidal maniac (Albert Cole) onto the body of a physically huge but mentally challenged man (John Bloom). The maniac takes over and the scientific monstrosity goes on a murderous rampage. Dern gives a typically weird performance as the doctor responsible for all the mayhem. The cast also includes longtime "American Top 40" host Casey Kasem and Pat Priest, who replaced Beverley Owen in the role of Marilyn on the TV series *The Munsters*. Screenwriter James Gordon White co-wrote a similar story for AIP the following year, *The Thing with Two Heads*, which is a lot more fun than *The Incredible 2-Headed Transplant*.

Song: "Incredible"

Alien invaders from *Invasion of the Saucer Men*.

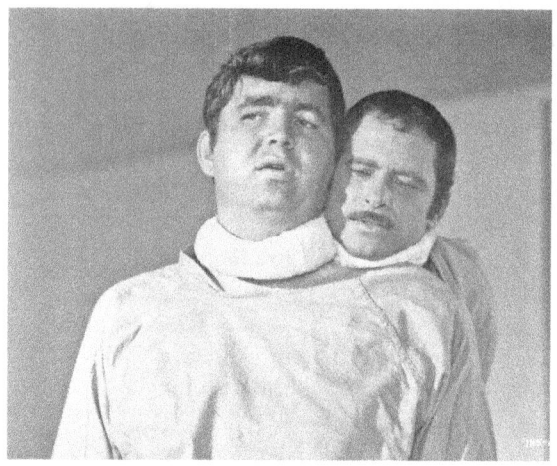

John Bloom and Albert Cole are *The Incredible 2-Headed Transplant*.

Invasion of the Saucer Men

"CREEPING HORROR ... FROM THE DEPTHS OF TIME AND SPACE!"

(June 1957) Black & White. A Malibu Production. Produced by James H. Nicholson and Robert Gurney Jr. Directed by Edward L. Cahn. Written by Al Martin, Robert Gurney Jr. Story: Paul Fairman. Starring Steve Terrell, Gloria Castillo, Frank Gorshin, Raymond Hatton. VHS: Columbia/TriStar (1.33) 69 min.

Albert Kallis' amazing poster art coupled with such catch-phrases as "See—Earth Attacked by Flying Saucers" and "See—Night the World Nearly Ended!" lead one to believe that *Invasion of the Saucer Men* is a serious endeavor. Such is not the case. Once again we have another AIP comedy but it does not quite sink to the depths of *Ghost of Dragstrip Hollow* or *Invasion of the Star Creatures*. Actually it is rather fun and does have some creepy moments such as "The Disembodied Hand That Crawls," which is also touted on the poster. A flying saucer lands in the lovers' lane outside of the town of Hicksburg (yes, the humor is on that level). Johnny Carter (Steve Terrell) and Joan Hayden (Gloria Castillo) accidentally run over one of the saucer's occupants ... an honest-to-goodness "little green man" from space. Of course the local authorities don't believe them so Johnny and Joan decide they are going to find proof on their own. Meanwhile the military has inadvertently blown up the saucer and is now trying to cover up the fact that it ever existed. Paul Blaisdell designed the iconic Saucer Men, which in color pro-

Gloria Castillo, monster maker Paul Blaisdell and newspaper columnist Buddy Mason behind the scenes of *Invasion of the Saucer Men*.

duction photos are not green at all but flesh-colored. The movie has some particularly graphic gore for the time. The abovementioned crawling hand is effectively gross, as is a close-up of a Saucer Man's eye being gored by the horn of a bull. AIP regulars Ed Nelson and Russ Bender can be spotted in minor roles. A fine quality Australian DVD unfortuntely censors all the horror effects.

Review: *Variety* (July 5, 1957), "Film suffers from poor use of attempted comedy."

Invasion of the Star Creatures

"EVIL ... BEAUTIFUL ... DEADLY.
IN THEIR EYES DESIRE, IN THEIR VEINS
THE BLOOD OF MONSTERS!"

(August 1962) Black & White. Produced by Berj Hagopian. Directed by Bruno VeSota. Written by Jonathan Haze. Starring Frankie Ray, Bob Ball, Dolores Reed, Gloria Victor. DVD: MGM (1.66) 70 min.; Extras: Theatrical trailer. Midnite Movies co-feature: *Invasion of the Bee Girls*.

Move over, *Ghost of Dragstrip Hollow*! This is the worst AIP film of all time! The groan-inspiring comedy team of Frankie Ray and Bob Ball play moronic army privates stationed at Fort Nicholson (wink, wink) missile base. They are selected to join a platoon of soldiers who are going to investigate a mysterious explosion at nearby Nicholson Mesa. Finding a cave where a spaceship is hidden, they are captured by Vegetable Men who take them to their leaders. These are a pair of Amazonian spacewomen named Poona and Tanga (which should provide a hint at the level of the comedy in this picture). Filmed on a scale the equal of *Plan 9 from Outer Space* or *Robot Monster*, *Invasion of the Star Creatures* is one of the cheapest looking movies ever made. The interior of the spaceship beggars description and the "monstrous" VegeMen wear costumes that consist of a burlap sack over a leotard with carrots for hair. Was this revenge on Nicholson and Arkoff by frequent AIP actors Jonathan Haze and Bruno VeSota, who respectively wrote and directed the film? But why make the audience suffer as well? *Invasion of the Star Creatures* was released on a mind-numbing double bill with *The Brain That Wouldn't Die* ... and, believe me, that was one unforgettable Saturday matinee. Although the advertising doesn't hint that the film is a "comedy," the trailer provides ample warning. Proceed at your own peril.

The Island of Dr. Moreau

"A TROPICAL PARADISE UNTOUCHED BY MAN ...
WHERE A BIZARRE CIVILIZATION EXISTS"

(July 1977) Color by Movielab. A Sandy Howard/Skip Steloff/Major Production. Produced by John Temple-Smith and Skip Steloff. Directed by Don Taylor. Written by John Herman Shaner and Al Ramrus. Starring Burt Lancaster, Michael York, Barbara Carrera, Nigel Davenport. DVD: MGM (1.85) 99 min.; Extras: Theatrical trailer.

A big disappointment at the time of its original release, this version of H.G. Wells' novel seems to have gotten better with the passage of time. It still never comes close to capturing the horror of the original version, *Island of Lost Souls* (Paramount, 1933) starring Charles Laughton, but it is better than the 1996 remake with Marlon Brando. The failure or success of the story depends on the portrayal of Dr. Moreau. The main problem with this Dr. Moreau is that he is played by Burt Lancaster, who never manages to convey the sinister madness necessary to pull off the part.

"Lionman" Gary Baxley is just one of many John Chambers makeup creations for *The Island of Dr. Moreau*.

Michael York, on the other hand, is an appealing hero and most of the footage features him. The main attributes of *The Island of Dr. Moreau* are the "manimal" makeup effects by John Chambers, who had created the makeup for the *Planet of the Apes* films. Preview showings of *The Island of Dr. Moreau* had Barbara Carrera reverting to a manimal (womanimal?) in the final scene, but this was scrapped when audiences deemed it too downbeat.

Review: *Time* (July 18, 1977), "The film gives promise of being a fairly gripping fantasy-adventure. But it answers all the questions too soon and then has nowhere to go."

It Conquered the World

"EVERY MAN ITS PRISONER ...
EVERY WOMAN ITS SLAVE!"

(July 1956) Black & White. Produced and Directed by Roger Corman. Written by Lou Rusoff. Starring Peter Graves, Beverly Garland, Lee Van Cleef, Sally Fraser. VHS: RCA/Columbia (1.33) 71 min.

A creature from the planet Venus hitches a ride to Earth on one of our satellites and then, with the help of a misguided scientist (Lee Van Cleef), attempts to subjugate the world. This was one of Roger Corman's early efforts and is also one of his best. The script by Lou Rusoff, with an uncredited dialogue assist from Charles Griffith (who also plays a scientist in the movie), is a fairly sophisticated piece of writing for a film of this type. The acting is also serious stuff, with the exception of some minor comic relief from Dick Miller and Jonathan Haze as bumbling soldiers. Beverly Garland steals the show as the disillusioned wife of Van Cleef. When she encounters the Venusian in its sulfurous cave, she tries to insult it to death ("So that's what you look like! You're ugly! Horrible!") before it does her in. If Best Actress awards were given for performances in B monster movies, Garland certainly deserved one for this. Much has been said in derision about the appearance of the creature itself. Another of Paul Blaisdell's imaginative creations, it is quite unlike anything seen on the screen before or since. You have to give Blaisdell credit for always trying something different ... and usually succeeding admirably on a very tight budget. It was people behind the scenes, like Blaisdell and composer Ronald Stein, who made such major contributions to these films but were given little credit for their efforts at the time. They have since received the attention they deserve, but unfortunately it was not in their lifetimes.

Review: *Variety* (Sept. 12, 1956), "This flying saucer pic is a definite cut above normal despite modest budget."

J.D.'s Revenge

"HE CAME BACK FROM THE DEAD TO POSSESS A MAN'S SOUL, MAKE LOVE TO HIS WOMAN, AND GET THE VENGEANCE HE CRAVED!"

(August 1976) Color by Movielab. Produced and Directed by Arthur Marks. Written by Jaison Starkes. Starring Glynn Turman, Lou Gossett, Joan Pringle, Carl Crudup. DVD: MGM (1.85) 96 min.; Extras: Theatrical trailer. Full-screen version.

In 1942, New Orleans gangster J.D. Walker and his sister Billy Jo are brutally murdered. Flash forward thirty years and hard-working law student Ike Hendricks (Glynn Turman) and his girlfriend Christella (Joan Pringle) attend a nightclub act in which Ike is hypnotized. Not long after this, Ike begins to act strangely and has violent blackout periods after which he remembers nothing. When he beats and rapes Christella, she understandably leaves him. He has his hair straightened, buys a forties style outfit, and begins to brandish a straight razor. Turns out he is possessed by the spirit of J.D. Walker, who is out to get revenge on the people whom he believes killed him and Billy Jo. One of them is gangster-turned-evangelist Elija Bliss (Lou Gossett). One night J.D./Ike picks up a girl in a bar and amazes her with his sexual prowess ("That was the best fuckin' I ever had!"). When her husband walks in unexpectedly, J.D. slices and dices him with the razor ("I'm the craziest nigger you ever gonna meet!"). Despite scenes such as this, *J.D.'s Revenge* seldom veers into the area of blaxploitation. It is basically a horror story about possession in which the char-

Close-up of another Paul Blaisdell creation, the alien from *It Conquered the World*.

acters happen to be black. Ike and Christella are sympathetic, well-defined characters and not the typical black stereotype caricatures which proliferate in the blaxploitation genre. Originally announced by AIP as *The Reincarnation of J.D. Walker*, this is a surprisingly well-made movie ... and one of the best black horror films of the period.

Jet Attack

"THE MOST AMAZING JET STORY TO EVER BLAST THE SCREEN!"

(February 1958) Black & White. Produced by Alex Gordon. Directed by Edward L. Cahn. Written by Orville H. Hampton. Starring John Agar, Audrey Totter, Gregory Walcott, James Dobson. VHS: Columbia/TriStar (1.33) 68 min.; VHS co-feature: *Paratroop Command*.

During the Korean War, a plane carrying scientist Dean Olmstead (Joe Hamilton) is shot down while making a test run involving a new radar system. Air Force Headquarters sends three men into enemy territory to try and find out if Olmstead survived the crash and, if so, bring him back to safety. The leader of the group is Tom Arnett (John Agar) and they are aided by a Russian nurse named Tonya (Audrey Totter) who is secretly working against the Red Army. *Jet Attack* is one of the best of the AIP war movies due to an interesting plot and fast-paced direction by the ubiquitous Edward L. Cahn. When did this man ever find time to sleep? Ronald Stein's score is a plus factor, as is the presence of B-movie icon John Agar in the lead.

Review: *Variety* (March 26, 1958), "A pretty good little war feature despite superficial characterizations in the screenplay."

Journey to the Seventh Planet

"WHAT IS THIS MONSTROUS THING? WITH THE POWER OF MIND OVER MATTER!"

(March 1962) Color. A Cinemagic Production. Produced and Directed by Sidney Pink. Written by Sidney Pink and Ib Melchior. Starring John Agar, Greta Thyssen, Carl Ottosen, Ann Smyrner. DVD: MGM (1.66) 77 min.; Extras: Theatrical trailer; Midnite Movies co-feature: *Invisible Invaders*.

Having "conquered" Mars in *The Angry Red Planet*, Sidney Pink decided to move on to the planet Uranus. The members of a United Nations space expedition land on the seventh planet to discover a world of their own imagination. A powerful alien intelligence is capable of entering the minds of the Earthmen and creating images based on their greatest desires and fears. The alien conjures up a bevy of beautiful babes (dressed in silly costumes) and some considerably less appealing monsters. The movie was filmed in Denmark; the monsters devised by local special effects man Bent Barfod were deemed so bad that, back home, AIP called on Projects Unlimited to try and improve the picture. A stop-motion giant rat-like creature was their main contribution. For another sequence, blue-tinted footage from *Earth vs the Spider* replaced a stalk-eyed Danish monster, which can still be glimpsed briefly. The "alien intelligence" is an enormous brain with one eye who lives in a cave. Curiously, in some scenes it seems to be a pile of tripe, rather than a brain. Several of the cast members (Carl Ottosen, Ann Smyrner, Mimi Heinrich) were also in Pink's AIP production *Reptilicus*. Although the background music is credited to Ib Glindemann, much of it is actually cribbed from scores by Ronald Stein. The end title song, crooned by somebody named Otto Brandenburg, is wonderfully awful.

Julius Caesar

"NEVER A CAESAR SO POWERFUL! NEVER SUCH A CAST OF INTERNATIONAL STARS!"

(September 1970) Panavision and Technicolor. A Commonwealth United Presentation. A Peter Snell Production. Produced by Peter Snell. Directed by Stuart Burge. Adapted by Robert Furnival. Starring Charlton Heston,

The large cast of *Julius Caesar* includes John Gielgud (front center, in dark toga), flanked by Jill Bennett and Charlton Heston. Directly behind Gielgud and Heston, left to right, are the clean-shaven Andre Morell and bearded Robert Vaughn and Derek Godfrey.

Jason Robards, John Gielgud, Richard Johnson. DVD: Lionsgate (1.33) 117 min.

Another of AIP's attempts at presenting more mainstream, bigger budget movies, this version of Shakespeare's play is done on a grand scale with an eclectic cast. Mark Antony seems to be the role Charlton Heston was born to play and he did so on a number of occasions. There can be little, if any, fault to be found with his performance. The same, unfortunately, cannot be said of Jason Robards. As Brutus, he delivers most of his lines in a monotone voice without any apparent grasp of Shakespeare's rhetoric. The rest of the cast ranges from excellent (Richard Johnson as Cassius) to lamentable (Robert Vaughn, all shifty eyes and sneers as Casca). Diana Rigg is outstanding in her one scene as Brutus' wife Portia. In her brief screen time she does more to demonstrate what Shakespearean acting is about than the rest of the cast combined. Also on hand are a number of familiar British supporting players in minuscule parts: Christopher Lee, Michael Gough, Derek Godfrey, and a wordless Andre Morell as Cicero. John Gielgud, who had played Cassius in the 1953 screen version of this play, was now elevated to the title role. Most technical aspects of the film are impressive save for the occasional bit of awkward costume design. One such example occurs during Mark Antony's "Friends, Romans, Countrymen" speech in which Heston's outfit resembles Carol Burnett's famous parody of *Gone with the Wind* in which she wears a dress made of curtains complete with curtain rod. Although the prologue and credits on the DVD are correctly letterboxed at 2.35, the rest of the film is fullscreen. Despite this, the color and clarity of picture are far superior to any of the VHS releases of this title. Regardless of whatever lofty ambitions AIP may have had for *Julius Caesar*, they apparently couldn't resist concocting some typically exploitative advertising for the publicity campaign. One such ad features images of JFK, Robert Kennedy, Martin Luther King Jr., and Abraham Lincoln. The text reads: "They were treacherous ... those who murdered Abe, John, Martin and Bobby but no more treacherous or twisted than those who plotted the assassination of *Julius Caesar*." Shameless!

Review: *Los Angeles Times* (September 23, 1970), "New film of Shakespeare's *Julius Caesar* is respectable rather than riveting and better suited to the classroom than the movie house."

Konga

"NOT SINCE KING KONG ...
HAS THE SCREEN EXPLODED WITH SUCH
MIGHTY FURY AND SPECTACLE!"

(March 1961) SpectaMation and Eastman Color. Produced by Herman Cohen. Directed by John Lemont. Written by Aben Kandel and Herman Cohen. Starring Michael Gough, Margo Johns, Jess Conrad, Claire Gordon. DVD: MGM/Sony (1.66) 90 min.

The most appealing aspect of many American International productions is the wildly absurd storyline. Even by sci-fi and horror standards they often stretch credibility to the limits. This is by no means a criticism as these loony plots are a big part of AIP's enduring charm. *Konga* is a prime example of an over-the-top AIP scenario. Dr. Charles Decker (Michael Gough at his most lunatic) returns from a year in the African jungle with a baby chimpanzee named Konga. Decker has perfected a growth serum that is derived from gigantic carnivorous plants.

The first injection of the serum turns Konga into an adult chimpanzee. The second turns him into a gorilla ... more accurately, a man in a bad gorilla costume. Another injection causes Konga to grow to skyscraper size and rampage through London with Dr. Decker

Producer Herman Cohen goes over the script with the star of *Konga*.

clutched in his hand. Actually, compared to the devastation wrought by *Gorgo* (another British monster movie released by MGM at the same time as *Konga*), the "rampage" is more like a stroll. The army decides to kill him anyway and brings Konga down in a barrage of gunfire next to Big Ben. Add to the plot a frustrated spinster housekeeper–lab assistant in love with Decker, a buxom blond biology student and her jealous boyfriend, and a greenhouse full of giant man- (or woman-) eating plants. What more could you ask for? This was producer Herman Cohen's last film for AIP. After a dispute over money he felt was owed him, Cohen severed his ties with the company but continued to produce movies in England, most notoriously Joan Crawford's last theatrical feature *Trog* (1970). *Konga* was released on a single disc in 2005. It has since been reissued as a MGM Midnite Movie double feature with *Yongary: Monster from the Deep*.

Review: *New York Herald Tribune* (September 16, 1961), "An extraordinarily talky and surprisingly draggy monster picture."

The Land That Time Forgot

"The Adventure You Will Never Forget!"

(April 1975) Color by Movielab (Technicolor). An Amicus Presentation. A Max J. Rosenberg and Milton Subotsky Production. Produced by John Dark. Directed by Kevin Connor. Written by James Cawthorn and Michael Moorcock. Starring Doug McClure, John McEnery, Susan Penhaligon, Keith Barron. DVD: MGM (1.85) 91 min.; Extras: Theatrical trailer. Midnite Movies co-feature: *The People That Time Forgot*.

As part of their ongoing effort to keep up with the competition, Amicus embarked on a series of more elaborate productions much as Hammer Films had done with *She* (1965) and *One Million Years B.C.* (1966). The first and best of these was an adaptation of Edgar Rice Burroughs' 1924 novel *The Land That Time Forgot* which had started off as a magazine story called "The Lost U-Boat." The book became the first installment in a trilogy of novels set on the forgotten island of Caprona (the others being *The People That Time Forgot* and *Out of Time's Abyss*). American International supplied some of the additional financing needed for Amicus' more costly endeavors in exchange for distribution rights in the United States. In 1916, the survivors of a torpedoed British ship manage to overcome the crew of the German submarine which fired on them. A wily German manages to steer them off course and they accidentally end up in a lost world in which prehistoric animals still survive. The dinosaur sequences were executed by Roger Dicken, who had also worked on Hammer's *When Dinosaurs Ruled the Earth* (1970). Instead of that film's stop-motion animation creatures, the dinosaurs in *The Land That Time Forgot* are cleverly conceived rod puppets—no substitute for animation, but effective nevertheless. There are quite a few monster sequences but in many of them the poor beasts seem to be just hanging around not menacing anybody. The humans still find it necessary to blow them to bits. If the voice of the German U-Boat captain played by John McEnery sounds familiar, it's because his dialogue was re-dubbed by Anton Diffring.

Review: *Time* (April 14, 1975), "The best Saturday matinee movie in much too long. It is an elaborate fantasy adventure with no bearing in reality whatsoever."

The Last Man on Earth

"How Much Horror Can You Face?"

(September 1964) Widescreen and Black & White. An Associated Producers Inc./Produzioni La Regina Presentation. Produced by Robert L. Lippert. Directed by Sidney Salkow. Written by Logan Swanson and William Leicester. Starring Vincent Price, Franca Bettoia, Giacomo Rossi-Stuart, Emma Danieli. DVD: MGM (2.35) 87 min.; Extras: Interview with Richard Matheson. Midnite Movies co-feature: *Panic in Year Zero!*

In 1965 a mysterious plague kills off the Earth's population and turns them into vampires. The only person who is immune to the disease is Robert Morgan (Vincent Price), who spends the next three years trying to survive in a world of the living dead. Richard Matheson's 1954 novel *I Am Legend* had a long, winding road to the screen. Britain's Hammer Films purchased the film rights in 1957 and brought Matheson to England to adapt his novel into a screenplay (to be called *Night Creatures*). Problems with the British film censorship board caused Hammer to abandon the project. The rights were then sold to Robert Lippert who brought in William Leicester to revise the script which eventually became *The Last Man on Earth*. Matheson asked that his name be removed from the movie but he finally settled on using the pseudonym Logan Swanson. Although produced in Italy, the film is set in an unnamed American city. Price gives a very understated performance with much of his dialogue as voiceover narration. The vampires of the novel are more like zombies in the movie version and scenes of them attacking

Morgan's home are a visual precursor to *Night of the Living Dead* (1968). Matheson's novel was filmed again in 1971 as *The Omega Man* starring Charlton Heston; it lacked the bleak end-of-the-world atmosphere of *The Last Man on Earth*. In 2007 yet another remake starred Will Smith and retained the original title of the novel. This time around the vampire theme was completely abandoned and the night dwellers are zombies. *The Last Man on Earth* is available from several DVD sources but the MGM Midnite Movie edition, with its flawless widescreen presentation, is definitely the one to buy. This transfer was reissued by MGM/Fox on a single disc in 2007 to capitalize on the release of the new film version.

Review: *Variety* (September 2, 1964), "A quickly-made, extremely low budgeter."

The Little Girl Who Lives Down the Lane

"What is Her Unspeakable Secret? Everyone Who Knows is Dead."

(May 1977) Color by Movielab. A Zev Braun Production. Produced by Zev Braun. Directed by Nicholas Gessner. Written by Laird Koenig. Starring Jodie Foster, Martin Sheen, Alexis Smith, Scott Jacoby. DVD: MGM (1.85) 92 min.

This quirky Canadian production offered Jodie Foster one of her earliest dramatic roles. She is in virtually every scene and gives an absolutely stunning performance, particularly when you consider she was only 13 years old at the time. Rynn (Foster) and her poet father rent a house on the outskirts of a small New England town. Some of the townspeople begin to suspect that all is not right in Rynn's household and that she may be hiding a terrible secret. Martin Sheen plays a creepy pedophile with designs on Rynn and Alexis Smith does a marvelous Joan Crawford–esque turn as his nosy mother. More a character study than a thriller, it still has its share of disquieting moments. It also has some touching ones between Foster and Scott Jacoby, who plays a crippled teenager she takes into her confidence ... and her bed. Foster's nude scene, which was cut from the theatrical prints, is reinstated here. She was presumably body-doubled by her 18-year-old sister.

Love at First Bite

"Just when you thought it was safe to go out in the evening."

(April 1979) Color by Movielab. A George Hamilton-Robert Kaufman Production. Presented by Melvin Simon. Produced by Joel Freeman. Directed by Stan Dragoti. Written by Robert Kaufman and Mark Gindes. Starring George Hamilton, Susan Saint James, Richard Benjamin, Dick Shawn. DVD: MGM (1.85) 96 min.; Extras: Theatrical trailer; Fullscreen version.

George Hamilton covered his preternatural tan with white pancake makeup for this vampire spoof. Nineteen seventy-nine was a good year for vampires what with Universal's big-budget version of *Dracula* starring Frank Langella and Werner Herzog's remake of *Nosferatu*. AIP decided to throw a bit of levity into

In *Love at First Bite*, George Hamilton plays Count Dracula.

the mix with *Love at First Bite*, which could also have been called "Disco Dracula." When Communists confiscate his castle in Transylvania, Count Dracula (Hamilton) goes to New York City where he prowls the discos in search of new blood. One night he meets pretty Cindy Sondheim (Susan Saint James) and falls in love with her, much to the dismay of her psychiatrist fiancé Jeffrey Rosenberg (Richard Benjamin). Also in the cast are Dick Shawn as an NYPD cop and Arte Johnson (of *Laugh-In* fame) hamming it up it as Renfield. Sherman Hemsley and Isabel Sanford, who were currently enjoying success in the television series *The Jeffersons*, also put in appearances. Although the humor is broad and a bit labored, this is a far better comedy than AIP's 1975 release *Old Dracula* which starred David Niven as the vampire count. Unfortunately the comedy highlight of *Love at First Bite* is ruined on the DVD by the replacement of Alicia Bridges' song "I Love the Nightlife." This was also true of the VHS version so apparently there was a problem securing the rights to this song.

Machine-Gun Kelly

"WITHOUT HIS GUN HE WAS NAKED YELLOW!"

(May 1958) Superama and Black & White. Produced and Directed by Roger Corman. Written by R. Wright Campbell. Starring Charles Bronson, Susan Cabot, Morey Amsterdam, Connie Gilchrist. VHS: RCA/Columbia (1.33) 84 min. DVD: Direct Video Distribution (1.33) 84 min.; Region-Free DVD

Flo (Susan Cabot) slaps *Machine-Gun Kelly* (Charles Bronson) under the approving gaze of her mother (Connie Gilchrist, standing at left).

from United Kingdom; Extras: Audio interview with Samuel Z. Arkoff; Trailers.

This highly fictionalized account of George "Machine-Gun" Kelly was released on a double bill with *The Bonnie Parker Story*. Together, they constituted AIP's initial foray into gangster pictures, a genre they would revisit over the years. *Machine-Gun Kelly* is tightly scripted, tautly directed, and well acted ... a typical example of Roger Corman's work for AIP. Future superstar Charles Bronson plays the title role, in a part originally slated for Corman regular Dick Miller. As Kelly's girlfriend Flo Eckert, Susan Cabot again shows why she was one of the best actresses ever to appear in B movies. Cabot oozes sexuality and evil in equal doses as the heartless bitch who goads Kelly to commit more and more crimes. Also on hand are a number of familiar Corman players including Barboura Morris, Richard Devon, and Frank De Kova. Special mention should also be made of Connie Gilchrist as Flo's brothel-running mother. Some of the best moments in the film occur when Ma Eckert berates Kelly for his cowardice. It's easy to see where Flo got her hard edge from, but Ma has a tender side too, something that is totally lacking in her heartless daughter. AIP reissued the *Machine-Gun Kelly/The Bonnie Parker Story* double bill in 1968 after the tremendous success of *Bonnie and Clyde* (1967).

Review: *Variety* (July 9, 1958), "A first rate little picture."

Madam Kitty

"SEX IS NOT ONLY AN ART BUT A WEAPON WITH MADAM KITTY"

(January 1977) Color by DeLuxe (Eastman Color). Produced by Coralta Cinematografica, Rome/Cinema Seven, Munich/Les Productions Fox Europa, Paris. A Trans-American Films Release. Directed by Tinto Brass. Written by Ennio de Concini, Maria Pia Fusco, and Tinto Brass. Starring Helmut Berger, Ingrid Thulin, Teresa Ann Savoy, John Steiner. DVD: Blue Underground (as *Salon Kitty*) (1.85) 133 min.; Extras: Theatrical trailers.

Helmut Berger is a duplicitous Nazi commander in *Madam Kitty*.

Could the Third Reich ever have existed without black stockings and garter belts? When did German officers have the opportunity to wage war when they apparently spent all their time in brothels and sleazy nightclubs? These are just two of the many questions that may come to mind after viewing *Madam Kitty* (a.k.a. *Salon Kitty*). In this curious combination of *The Damned* (1969) and *Cabaret* (1972), SS Officer Helmut Wallenberg (Helmut Berger) recruits loyal female Nazi supporters to work in a brothel as spies. Unbeknownst to Madam Kitty Kellerman (Ingrid Thulin), her new girls will be reporting every word spoken to them by their clients to root out any potential traitors to Hitler's cause. Their rooms will also be bugged with listening devices to record proof of any verbal infractions. When the beautiful Margherita (Teresa Ann Savoy) falls in love with German soldier Hans Reiter (Bekim Fehmiu), the plan begins to unravel. This may sound fairly straightforward but the movie is packed with bizarre imagery, over-the-top musical numbers, extreme overacting, and lots of gratuitous sex with full frontal nudity. The script is filled with "memorable" lines such as "When a problem is that shitty, you discuss it in a shit house." The movie seems like a warm-up for Tinto Brass' 1979 abomination *Caligula*. In fact, *Penthouse* publisher and *Caligula* producer Bob Guccione has said that his admiration for *Salon Kitty* is what led him to hire Brass to direct that film. One of the oddest things about *Salon Kitty* is the cast.

Helmut Berger and Ingrid Thulin both had starred in Luchino Visconti's *The Damned* and make a return to Nazi Germany in *Salon Kitty*. Bekim Fehmiu is surely the most ethnic-looking Nazi in memory. A popular star in his native Yugoslavia, he had made a failed bid for international stardom in the 1970 movie version of Harold Robbin's trashy novel *The Adventurers*. Also in the cast are John Ireland and the gorgeous Tina Aumont, who is completely wasted as Berger's dowdy wife. The striking production design is by Ken Adam, who was responsible for the design of many of the James Bond films. When AIP bought the U.S. rights to *Salon Kitty*, they changed the title to *Madam Kitty* and cut the running time to 110 minutes. Despite the editing, the film still received an X rating so it was released through the AIP subsidiary Trans-American Films.

Madhouse

"IF STARK TERROR WERE ECSTASY ...
LIVING HERE WOULD BE SHEER BLISS!"

(March 1974) Color by Movielab (Eastman Color). An American International–Amicus Co-Production. Produced by Max J. Rosenberg and Milton Subotsky. Directed by Jim Clark. Written by Greg Morrison and Ken Levison. Starring Vincent Price, Peter Cushing, Robert Quarry, Natasha Pyne. DVD: MGM (1.85) 91 min.; Extras: Theatrical trailer. Midnite Movies co-feature: *Theater of Blood*.

This British co-production between American International and Amicus Films was Vincent Price's final film for AIP. It was also the last truly "meaty" role he had in a horror movie. Although he did appear in several subsequent chillers, none of them were conceived as Price vehicles. Originally entitled *The Revenge of Dr. Death*, the story involves a former horror movie star, Paul Toombes (Price), who goes to London to appear in a TV series based on his most famous character, Dr. Death. Not long after he arrives, there is a series of killings with each duplicating a

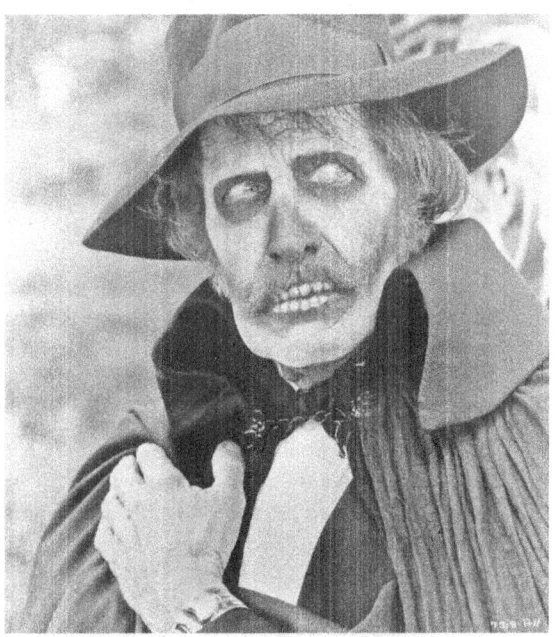

Vincent Price as Dr. Death in *Madhouse*.

method of murder from one of Toombes' old movies. At times *Madhouse* seems like a loving valentine to Price with many clips included from the Corman-Poe movies. Price is an extremely sympathetic figure as Paul Toombes and the sequence where his character is interviewed on a TV talk show is especially memorable. For once Price and Peter Cushing are given some "quality" screen time together rather than just having them both appear for the sake of marquee value. Hammer glamour girl Linda Hayden has a brief but effective role as one of the victims.

Review: *Variety* (March 26, 1974), "An inaptly titled but otherwise satisfactory horror entry."

The Masque of the Red Death

"WHAT EVILS LURK IN THIS
VILE FACE OF LUST?"

(June 1964) Panavision and Pathécolor. Produced and Directed by Roger Corman. Written by Charles Beaumont and R. Wright Campbell. Starring Vincent Price, Hazel

Court, Jane Asher, Patrick Magee. DVD: MGM (2.35) 89 min.; Extras: Theatrical trailer; Roger Corman interview. Midnite Movies co-feature: *The Premature Burial*.

The Masque of the Red Death was a story that Roger Corman had considered filming early in his Poe series. Although Charles Beaumont wrote a version of the script in 1961, Corman says he placed the project on a back burner to put more distance between it and Ingmar Bergman's *The Seventh Seal*, which shared similar plot elements. This was the seventh in the Poe cycle and AIP decided to produce the picture in England to give it a fresh approach but also because it could be filmed there more economically. Production designer Daniel Haller was able to make use of the elaborate sets from *Becket* which were stored at Elstree Studios where the picture was being shot. This, combined with Nicolas Roeg's sumptuous color cinematography, makes *The Masque of the Red Death* the most lavish of the Poe films. The themes involved are also more complex than the other movies in the series. Vincent Price's Satan-worshipping Prince Prospero is not the standard Poe movie villain. The character is written and performed with considerable shading and subtlety. The erudite script also cleverly incorporates another Poe story, "Hop-Frog," into the plotline. When filming was completed, the British Board of Film Censors insisted that Hazel Court's black mass sequence be excised or the movie could not be released in England. AIP reluctantly agreed, realizing that a British release would be necessary to insure maximum profitability. The scene was retained for the U.S. release.

Review: *Time* (May 15, 1964), "Dusts off a trifling Poe classic and adapts it to fit the collected smirks of Vincent Price."

Master of the World

"The Fabulous Adventures of the Man Who Conquered the Earth To Save It!"

(June 1961) MagnaColor by Pathé. Produced by James H. Nicholson. Directed by William Witney. Written by Richard Matheson. Starring Vincent Price, Charles Bronson, Henry Hull, Mary Webster. VHS: MGM (1.33) 104 min.; Extras: Theatrical trailer.

"In the tradition of *20,000 Leagues Under the Sea* and *Around the World in 80 Days*" announces the trailer for *Master of the World*, and it certainly is a conglomeration of ideas from both those pictures. Based on the Jules Verne novels *Robur the Conqueror* and *Master of the World*, the film was another bid by AIP to enter into more large-scale moviemaking. It was their most expensive production to date with a large part of the budget being spent on the construction of the intricate model flying ship, the *Albatross*. The special photographic

Vincent Price's face reflects "The Orgies of Evil" in the ad art for *The Masque of the Red Death*.

effects were created by Tim Barr, Wah Chang, and Gene Warren, who had worked on George Pal's *The Time Machine* the previous year. While the design of the *Albatross* is impressive, the rest of the effects are only adequate, particularly when the ship is shown dropping bombs on stock footage scenes from other movies. Vincent Price, fresh from his stint in *House of Usher*, gives a terrific performance as Robur, captain of the flying ship. He is a misguided genius who hopes to eradicate war by destroying the world's weapons of destruction. Also in the cast are Charles Bronson, taking another step up on the ladder to stardom, and a wildly over-acting Henry Hull. Hunky Richard Harrison is on hand as the navigator of the *Albatross*. Married at the time to Jim Nicholson's daughter, Harrison would soon depart for Italy where he would play leading roles in numerous sword-and-sandal films and Spaghetti Westerns. AIP accompanied their release of *Master of the World* with a typically lavish publicity campaign and, for the first time, several merchandise tie-ins. Ace Books issued a paperback movie edition featuring both of the Jules Verne novels in one volume; there was a Dell Movie Classics comic book adaptation; and Vee Jay Records released the soundtrack album of Les Baxter's melodic score. Despite all of this, the film failed to match the success of *House of Usher*, so it was back to Poe for Price and AIP. Although *Master of the World* has not yet been released on DVD, the MGM Midnite Movies VHS tape is an especially good-looking digital video transfer with stereophonic sound (AIP's first movie to have this). It also restores the pre-credits prologue showing man's early attempts at flying, which was missing on previous VHS releases of the film.

Review: *Time* (September 22, 1961), "Properly naive and lively subteen special."

Vincent Price in *Master of the World*.

Meteor

"IT'S FIVE MILES WIDE ... IT'S COMING AT 30,000 MPH ... AND THERE'S NO PLACE ON EARTH TO HIDE!"

(October 1979) Panavision and Color by Movielab. A Sandy Howard-Gabriel Katzka-Sir Run Run Shaw Production. Produced by Arnold Orgolini and Theodore Parvin. Directed by Ronald Neame. Written by Stanley Mann and Edmund H. North. Starring Sean Connery, Natalie Wood, Karl Malden, Henry Fonda. DVD: MGM (2.35) 107 min.; Extras: Theatrical trailer.

For better or worse (usually the latter), the seventies was the era of the "disaster movie," beginning with *Airport* (1970) and really taking off with *The Poseidon Adventure* (1972). Audiences couldn't seem to get enough of seeing a big-name cast in danger of losing their lives because of some large-scale natural

Director Ronald Neame, second from left, discusses a scene in *Meteor* with Sean Connery, left, Joseph Campanella, and Karl Malden.

or man-made cataclysm. By the time AIP got around to releasing *Meteor*, the decade was at an end and the genre was all but played out. Although it took a critical drubbing at the time of its release, *Meteor* is no worse than the majority of other films in this genre. It has all the major elements of the other pictures ... including the faults. In *Meteor*, Sean Connery is a crusty ex–NASA scientist who is called out of retirement to deal with an impending disaster. A huge meteor is heading toward Earth and the impact could destroy mankind, or at least a large part of it. Connery comes up with a plan to employ the nuclear defense rockets we have in space which are pointed at the U.S.S.R. He proposes we turn them around and use them to blast the meteor. Our rockets alone aren't enough to do the trick so it is suggested that the Russians do the same with their similar defense system. The problem is, the Russians refuse to admit they have such a system in place. Russian diplomat Brian Keith is sent to America with his language translator Natalie Wood to try and straighten things out. There are some decent special effects (despite an overuse of stock footage) including an avalanche which destroys a ski resort in the Alps, a hundred-foot tidal wave that levels Hong Kong, and a "meteor splinter" which hits the World Trade Center and reduces much of New York City to ruins. This last scene is particularly uncomfortable to watch now for obvious reasons. Also in the cast are Trevor Howard, Martin Landau (giving the worst performance of his career), and Richard Dysart. Henry Fonda is cast as "The President" and Sybil Danning is barely recognizable as a "Girl Skier" during the avalanche sequence. It was directed by Ronald Neame, who had helmed *The Poseidon Adventure*. AIP must have thought they had a surefire winner on their hands. Filmed at a cost of over $16 million, *Meteor* performed disappointingly at the box office and temporarily ended the series of disaster movies. In 1998, two movies with a similar premise to *Meteor* were released: *Deep Impact* and *Armageddon*.

Review: *Time* (November 19, 1979), "A tidal wave of sewage muck engulfs the New York subway system. When it comes to excrement, the makers of *Meteor* know their stuff."

The Mind Benders

"PERVERTED ... SOULLESS! ... EIGHT HOURS OF HELL IN THE TANK—AND HIS MEMORY OF HER WARM, LOVING BODY TURNED TO REPULSIVE CLAY!"

(May 1963) Black & White. A Michael Relph–Basil Dearden/Novus Production. Produced by Michael Relph. Directed by Basil Dearden. Written by James Kennaway. Starring Dirk Bogarde, Mary Ure, John Clements, Michael Bryant. DVD: Anchor Bay (1.66) 109 min.; Extras: Theatrical trailer; Dirk Bogarde bio.

Professor Sharpey (Harold Goldblatt) commits suicide and it is suspected that he was selling government secrets to the Communists. His friend and colleague Dr. Henry Longman (Dirk Bogarde) refuses to believe that Sharpey would knowingly betray his country and puts forth the theory that the professor was brainwashed. To prove his point, Longman subjects himself to treatment in a sensory deprivation tank. This results in nearly destroying his marriage and his mind. Fine direction and an excellent performance by Dirk Bogarde are only two of the good reasons for seeking out this intense British thriller. *The Mind Benders* was picked up by AIP for U.S. distribution, cut to 98 minutes, and given a minor release as a co-feature. It deserved better and finally got it with the excellent DVD release.

The Mini-Skirt Mob

"THEY'RE HOG STRADDLING FEMALE ANIMALS ON THE PROWL!"

(May 1968) Color by Perfect. A Maury Dexter Production. Produced and Directed by Maury Dexter. Written by James Gordon White. Starring Diane McBain, Jeremy Slate, Sherry Jackson, Patty McCormack. DVD: MGM (1.85) 86 min.; Extras: Theatrical trailer. Midnite Movies co-feature: *Chrome and Hot Leather*.

Shayne (Diane McBain), leader of the Mini-Skirt Mob, is a cold-hearted bitch. When her former boyfriend, rodeo cowboy Jeff Logan (Ross Hagen), gets married, Shayne and her friends decide to visit Jeff and his bride Connie (Sherry Jackson) on their wedding night. A fight ensues when Shayne goads gullible biker Lon (Jeremy Slate) into making a pass at Connie. At this point most of the gang decide to call it quits but hell hath no fury like Shayne scorned. She convinces a handful of minions to join her in following Jeff and Connie as they drive to their new home. Like that other Maury Dexter production *Hell's Belles*, *The Mini-Skirt Mob* never lives up to the promise of the "hog straddling female animals" of the publicity. Shayne and her girlfriends wear jackets with the name of the gang emblazoned

Diane McBain is a bitch on wheels in *The Mini-Skirt Mob*.

across the back but it never amounts to much. McBain's performance as Shayne, however, makes up for any lack of female gang action. Dressed in a gold mini-skirt outfit and black leather go-go boots, and sporting a gigantic blonde hairdo, she is definitely a force to be reckoned with. You do *not* want to get on her bad side. A former Warner Bros. ingénue, McBain also appeared in AIP's *Thunder Alley* (1967) and *Maryjane* (1968), both co-starring Fabian. The other two female leads also came from loftier beginnings. Sherry Jackson was a regular on the hit television series *Make Room for Daddy* as Danny Thomas' daughter Terry. Patty McCormack, who plays Shayne's kid sister Edie, gained fame as the evil Rhoda Penmark in the stage and movie versions of *The Bad Seed*. For the latter, she was nominated for a Best Supporting Actress Oscar. Oddly, the credits of *The Mini-Skirt Mob* list Patty McCormack as the singer of the title song but it is quite obviously sung by a man.

Motorcycle Gang

"WILD AND WICKED ...
LIVING WITH NO TOMORROW!"

(October 1957) Black & White. A Golden State Production. Produced by Alex Gordon. Directed by Edward L. Cahn. Written by Lou Rusoff. Starring Anne Neyland, Steve Terrell, John Ashley, Carl Switzer. VHS: Columbia/TriStar (1.33) 78 min. DVD: Direct Video Distribution (1.33) 78 min.; Region-Free DVD from United Kingdom; Extras: Audio interview with Samuel Z. Arkoff; Trailers.

A "retread" of *Dragstrip Girl* with motorcycles instead of hot rods; in fact, the original

Anne Neyland, right, attempts to stop Steve Terrell from giving John Ashley a much deserved thrashing in *Motorcycle Gang*.

title was *Motorcycle Girl*. In this film, a kindly cop (Russ Bender) does his best to keep a motorcycle gang on the straight and narrow. Randy (Steve Terrell) is on probation for an accident in which an old man was killed. Rival gang member Nick (John Ashley) served time for causing the accident and blames Randy for his conviction. Now Nick is out of jail and intends to get even with Randy for his fifteen months in the slammer. To complicate matters, the new girl in town, Terry (Anne Neyland), plays Randy and Nick against each other for her affections. When Nick and his bad boy bikers harass the members of a small community, the cop enlists Randy and his buddies to come to the rescue. Steve Terrell had a continuing role in the TV series *Life with Father* and also appeared in MGM's high-profile film version of *Tea and Sympathy* before becoming a contract player for American International. John Ashley had made his AIP debut earlier the same year in the aforementioned *Dragstrip Girl* and would have a long association with the company. Also in the cast are Paul Blaisdell in a rare appearance *sans* monster costume, Carl Switzer who had played "Alfalfa" in the *Our Gang* comedies, and Suzanne Sydney who would play the memorably weird "Dolly" in AIP's *High School Hellcats*. Top-billed Anne Neyland was an MGM contract player who had appeared with Elvis Presley in *Jailhouse Rock*. Producer Alex Gordon borrowed her from MGM to appear in *Motorcycle Gang*, which at the time was quite a casting coup for AIP.

Review: *Harrison's Reports* (November 30, 1957), "As indicated by the title, the action is loaded with thrills because of the risk to life and limb."

Murders in the Rue Morgue

"A SIGH ... A GASP ... A SCREAM! NIGHT HAS FALLEN ON THE RUE MORGUE"

(September 1971) Color by Movielab. Produced by Louis M. Heyward. Directed by Gordon Hessler. Written by Christopher Wicking and Henry Slesar. Starring Jason Robards, Christine Kaufmann, Herbert Lom, Michael Dunn. VHS: Lightning Video (1.33) 86 min. DVD: MGM (1.85) 98 min.; Extras: Theatrical trailer; Featurette "Stage Tricks and Screen Frights." Midnite Movies co-feature: *Cry of the Banshee*.

This was the last in the long series of AIP Edgar Allan Poe adaptations which began with *House of Usher* in 1960. As the series progressed, the scripts had less and less to do with Poe and this one is certainly no exception. Other than the title, little to nothing of the Poe story remains. Instead, there is a convoluted plot about a French theatre troupe menaced by a mysterious masked killer. The leading lady (Christine Kaufmann) is plagued by dreams which could be a reflection of her past or a glimpse into her future. These nightmares blend with reality until it is difficult to tell where one leaves off and the other begins. A confused screenplay is not the least of the problems here as leading man Jason Robards gives a performance which is indifferent at best. Displeased with the finished product, AIP cut the film to 86 minutes, tinted the dream sequences in monochrome, and drastically altered the final scene. The shorter theatrical cut was once available on VHS from Lightning Video and is now quite rare. After the wholesale tampering with his film, director Gordon Hessler refused to work for American International again.

Muscle Beach Party

"WHEN 10,000 BICEPS GO AROUND 5,000 BIKINIS ... YOU KNOW WHAT'S GONNA HAPPEN!"

(March 1964) Panavision and Pathécolor. Produced by James H. Nicholson and Samuel Z. Arkoff. Directed by William Asher. Written by Robert Dillion and William Asher. Starring Frankie Avalon, Annette Funicello, Luciana Paluzzi, Don Rickles. DVD: MGM (2.35) 95 min.; Extras: Theatrical trailer. Midnite Movies co-feature: *Ski Party*.

The second in the "Beach Party" series is notable for the absence of Harvey Lembeck and his Rat Pack. Instead the beach gang has to contend with a neighboring colony of musclemen, led by coach Don Rickles, who are infringing on their territory. Once again Frankie and Dee Dee are at romantic odds, this time because of a wealthy Italian heiress (Luciana Paluzzi) who has set her sights on the singing surfer. Rock Stevens, who plays "Mr. Galaxy," starred in several European sword-and-sandal films. He later appeared in the television series *Mission Impossible* using his real name, Peter Lupus. Peter Lorre provides an extended cameo at the finale. Surprisingly, in one scene Frankie Avalon smokes a cigarette, despite the claims of both director William Asher and producer Sam Arkoff that none of the kids ever smoked in these films. *Muscle Beach Party* also introduces Little Stevie Wonder.

Songs: "Muscle Beach Party," "Runnin' Wild," "Muscle Hustle," "My First Love," "Surfin' Woodie," "Surfer's Holiday," "Happy Street," "A Girl Needs a Boy"

Review: *Variety* (March 25, 1964), "Sequels rarely match the drawing power of an original, especially when the cycle is linked to a passing fad."

Luciana Paluzzi admires Peter Lupus' pecs in *Muscle Beach Party*.

The Night Evelyn Came Out of the Grave

"THE WORMS ARE WAITING!"

(July 1972) Techniscope and Technicolor. A Phoenix Cinematografica Production. A Phase One Films Release. Produced by Antonio Sarno. Directed by Emilio P. Miraglia. Written by Fabio Pittorru, Massimo Felisatti, Emilio P. Miraglia. Starring Anthony Steffen, Marina Malfatti, Erica Blanc, Giacomo Rossi Stuart. DVD: No Shame (2.35) 100 min.; Extras: Erica Blanc and Lorenzo Baraldi interviews; Italian and English theatrical trailers; Photo and still gallery.

A wealthy English lord, Alan Cunningham (Anthony Steffen) is also a psychopath who is haunted by the death of his redheaded wife Evelyn. As a result he picks up girls with red hair, takes them to his remote estate, and kills them. Pseudo-supernatural elements lead the audience to believe this is a movie about the living dead but in reality it is another murder mystery motivated by money. This entry in the Italian Giallo genre has a typically convoluted plot tricked out with atmospheric direction and stylish production values. The oddest thing about *The Night Evelyn Came Out of the Grave* (and there are many of them) is that the film begins with main character Alan Cunningham killing one girl and attempting to kill another. Then it shifts gears mid-point and the audience is expected to sympathize with all the mayhem being inflicted on a person whom we have already seen is a crazed killer. No further mention of the murders is made. It's as if the screenwriters forgot all about this particular aspect of the story. Nevertheless, it is an entertaining mishmash and Erica Blanc's now infamous striptease (while emerging from a coffin) is as deliriously outrageous as it sounds. *The Night Evelyn Came Out of the*

Grave was produced in Italy in 1971 and released in the States the following year by one-off AIP subsidiary Phase One Films. The U.S. theatrical release ran 90 minutes and eliminated, among other things, the pre-credits prologue. Although this movie has been available from several PD companies over the years both on VHS and DVD, quality-wise all the prints have left much to be desired. The DVD from No Shame is a fine uncut version presented in the correct 2.35 aspect ratio. It is available in "The Emilio Miraglia Killer Queen Box Set" which also includes the director's Giallo *The Red Queen Kills 7 Times*, which is the better film of the two, though the plotting is just as absurd. But, hey, that's part of what makes watching a Giallo so much fun.

Night of the Blood Beast

"No Girl Was Safe as Long as this Head Hunting Thing Roamed the Land!"

(August 1958) Black & White. Produced by Gene and Roger Corman. Directed by Bernard L. Kowalski. Written by Martin Varno. Starring Ed Nelson, Michael Emmet, Angela Greene, John Baer. DVD: Retromedia (1.33) 62 min.

This is the first of a pair of sci-fi movies directed by Bernard Kowalski for Gene and Roger Corman. Originally the Corman brothers had approached Jerome Bixby to write the screenplay for this film. Bixby was involved in another project at the time and suggested his 21-year-old friend Martin Varno. Varno, whose agent was Forrest J Ackerman, took the assignment and drafted a script entitled *The Creature*

In *Night of the Blood Beast*, "The Beast" (Ross Sturlin) attacks Michael Emmet outside of Bronson Caves in Los Angeles.

from *Galaxy 27*. During the production, Varno's script was altered so drastically that he went to the Screen Writers Guild and demanded restitution for the damages done to his work. In the finished film, a manned rocket crashes on its return to Earth and the pilot is killed. A scientific recovery team retrieves the body, not knowing that a creature from outer space hitched a ride on the rocket and has followed them back to their home base. When the pilot miraculously returns to life, the scientists discover that he has been impregnated by the alien and is now carrying its young within his body. *Night of the Blood Beast* runs barely over an hour and is a tad slow-moving at times, but the serious tone never lets up and it has some truly unsettling moments. In keeping with the film's meager $87,000 budget, the creature costume is a leftover from Roger Corman's *Teenage Caveman* which had finished filming a couple of weeks before *Night of the Blood Beast* went into production. With some minor alterations, the costume is used to even greater effect than it was in the previous movie and makes for a memorable monster.

Review: *Variety* (December 10, 1958), "Respectfully suspenseful picture."

Night of the Blood Monster

"Horror Will Hold You Helpless!"

(May 1972) Widescreen and Color by Movielab. A Towers of London Production. Produced by Harry Alan Towers. Directed by Jess Franco. Written by Anthony Scott Veitch. Starring Christopher Lee, Leo Genn, Maria Schell, Maria Rohm. DVD: Blue Underground (as *The Bloody Judge*) (2.35) 104 min.; Extras: Theatrical and TV trailers; Interview with Christopher Lee and Jess Franco; Deleted and alternative scenes; Poster and still galleries.

This 1970 Spanish-Italian-West German co-production is set in 17th century England during the reign of King James II, a time of tremendous civil upheaval. Harry (Hans Hass), son of the Earl of Wessex (Leo Genn), is in love with Mary Gray (Maria Rohm). Her sister Alicia (Margaret Lee) was condemned to death as a suspected witch by Judge George Jeffreys (Christopher Lee). The malefic Jeffreys begins to persecute Mary and her lover as well. The film is known under various titles such as *The Bloody Judge* and *Il trono di fuoco/The Throne of Fire*. When it was released in the U.S. by AIP in 1972, it was cut to 81 minutes and given the ridiculous title *Night of the Blood Monster*. The movie is much in the mode of Michael Reeves' historical horror *Witchfinder General* (a.k.a. *Conqueror Worm*). It is also one of Spanish director Jess Franco's most accomplished productions. Although the uncut version displays some of the director's "excesses," it is still one of the more subdued entries in his body of work. Christopher Lee gives a very good performance as Judge Jeffreys and Bruno Nicolai contributes a marvelous score. The excellent quality DVD from Blue Underground is the most complete version available. Unfortunately, some utterly gratuitous nude scenes from the German-language version are included. They stop the film dead in its tracks and all but rob it of what class it has.

Night Tide

"Was She Human ... or Was She a Beautiful Temptress from the Sea, Intent Upon Loving, Consuming, and Killing?"

(April 1963) Black & White. A Filmgroup Presentation. Produced by Aram Kantarian. Written and Directed by Curtis Harrington. Starring Dennis Hopper, Linda Lawson, Gavin Muir, Luana Anders. DVD: Image (1.85) 85 min.; Extras: Theatrical trailer; Audio commentary by Curtis Harrington and Dennis Hopper.

In Curtis Harrington's first feature film, Dennis Hopper is Johnny, a naive sailor who falls in love with Mora (Linda Lawson), a fake sideshow mermaid. As it turns out, Mora might not be such a fake after all. She just may

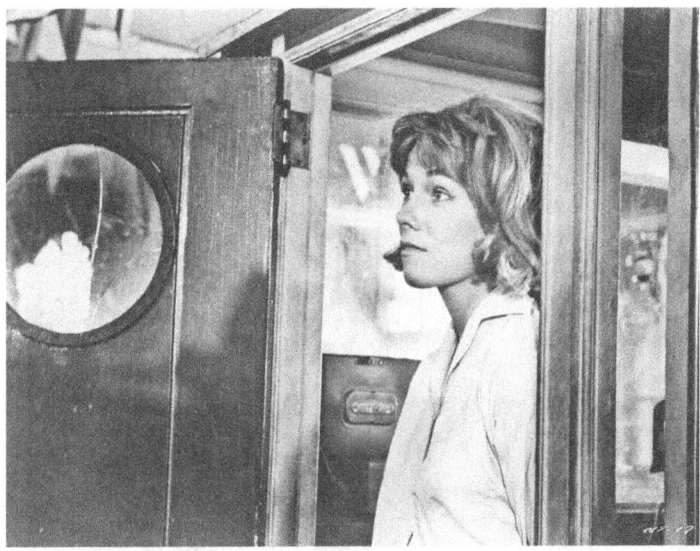

Luana Anders, shown here in *Night Tide*, gave many memorable performances in AIP movies.

be a descendant of the Sirens of Greek mythology who lured unsuspecting men to their deaths. Mora's two previous boyfriends have died under mysterious circumstances and Johnny seems a likely candidate to become number three. Filmed in and around Venice, California, *Night Tide* is haunting and atmospheric; more arthouse than grindhouse, although AIP tended to lean toward the latter in promotion. Hopper gives a sympathetic performance that is "Method" all the way while Linda Lawson is beautiful and mysterious as Mora. Also on hand is the wonderful Luana Anders as the uncomplicated "good girl" also in love with Johnny. "Laura" composer David Raksin supplied the spare background score. Although also available from other DVD companies, the Image disc of *Night Tide* boasts a widescreen presentation with pristine picture quality.

Review: *Time* (December 6, 1963), "The film emits an uncommon glow of freshness and imagination."

The Norseman

"Before Columbus was born, a reckless band of blonde giants sailed to an unknown land we now call America."

(November 1978) Color by Movielab. A Charles B. Pierce-Fawcett-Majors Film Production. Written, Produced, and Directed by Charles B. Pierce. Starring Lee Majors, Cornel Wilde, Mel Ferrer, Susie Coelho. VHS: MGM/Amazon (1.33) 90 min.

At the height of his bionic popularity on television, Lee Majors unwisely chose this uninspired potboiler as his pathway to big screen stardom. Thorvald the Viking (Majors) sails with his men to the New World to search for his father King Eurich (Mel Ferrer). Eurich and his men are being held captive by a fierce Indian tribe and it's up to Thorvald to rescue them. It's Vikings vs. Indians with beautiful squaw Susie Coelho caught in the middle. Cornel Wilde and Mel Ferrer seem bewildered as to how they ended up in this cheap made-in-Florida turkey.

The Oblong Box

"Edgar Allan Poe's Classic Tale of the Living Dead!"

(June 1969) Color by Berkey Pathé. Produced and Directed by Gordon Hessler. Written by Lawrence Huntingdon and Christopher Wicking. Starring Vincent Price, Christopher Lee, Hilary Dwyer, Rupert Davies. DVD: MGM (1.85) 97 min.; Extras: Theatrical trailer. Midnite Movies co-feature: *Scream and Scream Again*.

A hodgepodge of ideas including premature burial, grave robbing, the evils of Colonialism, black magic, and a twisted killer in a mask ... to name only a few of the plot elements. And all of this attributed to poor Edgar Allan Poe! Michael Reeves was set to direct but when illness forced him to abandon the project, executive producer Louis M. Heyward recruited Gordon Hessler to take over. Although there has been much speculation about what Reeves would have done with the film, it's doubtful he could have salvaged this mostly unpromising material. The plot concerns Edward and Julian Markham (played respectively by Alister Williamson and Vincent Price), two brothers who have returned to England after living many years on their plantation in Africa. Edward, the victim of a witch doctor's sorcery, is now a crazed, disfigured lunatic who is kept a prisoner by Julian. Hessler has said AIP was so delighted with a rough cut of the movie that they gave him additional money to "give the picture a more impressive look." Actually they wanted more boobs and blood so a largely superfluous scene in a tavern-brothel was added. The story revolves around the character of Edward Markham so Price and Christopher Lee are mainly used for window dressing. They have only one brief scene together and in it Lee is lying on a floor with his throat cut. Theatrical prints of *The Oblong Box* ran 91 minutes. The DVD adds some dialogue sequences between Price and Hilary Dwyer plus additional nudity and bloodletting.

Review: *New York Times* (July 24, 1969), "*The Oblong Box* (the coffin in this cheerless charade) might have been better left interred."

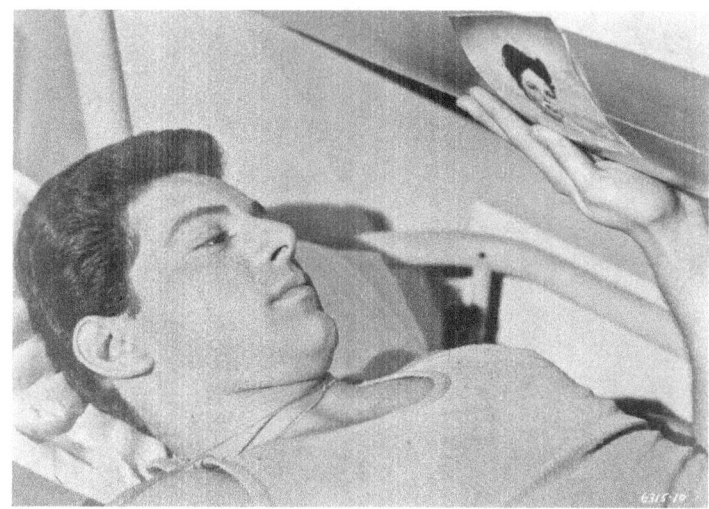

In *Operation Bikini*, Frankie Avalon dreams of his "Girl Back Home."

Operation Bikini

"ON A BEACHHEAD OR IN A BEACH HOUSE ... THEY ALWAYS MADE A PERFECT SCORE!"

(April 1963) Black & White (with color sequences). Produced by James H. Nicholson and Lou Rusoff. Directed by Anthony Carras. Written by John Tomerlin. Starring Tab Hunter, Frankie Avalon, Scott Brady, Eva Six. VHS: MGM/Amazon (1.33) 84 min.

This odd little film is a World War II drama, although the advertising would lead you to believe it was more about two-piece bathing suits. In 1943, an underwater demolition team is taken aboard a submarine. Their assignment is to destroy a recently sunk U.S. sub before the Japanese can salvage its advanced radar equipment. This would seem like a fairly straightforward plotline but the movie is filled with a strange mix of elements. Frankie Avalon is a lovesick sailor who dreams about his girlfriend Roxanne ... in color. Lying in his bunk and gazing at a photo of his girl, Frankie drifts off to a land of colorful tropical island sunsets where he suddenly bursts into song. This happens twice, as if one time wasn't weird enough. Blonde Hungarian bombshell Eva Six is "introduced" in this film but she plays an Asian girl wearing a black fright wig. She and Tab Hunter get into a brawl; she slugs him in the face and he slugs her right back. This apparently turns her on because that same night she visits Tab in his sleeping bag, rips off his shirt, and oils him up for a "massage" (this scene is conspicuously absent from the Dell Movie Classics comic book adaptation). The next day she is machine-gunned to death by the enemy. Illicit massages apparently must be atoned for. The movie is in black and white, obviously to make use of World War II stock footage, but, in addition to the dream sequences, there is a full color epilogue as well.

A narrator tells us that Bikini Island won't be remembered for a battle or the A-bomb but a bathing suit. Cut to sexy babes in bikinis frolicking on a beach throughout the end credits. What were the producers thinking? Maybe this was the inspiration for *Beach Party*, which came out a few months later. The mostly all-male cast includes Jim Backus, Michael Dante, and Jody McCrea in the first of his many roles for AIP. *Operation Bikini* was available on VHS from MGM exclusively through Amazon.com, as were several other AIP titles. It is now an expensive collector's item.

Song: "The Girl Back Home"

Operation Dames

"No Fury Like Four Girls Trapped Behind Enemy Lines!"

(March 1959) Black & White. A Camera Eye Pictures Inc. Production. Produced by Stanley Kallis. Directed by Louis Clyde Stoumen. Written by Ed Lakso. Starring Eve Meyer, Chuck Henderson, Don Devlin, Ed Craig. VHS: Columbia/TriStar (1.33) 73 min.

In 1950 during the Korean War, a group of U.S.O. entertainers gets lost behind enemy lines. A small band of soldiers, led by hard-boiled Sergeant Jeff Villeto (Chuck Henderson), finds them and must try to lead them to safety. Along the way, Jeff falls for buxom dancer Lorry (Eve Meyer) much to the chagrin of his second-in-command Billy (Chuck Van Haren). In one scene, Billy arrives to take over the night watch right after Jeff and Lorry have made love. He berates his sergeant for taking advantage of Lorry, referring to her as "a decent Christian girl." Jeff replies "So are you." Huh? This is the high point of yet another unremarkable AIP war movie. The most memorable aspect of the picture is the presence of busty Eve Meyer. Ms. Meyer married director Russ Meyer in 1952 and was the Playboy Playmate of the Month in June 1955. She also adorned the covers of several men's magazines of the period. Her only other acting role was in her husband's film *Eve and the Handyman* (1961). Eve produced many of Russ Meyer's films until their divorce in 1969. Tragically, she died in a 1977 plane crash.

Songs: "Girls Girls Girls," "Regular Man"

Review: *Variety* (March 4, 1959), "Has an interesting premise that doesn't come off."

Pajama Party

"The Party Picture That Takes Off (Way Off) Where the Others Stopped!"

(November 1964) Panavision and Pathécolor. Produced by James H. Nicholson and Samuel Z. Arkoff. Directed by Don Weis. Written by Louis M. Heyward. Starring Tommy Kirk, Annette Funicello, Jody McCrea, Harvey Lembeck. DVD: MGM (2.35) 84 min.; Extras: Theatrical trailer; Fullscreen version.

Connie (Annette Funicello) is tired of being neglected by her sports-obsessed boyfriend Big Lunk (Jody McCrea), so she decides to make him jealous. The guy she picks to do this with is a Martian named Go-Go (Tommy Kirk) who has been sent to Earth to pave the way for an invasion. *Pajama Party* is even silly by AIP standards. There is lots of slapstick, singing, and dancing but very little in the way of a story. Louis M. Heyward said he based his script, originally entitled *The Maid and the Martian*, on the antics of his son (was he a Martian?). Whatever the case, this began a long and fruitful relationship between AIP and "Deke" Heyward, who eventually became vice-president in charge of European production for the company. As such, he contributed to some of their most memorable movies. Reunited in *Pajama Party* are Walt Disney veterans Tommy Kirk and Annette Funicello who had just starred together in Disney's *The Misadventures of Merlin Jones* (also 1964). "Beach regulars" Jody McCrea, Candy Johnson, Don Rickles, and Harvey Lembeck are all on hand. Veteran performers Elsa Lanchester, Buster Keaton, and Dorothy Lamour are robbed of their dignity, but at least they were working. Susan Hart, who quickly became Mrs. James H. Nicholson, makes her AIP debut herein.

Frankie Avalon has a cameo as the leader of the invading Martians. And Jesse White, as the villainous J. Sinister Hulk, is a dead ringer for cigar-chomping Samuel Z. Arkoff ... coincidence? AIP's decision to change the title to *Pajama Party* came at such a late date that Annette had already recorded the title song "The Maid and the Martian" which then had to be scrapped.

Songs: "It's That Kind of Day," "There Has to Be a Reason," "Pajama Party," "Where Did I Go Wrong?," "Beach Ball," "Among the Young," "Stuffed Animal"

Panic in Year Zero!

"AN ORGY OF LOOTING AND LUST ... A-DAY
WHEN CIVILIZATION CAME TO AN END!"

(June 1962) Widescreen and Black & White. Produced by Arnold Houghland and Lou Rusoff. Directed by Ray Milland. Written by Jay Simms and John Morton. Starring Ray Milland, Jean Hagen, Frankie Avalon, Richard Garland. DVD: MGM (2.35) 92 min. Midnite Movies co-feature: *The Last Man on Earth*.

Harry Baldwin (Ray Milland) and his family are taking a vacation away from Los Angeles when they learn that a nuclear holocaust has destroyed that city, and many of the world's other great cities. Harry must fight to keep his family safe in a world gone crazy, and keep from losing his own moral values as well. This thoughtful and remarkably non-exploitative movie is a real departure from the typical AIP sensationalistic approach. Milland both directs and stars in the film, and does a fine job wearing both hats. The shooting title was *Survival* and this was later changed to *End of the World*. A paperback novelization of the screenplay was issued under that title at the time of the original theatrical release but the film finally showed up in theatres as *Panic in Year Zero!* A potent motion picture by any title.

Review: *Harrison's Reports* (July 14, 1962), "Good. While this is not an outstanding success, it does acquit itself rather admir-

Frankie Avalon studies his script for "Survival," which became *Panic in Year Zero!*

ably. The net result is an interesting item of entertainment."

Paratroop Command

"KIDS LIVING TO THE DEADLY THRILL
OF JUMP AND KILL!"

(February 1959) Black & White. A James H. Nicholson and Samuel Z. Arkoff Production. Produced and Written by Stan Shpetner. Directed by William Witney. Starring Richard Bakalyan, Ken Lynch, Jack Hogan, Jimmy Murphy. VHS: Columbia/TriStar (1.33) 83 min.; VHS co-feature: *Jet Attack*.

The story opens in 1942 when a battalion of paratroopers is dropped in North Africa. The six guys are Lieutenant (Ken Lynch), Sergeant (Jimmy Murphy), Ace (Jack Hogan), Cowboy (Jim Beck), Pigpen (Jeffry Morris), and Charlie (Richard Bakalyan). They soon encounter Nazis. When Charlie's gun jams, Cowboy accuses him of freezing up. Charlie gets separated from the rest of the group and, not knowing that Cowboy has donned a Nazi uniform to act as a decoy, inadvertently shoots him dead. Ace, who has been Cowboy's friend since childhood, vows to avenge his buddy's death. The action moves to Sicily and Salerno with Ace waiting all the while for a chance to kill Charlie. Richard Bakalyan, who also appeared in *The Cool and the Crazy*, was a fine actor who could always be counted on to bring nuances to the characters he played. The previous year he had appeared with Jack Hogan in *The Bonnie Parker Story* which was made by the same team of Stan Shptner and William Witney. Bakalyan later proved himself an adept comedian and his versatility insured him a lengthy career in both movies and television.

Review: *Harrison's Reports* (January 31, 1959), "Of the program war melodramas thus far released by American International, this one shapes up as the best."

The People That Time Forgot

"HIDDEN BEHIND A WALL OF ICE AND DOOMED TO VANISH IN FLAMES!"

(July 1977) Color by Movielab. A Max J. Rosenberg Production. Produced by John Dark. Directed by Kevin Connor. Written by Kevin Tilley. Starring Patrick Wayne, Doug McClure, Sarah Douglas, Dana Gillespie. DVD: MGM (1.85) 90 min.; Extras: Theatrical trailer. Midnite Movies co-feature: *The Land That Time Forgot*.

Ben McBride (Patrick Wayne) mounts an expedition to the lost continent of Caprona to rescue his friend Bowen Tyler who became trapped there in the previous movie *The Land That Time Forgot*. When their amphibious bi-plane is attacked by a Pterodactyl, McBride and company are in danger of being stranded themselves. After being befriended by a curvaceous cave girl (Dana Gillespie), they all end up prisoners in the City of Skulls whose rotund ruler (Milton Reid covered in green body makeup) plans to sacrifice them to the volcano god. In the end, the volcano erupts and the lost world belches and farts flames endlessly as the adventurers run back to their repaired plane. This is the third in a series of British movies based on novels by Edgar Rice Burroughs which AIP produced in conjunction with Amicus Films. The first of these (the aforementioned *The Land That Time Forgot*) was a well-made and exciting adventure fantasy which benefited from a well-written script. It also had an extensive menagerie of prehistoric monsters, cleverly designed by Roger Dicken. This time around, the poorly conceived monsters are few and far between and most of the story consists of

Thorley Walters, Doug McClure, and Patrick Wayne stand ready to fight *The People That Time Forgot*.

going from one place to another and back again. There is also some misguided production and costume design. The soldiers of the City of Skulls look like Shogun warriors and the walls of the palace are decorated with tapestries which appear to have been woven by artist Frank Frazetta.

The Phantom from 10,000 Leagues

"From the Depths of the Sea ... Horrifying! Terrifying!"

(January 1956) Black & White. A Milner Bros. Production. Produced by Jack and Dan Milner. Directed by Dan Milner. Written by Lou Rusoff. Starring Kent Taylor, Cathy Downs, Michael Whalen, Rodney Bell. DVD: MGM/Fox (1.85) 80 min. Midnite Movies co-feature: *The Beast with a Million Eyes*.

Although Jim Nicholson and Sam Arkoff had promised their exhibitors a new sci-fi–horror double bill, they found themselves without a companion feature to Roger Corman's *Day the World Ended*. They enlisted the services of the Milner Brothers (Jack and Dan) to inexpensively film a script by Arkoff's brother-in-law, Lou Rusoff. The plot involves a radioactive ball of light, located in the waters off the California coast, which is guarded by a hideous aquatic monster. A number of people, including an agent of a foreign government, are attempting to discover the secret of the powerful energy source. The story is slow-moving and the monster is especially unconvincing (it looks somewhat like a dragon in a Chinese New Year parade) but the writing and acting are respectable. Both Kent Taylor and Michael Whalen had played romantic leads at Fox in the Thirties and now they found themselves cast opposite a sea monster. Ronald Stein provides a good score with an especially memorable piano piece for the opening credits. *The Phantom from 10,000 Leagues* has long been available as a PD title from a variety of sources but the MGM Midnite Movies edition is a beautifully remastered transfer. Although it appears to be a bit overly letterboxed at 1.85, this is definitely the one to get.

Review: *Harrison's Reports* (January 21, 1956), "As an entertainment it shapes up as a weak and tedious science-fiction mish-mash."

Pit and the Pendulum

"The Greatest Terror Tale Ever Told!"

(August 1961) Panavision and Pathécolor. Produced and Directed by Roger Corman. Written by Richard Matheson. Starring Vincent Price, Barbara Steele, John Kerr, Luana Anders. DVD: MGM (2.35) 80 min.; Extras: Theatrical trailer; TV prologue; Audio commentary by Roger Corman. Midnite Movies co-feature: *The Fall of the House of Usher*.

The second of Roger Corman's Edgar Allan Poe adaptations is arguably the best in the series and was even more financially successful than *House of Usher*. Francis Barnard (John Kerr) travels to the forbidding Spanish castle of Nicholas Medina (Vincent Price) to learn the circumstances surrounding the death of his sister Elizabeth (Barbara Steele), Nicholas' wife. As the truth is revealed, the situation becomes more sinister for all involved, ending in betrayal, insanity and death. Daniel Haller's art direction and production design are especially impressive, considering that the entire budget for the film was only about $200,000. Barbara Steele, in her first film after *Black Sunday*, is wonderful as the beautiful but scheming Elizabeth, despite the fact that her dialogue was revoiced by another actress. Price was taken to task by critics at the time of the film's original release for what they considered a hammy performance but in reality he expertly assays the part of a man gradually being driven insane. For the network television release, a special prologue was filmed to pad the running time. This prologue, featuring Luana Anders, is included on the DVD release but it is incorrectly listed as the "theatrical prologue." In recent years, actor-producer Mark Damon has taken credit for bringing the Poe stories to the attention of Roger Corman

Luana Anders, Vincent Price, John Kerr, and Antony Carbone are about to make a startling discovery in Pit and the Pendulum.

and also claims that he, not Corman, directed *Pit and the Pendulum*. Sure you did, Mark.

Review: *Films in Review* (October 1961), "Roger Corman is as inventive as he was on *Usher*, and effectively employs all the stock-shocks, and a few new ones."

Planet of the Vampires

"10,000 YEARS AGO OR 10,000 YEARS TO COME"

(November 1965) ColorScope (Technicolor). Produced by Fulvio Lucisano. Directed by Mario Bava. Written by Ib Melchior and Louis M. Heyward. Starring Barry Sullivan, Norma Bengell, Angel Aranda, Evi Marandi. DVD: MGM (1.85) 88 min.; Extras: Theatrical trailer.

Mario Bava's colorful and atmospheric *Terror nella spazio/Terror in Space* became *Planet of the Vampires* for its AIP theatrical release. No matter what the title, this is a fascinating excursion into the unknown. A spaceship lands on a distant planet where one by one the crew members are killed and their bodies reanimated by an alien force. There isn't much more to the plot than that but Bava manages to turn the movie into a directorial *tour de force*. The film is filled with a succession of haunting images and unexpected jolts which transform the simple plot into a triumph of style over substance. A distress signal lures an unsuspecting spaceship to a fog-shrouded planet where the crew finds a derelict spacecraft containing the fossilized remains of an alien crew. Sound familiar? These elements were borrowed from *Planet of the Vampires* for Ridley Scott's *Alien* (1979). When AIP sold the film to television they changed the title to *The Demon Planet*. The MGM DVD includes two minutes which were cut from the theatrical release. It also restores the original electronic score by Gino Marinuzzi Jr. which had been replaced on the HBO video version with a new score by Kendall Schmidt because of a dispute over the music rights.

The Premature Burial

"WITHIN THIS COFFIN LIES A MAN ... YET ALIVE!"

(March 1962) Panavision and Eastman Color by Pathé. Produced and Directed by Roger Corman. Written by Charles Beaumont and Ray Russell. Starring Ray Milland, Hazel Court, Heather Angel, Richard Ney. DVD: MGM (2.35) 81 min.; Extras: Theatrical trailer; Roger Corman interview. Midnite Movies co-feature: *The Masque of the Red Death*.

Roger Corman had originally planned *The Premature Burial* as an independent production to be released by Pathé. Because of this, he could not use Vincent Price in the lead (the actor was under contract to AIP). In his place, Ray Milland was chosen to star. The first day of shooting, Jim Nicholson and Sam Arkoff turned up on the set and informed Roger that AIP had just bought Pathé's interest in the picture and he was once again working for them. Of all the Corman-Poe films, *The Premature Burial* most resembles the "drawing room horror" of a Hammer film due to the primarily British cast and the splendid production design by Daniel Haller. Guy Carrell (Milland) has an obsessive fear of being buried alive. His phobia leads him to build an elaborate tomb filled with various contraptions which would enable him to escape should he accidentally be interred prematurely. This all puts a considerable strain on his marriage to the beautiful Emily (Hazel Court) and an even greater strain on his mental condition. This was the first of many AIP films for Ray Milland, yet another actor whose career was resuscitated by the company. Ronald Stein provides an excellent, eerie score which incorporates the sea chanty "Molly Malone" with haunting results.

Review: *Variety* (March 14, 1962), "Too familiar to generate much shock."

Ray Milland in his first film for AIP, *The Premature Burial*.

Psych-Out

"THESE ARE THE PLEASURE LOVERS! THEY'LL ASK FOR A DIME WITH HUNGRY EYES ... BUT THEY'LL GIVE YOU LOVE—FOR NOTHING!"

(April 1968) Pathécolor. Produced by Dick Clark. Directed by Richard Rush. Written by E. Hunter Willett and Betty Ulus. Starring Jack Nicholson, Susan Strasberg, Dean Stockwell, Bruce Dern. VHS: HBO Video (1.33) 98 min. DVD: MGM (1.85) 89 min.; Extras: Theatrical trailer; Featurette "Love and Haight." Midnite Movies co-feature: *The Trip*.

A deaf girl (Susan Strasberg) goes to San Francisco's Haight/Ashbury district in search of her brother (Bruce Dern) and becomes involved in the "Flower Power" drug scene. The movie was originally called *The Love Children*, but producer Dick Clark says that Sam Arkoff changed the title because he was afraid

Susan Strasberg is a deaf girl on a "bum trip" in *Psych-Out*.

people would think it was a movie about "bastards." Although films like this may seem silly now, they are chronicles of a fleeting bit of history which often effectively capture the mood and images of that time. Jack Nicholson seems impossibly young here. Watching this, it's hard to imagine the heights he would climb to and the longevity of his career. Biker movie regular Adam Roarke also puts in an appearance as a drugged-up hippie. The theatrical version of this film ran 98 minutes, with the addition of extended nude scenes not in the director's original cut. The theatrical version was available on video but the DVD is the director's cut without the nudity.

Psycho-Circus

"THE MOST HORRIFYING SYNDICATE OF EVIL IN HISTORY!"

(May 1967) Eastman Color. Produced by Harry Alan Towers. Directed by John Moxey. Written by Peter Welbeck (a.k.a. Harry Alan Towers). Starring Christopher Lee, Leo Genn, Anthony Newlands, Suzy Kendall. DVD: Blue Underground (as *Circus of Fear*) (1.66) 91 min.; Extras: Audio commentary by John Moxey; Theatrical trailers; Poster and still gallery.

A £750,000 armored car heist occurs on London Bridge. The police trace some of the bank notes to the winter quarters of Barberini's Circus. Here, suspicious characters abound, each seemingly with an ax to grind. Three murders and much talk later, the identity of the man who masterminded the job is revealed. But by this time, does anybody care? The circus act footage herein is cribbed from *Circus of Horrors* but anyone expecting the lurid thrills of that film is doomed to disappointment. What we have here is a not-very-exciting mystery punctuated with deadly dull interludes in which the police discuss the case endlessly. The interesting cast includes Christopher Lee as Gregor the lion tamer, whose face is hidden behind a black hood for most of the film. Klaus Kinski skulks around until somebody offs him with a knife. Margaret Lee, who appears in many of Harry Alan Towers' films, is similarly dispatched. Skip Martin plays "Mr. Big," a dwarf with a penchant for blackmail. All of this amounts to next to nothing. Shot at England's Bray Studios, former home of Hammer Films, the film's original title was *Circus of Fear*. AIP, apparently realizing they had a real dud on their hands, tried to salvage something from this fiasco by changing the title to *Psycho-Circus*. They also cut the color movie to 65 minutes and, trying to reduce print costs, released it in black and white. The excellent quality DVD from Blue Underground is the original British version of the film, full-length and in color.

Barry Sullivan is a badly scarred man bent on revenge in *Pyro*.

Pyro

"LOOK AT THIS MAN AND BEWARE ...
THERE IS NOTHING HUMAN ABOUT HIM ...
EXCEPT HIS DESIRES!"

(April 1964) Panacolor. A Sidney Pink and Harry Eller Production. Produced by Sidney Pink and Richard C. Meyer. Directed by Julio Coll. Written by Luis de los Arcos and Sidney Pink. Starring Barry Sullivan, Martha Hyer, Luis Prendes, Soledad Miranda. DVD: Troma (1.66) 99 min.; Extras: Troma trailers; Interview with Sidney Pink.

Engineer Vance (Barry Sullivan) gets a job in Spain and moves there with his wife and daughter. He meets beautiful, amoral Laura (Martha Hyer) and they begin a torrid romance. Vance comes to his senses and ends the affair but Laura reckons that with his wife and child out of the way, he will return to her. She sets their house on fire but Vance goes in to save his family and is horribly burned. Disfigured beyond recognition, Vance swears vengeance on Laura for the death of his loved ones. This is a very odd film ... particularly when you consider that it came from the same man who gave the world *The Angry Red Planet* and *Reptilicus*. It was filmed in Spain as *A Cold Wind from Hell*; AIP found limited marketability in that title and changed it to *Pyro*. Although there is little true horror, the story has a number of disturbing moments. One of these is the revelation that Laura's child is actually the offspring of Laura and her own father (shades of *Chinatown*). This is apparently mentioned to help account for Laura's extremely disturbed mental state. Barry Sullivan's burn makeup is very effective, recalling that of Vincent Price in *House of Wax*.

Review: *San Diego Evening Tribune* (April 1964), "The story drags desultorily and after the first half-hour or so turns into formula fare which is completely predictable."

Queen of Blood

"Hideous Beyond Belief ... with an Inhuman Craving!"

(March 1966) Pathécolor. Produced by George Edwards. Written and Directed by Curtis Harrington. Starring Basil Rathbone, John Saxon, Judi Meredith, Dennis Hopper. VHS: Star Classics (as *Planet of Blood*) (1.33) 81 min. DVD: Stax Entertainment (1.33) 81 min. Region 0 DVD from the United Kingdom.

Yet another film which resulted from the acquisition of the 1962 Russian space epic *Planeta Burg/Planet of Storms* (see *Voyage to the Prehistoric Planet*). In the far distant future of 1990 when space travel is commonplace, Earth receives a distress signal from a spaceship from another galaxy which has crash-landed on Mars. The rescue team sent from Earth finds the sole survivor, a strange alien woman with green skin. On the flight back to Earth, the crew members are horrified to discover that the alien needs human blood to survive. Writer-director Curtis Harrington successfully managed to concoct an interesting plot using the effects footage from *Planeta Burg* as the framework. Although the Russian footage is well integrated into the scheme of things, the quality of *Planeta Burg* is vastly superior to that of the U.S. additions, making these insertions all the more obvious. The first two-thirds of *Queen of Blood* rely heavily on this footage but once the alien woman has been brought aboard the earthship the real story kicks in. Florence Marly plays the space vampire without a line of dialogue but she nevertheless exudes an aura of total malevolence. Although the background score is credited to Leonard Morand, much of the music is recycled from old Ronald Stein scores such as *Not of This Earth* and *Attack of the 50 Foot Woman*. In the U.S., *Queen of Blood* was released commercially on laser disc by Image Entertainment, paired with *Planet of the Vampires*. It was also out on a poor quality, slow-speed VHS tape from Star Classics using the television title *Planet of Blood*. The U.K. DVD, though far from perfect, is much better quality than the VHS tape. However it is not as good as the beautiful remastered transfer from MGM which has been shown on cable television.

The Raven

"The Terror Began at Midnight!"

(January 1963) Panavision and Pathécolor. Produced and Directed by Roger Corman. Written by Richard Matheson. Starring Vincent Price, Peter Lorre, Boris Karloff, Hazel Court. DVD: MGM (2.35) 86 min.; Extras: Theatrical trailer; Richard Matheson and Roger Corman featurettes; Promotional record. Midnite Movies co-feature: *The Comedy of Terrors*.

Wanting to do something different in his series of Poe films and encouraged by the positive response to the seriocomic tone he used for the episode "The Black Cat" in *Tales of Terror*, Roger Corman approached screenwriter Richard Matheson with the idea of making *The Raven* a comedy. Certainly, with only the poem as a basis, Matheson had considerable freedom in his creation of a story. In England during the Middle Ages, Dr. Erasmus Craven (Vincent Price) is visited by a raven tap-tap-tapping at his window. In this case it is inept magician Dr. Bedlo (Peter Lorre) under a spell which has turned him into the bird of the title. This was accomplished by the superior magic of the evil Dr. Scarabus (Boris Karloff). Craven, also a magician, restores Bedlo to human form. When Bedlo says that he has seen Craven's supposedly dead wife Leonore (Hazel Court) at the castle of his foe, the two set out to confront Scarabus in his lair. Also along for the ride are Craven's daughter Estelle (Olive Sturgess) and Bedlo's son Rexford (Jack Nicholson, in his first AIP film). Although none of the publicity would suggest it, this is all played as a comedy. Even the comic book and paperback tie-ins don't let on that this is not a horror film. Nevertheless, *The Raven* was a tre-

Stunning poster art for *The Raven*.

mendous hit at the box office, encouraging AIP to make *The Comedy of Terrors* which came out eleven months later. Much of the reason for the success of *The Raven* is no doubt due to the wonderful performances of Price, Lorre, and Karloff. In his first of several films for AIP, Karloff is far more ambulatory than he would be in later roles. His studied dry humor is a perfect foil for the far broader comedy of Lorre and the charmingly bemused Price, whose technique falls somewhere in between the two. By all accounts, these three masters of horror had a wonderful time making the film and it shows. Also worth mentioning are the marvelous sets by Daniel Haller, who outdoes himself this time, particularly with the flame-spewing gargoyles of Dr. Scarabus' castle.

Review: *Time* (February 1, 1963), "It's fun to see the old horrors all together—sort of like watching an Ugly Contest."

Raw Meat

"Neither Men Nor Women, They Are Less Than Animals"

(September 1973) Technicolor. A Jay Kanter-Alan Ladd, Jr. Production. Produced by Paul Maslansky. Directed by Gary Sherman. Written by Ceri Jones. Starring Donald Pleasence, David Ladd, Sharon Gurney, Christopher Lee. DVD: MGM (1.85) 88 min.; Extras: Theatrical trailer.

When a government official disappears in a London Underground station, police investigate and uncover a series of similar occurrences. Nearly a century before, workers digging a new tunnel were trapped in a cave-in. Some of these people survived by eating their dead. Now the last of their descendants has come to the surface in search of food and a new mate.

Originally called *Death Line* and tastefully retitled by AIP, this British production has an original premise and some genuine shocks. The film is marred somewhat by the over-use of gruesome gore effects but, as a whole, it is very effective. Christopher Lee has one scene, which amounts to little more than an extended cameo. During its original U.S. release, *Raw Meat* was rated R but the DVD is an unrated version. The print quality of the DVD is also superior to the theatrical version.

Reform School Girl

"A Shocking True Story of Delinquent Girls!"

(August 1957) Black & White. A Carmel Production. Produced by Robert Gurney Jr. and Samuel Z. Arkoff. Written and Directed by Edward Bernds. Starring Gloria Castillo, Ross Ford, Edward Byrnes, Yvette Vickers. VHS: Columbia/TriStar (1.33) 71 min. DVD: Direct Video Distribution (1.33) 71 min.; Region-Free DVD from United Kingdom; Extras: Audio interview with Samuel Z. Arkoff; Trailers.

Poor Donna (Gloria Castillo) just can't win. When she isn't defending herself against the advances of her disgusting uncle (Jack Kruschean), she's fending off creeps like Vince (Edward Byrnes). When Vince steals a car and runs over an innocent bystander, he escapes the scene and leaves Donna to face the music. Donna ends up at the Hastings Reform School for Girls. Actually, compared to the rest of her life, the Hastings School is a definite improvement. The girls attend classes, play volleyball, grow tomatoes, and have dance parties with the local boys. A bunch of ineffectual old battleaxes are in charge and, as one inmate aptly puts it, they are so old they creak. Unfortunately, Vince gets his ex-girlfriend Josie (Luana Anders) put into Hastings and manages to lay the blame on Donna. From then on, Donna's life is utter hell as Josie and the other girls torment her for being that lowest form of life ... a "squealer." The most interesting thing about *Reform School Girl* is the cast. Edward Byrnes is slimy sociopath Vince, the year before he became a teen heartthrob as "Kookie" on the TV series *77 Sunset Strip*. Luana Anders, as the dangerous Josie, appears in the first of many AIP films. Other inmates include Yvette Vickers (so memorable in *Attack of the Giant Leeches* and *Attack of the 50 Foot Woman*) as hardboiled troublemaker Roxy and an amazonian Sally Kellerman as Roxy's nearly mute stooge. Composer Ronald Stein contributes a very memorable main title theme.

Review: *Harrison's Reports* (August 31, 1957), "Although of program quality, *Reform School Girl* is so capably directed and acted that the characters seem genuine."

Reptilicus

"What Was This Beast Born Fifty Million Years Out of Time?"

(October 1961) Pathécolor. A Cinemagic Inc. Production. Produced and Directed by Sidney Pink. Written by Ib Melchior and Sidney Pink. Starring Carl Ottosen, Ann Smyrner, Mimi Heinrich, Asbjorn Anderson. DVD: MGM (1.85) 82 min.; Extras: Theatrical trailer.

Reptilicus gets off to a good start. Danish miners drilling for copper unearth the frozen tail of a prehistoric creature. It is taken to the Copenhagen "akvarium" to be studied by scientists. Said scientists concur that it is part of a hitherto unknown species of giant reptile which is capable of regenerating itself. Example: a lizard loses its tail and grows a new one but Reptilicus grows a new body from just the tail. While the tail is busy regenerating, the audience is subjected to a travelogue of Copenhagen complete with a dreadful musical interlude at the Tivoli Gardens. After this unwanted respite, lightning strikes the aquarium and accelerates the growth of Reptilicus. Soon the enormous monster escapes to terrorize Copenhagen. Now is when the trouble really begins for the film itself because after all the buildup, Reptilicus looks like the puppet Ollie on the old *Kukla, Fran, and Ollie* children's program. Actually, not even that good.

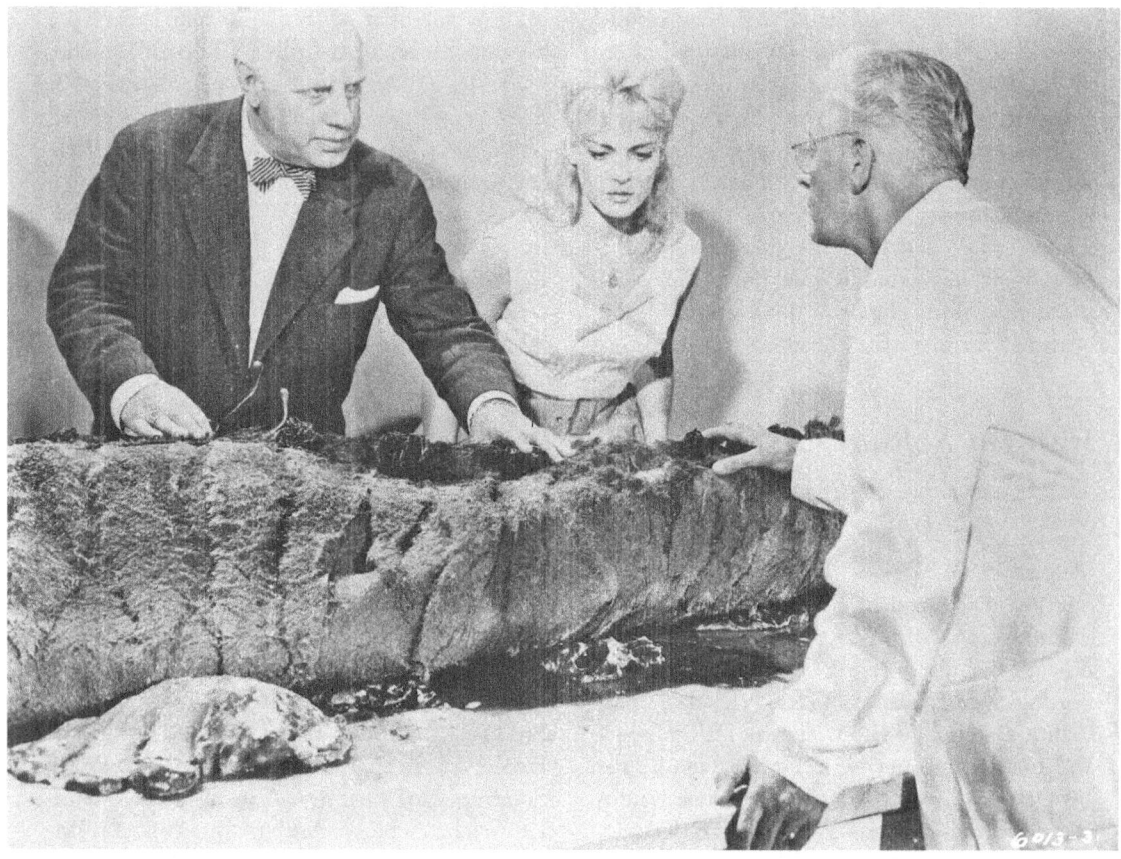

Asbjorn Anderson, Ann Smyrner, and Poul Wildaker examine the frozen tail of *Reptilicus*.

Reptilicus is the most unconvincing monster since *The Giant Claw* (Columbia, 1957). All the "special" effects are equally awful. Reptilicus devours a "cartoon man" at one point and disgorges cartoon green acid slime at several others. Apparently the producer was able to convince the entire population of Copenhagen to participate in this fiasco as much footage is devoted to huge crowds of people running through the streets. When Nicholson and Arkoff got a load of the finished movie, even they were appalled and promptly sued producer Sidney Pink for misrepresentation of product. After editing out some of the more dire special effects (such as Reptilicus flying), AIP finally released the movie. In truth, *Reptilicus* is certainly no worse than many of their other films and actually is quite fun, if you're in the right mood.

The Return of Count Yorga

"A Terrifying Tale of Unearthly Hungers!"

(August 1971) Color by Movielab. A Michael Macready–Bob Kelljan Production. Produced by Michael Macready. Directed by Bob Kelljan. Written by Bob Kelljan and Yvonne Wilder. Starring Robert Quarry, Mariette Hartley, Roger Perry, Yvonne Wilder. DVD: MGM (1.85) 97 min.; Extras: Theatrical trailer. Midnite Movies co-feature: *Count Yorga, Vampire*.

Despite having been staked through the heart and turned into dust, Count Yorga (Robert Quarry) is back. So is his disfigured manservant Brudah (Edward Walsh), who was also "permanently" dispatched in the previous film. No explanation is given as to their return and there is really no connection at all with the first story. Roger Perry is also back but he plays a different character than he did in *Count Yorga, Vampire*. Yorga now lives outside of San Francisco, in a mansion located in close proximity to an orphanage. Mariette Hartley is Cynthia, the girl Yorga meets and falls in love with. With a budget more than double that of its predecessor, *The Return of Count Yorga* is definitely a much more polished production. It also has some truly creepy moments. A young boy is playing ball in a deserted graveyard at dusk and Count Yorga's vampire brides crawl out of their graves to menace him. The same "brides" invade the home of Cynthia's family and slaughter them in a sequence which brings to mind the Charles Manson murders. In an amusing touch, Count Yorga is seen watching a Spanish-language version of *The Vampire Lovers* on television. Producer Michael Macready's father, actor George Macready, has a cameo role as a somewhat addled "vampire expert."

Review: *Cinefantastique* (Spring 1972), "As a follow-up film, it suffers a familiar stigma; too much money but too little inspiration."

Robert Quarry prepares to make Mariette Hartley his undead consort in *The Return of Count Yorga*.

Roadracers

"SCREECHING HELL ON WHEELS ...
IS IT SPORT OR MURDER?"

(March 1959) Black & White. Produced by Stanley Kallis. Directed by Arthur Swerdloff. Written by Ed Lakso and Stanley Kallis. Starring Joel Lawrence, Sally Fraser, Skip Ward, Mason Alan Dinehart, Jr. VHS: Columbia/TriStar (1.33) 73 min. DVD: Direct Video Distribution (1.33) 73 min.; Region-Free DVD from United Kingdom; Extras: Audio interview with Samuel Z. Arkoff; Trailers.

Rob "Leadfoot" Wilson (Joel Lawrence) is a race car driver who has been off the circuit because of a fatal accident caused by his overzealous driving. In reality, Rob hates racing but he has persisted in the sport to try and win the love of his race car–obsessed father. Daddy Wilson (John Shay) has found a new driver, Greg (Skip Ward), who also just happens to be the ex-boyfriend of Rob's current girlfriend, Liz (Marian Collier). When Rob's father rejects him yet again and Liz returns to Greg, "Leadfoot" takes to drink and threatens to kill Greg during the upcoming Grand Prix race. Joel Lawrence is a Tony Curtis type who manages to make his disturbed character tragic and sympathetic, although his part is ostensibly the heavy of the piece. Actually there is far more complexity to the characters than one would expect in a picture of this type. Likable AIP regular Sally Fraser is Rob's concerned sister Joanie. The main title song "Leadfoot" (written by Ed Lakso and sung by Jimmie Madden) is incredibly weird, as are the images which accompany the credits. Unlike most of the other Arkoff titles they released, the Columbia/TriStar video of *Roadracers* is taken from a particularly rough source. The U.K. DVD is far superior quality.

Songs: "Here You Are," "Leadfoot," "Liz"

Rock All Night

"SOME HAVE TO DANCE ... SOME HAVE TO KILL!"

(April 1957) Black & White. Produced and Directed by Roger Corman. Written by Charles B. Griffith. Starring Dick Miller, Abby Dalton, Russell Johnson, Mel Welles. VHS: Columbia/TriStar (1.33) 65 min. DVD: Direct Video Distribution (1.33) 65 min.; Region-Free DVD from United Kingdom; Extras: Audio interview with Samuel Z. Arkoff; Trailers.

Shorty (Dick Miller) is an aptly named guy with a chip on his shoulder who hangs out at Hal's Cloud Nine club. One night Jigger and Joey (Russell Johnson and Jonathan Haze), a pair of murderous thugs who have just pulled a robbery, come into the club. They hold the customers hostage in an attempt to ward off the police. Abby Dalton (with songs dubbed by Nora Hayes) is a nervous singer auditioning for a gig on the night this all comes down. The cast is made up of many of the Corman regulars including Bruno VeSota, Mel Welles, Barboura Morris, Beach Dickerson and Ed Nelson. All of them are given their moment to shine and make the most of it. But it is Dick Miller who makes the greatest emotional impact as the bitter but brave Shorty. The origin of Rock All Night goes back to a 1955 episode of the television series *Jane Wyman Presents The Fireside Theatre* called "The Little Guy." It was written by David Harman, who gets a story credit on the film, and starred Dane Clark as Shorty and Lee Marvin as Jigger. Roger Corman and writer Charles Griffith expanded the 30-minute TV program into a feature-length film by adding a number of musical numbers by The Platters and The

Dick Miller had one of his best roles ever as Shorty in *Rock All Night*.

Blockbusters. The songs are all in the first part of the movie and the remaining half is basically the same as the TV show. In fact, *Rock All Night* looks very much like an early TV drama with the action mostly confined to one set and captured by some uncharacteristically static camerawork by the great Floyd Crosby.

Songs: "I'm Sorry," "He's Mine," "Rock All Night," "I Wanna Rock Now," "Rock and Roll Guitar," "I Guess I Won't Hang Around Here Anymore," "The Great Pretender."

Review: *Harrison's Reports* (May 4, 1957), "An ordinary program picture. There are several musical interludes of the popular variety, but these are not too impressive."

Runaway Daughters

"TEENAGE REBELS! A SHOCKING STORY THAT COULD HAPPEN TO YOU!"

(October 1956) Black & White. A Golden State Production. Produced by Alex Gordon. Directed by Edward L. Cahn. Written by Lou Rusoff. Starring Marla English, Anna Sten, Lance Fuller, Adele Jergens. DVD: Direct Video Distribution (1.33) 91 min.; Region-Free DVD from United Kingdom; Extras: Audio interview with Samuel Z. Arkoff; Trailers.

Audrey (Marla English), Mary (Mary Ellen Kaye) and Angela (Gloria Castillo) are teenage girls with problem parents. Audrey's folks (Anna Sten and John Litel) have got big bucks and they are permissive in the extreme. They will give their daughter anything just as long as she leaves them alone to have a cock-

Runaway Daughters Marla English (left), Mary Ellen Kaye, and madcap Gloria Castillo with their benefactress Adele Jergens.

tail and enjoy themselves. Mary's dad (Jay Adler) is a sick twist who is bitter about the wife who walked out on him. He takes it out on their daughter by being fanatically strict. Angela's much-married mother is off in Acapulco with her new husband, leaving Angela on her own with her ex-con brother Tony (Lance Fuller). Any wonder why these girls are really screwed up? When the girls ditch high school and run off to Los Angeles, Tony's girlfriend Dixie (Adele Jergens) gives them work as "taxi dancers" in her club. Dixie is a tough dame with the requisite heart of gold. She does her best to solve the girls' problems and get them back on the right track. She manages to succeed with two of them. Producer Alex Gordon had a penchant for casting oldtimers in his films whenever possible. This angered Sam Arkoff, who insisted that the youth market couldn't care less. When Gordon cast former Goldwyn star Anna Sten in the mother role in *Runaway Daughters*, Arkoff screamed, "You're casting from the graveyard!" Also in the cast is John Litel, who replaced an ailing Tom Conway at the last minute. The more youthful players include Steve Terrell and Frank Gorshin, who would both reunite with Gloria Castillo and director Edward L. Cahn for *Invasion of the Saucer Men* the following year. Of all the titles in the Direct Video Distribution "Arkoff Film Library," *Runaway Daughters* is taken from the roughest source. The picture is sharp but there are lines and scratches present throughout. Nevertheless it is a fun movie and well worth having.

Samson and the Seven Miracles of the World

"The Wonder Film of the Year!"

(December 1962) ColorScope (Dyaliscope and Technicolor). A Panda Film, Rome-Gallus Film, Paris Production. Produced by Ermanno Donati and Luigi Carpentieri. Directed by Riccardo Freda. Written by Oreste Biancoli and Duccio Tessari. Starring Gordon Scott, Yoko Tani, Helene Chanel, Gabriele Antonini. DVD: Alpha (1.66) 90 min.

In 1959, AIP imported the Italian epic *Nel signo de Roma/The Sign of Rome* and changed the title to *Sign of the Gladiator*. The movie was recut, dubbed into English, and given a wide release. Its subsequent success prompted AIP to import more European costume spectaculars, which could be acquired inexpensively and converted into big bucks at the box office. *Samson and the Seven Miracles of the World* was one of these. Originally titled *Maciste alla corte del gran khan/Maciste in the Court of the Grand Khan*, the plot is a departure from the rest of its sword-and-sandal brethren only by virtue of the pseudo–Chinese locale. An evil Tartar has taken over a Chinese kingdom and is now attempting to do away with the rightful heirs to the throne. Samson appears out of nowhere to aid the oppressed and make mincemeat of their oppressors. To say that Samson, dressed only in a brief red loincloth, looks out of place in a sea of over-dressed extras, is an understatement. Gordon Scott, a former Tarzan, is Samson and he proved to be one of the most popular of the American musclemen to star in European sword-and-sandal films. The Alpha DVD is incorrectly letterboxed at 1.66 instead of 2.35. The Retromedia DVD of this film is the correct 2.35 aspect ratio but has poor color and is missing 10 minutes of footage.

The Savage Seven

"Your town could be their next killing ground..."

(May 1968) Color by Perfect. A Dick Clark Production. Produced by Dick Clark. Directed by Richard Rush. Written by Michael Fisher and Rosalind Ross. Starring Robert Walker Jr., Adam Roarke, Larry Bishop, Joanna Frank. VHS: MGM/Amazon (1.33) 97 min.

Motorcycle gang leader Kisum (Adam Roarke) steers his bikers into an Indian reservation where they cause all manner of mayhem and destruction. Kisum earns the ire of Johnnie Blue Eyes (Robert Walker Jr.) when he makes a pass at Johnnie's sister (Cher lookalike Joanna Frank). The local "white oppressor" starts to throw his weight around (literally) and the bikers join forces with the Indians to fight him. But when an Indian girl is found raped and murdered, the tribe blames the bikers and a bloody battle ensues. There are a number of interesting elements involved in this production: a pre–Laverne Penny Marshall as a biker chick, rock 'n' roll Hall of Fame inductee Duane Eddy as the leader of a biker gang, cinematography by the great Laszlo Kovacs, songs by Cream and Iron Butterfly, and Roger Corman regular Beach Dickerson in a supporting role (and also serving as production assistant). Unfortunately, this all adds up to very little and the end result is just another moderately entertaining biker flick filled with lots of beer-swilling and furniture-smashing.

Review: *Time* (May 24, 1968), "It all ends as it began, in chaos, proving itself ideal kapok to fill out the lower end of double bills in drive-ins."

Schizoid

"BITING, GNAWING TERROR CLAWS AT YOUR BRAIN!"

(March 1973) Technicolor. Produced by Edmondo Amati. Directed by Lucio Fulci. Written by Lucio Fulci, Roberto Gianviti, Jose Molla, Andre Tranche. Starring Florinda Bolkan, Stanley Baker, Jean Sorel, Leo Genn. DVD: Shriek Show (as *Lizard in a Woman's Skin*) (1.85) 96 min.; Extras: Theatrical trailer; Cast and crew interviews; Documentary; Full-screen version.

The 1971 European Giallo *Una lucertola con la pelle di donna/A Lizard in a Woman's Skin* was picked up by AIP and released two years later as *Schizoid*. It was also shown under the original title for some engagements. Carol Hammond (Florinda Bolkan) is plagued by nightmares involving her fast-living neighbor Julia (Anita Strindberg). One night Carol dreams that she murders Julia and the next day the woman is found stabbed to death. Near the corpse is Carol's fur coat and a bloody letter opener. Is Carol the killer or has she been set up by person or persons unknown? This is an especially well-made thriller and one of the most stylish films by Lucio Fulci, a director whose work is often compromised by his use of excessive gore. The full-screen version on the DVD is in Italian with English subtitles and runs about three minutes longer but the print quality is inferior to the letterboxed version.

Scream and Scream Again

"TRIPLE DISTILLED HORROR ... AS POWERFUL AS A VAT OF BOILING ACID!"

(February 1970) Color by Movielab. An Amicus Production. Produced by Max J. Rosenberg and Milton Subotsky. Directed by Gordon Hessler. Written by Christopher Wicking. Starring Vincent Price, Christopher Lee, Peter Cushing, Michael Gothard. DVD: MGM (1.85) 95 min.; Extras: Theatrical trailer. Midnite Movies co-feature: *The Oblong Box*.

Three separate and seemingly unrelated plotlines come together at the clinic of Dr. Browning (Vincent Price), a research scientist who is experimenting to create composite beings, half human and half synthetic. Based on *The Disoriented Man* by Peter Saxon, the film was originally announced under the title *Screamer*. The script jettisons the invading aliens of the novel and improves on it by instead playing up the political ramifications of the plot. Producers Rosenberg and Subotsky had the rights to the book and brought it to the attention of Louis M. Heyward at AIP, but apparently neither of them cared much for the finished product. This may have been because executive producer Heyward eventually banished Subotsky from the set because of his continual interference with the production. Although the three great horror stars of the period are given star billing, none of them has much screen time. Peter Cushing appears in what is little more than a cameo. Price and Christopher Lee fare somewhat better. Price makes the most of his part and manages, once again, to give a memorable performance with very little to work with. The most frightening and disturbing aspect of *Scream and Scream Again* deals with a half human serial killer who preys on girls who are part of the mod club scene. The DVD restores the original score by David Whitaker, which had been replaced in some video versions of the film.

Review: *Variety* (February 4, 1970), "Very effective, suspensefully developed and gory horror story with spy and sci-fi overtones."

Scream Blacula Scream

"THE BLACK PRINCE OF SHADOWS STALKS THE EARTH AGAIN!"

(June 1973) Color by Movielab. Produced by Joseph T. Naar. Directed by Bob Kelljan. Written by Joan Torres, Raymond Koenig, and Maurice Jules. Starring William Marshall, Pam Grier, Don Mitchell, Michael Conrad. DVD: MGM (1.85) 96 min.; Extras: Theatrical trailer.

In this sequel, the vampire Blacula (William Marshall) is resurrected by a voodoo ritual. Dismayed at having been brought back to a life of the undead, he attempts to have Lisa (Pam Grier), the leader of a voodoo cult, exorcise him of the vampire curse. Although the formula is similar to the first film, this is the better of the two. Marshall is given more dialogue and manages to elicit some sympathy for his character. The wonderful Grier, queen of blaxploitation cinema, gets to display a venerability that is usually lacking in her more "baadasssss" roles of the period. This time around the direction is by Bob Kelljan who had plenty of experience with vampires, having previously helmed AIP's two "Count Yorga" movies. In the last scene, the police raid a mansion full of Blacula's vampire minions who all have big fangs as well as even bigger hair. Blacula's demise is less conclusive than in the previous film, leaving the way open for another sequel that never happened.

The Screaming Skull

"THE TORTURED GHOST WHO CLAIMED VENGEANCE IN THE BRIDE'S BEDROOM!"

(August 1958) Black & White. A Madera production. Produced and Written by John Kneubuhl. Directed by Alex Nicol. Starring John Hudson, Peggy Webber, Alex Nicol, Russ Conway. DVD: Goodtimes (1.33) 67 min.

Newlyweds Eric and Jenni Whitlock return to the mansion he shared with his first wife, who died under mysterious circumstances. Before long, Jenni begins to fear that the ghost of the deceased wife has returned to haunt her. Is it really a supernatural occurrence or a plot to drive the new bride insane? John Hudson is the look-alike brother of actor William Hudson, who appeared in *Attack of the 50 Foot Woman* and *The Amazing Colossal Man*.

Alex Nicol does double duty, directing and playing Mickey, the dimwitted caretaker of the estate. *The Screaming Skull* is available from a number of sources but the Goodtimes DVD is better quality than the others,

Don Mitchell and Pam Grier share a rare peaceful moment in *Scream Blacula Scream*.

although a few seconds of Peggy Webber undressing is missing from this print.

Review: *Variety* (November 12, 1958), "[Alex] Nicol's direction isn't able to rise above static qualities of the script."

Shake, Rattle and Rock!

"The Rockin', Rollin', Boppinest Jam Session You've Ever Seen!"

(October 1956) Black & White. A Sunset Production. Produced by James H. Nicholson. Directed by Edward L. Cahn. Written by Lou Rusoff. Starring Touch Connors, Lisa Gaye, Sterling Holloway, Raymond Hatton. VHS: Columbia/TriStar (1.33) 77 min. DVD: Direct Video Distribution (1.33) 77 min.; Region-Free DVD from United Kingdom; Extras: Audio interview with Samuel Z. Arkoff; Trailers.

"Local Disc Jockey Faces Possible Arrest for Complicity in Rock and Roll Orgy" screams the newspaper headline in *Shake, Rattle and Rock!* and that just about sums up the plot of the movie. Deejay and TV rock and roll dance show host Garry Nelson (Touch Connors) just wants to help keep his teenage audience out of trouble. A group of "concerned" citizens (a.k.a. conservative fuddy duddies) wants to eradicate the evils of rock and roll which inevitably leads to "lust and crime." This group is led by Douglass Dumbrille, Raymond Hatton, Percy Helton, and frequent Marx Brothers foil Margaret Dumont. Out to get rid of Nelson's positive influence on the teenagers and lead them into lives of crime is gangster Bugsy Smith. The climax of the movie is a televised trial in which the home audience is asked to phone in their verdict. Kind of like *American Idol* without the singers. Bugsy is played by Paul Dubov, who seems to be the direct prototype for Harvey Lembeck's character Eric Von Zipper in the "Beach Party" movies. Also in the cast are Lisa Gaye (Debra Paget's look-alike sister) and the incredibly annoying Sterling Holloway. The one reason that this film deserves a place in motion picture history is the presence of the great Fats Domino performing three numbers, including his big hit "Ain't That a Shame." The other performers on hand are Joe Turner, Choker Campbell and His Band, Tommy Charles, and Annita Ray.

Songs: "I'm in Love Again," "Honey Chile," "Ain't That a Shame," "Feelin' Happy," "Lipstick Powder and Paint," "Rock Rock Rock," "Sweet Love on My Mind," "Rockin' Saturday Night"

The She-Creature

"Hypnotized ... Reincarnated as a Monster from Hell!"

(July 1956) Black & White. A Golden State Production. Produced by Alex Gordon. Directed by Edward L. Cahn. Written by Lou Rusoff. Starring Chester Morris, Marla English, Cathy Downs, Lance Fuller. DVD: Lionsgate (1.33) 77 min.; DVD co-feature: *Day the World Ended*.

Yet another Paul Blaisdell creation: *The She-Creature*.

In the early 1950s, hypnotism, reincarnation, and age regression were in the headlines thanks to the highly publicized case of "Bridey Murphy." In 1952 a Colorado housewife named Virginia Tighe recalled, while under hypnosis, her past life as a 19th century woman from Cork, Ireland, named Bridey Murphy. The book-length account of this, *The Search for Bridey Murphy* by Morey Bernstein, was published in 1956 and became a bestseller. That same year Hollywood jumped on the reincarnation bandwagon and released three films on the subject: *I've Lived Before* (Universal), *The Search for Bridey Murphy* (Paramount), and *The She-Creature*, which beat both of the others into theatres by several months. In *The She-Creature* a carnival hypnotist named Lombardi (Chester Morris) is able to regress his lovely assistant Andrea (Marla English) into an amphibious prehistoric monster with murderous tendencies. *The She-Creature* has a very grave tone and an exceptionally strong cast. Both John Carradine and Peter Lorre were approached to play Lombardi and both declined. Former "Boston Blackie" Chester Morris eventually ended up with the part. Other veteran performers on hand are Tom Conway and Frieda Inescort. Also in the cast is one of the Hudson brothers, William, in a supporting role as Cathy Downs' drunken former fiancé. The She-Creature itself is one of Paul Blaisdell's most memorably over-the-top creations and has become an icon of fifties horror movies.

Review: *Variety* (September 5, 1956), "Director Edward L. Cahn manages to mix in a good quota of chills."

She Gods of Shark Reef

"Beautiful Maidens in a Lush Tropical Paradise Ruled by a Hideous Stone God"

(August 1958) Pathécolor. Produced by Ludwig Gerber. Directed by Roger Corman. Written

Don Durant, Bill Cord, Lisa Montell, and Jeanne Gerson spot something in the tide pools in *She Gods of Shark Reef*.

by Robert Hill and Victor Stoloff. Starring Don Durant, Bill Cord, Lisa Montell, Jeanne Gerson. DVD: Alpha (1.33) 63 min.

Two brothers, one good and one bad, are shipwrecked on a Polynesian island populated by female pearl divers. When one of the local girls falls in love with the good brother, the angry gods demand sacrifice. She is chosen to be thrown into the shark-infested waters surrounding the stone idol of their vengeful god. If this sounds intriguing, it isn't. While Roger Corman was in Hawaii making *Naked Paradise*, independent producer Ludwig Gerber hired him to direct the existing script for this one. Released with typically spectacular AIP poster art, which belies the dull content of the actual movie, this was an uncharacteristic misfire for Corman. The Alpha DVD is an abysmal transfer, which certainly doesn't help the situation.

Review: *Variety* (December 10, 1958), "Film boasts fine color, rich red blood, capable underwater photography and very little story."

Sheba, Baby

"Hotter 'n 'Coffy' ...
Meaner 'n 'Foxy Brown'"

(March 1975) Color by Movielab. A William Girdler/David Sheldon Production. Produced by David Sheldon. Directed by William Girdler. Written by William Girdler and David Sheldon. Starring Pam Grier, Austin Stoker, D'Urville Mason, David Merrifield. DVD: MGM (1.85) 91 min.; Extras: Theatrical trailer.

Sheba Shayne (Pam Grier) is a classy private eye who is determined to get even with the local crime lord responsible for the death of her father. *Sheba, Baby* never comes close to reaching the delirious heights of that ultimate Pam Grier vehicle, *Foxy Brown*. In fact, it is surprisingly subdued by blaxploitation standards. Grier still manages to kick some ass but she remains sensibly clothed throughout ... and with nary an Afro in sight. Actually, to the movie's credit, *Sheba, Baby* plays more like an action flick which just happens to have a black heroine. The one major lapse into typical blaxploitation territory comes in the person of Christopher Fry, whose performance as a petty loan shark in a pimp suit is embarrassing, to put it mildly. The director of *Sheba, Baby* was William Girdler, who was soon to become famous (or infamous, depending on your point of view) for such pictures as *Grizzly* (1976) and *Day of the Animals* (1977). Prior to *Sheba, Baby*, Girdler had directed AIP's *Abby* (1974), a blaxploitation take on *The Exorcist*. Girdler's final movie was *The Manitou* (1978); he died in a helicopter crash before the film was released. He was only 30 years old. He had stated that *Sheba, Baby* was his least favorite of the films he had directed, although it is actually a more accomplished effort than some of his other movies.

Sign of the Gladiator

"Wondrous Spectacle Bigger Than
Anything You Have Ever Seen!!!"

(October 1959) ColorScope (Dyaliscope and Eastman Color). A Glomer Film Production. Produced by Vittorio Musy-Glory. Directed by Guido Brignone. Written by Sergio Leone, Guido Brignone, Giuseppe Mangione, Francisco Thellung, Francesco De Feo. Starring Anita Ekberg, Georges Marchal, Lorella De Luca, Jacques Sernas. VHS: Meteor Video (1.33) 80 min.

American International's first Euro-epic import was originally titled *Nel signo de Roma/The Sign of Rome*. Both Nicholson and Arkoff thought the film had exploitation potential so they purchased the U.S. distribution rights, shortened it by 18 minutes, dubbed it into English, and retitled it *Sign of the Gladiator*. The fact that there was no gladiator in the film did not deter them. The title change was justified when AIP supplied narration in which Roman counsel Marcus Valerius (Georges Marchal) is said to have been a former gladiator. In Sam Arkoff's autobiography he claims "we also spliced in a shot of a gladiator from another film," but there is no evidence of this in the movie. Cunning Marcus Valerius allows himself to be captured by Xenobia (Anita Ekberg), queen of Palmyra. He convinces her that he has deserted the Romans and wishes to aid her in a war against Rome. Meanwhile her evil advisor is planning to sell her out to the Persians. Also thrown into the mix is a subplot involving another Roman officer (Jacques Sernas) who is in love with a virgin priestess in the Palmyra temple. When Marcus Valerius and Queen Xenobia fall in love, things really get complicated. *Sign of the Gladiator*, while no work of art, is fairly diverting entertainment. At the time of its release, the U.S. market had not yet been saturated with dubbed imports (as it soon would be) and the movie did respectable business at the box office. Production values are of a generally high caliber, in particular the impressive costumes designed by Vittorio Nino Novarese. The cast is an interesting one. In addition to the leads, it also includes genre regulars Folco Lulli, Chelo Alonso, Arturo Dominici, and Mimmo Palmara. AIP filmed new opening credits showing a dancing girl and closing credits featuring the song "Xenobia" sung by Bill Lee. The rare Meteor Video VHS tape is a poor transfer but it does letterbox the opening and closing AIP credits.

Review: *New York Herald Tribune* (December 3, 1959), "The plot is as thin as some of the costumes Miss Ekberg wears."

Georges Marchal romances Anita Ekberg in AIP's first sword-and-sandal import, *Sign of the Gladiator*.

Sisters

"WHAT THE DEVIL HATH JOINED TOGETHER LET NO MAN CUT ASUNDER!"

(March 1973) Color by Movielab. A Pressman-Williams Production. Produced by Edward R. Pressman. Directed by Brian De Palma. Written by Brian De

Bill Finley fights Margot Kidder in Brian De Palma's *Sisters*.

Palma and Louisa Rose. Starring Margot Kidder, Jennifer Salt, Charles Durning, Bill Finley. DVD: Criterion (1.85) 92 min.; Extras: Various print articles, essays, and publicity galleries.

Although he had already directed six features prior to Sisters, Brian De Palma truly hit his stride with this stylish shocker. Journalist Grace Collier (Jennifer Salt) witnesses a murder from the window of her apartment. When the police arrive, there is no evidence of a crime having been committed. Grace decides to do some investigating on her own and discovers a terrifying secret about her seemingly sweet and innocent neighbor Danielle Breton (Margot Kidder). Alternating between humor and horror, Sisters is an audacious and fascinating motion picture. There are a number of wonderful set pieces but the most memorable, and disturbing, is a hallucinatory dream sequence in which Salt imagines herself as the Siamese Twin of Margot Kidder. Bernard Herrmann contributes a typically excellent score which greatly enhances the impact of the images it accompanies.

Review: *Time* (April 30, 1963), "It is a homage by a gifted, if erratic, young director [De Palma] to one of the cinema's genuine masters, Alfred Hitchcock."

Ski Party

"IT'S WHERE THE HE'S MEET THE SHE'S ON SKIS AND THERE'S ONLY ONE WAY TO GET WARM!"

(June 1965) Panavision and Pathécolor. Produced by Gene Corman. Directed by Alan Rafkin. Written by Robert Kaufman. Starring Frankie Avalon, Dwayne Hickman, Deborah Walley, Yvonne Craig. DVD: MGM (2.35) 91 min.; Extras: Theatrical trailer. Midnite Movies co-feature: *Muscle Beach Party*.

The Beach Party gang give up "surf" for "snow" in this nonsensical outing. Todd (Frankie Avalon) and Craig (Dwayne Hickman) are a couple of sexually frustrated college buddies who constantly strike out with their prospective girlfriends Linda (Deborah Walley) and Barbara (Yvonne Craig). Determined to impress the girls with their skiing prowess, Todd and Craig head off to the mountains for the college weekend ski party. Once there, the boys' ski class proves to be too much for them so they join the slower paced girls' class. However, to do this they have to dress up like girls. When Todd and Craig become Jane and Nora, the movie becomes the AIP version of *Some Like It Hot*. Lesley Gore and James Brown are on hand to sing some songs; watch for Dick Miller in the small part of a taxi driver. Annette Funicello even has two brief scenes at the beginning as a sex education instructor. The film closes with a plug for the forthcoming *Cruise Party*, which was never made.

Mike Nader, who appears in most of the Beach Party films, was the nephew of actor George Nader. Much later, as Michael Nader, he had the recurring role of Dex Dexter in the TV series *Dynasty*.

Songs: "Ski Party," "The Gasser," "Paintin' the Town," "Lots Lots More," "We'll Never Change Them," "Sunshine Lollipops and Rainbows," "I Got You"

Sorority Girl

"SABRA—SMART ... PRETTY ... AND ALL BAD!"

(October 1957) Black & White. Produced and Directed by Roger Corman. Written by Ed Waters and Leo Lieberman. Starring Susan Cabot, Dick Miller, Barboura O'Neill, June Kenney. VHS: Columbia/TriStar (1.33) 60 min. DVD: Direct Video Distribution (1.33) 60 min.; Region-Free DVD from United Kingdom; Extras: Audio interview with Samuel Z. Arkoff; Trailers.

Although he is mostly known for his sci-fi–horror films, Roger Corman has also directed a number of lesser known gems such as *Sorority Girl*. Corman assembled his familiar group of actors for this tragic story of a disturbed young woman and the havoc she attempts to wreak on her sorority sisters. Susan Cabot gives a powerhouse performance as

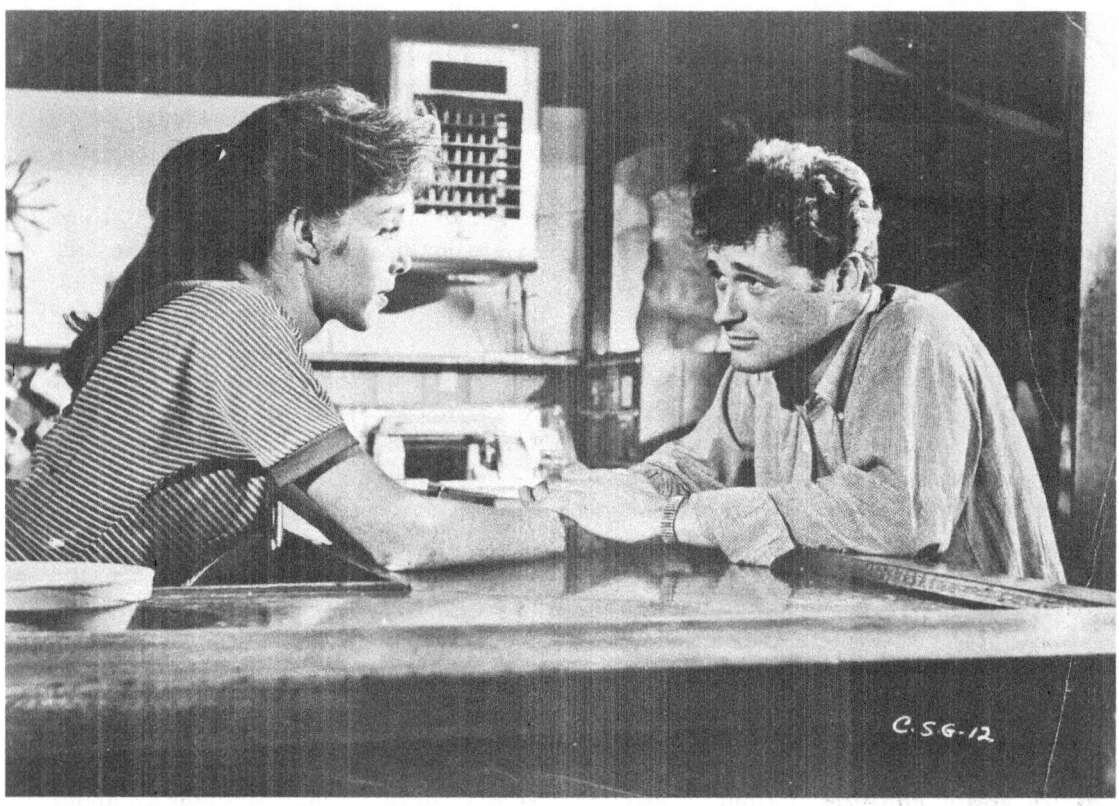

Barboura O'Neill (a.k.a. Barboura Morris) shares a tender moment with Dick Miller in *Sorority Girl*.

Sabra, a miserable and misunderstood member of Xi Sigma sorority. Although her peers think Sabra has it all, she is really an unloved, unhappy product of a neglectful upbringing. Also on hand is Barboura O'Neill (later Barboura Morris) as Sabra's highly principled roommate Rita. Rounding out a trio of excellent performances is Dick Miller, for once cast as a handsome leading man. Cabot always managed to outact whoever she was in a scene with, and this film is no exception. Early in Cabot's film career she was under contract to Universal-International where she was cast in a variety of lightweight costume pictures and Westerns. Fed up with the roles she was given, she left Universal and moved to New York where Corman saw her in a stageplay. He convinced her to return to Hollywood and, although the films she made for him were no more prestigious than those she had done at Universal, she was given a wide variety of roles in which she could and did shine. Now she is best remembered for her bizarre death at the hands of her son in 1986. Special mention should be made of the wonderful main title design by Bill Martin which basically relates, in abstract images, the plot of the movie to follow. The original shooting title was *Confessions of a Sorority Girl*.

Review: *Harrison's Reports* (November 30, 1957), "Though the story is not a knockout *Sorority Girl* is fairly interesting."

Spirits of the Dead

"EDGAR ALLAN POE'S ULTIMATE ORGY!"

(July 1969) Color by Berkey Pathé (Eastman Color). Les Films Marceau-Cocinor (Paris) and Produzioni Europee Associate (Rome). Three episodes that make up the movie: "Metzengerstein"—Directed by Roger Vadim. Written by

Roger Vadim, Pascal Cousin, and Clement Biddlewood. Starring Jane Fonda, Peter Fonda, James Robertson-Justice, Anny Duperey; "William Wilson"—Directed by Louis Malle. Written by Louis Malle, Clement Biddlewood, and Daniel Boulanger. Starring Alain Delon, Brigitte Bardot, Umberto D'Orsi, Daniele Vargas; "Toby Dammit"—Directed by Federico Fellini. Written by Federico Fellini and Bernardino Zapponi. Starring Terence Stamp, Salvo Randone, Fabrizio Angeli, Marina Yaru. DVD: Home Vision Entertainment (1.75) 121 min.; In French with English subtitles.

One of the most unusual movies in AIP's long history is *Spirits of the Dead*, a French-Italian co-production originally entitled *Histoires Extrordinaires d'après Edgar Allan Poe*. Apparently feeling they had a monopoly on cinematic interpretations of Poe's work, AIP bought the U.S. distribution rights and changed the title to *Spirits of the Dead*. They cut out four minutes of potentially questionable material and added Vincent Price reciting a bit of the Poe poem to justify the title change. Presto! We have another AIP Poe horror film! Helmed by three of European cinema's most esteemed directors, the movie is a mixed bag and definitely more of an art film. The first, and weakest, segment is Roger Vadim's "Metzengerstein" starring his then-wife Jane Fonda. It tells the tale of dissolute Countess Frederica Metzengerstein (Fonda), who falls in love with her cousin Wilhelm (a very uncomfortable acting Peter Fonda). When Wilhelm spurns her, Frederica has his barn set ablaze but he is accidentally killed in the conflagration. A mysterious black horse appears shortly thereafter and Frederica becomes obsessed with it. Dressed in outlandish costumes which make her look like a medieval Barbarella, Jane Fonda gives one of her worst performances

Spirits of the Dead: James Robertson-Justice and Jane Fonda in "Metzengerstein."

Spirits of the Dead: Terence Stamp in "Toby Dammit."

ever. Director Vadim worships her in every scene as the slight story crawls to its eagerly anticipated conclusion. Louis Malle fares better with his segment, "William Wilson." Alain Delon portrays the title character, a cruel and ruthless man who discovers that he has a doppelganger with a conscience. Brigitte Bardot, smoking a cigar and wearing a terrible black wig, becomes the object of Wilson's scorn and duplicity. The highlight of *Spirits of the Dead* is the final segment directed by Federico Fellini. Filled with typically bizarre Fellini imagery, "Toby Dammit" stars Terence Stamp as a British movie star on the skids; he comes to Rome to make a Spaghetti Western to be financed by the Catholic Church. But Toby can't seem to shake the devil which is driving him to self-destruction. The DVD of *Spirits of the Dead* is the full-length European version minus the Vincent Price voiceover and with far superior color than the AIP theatrical prints.

Review: *Motion Picture Herald* (July 23, 1969), "AIP, in picking up the American distribution rights, has apparently tried to tailor it to a less sophisticated shocker-exploitation audience."

Squirm

"THIS WAS THE NIGHT OF THE CRAWLING TERROR!"

(July 1976) Color by Movielab. An Edgar Lansbury-Joseph Beruh Production. Produced by George Manasse. Written and Directed by Jeff Lieberman. Starring Don Scardino, Patricia Pearcy, R.A. Dow, Jean Sullivan. DVD: MGM (1.85) 93 min.; Extras: Theatrical trailer; TV spot; Audio commentary by Jeff Lieberman.

Squirm is one of several "nature strikes back" horror films of the seventies (including AIP's *Frogs*). A terrible storm brings down the power lines near Fly Creek, Georgia, sending millions of volts of electricity into the wet ground. The following morning, New York City boy Mick (Don Scardino) arrives in Fly Creek to visit his new girlfriend Geri (Patricia Pearcy). He immediately runs afoul of the town's redneck sheriff and a slow-witted handyman who also has designs on Geri. A series of horrible incidents causes Mick to realize that the electrically charged earth is stirring up the local worm population. When night falls, the worms begin to crawl out of the mud in countless numbers, devouring anybody who gets in their way. The DVD of *Squirm* actually looks far better than the murky theatrical prints which circulated at the time of the film's original release. The effectively gruesome makeup effects were provided by Rick Baker, the same year he played the title role in Dino De Laurentiis' excessively maligned remake of *King Kong*. A very busy year indeed for the talented Mr. Baker as he also did uncredited work on Bert I. Gordon's *The Food of the Gods* for AIP.

Submarine Seahawk

"Sliding Through Cold, Murky Depths ... The Secret Sub Than Won a War!"

(February 1959) Black & White. A Golden State Production. Produced by Alex Gordon. Directed by Spencer G. Bennet. Written by Lou Rusoff. Starring John Bentley, Brett Halsey, Wayne Heffley, Steve Mitchell. VHS: Columbia/TriStar (1.33) 83 min.

In this tepid World War II tale, the submarine *Seahawk* is given a new commanding officer and an important assignment. Although Capt. Paul Turner (John Bentley) is considered cold-hearted and aloof, his military savvy makes him the most qualified officer for a top secret reconnaissance mission. Turner's task is to locate a hidden harbor where the Japanese fleet is docking its warships. The other senior officers aboard are Bill Hallohan (Paul Maxwell), who has been passed over for the command of the *Seahawk* in favor of Turner, and neurotic newcomer David Shore (Brett Halsey), a human time bomb waiting to explode. You can tell this because he is always sweating and there are dark circles around his eyes. The bulk of this film consists of the officers hashing it out in one room of the sub while the fun-loving, goofy crew makes wisecracks in another. Every once in a while they throw in some World War II stock footage or a scene from another war movie to provide some much-needed action. Typical of AIP publicity, the minor character of Maizie (Mabel Rea), a B-girl in a Honolulu bar, shows up prominently in the advertising as "Maizie: She had been through hell so war was heaven!" Sounds like her story is more interesting than the one in the movie.

Review: *Variety* (January 28, 1959), "It's been done before but it's still engrossing."

Succubus

"This Motion Picture is the Story of a Kind of Woman You May Not Have Known Even Existed."

(April 1969) Eastman Color. An Aquila Film Enterprises Production, Berlin. A Trans-American Films Release. Produced by Adrian Hoven. Directed by Jess Franco. Written by Pier A. Caminneci. Starring Janine Reynaud, Jack Taylor, Adrien Hoven, Michel Lemoine. DVD: Anchor Bay (1.33) 76 min.; Extras: Theatrical trailer.

Wikipedia defines a Succubus as "a female demon which comes to men in their dreams to seduce them ... drawing energy from the men to sustain themselves often until the point of exhaustion or death." Lorna Green (Janine Reynaud) is a performer in a pseudo S&M nightclub act staged by her lover, William (Jack Taylor). Lorna has nightmares in which she kills her lovers, both male and female and, seemingly, these people turn up dead the next morning. You never really know what is real and what isn't in this picture. Dwarfs, drags, drugs, and debauchery ... *Succubus* has it all. All, that is, except for a coherent plot. Spanish director Jess Franco is one of the most prolific, and erratic, filmmakers of all time. This was one of his attempts to make an "art house" exploitation movie. He does successfully maintain a hallucinatory atmosphere throughout. Filmed in West Germany under the title *Necronomicon* and running 84 minutes, the film was first shown at the Berlin Film Festival. According to a press release at the time, Janine Reynaud announced there that she hoped to become "first lady of the horror sex film." She quickly followed *Succubus* with Adrian Hoven's *Castle of Bloody Lust* and Jess Franco's *Kiss Me Monster*. Later she appeared in Sergio Martino's excellent Giallo *The Case of the Scorpion's Tail* (1971). She may not have become "the first lady of the horror sex film" but she certainly gave it her best shot. In *Succubus* she is a striking presence. When clothed, which isn't often, she wears outfits created by designer Karl Lagerfeld. The film was given an "X" rating by the MPAA so AIP released it through their sleazy movie division, Trans-American Films. In 2006, Blue Underground DVD reissued *Succubus* remastered in 1.66 aspect ratio.

Sugar Hill

"Devil Woman with Voodoo Powers to Raise the Savage Dead!"

(February 1974) Color by Movielab. Produced by Elliot Schick. Directed by Paul Maslansky. Written by Tim Kelly. Starring Marki Bey, Robert Quarry, Don Pedro Colley, Richard Lawson. VHS: Orion (1.33) 91 min.

Sugar Hill's (Marki Bey) boyfriend Langston (Larry D. Johnson) refuses to sell his successful nightclub to crimelord Morgan (Robert Quarry), so Morgan has his henchmen beat Langston to death. Sugar, of course, vows to get revenge and enlists the aid of local voodoo queen Mama Maitresse (Zara Culley) to help her. Mama conjures up the spirit of Baron Samedi (Don Pedro Colley) and his army of blank-eyed, machete-wielding zombies who become the instruments of Sugar's vengeance. This rather deft combination of blaxploitation and horror seems far less contrived than the *Blacula* films and there are some effective sequences in which the undead kill their victims while Sugar gloats on the sidelines. Bey may lack Pam Grier's strong presence but she is quite a looker and does reasonably well in the title role. Quarry is as hammy as ever but this time with the added bonus of a Southern accent.

Song: "Supernatural Voodoo Woman"

Suicide Battalion

"To hell with orders ... we attack!"

(February 1958) Black & White. A Zuma Production. Produced and Written by Lou Rusoff. Directed by Edward L. Cahn. Starring Michael Connors, John Ashley, Russ Bender, Jewell Lain. VHS: Columbia/TriStar (1.33) 79 min.; VHS co-feature: *Hell Squad*.

In addition to their sci-fi–horror movies and teenage angst films, AIP also made a number of black and white World War II dramas during the late fifties and early sixties. Armed with hours of actual World War II stock footage, AIP produced these films employing tiny casts and minuscule budgets (even for them). Most of the plots concern a small group of men who must undertake a top secret, dangerous mission which will almost certainly result in death for some or all involved. That's the plot of *Suicide Battalion* as well. Tough-talking Major Matt McCormick (Michael Connors) takes five volunteers to blow up a building housing important military documents which is now in Japanese occupied territory on a South Pacific island. Interspersed with poorly matched World War II footage are zany scenes in which McCormick's madcap lunks attempt to help lovesick teenager Tommy Novello (John Ashley) get engaged to his native sweetheart Cho Cho (Jackie Joseph ... several years before her turn as Audrey in the original *Little Shop of Horrors*). Predictably, when things start to get serious, Tommy is the first casualty. In this, his last movie for AIP, Touch Connors had finally graduated to using his real name, Michael. Sometime-singer John Ashley had, according to the press book for *Suicide Battalion*, "just finished a rock and roll tour of Texas and Oklahoma." Also in the cast is camp Hawaiian icon Hilo Hattie, the woman who helped put the Muumuu on the fashion map.

Review: *Variety* (March 26, 1958), "For its class is a well-produced little feature."

Super Stooges vs. the Wonder Women

"SHUDDER AT INCREDIBLE FEATS OF SUPER HUMAN STRENGTH!"

(February 1975) Techniscope and Technicolor. Produced by Ovidio Assonitis and Giorgio Carlo Rossi. Directed by Al Bradley (a.k.a. Alfonso Brescia). Written by Alfonso Brescia and Aldo Crudo. Starring Nick Jordon (Aldo Canti), Marc Hannibal, Yueh Hua, Malisa Longo. DVD: Rarescope/BCI (as *Amazons vs. Supermen*) (2.35) 105 min.; Extra: Trailers.

AIP picked up the Italian feature *Superuomini, Superdonne, Superbotte* for a planned 1974 release but held it back until the following year. It's amazing that it was released at all. When his friend is killed by the queen of the Amazons (Magda Konopka) and her warrior women, Aru (Nick Jordon) swears to avenge him. With the help of African warrior Mug (Marc Hannibal) and Chinese martial arts expert Chang (Yueh Hua), Aru sets off to put an end to the cruel rule of the Amazons forever. The slim plot is merely an excuse for kung fu hijinks and lowbrow comedy. As if the content of the film wasn't bad enough, the DVD has poor color and substandard image.

Yueh Hua, left, demonstrates his martial arts skills in the insufferable *Super Stooges vs. the Wonder Women*.

Tales of Terror

"A TRILOGY OF SHOCK AND HORROR!

(August 1962) Panavision and Pathécolor. Produced and Directed by Roger Corman. Written by Richard Matheson. Starring Vincent Price, Basil Rathbone, Peter Lorre, Debra Paget. DVD: MGM (2.35) 80 min.; Extras: Theatrical trailer. Midnite Movies co-feature: *Twice Told Tales*.

In this, the third of Roger Corman's series of Edgar Allan Poe movies, Vincent Price gives three effective and varied performances. "Morella" has him as a man whose dead wife returns for revenge. Price is the victim of his mistress' vengeful husband (Peter Lorre) in a wry telling of "The Black Cat." "The Case of M. Valdemar" finds him as a terminally ill man who is hypnotized at the point of death with horrifying results. Price is given wonderful support by those outstanding screen veterans Peter Lorre and Basil Rathbone, who would return to appear with him in subsequent AIP productions. Joyce Jameson does a delightful comic turn in the "Black Cat" sequence as Lorre's sweet but empty-headed wife. And the beautiful Debra Paget plays Price's devoted spouse in "The Case of M. Valdemar." The single release MGM DVD has both fullscreen and widescreen versions.

Review: *New York Times* (July 5, 1962), "A dull, absurd and trashy adaptation of three Edgar Allan Poe stories."

Publicity sketch for the sequence "The Black Cat" in *Tales of Terror*.

Unless you are a martial arts fanatic, this is definitely a movie to skip.

Tank Commandos

"BATTLE BORN PASSIONS OF DEFIANT MEN AT WAR!"

(March 1959) Black & White. A James H. Nicholson and Samuel Z. Arkoff Production. Produced, Directed and Written by Burt Topper. Starring Wally Campo, Maggie Lawrence, Robert Barron, Donato Farretta. VHS: Columbia/TriStar (1.33) 79 min.

American soldiers fight Nazis in 1944 Italy in this war film. Lieutenant Jim Blaine (Robert Barron) leads a small group of demolition experts on a mission to discover how German tanks are crossing a seemingly unfordable river. The troop has adopted an Italian war orphan named Diano (Donato Ferretta) who seems to be inspired by the character of "Dondi" in the comic strip of the same name. But *Tank Commandos* is certainly no comic strip. It is one of the bleakest and most hard-hitting of the AIP war movies. Decent characterization and acting plus a melancholy Ronald Stein score all contribute to making this film an above-average endeavor. On the downside, Jo Ann Hill sings a sappy song called "Diano" over the beginning and end credits.

Review: *Harrison's Reports* (March 7, 1959), "A fair program war melodrama. Has considerable action and suspense but is somewhat lacking in appreciable human interest."

Teenage Caveman

"PREHISTORIC REBELS AGAINST PREHISTORIC MONSTERS!"

(July 1958) Superama and Black & White. Produced and Directed by Roger Corman. Written by R. Wright Campbell. Starring Robert Vaughn, Darrah Marshall, Leslie Bradley, Frank De Kova. DVD: Lionsgate (1.33) 66 min.; DVD co-feature: *Viking Women and the Sea Serpent*.

Leslie Bradley and Robert Vaughn examine the body of "The God Who Gives Death with a Touch" in *Teenage Caveman*.

Teenage Caveman and its DVD companion feature were each filmed with a budget of $70,000 and a ten-day shooting schedule. The big difference is that *Teenage Caveman* never attempts to go beyond its humble means. This is not to suggest that it doesn't suffer from its economies. As with *Viking Women and the Sea Serpent*, many of the costumes look as if they were fashioned from bath mats. The prehistoric animal sequences are stock footage from the 1940 version of *One Million B.C.* The movie also manages to incorporate some scenes from *Day the World Ended* and *The She-Creature*. Despite this economizing, the film works and has much to recommend it. The screenplay by R. Wright Campbell has more than a few speculative ideas and there are some sincere performances. On hand are Corman regulars Jonathan Haze, Ed Nelson, Beach Dickerson and, in one brief shot, Barboura Morris. Dickerson gets a real workout as he appears in a number of roles in various guises, including a bear. Robert Vaughn, years before his success in the *Man from U.N.C.L.E.* television series, plays the "teenage" title character, although his age was twenty-six at the time. He is "The Boy" who questions the laws of his clan and dares to venture into the forbidden territory beyond the river where the fearsome "God Who Gives Death with a Touch" dwells. Bronson Caves, one of the most overused locations in Hollywood during the fifties, has seldom been shown to greater effect and makes for a perfect primitive terrain. Originally the film was called *Prehistoric World* but it was changed to *Teenage Caveman* by Nicholson and Arkoff just before its release. Publicity photos issued at the time still bear the original title. The movie was shot in Superama but the DVD is a standard version that all too often betrays its 2.35 widescreen origins.

Review: *Variety* (September 7, 1958), "The 'message' is handled with restraint and good taste, and gives substance to the production."

Tentacles

"Each year 10,000 tourists visit Ocean Beach. This Summer Ocean Beach has attracted SOMETHING ELSE!'

(June 1977) Widescreen and Color by Movielab (Technovision and Technicolor). An

John Huston and Shelley Winters have a pajama party in *Tentacles*.

Ovidio Assonitis Production. Produced by Enzo Doria. Directed by Oliver Hellman (a.k.a. Ovidio Assonitis). Written by Jerome Max, Tito Carpi, and Steve Carabatsos. Starring John Huston, Shelley Winters, Bo Hopkins, Henry Fonda. DVD: MGM (2.35) 102 min.; Extras: Theatrical trailer. Midnite Movies co-feature: *Empire of the Ants*.

Tentacles (or *Tentacoli*) is the worst of the many *Jaws* rip-offs to surface (or sink) in the wake of that blockbuster hit. It is an Italian-American co-production which was filmed primarily at various locations in Southern California and features a variety of actors familiar to U.S. audiences. A series of unusual occurrences off the California coast sets reporter John Huston to wondering if the offshore work being done by Henry Fonda's company has stirred up something unpleasant. Turns out it has ... a giant octopus that is making a meal of anyone unfortunate enough to get in its general vicinity. When the wife (Deli Boccardoa) of a marine biologist (Bo Hopkins) is killed, he turns into Captain Ahab bent on killing the horrible sea creature. He concocts a plan to destroy the monster with the help of two friendly killer whales from Sea World. Shelley Winters does not play one of the whales. Instead she is cast as the sister of John Huston. Her ten-year-old son (huh?) is a contestant in a local sailboat race which of course puts him in peril of the giant octopus and gives Shelley ample opportunity to fret and suffer. Also on hand are Claude Akins as a local law enforcement officer and Cesare Danova (dubbed with someone else's voice) as one of Fonda's flunkies. The movie is slow-moving, unfocused, and unexciting. The MGM Midnite Movies DVD runs 102 minutes, which is twelve excruciating minutes more than the AIP theatrical release and the MGM VHS tape.

The Terror

"FROM THE DEPTHS OF AN EVIL MIND CAME A DIABOLICAL PLAN OF TORTURE ... INCONCEIVABLE ... UNBELIEVABLE!"

(September 1963) VistaScope and Pathécolor. A Filmgroup Production. Produced and Di-

In *The Terror*, Jack Nicholson threatens Dorothy Neumann.

rected by Roger Corman. Written by Leo Gordon and Jack Hill. Starring Boris Karloff, Jack Nicholson, Sandra Knight, Dick Miller. DVD: Ovation (1.33) 79 min. Extras: Theatrical trailer.

When Roger Corman finished shooting *The Raven* ahead of schedule, Boris Karloff still owed him a couple of days work. Corman hastily assembled a few pages of dialogue and, over a weekend, filmed Karloff on the still standing sets from *The Raven*. With this initial Karloff footage in the can, Corman put Leo Gordon and Jack Hill to the task of developing a feature-length script, using the existing Karloff sequences as the core of the plot.

Although touted as being made in three days, *The Terror* actually took longer than most Corman films to complete. In addition to Corman, five other people (Francis Coppola, Dennis Jakob, Monte Hellman, Jack Hill, and Jack Nicholson) directed various scenes, creating a real patchwork of material. That the movie makes what little sense it does is a minor miracle. The story has Andre (Jack Nicholson), a young soldier from Napoleon's army, meet a beautiful girl (Sandra Knight) who draws him into a mysterious vortex of death and the supernatural. Karloff plays the sinister Baron Von Leppe, who holds the secret to the horrific events which transpire. Also in the cast are "Cormanites" Dick Miller, Jonathan Haze and Dorothy Neumann. *The Terror* has the feel of the Corman Poe films and the last scene is effectively shocking. This title is available from a variety of sources of varying quality. None of them is as good-looking as the print which has aired on some of the cable television networks but the DVD from Ovation is acceptable until something better comes along.

The Thing with Two Heads

"THE DOCTOR BLEW IT—HE TRANSPLANTED A WHITE BIGOT'S HEAD ON A SOUL BROTHER'S BODY!"

(July 1972) Color by DeLuxe. A Saber Production. Produced by Wes Bishop. Directed by

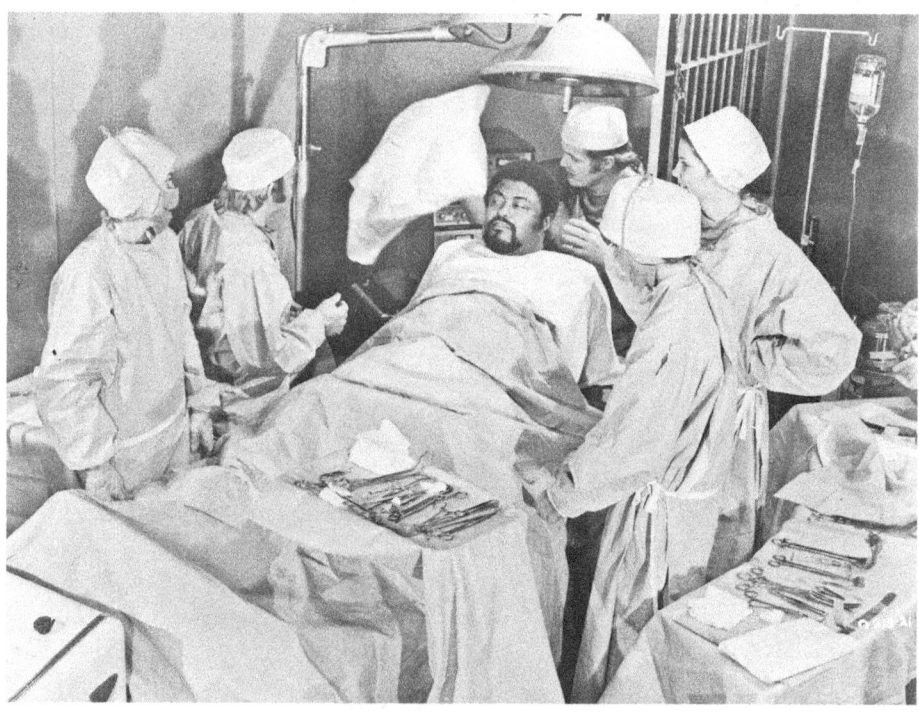

Rosey Grier prepares to have Ray Milland's head grafted onto his body in *The Thing with Two Heads*.

Lee Frost. Written by Lee Frost, Wes Bishop and James Gordon White. Starring Ray Milland, Roosevelt "Rosey" Grier, Don Marshall, Chelsea Brown. DVD: MGM (1.85) 91 min.; Extras: Theatrical trailer. Midnite Movies co-feature: *The Incredible 2-Headed Transplant*.

Surely one of the oddest films of AIP's entire output, *The Thing with Two Heads* has to be seen to be believed. Dr. Max Kirshner (Ray Milland) is a brilliant surgeon who has perfected an operation to transplant heads onto other bodies. He is also a rabid bigot with a fatal disease. A search is made to find a condemned prisoner who is willing to donate his body so that Kirshner's head may survive. The donor turns out to be Jack Moss (Rosey Grier), who has been framed for a crime he didn't commit. The operation is a success until Kirshner's head awakens to find himself sharing the body of a black man. Racial slurs and stereotypes abound. Chelsea Brown has some good scenes as Jack's girlfriend Lila. A chase scene with police cars pursuing Jack/Max on a motorcycle goes on for far too long and has a seemingly endless amount of car crashes. *The Thing with Two Heads* features the onscreen debut of master gorilla suit maker Rick Baker performing in one of his creations. This appearance was instrumental in his being cast in the title role of Dino De Laurentiis' 1976 *King Kong*.

Thunder Alley

"Days of Screaming Wheels ...
Nights of Reckless Pleasure!"

(March 1967) Panavision and Pathécolor. Produced by Burt Topper. Directed by Richard Rush. Written by Sy Salkowitz. Starring Annette Funicello, Fabian, Diane McBain, Warren Berlinger. DVD: MGM (2.35) 89 min.; Extras: Theatrical trailer. Midnite Movies co-feature: *Fireball 500*.

Champion stock car racer Tommy Callahan (Fabian) has a blackout which causes a fatal accident so he is prohibited from professional racing. To get back onto the circuit he takes a job stunt racing with "Madsen's Thrill Circus." Pete Madsen (Jan Murray) has a daughter named Francie (Annette Funicello) who quickly falls head over heels for Tommy, despite his already having a girlfriend (Diane McBain). In her last AIP role, Annette is still pretty much playing her standard good girl part but does get drunk in one scene. She also sings a nice ballad called "When You Get What You Want." Fabian, on the other hand, is no clean-cut Frankie Avalon type. He drinks, smokes, and shares a hotel room bed with his onscreen girlfriend. *Thunder Alley* is fairly innocuous entertainment except for a truly ridiculous, and totally out of place, drunken party scene with a mob of gyrating dancers, gallons of booze, and close-ups of countless pairs of jiggling boobs. Diane McBain started as a contract star at Warner Bros. where she appeared in such high profile big screen soap operas as *Parrish* and *Claudelle Inglish* (both 1961). She ended up doing several films at AIP, mostly in thankless roles like the one she plays in this film. Diane Varsi, a former Academy Award nominee for *Peyton Place* (1957), would suffer a similar fate at AIP in movies like *Bloody Mama*. Pre-production promotional material for *Thunder Alley* listed Fred Clark and Donna Loren in the parts which eventually were played by Jan Murray and McBain.

Songs: "When You Get What You Want," "Thunder Alley"

The Time Travelers

"You are in the Future before it happens!"

(October 1964) Color. A Dobil Production. Produced by William Redlin. Directed by Ib Melchior. Written by David Hewitt and Ib Melchior. Starring Preston Foster, Philip Carey, Merry Anders, John Hoyt. VHS: Thorn EMI/HBO (1.33) 82 min.

Three scientists (Preston Foster, Philip Carey, Merry Anders) inadvertently create a "time portal" which transports them and a

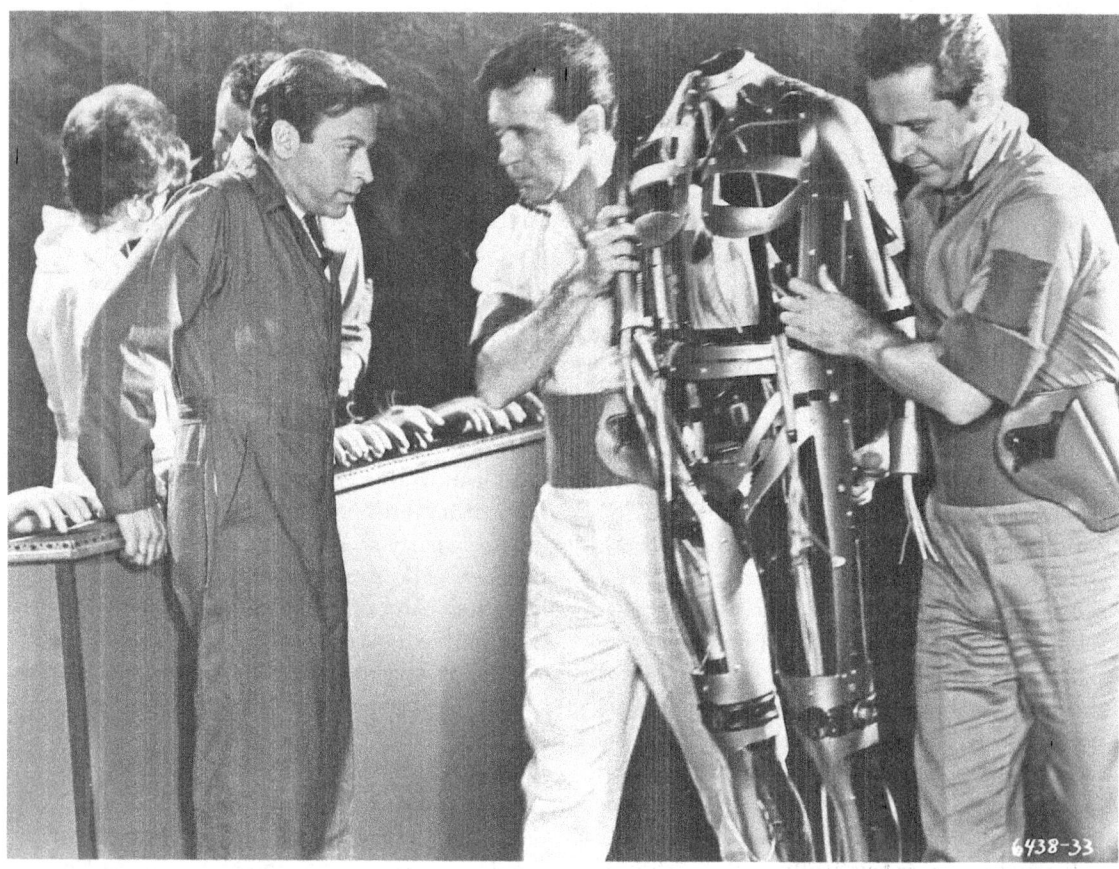

Workers assemble androids as Steve Franken looks on in *The Time Travelers*.

goofy handyman (Steve Franken) to the year A.D. 2071. There they find a desolate terrain laid waste by atomic warfare and populated by mutants. The few remaining members of a scientifically advanced race of humans dwell in tunnels beneath the earth. A similar premise was used in the 1956 Allied Artists film *World Without End* with far greater effect. *The Time Travelers* is hopelessly old-fashioned even by 1963 standards. The sets and costumes are on a par with those in such fifties sci-fi gems as *Fire Maidens from Outer Space* and *Missile to the Moon*. At least those movies were fun but *The Time Travelers* is merely dull. The special effects look like they were taken from a second-rate magician's stage act and have little or nothing to do with the story being told. One interminable sequence takes place in a factory where Androids are being assembled. The scene is stupid enough on its own without the added horror of Richard LaSalle's truly awful background music. As if once wasn't bad enough, the climax of the film is a speeded-up recapitulation of the entire movie. Forrest J Ackerman was able to parlay his position as editor of *Famous Monsters of Filmland* into a bit part in *The Time Travelers*. Unsurprisingly, the magazine touted the film's release in glowing terms. Director Ib Melchoir's previous directorial effort for AIP was *The Angry Red Planet* and, although certainly no masterpiece, it is an infinitely more entertaining film than this one.

Review: *Variety* (December 2, 1964), "Poor acting performances, stilted writing and generally uneven direction."

Tomb of Ligeia

"CAT OR WOMAN OR A THING
TOO EVIL TO MENTION?"

(January 1965) ColorScope. A Roger Corman Production. Produced by Pat Green and Roger Corman. Directed by Roger Corman. Written by Robert Towne. Starring Vincent Price, Elizabeth Shepherd, John Westbrook, Derek Francis. DVD: MGM (2.35) 81 min.; Extras: Audio commentaries by Roger Corman and Elizabeth Shepherd; Theatrical trailer. Midnite Movies co-feature: *An Evening of Edgar Allan Poe*.

Toward the end of his life, Vincent Price told director Tim Burton that of all the films he had appeared in, *Tomb of Ligeia* came closest to being a work of art. This was the last of eight Edgar Allan Poe adaptations that Roger Corman directed for AIP. Although AIP continued to evoke the name of Poe on subsequent horror movies, few of them came close to equaling what Corman had accomplished. As written by Robert Towne (who later wrote *Chinatown*), *Tomb of Ligeia* is very much a mood piece with the story being rather incidental. Instead the audience is given a succession of haunting, and sometimes disturbing, images tied together with a slim plotline. Lady Rowen Travanion (Elizabeth Shepherd) becomes infatuated with the mysterious and troubled Vernon Fell (Vincent Price). She hastily marries him only to discover that he is still under the spell of his dead first wife Ligeia (also played by Shepherd). The set-up is very similar to *Jane Eyre*, *Rebecca*, and *Dragonwyck*, with a second wife unable to comprehend the secretive husband she has so impulsively married. Price's performance as Vernon Fell at times recalls Nicholas Van Ryn, the character he played in *Dragonwyck* (1946) and, at others, Roderick Usher. Knowing this would be the last of his Poe films, Corman obviously tried to do something different with *Tomb of Ligeia*. Eschewing the studio-bound sets of the previous films in the series, Corman took this movie outdoors to the expansive English countryside. The ruined abbey where much of the story takes place has an atmosphere of decay that perfectly suits this tale of possession and necrophilia. The uncredited black cat which plays a large part in the proceedings is certainly put through its paces and deserves honorable mention.

Review: *Films and Filming* (March 1965), "It is certainly the most sensitive of the Poe stories that Corman has directed, and in some ways is probably his best work. Very Impressive."

The Trip

"A LOVELY SORT OF DEATH"

(August 1967) Pathécolor. Produced and Directed by Roger Corman. Written by Jack Nicholson. Starring Peter Fonda, Bruce Dern, Susan Strasberg, Dennis Hopper. DVD: MGM (1.85) 85 min.; Extras: Theatrical trailer; Audio commentary by Roger Corman; Featurette "Tune In, Trip Out." Midnite Movies co-feature: *Psych-Out*.

This nearly plotless film stars Peter Fonda as a director of television commercials who is at a turning point in his life. He decides to take an LSD trip with the hope of getting a clearer insight into his feelings. The drug guru who assists him on the trip is played by Bruce Dern. The trip itself often seems to be a pastiche of images which recall Bergman, Fellini, and Roger Corman's own horror films. Fonda plays his part convincingly, projecting an innocence which instantly elicits sympathy for his character. Corman stock company regulars Luana Anders, Beach Dickerson, Dick Miller, and Barboura Morris all put in appearances. As part of his preparation for directing *The Trip*, Corman took LSD to familiarize himself with the effects of the drug. Although Corman attempted to treat the drug experience objectively, AIP added a prologue condemning the use of LSD and ended the film with a shattered image of Peter Fonda, suggesting that the trip affected his life in an adverse way. Thirty years later, both Fonda and Corman are still regretting that the original film was compromised. Said Fonda in a November 8, 2007, *Daily Variety* interview: "It was a copout. The audience should have been permitted to make its own decision. It's very important for the moral commitment of the story."

Peter Fonda in *The Trip*.

Review: *Films and Filming* (June 1969), "Corman brings off the stunning effects with a skill that places him securely among the most interesting of all 'visual' directors."

The Undead

"Terror ... That Screams from the Grave!"

(March 1957) Black & White. Produced and Directed by Roger Corman. Written by Charles Griffith and Mark Hanna. Starring Pamela Duncan, Richard Garland, Allison Hayes, Val Dufour. DVD: Direct Video Distribution (1.33) 75 min.; Region-Free DVD from United Kingdom; Extras: Audio interview with Samuel Z. Arkoff; Trailers.

Inspired by the "Bridey Murphy" case, Roger Corman directed a reincarnation chiller to be called *The Trance of Diana Love*. By the time it was ready for release, the fad had run its course so the title was changed to the more exploitative, but totally misleading, *The Undead*. Shot in ten days in a supermarket which had been converted into sound stages, this is one of Corman's most unusual and imaginative pictures. A prostitute (Pamela Duncan) is hypnotized by a psychiatrist (Val Dufour) and regressed to a past life in which she was wrongly condemned to death for being a witch. The majority of the story is set in medieval times and, despite a very small budget, Corman manages to create an atmosphere that seems like an extremely grim Grimm's fairy tale. The cast is filled with Corman repertory players. Pamela Duncan, Richard Garland, and Mel Welles had just starred in *Attack of the Crab Monsters* (Allied Artists, 1957). Bruno VeSota, Richard Devon, Dick Miller, and Dorothy Neumann would work in future Corman productions. Allison Hayes, who had previously appeared in Corman's *Gunslinger*, here plays Livia, the most buxom sorceress ever to attend a Witches' Sabbath. The following year she would be forever immortalized in *Attack of the 50 Foot Woman* (Allied Artists, 1958). Although *The Undead*

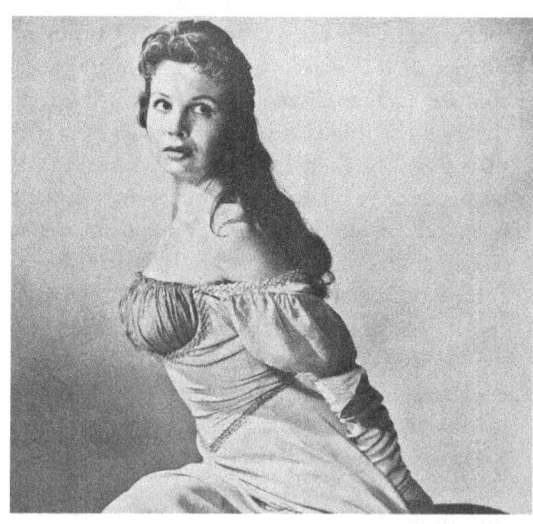

In *The Undead*, Pamela Duncan portrays a prostitute who is regressed to a past life.

has been released on both VHS and DVD in the United Kingdom, it has never been commercially available in the U.S.

Review: *Harrison's Reports* (May 2, 1957), "The story, such as it is, is highly unpleasant and fantastic, let alone mixed up."

The Vampire Lovers

"IF YOU DARE ... TASTE THE DEADLY PASSION OF THE BLOOD-NYMPHS!"

(October 1970) Color by Movielab (Technicolor). An American International–Hammer Film Production. Produced by Harry Fine and Michael Style. Directed by Roy Ward Baker. Written by Tudor Gates. Starring Ingrid Pitt, Peter Cushing, George Cole, Kate O'Mara. DVD: MGM (1.85) 91 min. Extras: Theatrical trailer. Audio commentary by Roy Ward Baker, Ingrid Pitt, and Tudor Gates. Midnite Movies co-feature: *Countess Dracula*.

Ingrid Pitt has just drained the life out of Kate O'Mara in the AIP-Hammer co-production *The Vampire Lovers*.

The Vampire Lovers was the only official co-production between Hammer Films and American International, although over the years AIP did pick up other Hammer titles for U.S. distribution. Producers Harry Fine and Michael Style (working with writer Tudor Gates) took their proposed project based on the vampire novella *Carmilla* to Hammer, who then approached AIP with the idea of a co-production. *The Vampire Lovers* was the first Hammer film to fully indulge in the sexually liberated cinematic trend of the times with lesbianism and a great deal of female nudity. Hammer said that AIP insisted on including the nudity while AIP executive producer Louis "Deke" Heyward claimed that it was Hammer's idea and he fought against it. Whoever was responsible, the film was rather shocking at the time of its original release and earned an R rating in the U.S. This R was only given after AIP had made some cuts, not for sexual content but for violence. When *Vampire Lovers* was first released, few critics managed to get past its exploitative aspects, for which it was severely criticized. Now the movie has gained a loyal cult following and is considered a classic of its kind. Most of the contemporary publicity for the film centered on leading lady Ingrid Pitt. Ms. Pitt had already appeared in a few forgettable movies when she was cast in a flashy supporting role opposite Richard Burton and Clint Eastwood in *Where Eagles Dare* (1969). Hammer and AIP both touted her as the new "Sex Symbol of the seventies." Although she never became a mainstream star, she did achieve the status of an enduring horror icon. AIP and Hammer never again joined forces although in 1975 Hammer's Michael

Carreras approached Sam Arkoff with the idea of co-producing a movie version of *Vampirella*, based on the popular comic book character of the time. After briefly considering the proposal, Arkoff withdrew and the film was never made by Hammer. For the outstanding MGM Midnite Movies DVD, the inferior AIP "Color by Movielab" was replaced by an original British Technicolor transfer and two minutes of excised footage was reinstated.

Review: *L'Incroyable Cinema* (Spring 1971), "Roy Ward Baker has directed it with such lack luster effort that shows in the dullness of so many scenes."

Venus in Furs

"THE COAT THAT COVERED PARADISE, UNCOVERED HELL!"

(May 1970) Color. A Commonwealth United Presentation. Produced by Harry Alan Towers. Directed by Jess Franco. Written by Jess Franco and Malvin Wald. Starring James Darren, Barbara McNair, Maria Rohm, Klaus Kinski. DVD: Blue Underground (1.85) 86 min.; Extras: Interview with Jess Franco; Audio interview with Maria Rohm; Theatrical trailer; Poster and still gallery.

Trumpet player Jimmy (James Darren) finds the half-nude body of beautiful Wanda Reed (Maria Rohm) on the beach in Istanbul. He remembers seeing her the previous night at a jet set party where he had played a gig. Later that evening, he inadvertently witnessed a violent S&M sex scene involving Wanda with partygoers Kapp (Dennis Price), Olga (Margaret Lee), and Ahmed (Klaus Kinski) ... "Man, it was a wild scene but if they wanted to go that route, it was their bag." Jimmy can't get the memory of Wanda out of his mind. He flees Istanbul, eventually ending up in Rio de Janeiro where he becomes involved with a singer named Rita (Barbara McNair). For awhile everything seems to be okay but one night during Carnival, Wanda walks into the club where he is playing trumpet in a jazz band. Is this a lookalike or is it the real Wanda Reed come back from the dead to take revenge on the people responsible for her death? Whichever it might be, Jimmy immediately falls under her spell, to the dismay of Rita. Fans of Jess Franco often cite *Venus in Furs* (also known as *Proximus*) as his masterpiece, and not without good reason. It certainly contains some of his best work on film and has a surreal quality that haunts the viewer long after the movie is over. Franco says that the movie began as an idea he and renowned trumpeter Chet Baker had in which the character of Jimmy was a black musician. This concept didn't pan out but Franco does include an interracial romance between Darren and McNair which was still something uncommon in films at the time. Rohm has never looked more gorgeous than she does as the Venus in Furs of the title ... although she could also be called "Venus in Wigs" as she certainly wears a wide variety of them throughout the course of the story. The jazz background score by the British group Manfred Mann adds greatly to the atmosphere of this "wild, paranoiac trip." One of Harry Alan Towers' international co-productions, *Venus in Furs* was released in Europe in 1969 and in the U.S. the following year. Surprisingly, despite its strong sexual content, AIP did not cut the film for the Stateside release or relegate it to their Trans-American Films distribution subsidiary. The DVD from Blue Underground is an excellent quality transfer with beautiful color which does the movie full justice. "Venus in Furs will be smiling..."

Viking Women and the Sea Serpent

"THE RAW COURAGE OF WOMEN WITHOUT MEN LOST IN A FANTASTIC HELL-ON-EARTH!"

(December 1957) Black & White. Produced and Directed by Roger Corman. Written by Lawrence L. Goldman and Irving Block. Starring Abby Dalton, Brad Jackson, June Kenney, Richard Devon. DVD: Lionsgate (1.33) 70 min.; DVD co-feature: *Teenage Caveman*.

The Viking women practice spear-throwing while Abby Dalton, third from left, Betsy Jones-Moreland, second from right, and Susan Cabot, right, look on in *Viking Women and the Sea Serpent.*

How do you make an epic motion picture in ten days with a $70,000 budget? You don't ... but Roger Corman deserves some credit for trying. To be fair, Corman shouldn't take all the blame for this failure. He says he was "taken in" by the promises of special effects men Jack Rabin and Irving Block, who claimed they could deliver spectacular visuals for next to no money. With *Viking Women and the Sea Serpent*, Rabin and Block were clearly in over their heads. Actually they did manage to provide some impressive matte paintings, and the "Monster of the Vortex" is effective, though glimpsed all too briefly. Where the film really falls short is in the quality of the costuming and some truly awful anachronistic dialogue. If you can forgive this, the movie can be lots of fun. The cast is a "who's who" of Roger Corman-AIP stock players including Jonathan Haze, Betsy Jones-Moreland, Michael Forest and Gary Conway. Best of all is the divine Susan Cabot once again giving a performance worthy of far better material. The full title of the film is *The Saga of the Viking Women and Their Voyage to the Waters of the Great Sea Serpent*, which just about says it all as far as plot goes. The impressive credits accompanied by Albert Glasser's dramatic main title music certainly would lead one to believe they are about to see an epic tale filmed on a grand scale. The first shot of a Malibu beach doubling for Scandinavia quickly bursts that bubble.

Review: *Harrison's Reports* (April 26, 1958), "Plentiful action and the scantily clad women are attractive and resourceful. The direction and acting meet the demands of the script."

Voodoo Woman

"CREEPING TERROR ... STRIKING FROM THE DEPTHS OF HELL! A WOMAN BY DAY ... A MONSTER BY NIGHT!"

(March 1957) Black & White. A Carmel Production. Produced by Alex Gordon. Directed by Edward L. Cahn. Written by Russ Bender and V.I. Voss. Starring Marla English, Tom Conway, Lance Fuller, Touch Connors. VHS: Columbia/TriStar (1.33) 75 min. DVD: Direct Video Distribution (1.33) 75 min.; Region-Free DVD from United Kingdom; Extras: Audio interview with Samuel Z. Arkoff; Trailers.

Hard-bitten and avaricious Marilyn Blanchard (Marla English) is determined to locate an African tribe which is rumored to use solid gold objects in their voodoo rituals. With boyfriend Rick (Lance Fuller) and reluctant guide Ted Bronson (Touch Connors), she sets off into the African jungle on her quest. At the same time, Dr. Roland Gerard (Tom Conway) has ingratiated himself with this tribe and, using a mixture of "black voodoo" and "white science," he attempts to create a new being, half human and half beast. When Marilyn arrives at the native village, Dr. Gerard realizes that because of her ruthless nature she is the perfect subject for his experiments. *Voodoo Woman* was the last AIP picture starring their resident glamour girl Marla English, who soon retired from films. Paul Blaisdell wears a modified version of his "She-Creature" costume; the head was replaced with a skull outfitted with ping pong ball eyes and a white fright wig. This is definitely not his most imaginative creation and it is wisely kept in the shadows most of the time to conceal its limitations. Slow-moving and with the "action" confined to studio jungle sets, *Voodoo Woman* is one of AIP's weaker horror entries of the fifties, but it's still lots of fun.

Song: "Black Voodoo"

Review: *Harrison's Reports* (March 2, 1957), "A very ordinary program horror melodrama, based on a story that is confused and confusing."

Lance Fuller and Marla English, frequent stars of early AIP films, appeared in *Voodoo Woman*.

War Goddess

"WOMEN WARRIORS AS SENSUOUS AS THEY ARE SAVAGE"

(March 1975) Technicolor. Produced by Nino Krisman. Directed by Terence Young. Written by Richard Aubrey, Dino Maiuri, Massimo De Rita, Serge De La Roche. Starring Alena Johnston, Sabine Sun, Angelo Infanti, Rossana Yanni. DVD: Retromedia (1.33) 89 min.; DVD co-feature: *War Gods of Babylon*.

In 1973, AIP sent an elaborate promotional book to exhibitors announcing their forthcoming spectacular: "American International Pictures' *The Amazons* will be hitting theatre circuits as one of the most heavily pre-sold and showmanship backed properties in the company's history. The big year for AIP is 1974 ... the year of Terence Young's *The Amazons*." The colorful brochure tastefully avoids mentioning that the movie is basically nothing more than a low-budget sword-and-sandal "boob-a-thon." The fact that Young directed the picture is heavily promoted, with good reason since he had previously helmed *Dr. No*, *From Russia with Love*, *Thunderball* and *Wait Until Dark*. Why he got involved with *The Amazons* is a mystery. Somewhere along the line, someone at AIP must have actually watched the film because the planned "hoopla" was abandoned, the title was changed to *War Goddess*, and the film barely got any release at all. Sisters Antione (Alena Johnston) and Oreitheia (Sabine Sun) are rivals to rule the "queen-dom" of the Amazons. Antione wins a naked girlfight and becomes queen, thereby incurring the enmity of her sibling. Once a year the Amazons must mate with the repulsive male of the species in order to propagate their race ("They pay in copper for good male seed," observes a prospective doner). After their sexual encounter, Antione falls in love with the Greek king Theseus (Angelo Infanti), which provides even more fuel for her sister's fire. When Antione is tricked into believing that Theseus has betrayed her, there is another naked girlfight and the two sisters join forces to march against the Greeks with "Freedom from Male Tyranny" as their mantra. Totally silly, but lots of fun for the undemanding.

Filmed in England as *City Under the Sea*, Edgar Allan Poe's poem of the same name is misquoted several times during the course of the movie. Curiously, when the film was released in the U.S. as *War-Gods of the Deep* there was no mention of Poe in the advertising. The plot is much closer in spirit to Jules Verne than Poe with Vincent Price playing the Captain, a Nemo-like ruler of an underwater city off the coast of Cornwall. The Captain has a young girl (Susan Hart) kidnapped and taken to his sunken city because she resembles his long-dead wife. Her friends (Tab Hunter and David Tomlinson) brave the depths to rescue her. Following in the footsteps of Gertrude the Duck (*Journey to the Center of the Earth*) and Frosty the Poodle (*The Lost World*), Herbert the Chicken is another co-star. Why annoying pets are frequently taken along on cinematic quests to lost worlds is anybody's guess. Although *War-Gods of the Deep* has the typically fine production values of AIP's British films, it is basically a silly and plodding affair with the cast floundering throughout. Price tries gamely but he can't seem to muster much enthusiasm for his part. In a *Films and Filming* article which came out at the time of the movie's release, Price complained that the Poe poem "had nothing to do with what was in the script." He continued: "And that is very bad, because if

War-Gods of the Deep

"THEY DARED THE MOST FANTASTIC JOURNEY THAT HAS EVER CHALLENGED IMAGINATION!"

(May 1965) ColorScope. Produced by Daniel Haller and George Willoughby. Directed by Jacques Tourneur. Written by Charles Bennett, Louis M. Heyward, and David Whittaker. Starring Vincent Price, Tab Hunter, Susan Hart, David Tomlinson. DVD: MGM (2.35) 85 min.; Extras: Theatrical trailer. Midnite Movies co-feature: *At the Earth's Core*.

Tab Hunter and Susan Hart face *War-Gods of the Deep*.

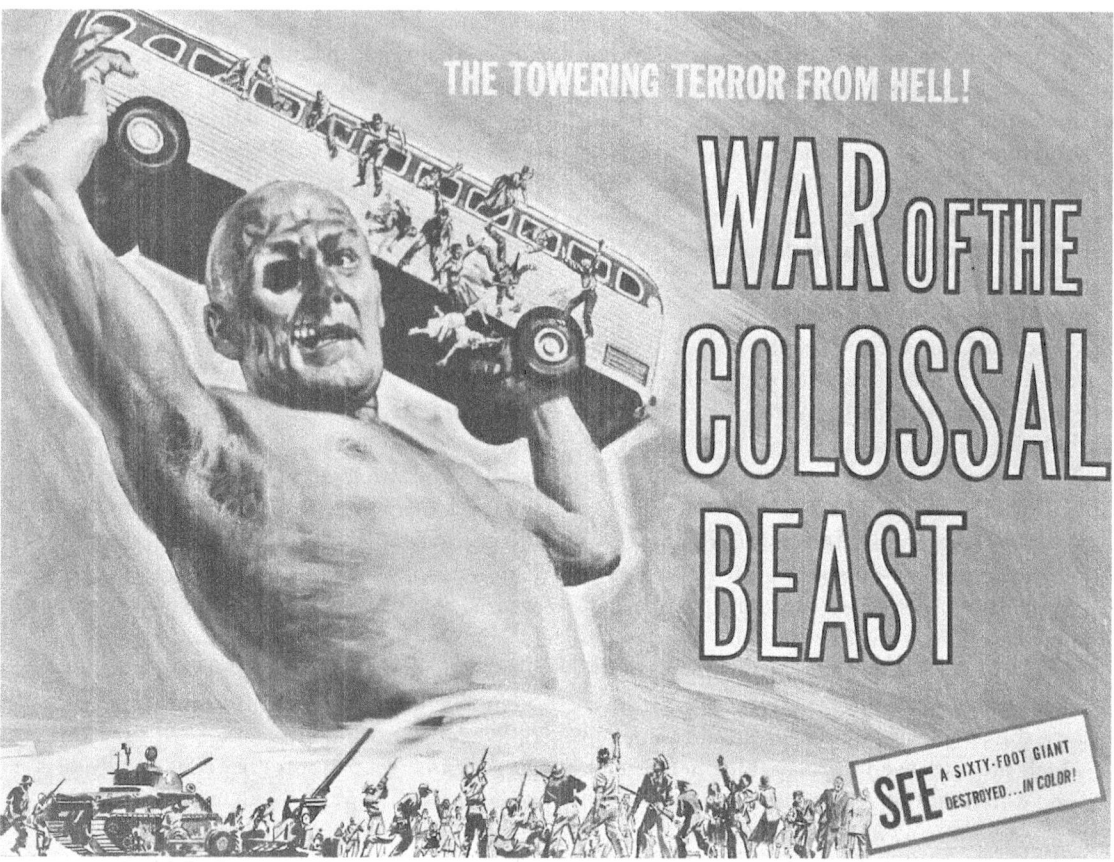

Exciting poster art for Bert I. Gordon's *War of the Colossal Beast*.

there are twenty people in a cinema who know Poe's poem you've lost them. There is an atmosphere of a lack of genuineness ... and it dies." This was the final film of director Jacques Tourneur, who did not go out on a high note with this picture.

Review: *Variety* (June 1, 1965), "Excellent direction and special effects, plus good performances, provide zip for standard plot."

War of the Colossal Beast

"The Towering Terror from Hell!"

(July 1958) Black & White. Produced and Directed by Bert I. Gordon. Written by George Worthing Yates. Starring Sally Fraser, Roger Pace, Dean Parkin, Russ Bender. DVD: Lionsgate (1.33) 69 min.; DVD co-feature: *Earth vs the Spider*.

Following giant Col. Glenn Manning's fall off of Boulder Dam in *The Amazing Colossal Man* (1957), he ends up South of the Border somewhat the worse for wear. Not only is his face horribly disfigured but his brain has also been damaged. His sister Joyce (Sally Fraser) still believes there is hope for her brother and convinces a U.S. army officer to capture Glenn and bring him back to the United States. He eventually escapes from an airplane hangar at Los Angeles Airport and ends up cornered by the military at Griffith Park Observatory where the film swiftly comes to its colorful (literally) climax. Though sorely missing the dramatic presence of Glenn Langan, who played Col. Manning in the previous film, *War of the Colossal Beast* (filmed as *Revenge of the Colossal Man*) is an entertaining, if unremarkable, sequel. This time around Dean Parkin plays the Colossal One, in a performance similar to the one he gave as Bert I. Gordon's *The Cyclops* (Allied Artists, 1957).

Review: *Variety* (August 20, 1958), "Lack of novel situations but good special effects and properly horrible makeup."

War of the Zombies

"Unconquerable Warriors of the Damned!"

(March 1965) ColorScope (Eastman Color). A Galatea Production. Produced by Ferruccio de Martino and Massimo de Rita. Directed by Giuseppe Vari. Written by Piero Pierotti and Marcello Sartarelli. Starring John Drew Barrymore, Ettori Manni, Susy Anderson, Ida Galli. DVD: Substance (as *Rome Against Rome*) (1.66) 85 min.

By 1965, American audiences had grown tired of the constant parade of dubbed Euro-epics which were being shown in theatres and on television. AIP had purchased *Roma contro Roma/Rome Against Rome*, which had a strong fantasy element in addition to the usual swords and sandals. They decided to focus on the fantastic ingredients and market it as a horror movie. Cut from 110 to 85 minutes and retitled *War of the Zombies*, the plot concerns Roman Centurion Gaius (Ettori Manni) who discovers treachery and black magic in ancient Armenia. Aderbal (John Drew Barrymore) is a sorcerer who steals the bodies of Roman soldiers killed in battle and resurrects them as mindless automatons to fight against their former countrymen. This is accomplished with the aid of a powerful one-eyed goddess. Although the film does boast some lavish costumes and imaginative sets, most of the large-scale scenes were cribbed from *Hannibal* and *Constantine and the Cross*. Handsome hero Ettori Manni was a frequent player in Euro-epics whose days in Roman armor go back to *Due Notte con Cleopatra/Two Nights with Cleopatra* (1954), one of Sophia Loren's early films. *War of the Zombies* was released on a particularly duplicitous double-bill with a Japanese samurai movie which AIP had rechristened *The Lost World of Sinbad* to create "The Double Shock Show of the Year!" When *War of the Zombies* appeared on television, AIP changed the title yet again, this time to *Night Star, Goddess of Electra*.

What's Up, Tiger Lily?

"Woody Allen's lowdown on how to make a Chinese fortune KOOKIE"

(September 1966) TohoScope and Color. A Henry G. Saperstein–Reuben Berkovitch Production. Produced by Henry G. Saperstein and Woody Allen. Special Material by Woody Allen. With Writing and Vocal Assists by Julie Bennet, Frank Buxton, Louise Lasser, Len Maxwell, Mickey Rose, and Bryna Wilson. Starring Tatsuya Mihashi, Akiko Wakabayashi, Mie Hama, Tadao Nakamuru. DVD: Image (2.35) 80 min.; Extras: Alternate television audio track; Woody Allen filmography.

A one-joke wonder perpetrated by Woody Allen … but the joke is often hilarious. The original movie (*Kai No Kag*) was a Japanese spy spoof produced by Toho Company Ltd., directed by Senkichi Taniguchi and written by Hideo Ando. Allen and Henry G. Saperstein bought the rights for $66,000 and Allen proceeded to re-edit the film and redub the voices to make it into a zany comedy involving a secret formula for the ultimate egg salad. Secret agent Phil Moscowitz (Tatsuya Mihashi) gets involved in all manner of dangerous situations during his quest to retrieve the stolen recipe. He is assisted by the beautiful Suki Yaki (Akiko Wakabayashi) and her sister Teri (Mie Hama). The Lovin' Spoonful provide the background music and appear in two scenes which were filmed for the U.S version.

Review: *Time* (October 14, 1966), "The joke of course goes on too long, and when the spectator tires of it he can't help noticing what Allen's annotations cannot entirely conceal; the original film. It's terrible."

White Huntress

"WHITE WOMAN VS. THE DEADLY PYTHON"

(August 1957) Black & White. A Majestic Production. Produced by C. Ray Stahl. Directed by George Breakston. Written by Dermot Quinn. Starring Robert Urquhart, John Bentley, Susan Stephan, Alan Tarlton. DVD: RetroMedia (1.37) 69 min.; Bonus feature: *Jungle Siren*.

In 1890, two brothers of very different temperaments lead a wagon train of settlers across British East Africa to an area they hope to colonize. When they arrive at their destination, they are met with opposition from the Masai tribe. The simple plot plays more like an American Western rather than a "jungle picture." Filmed entirely on location in Kenya, this British production was AIP's first import and suffered the fate of future pickups. The original title was *Golden Ivory*, the running time was 86 minutes, and it was filmed in color. All of this changed once AIP got their hands on it. First it was given the far more exploitative title of *White Huntress*, although the closest character to qualify is a naive pioneer girl. Then it was shorn of some 17 minutes and released in black-and-white on a double bill with the documentary *Naked Africa* for "Double Dynamite Action Thrills!" You have to give them credit for trying.

Who Slew Auntie Roo?

"SAY GOODNIGHT TO AUNTIE ROO, KIDDIES ... IT'S DEAD TIME!"

(December 1971) Color by Movielab. An American International–Hemdale Production. Produced by Samuel Z. Arkoff and James H. Nicholson. Written by Robert Blees, James (Jimmy) Sangster, David Osborn, and Gavin Lambert. Starring Shelley Winters, Mark Lester, Ralph Richardson, Michael Gothard. DVD: MGM (as *Whoever Slew Auntie Roo?*) (1.85) 92 min.; Extras: Theatrical trailer. Midnite Movies co-feature: *What's the Matter with Helen?*

According to Louis "Deke" Heyward, Jim Nicholson had seen and enjoyed the movie *What's the Matter with Helen?* (1971) very much. AIP had recently acquired a screen story by David Osborn called "The Gingerbread House" and Nicholson felt that it would be a good vehicle to reunite *Helen* director Curtis Harrington and star Shelley Winters. What Nicholson ended up with was a rather mean-spirited and lackluster thriller with Winters at her most shrill and Harrington at his most uninspired. In defense of Harrington, the material is not very inspiring and doing two pictures in a row with the virtually undirectable Ms. Winters must have been draining. As with the other British American International productions, *Who Slew Auntie Roo?* is technically impressive and has a fine roster of British character actors including Lionel Jeffries, Hugh Griffith, Judy Cornwell, Rosalie Crutchley, and Pat Heywood. Griffith became a fixture in the AIP British productions. Although Griffith was well known to be a hard drinker, "Deke" Heyward always tried to find a part for him and later said that he continually behaved in a professional manner on their pictures. The same cannot be said for Winters. According to Heyward, she insisted that they approach Laurence Olivier for the part which eventually was played by Ralph Richardson. She was not at all happy with the

In *Who Slew Auntie Roo?*, Shelley Winters is about to take a bite out of an apple and the scenery.

replacement ("You got the wrong 'Sir'" she told Heyward). Shelley also made unwanted advances toward Michael Gothard which made him extremely uncomfortable throughout the shoot. The plot of *Who Slew Auntie Roo?* concerns Christopher (Mark Lester) and his sister Katy (Chloe Franks), two orphans who attend a Christmas party for destitute children given by Mrs. Forrest (Winters), a wealthy eccentric. It turns out that kindly Mrs. Forrest (a.k.a. Aunt Roo) is a bit more than eccentric ... she's totally bonkers. Katy reminds Aunt Roo of her long-dead daughter and she plans to keep the little girl to take her place. When Christopher spies Aunt Roo talking to the rotting corpse of her daughter, he knows that he must rescue Katy from the madwoman's clutches. This "Hansel and Gretel" allegory could have been fun if it had been given a lighter treatment.

Diane Ladd is the biker mama of Loser (Bruce Dern) in *The Wild Angels*.

The Wild Angels

"THEIR CREDO IS VIOLENCE...
THEIR GOD IS HATE!"

(July 1966) Panavision and Pathécolor. Produced and Directed by Roger Corman. Written by Charles B. Griffith. Starring Peter Fonda, Nancy Sinatra, Bruce Dern, Diane Ladd. DVD: MGM (2.35) 93 min.; Extras: Theatrical trailer. Midnite Movies co-feature: *Hell's Belles*.

Heavenly Blues (Peter Fonda) is the leader of the San Pedro branch of the Hell's Angels (the actual Angels cast in the film are from the Venice club). He, Loser (Bruce Dern) and the rest of the gang go to a Mexican border town in search of a missing bike. When they get there, the bikers aren't terribly kind to the locals ("Which one of you taco venders stole an Angel's machine?") and a fight ensues. The cops arrive to break it up and Loser steals one of the police motorcycles. He ends up getting shot by a pursuing officer and put in the hospital. Blues and the gang decided to "spring him," a rash act which results in the death of Loser. Loser's wake in the small mountain community of Sequoia Groves turns into the inevitable drunken brawl with his girlfriend (Diane Ladd) getting gang-banged behind the church altar. Blues ends up burying Loser alone, pondering over why he can't be "free to get loaded and have a good time." The release of *The Wild Angels* heralded the beginning of an anti-establishment trend in motion pictures which reached its apex with *Easy Rider* in 1969. *The Wild Angels* also was a drastic departure from AIP's horror films and Beach Party movies. *Newsweek* noted this in an article entitled "Fallen Angels," saying: "The company has lost its sense of humor, and its innocence, in the process of growing up and undertaking supposedly adult themes." The article went on to vilify *The Wild Angels* in no uncertain terms. Originally the film was to have been entitled *All the Fallen Angels* with

George Chakiris starring as Heavenly Blues with Peter Fonda as Loser. When Chakiris balked at doing his own motorcycle riding, he left the picture and Fonda was moved up to the lead. Bruce Dern was then cast as Loser in the first of many scene-stealing roles for AIP. Nancy Sinatra, as Blues' lady Mike, is incongruously clean-cut for a biker's moll. Other members of the gang include Michael J. Pollard, Gayle Hunnicutt and Joan Shawlee as a particularly "long of tooth" biker mama.

Review: *Time* (September 9, 1966), "*The Wild Angels* is a sleazy synthetic retread that will probably take a long skid through U.S. grind houses."

Wild in the Streets

"IF YOU'RE THIRTY, YOU'RE *THROUGH!*"

(May 1968) Pathécolor. Produced by James H. Nicholson and Samuel Z. Arkoff. Directed by Barry Shear. Written by Robert Thom. Starring Christopher Jones, Shelley Winters, Diane Varsi, Hal Holbrook. DVD: MGM (1.85) 97 min.; Extras: Theatrical trailer; Midnite Movies co-feature: *Gas-s-s-s*.

This cultural artifact was a tremendous success at the time of its original release and is the ultimate example of the "social protest" movies which were being produced by AIP. Max Jacob Flatow Jr. (Christopher Jones) runs away from home and becomes the incredibly popular rock star "Max Frost." He is asked to publicly endorse a candidate (Hal Holbrook) who is running for Senator, but Max makes the platform his own by calling for legislation to lower the voting age to fourteen. Youths across the country stage protests and the voting age is eventually lowered. The result is that Max Frost is elected president of the United States. One of his first acts is to have all people over 30 put into interment camps where they are kept docile by continual doses of LSD in their drinking water. *Wild in the Streets* has a cast filled with famous and soon-to-be famous performers. Christopher Jones seemed destined for stardom. After this picture, he

Christopher Jones is rock star Max Frost in *Wild in the Streets*.

starred in AIP's *Three in the Attic* which also proved to be a big hit. In 1970 he played a leading role in David Lean's *Ryan's Daughter* but afterwards he dropped out of movies entirely. In 1996 Jones returned to the screen in *Mad Dog Time*, which was directed by his *Wild in the Streets* co-star Larry Bishop. Shelley Winters, in her first AIP role, gives her usual over-the-top performance as Max's scary mother, Daphne Flatow. A pre-credits montage showing Max's horrifying childhood gives Shelley plenty of opportunity to chew the scenery even before the movie proper begins. Also on hand in major roles are Ed Begley, Richard Pryor, Diane Varsi (completely wasted) and Millie Perkins, who was married to screenwriter Robert Thom.

A number of celebrities are also on view in cameo parts: Army Archerd, Walter Winchell, Pamela Mason, Melvin Belli, Bobby Sherman and Dick Clark. "Max Frost and The Troopers" perform the song "Shape of Things to Come" by Barry Mann and Cynthia Weil, which went on to become a hit single. The following year, Robert Thom wrote and directed another anti-establishment movie for AIP, *Angel, Angel Down We Go* (a.k.a. *Cult of the Damned*) starring Jennifer Jones and Jordon Christopher. *Wild in the Streets* was nominated for an Academy Award for Best Film Editing.

Songs: "Love to Be Your Man," "Free Lovin'," "Fifty Two Percent," "Shape of Things to Come," "Fourteen or Fight"

Review: *Time* (May 24, 1968), "Some pictures are put-ons that seem to plead for a tacit agreement with their audience: what is to be viewed is beneath contempt, therefore it is beyond criticism."

The Wild Party

"TALK ABOUT WILD!"

(June 1975) Color by Movielab. An Edgar Lansbury-Joseph Beruh/Merchant Ivory Production. Produced by Ishmail Merchant. Directed by James Ivory. Written by Walter Marks. Starring James Coco, Raquel Welch, Perry King, David Dukes. VHS: Embassy (1.33) 95 min. DVD: MGM (1.85) 109 min.; Extras: Theatrical trailer; Featurette "Hollywood Hoopla."

This early Merchant Ivory Production, based on the 1928 poem by Joseph Moncure March, recounts the tragic incidents that occur at a party given by a fading silent film star (James Coco) and his beautiful mistress (Raquel Welch). Although highly publicized by AIP while in production, the finished product failed to meet with Sam Arkoff's approval. The film was cut to 95 minutes and extensively restructured, which only succeeded in making it a confusing mess. Now restored to the original length for DVD, *The Wild Party* has its moments but somehow still fails as a whole, despite some good performances (by Welch in particular) and lavish production values. Former porn star Paul Barresi, who once claimed

Raquel Welch and James Coco in *The Wild Party*.

to have had a two-year affair with John Travolta, can be spotted as the party bartender. The truncated theatrical version was available on VHS from Embassy Home Video.

Review: *Time* (August 18, 1975), "*The Wild Party* never develops the fine frenzy it needs. There is all manner of period decadence festooning the screen, rendered too campily to have much force."

Wuthering Heights

"THE POWER, THE PASSION, THE TERROR OF EMILY BRONTE'S IMMORTAL STORY OF YOUNG LOVE."

(January 1971) Color by Movielab. Produced by James H. Nicholson, Samuel Z. Arkoff, and Louis M. Heyward. Directed by Robert Fuest. Written by Patrick Tilley. Starring Timothy Dalton, Anna Calder-Marshall, Harry Andrews, Ian Ogilvy. DVD: MGM (1.85) 104 min.; Extras: Fullscreen version.

When producer Louis M. Heyward agreed to go to England to supervise AIP's British production unit, it was with the condition that he could do a version of Emily Bronte's *Wuthering Heights*. Although Sam Arkoff attempted to renege on the deal, Heyward eventually convinced him to go ahead with the project by presenting it as a horror movie. The end result is one of AIP's finest productions. Although Heyward and director Robert Fuest had originally envisioned a much longer film, the outcome doesn't seem all that compromised save for some rather accelerated pacing. Timothy Dalton and Anna Calder-Marshall are excellent as the star-crossed lovers Heathcliff and Cathy. The supporting cast includes the lovely Hilary Dwyer, who was under contract to AIP. She was a particular favorite of producer Heyward and appeared in four of the British AIP productions. Michel Legrand contributes a memorable background score which was released on American International Records. Although its reputation is overshadowed by the 1939 version, *Wuthering Heights* can certainly stand on its own as a powerful film adaptation of the novel. There are liberties taken

Anna Calder-Marshall is Cathy in AIP's excellent version of Emily Bronte's classic novel *Wuthering Heights*.

with the original text but, in the end, they seem perfectly in keeping with the spirit of the book. John Coquillon's outstanding color cinematography helps to make this the classiest-looking AIP film ever. So classy, in fact, that it was the first American International movie to open at New York's prestigious Radio City Music Hall. In 1972, a sequel based on the second half of the book was announced as *Return to Wuthering Heights* but nothing ever came of it. That same year, Nathaniel Hawthorne's *The House of Seven Gables* was also on AIP's production schedule, to be directed by Robert Fuest. Although scripts were written by both Gary Elmes and Gerry DePego, this project also fell by the wayside.

Review: *Time* (March 1, 1971), "Though [Robert] Fuest seems to leave his players to their own devices, he has a fine camera eye."

"X" the Man with the X-Ray Eyes

"HE STRIPPED SOULS AS BARE AS BODIES!"

(September 1963) Pathécolor. Produced and Directed by Roger Corman. Written by Robert Dillon and Ray Russell. Starring Ray Milland, Diane van der Vlis, Harold J. Stone, Don Rickles. DVD: MGM (1.85) 80 min.; Extras: Theatrical trailer; Audio commentary by Roger Corman, TV prologue.

A modern fable illustrating the adage that too much knowledge can be a dangerous thing. Dr. James Xavier (Ray Milland) has developed a formula which enables him to greatly increase the range of his vision. Unfortunately he cannot control it and the effects are cumulative. Eventually the unpredictable influence of the drug unbalances Xavier's mind and he suffers the consequences. Although a three-week shooting schedule and $300,000 budget seem minuscule by today's standards of filmmaking, at the time they were even more generous than the time and money spent on some of the Poe movies. Jim Nicholson thought up the title and then asked Roger Corman to help him develop the plot. It was Corman who came up with the idea of making the central character an altruistic research scientist instead of a criminal, which had been Nicholson's first inclination. Ray Russell and Robert Dillion took this idea and turned it into a sober and thought-provoking screenplay. Corman has expressed dissatisfaction with the special effects but, given the budget, the X-Ray visuals (dubbed "Spectarama") are very effective. In the lead role, Milland seems rather cold and unsympathetic, much as he

Ray Milland confesses to Diane van der Vlis that he has seen too much in "X" the Man with the X-Ray Eyes.

had the previous year in *The Premature Burial.* The only time Milland's cranky character cracks a smile and seems to be enjoying himself is when he suddenly gets the ability to see through clothing at a twist party. Milland aside, the film is well cast and includes a number of familiar faces. Sci-fi–horror movie stalwarts John Hoyt, Morris Ankrum and John Dierkes are on hand. Corman also finds small roles for his reliable players Jonathan Haze, Barboura Morris and Dick Miller. The extras on the DVD include a prologue which was expressly filmed for the network television showings. As with the MGM DVD of *Pit and the Pendulum*, this is incorrectly identified as the "Theatrical Prologue." This film is also available in the Roger Corman Collection boxed set but without any of the extras.

Yog—Monster from Space

"THE MIGHTIEST MONSTER EVER ...
RUNS AMOK THROUGH OUR UNIVERSE!"

(August 1971) ColorScope (TohoScope and Eastman Color). A Toho Co. Ltd. Production. Produced by Tomoyuki Tanaka and Fumio Tanaka. Directed by Ishiro Honda. Written by Ei Ogawa. Starring Kenji Sahara, Akira Kubo, Yoshio Tsuchiya, Tetsu Nakamura. DVD: Media Blasters (as *Space Amoeba*) (2.35) 84 min.; Extras: Japanese with English subtitles or English-language options; Audio commentary by Fumio Tanaka; Documentary "Meet the Marine Animals Behind the Monsters"; Theatrical trailer.

A Japanese rocket is sent into space to orbit Jupiter. On the way it is waylaid by a mysterious blue substance which steers the rocket back to Earth where it crashes into the ocean off an island near Japan. This island is being considered as a future vacation resort. Two representatives of the development company, a photographer, and a scientist have been sent there to consider the feasibility of this venture. The blue substance from the rocket infiltrates the bodies of some of the local marine life and causes them to grow to gigantic size. These monsters are Gezora (a giant squid), Ganimes (a giant crab), and Kamoebas (a giant turtle). After menacing the humans in its various giant guises, the alien presence is eventually defeated by the sound waves made by bats. The explanation for this makes no sense whatsoever but then not much does in this completely weird movie. *Yog—Monster from Space* is one of the later films in the first cycle of Japanese monster films. It differs from many other Toho productions in that it features three new creatures who do not appear in any other movies. Confined to the island setting, these creatures are also given no opportunity to stomp Tokyo and must make do with palm trees and native huts. This highly entertaining movie was released in Japan in 1970 under the title *Kessen Nanki No Daikaiju.* The excellent quality DVD from Media Blasters is not the AIP dub.

The Young Racers

"A LITTLE DEATH EACH DAY ...
A LOT OF LOVE EVERY NIGHT!"

(January 1963) Pathécolor. Produced and Directed by Roger Corman. Written by R. Wright Campbell. Starring Mark Damon, William Campbell, Luana Anders, Robert Campbell. DVD: MGM/Fox Roger Corman box set (1.66) 83 min.

Despite the title, *The Young Racers* is not about hot-rodding teens. It is a well-written and competently acted adult drama. Race car driver Joe Machin (William Campbell) is a womanizing heel who is determined to become Grand Prix champion. Ex-driver turned writer Stephen Children (Mark Damon) finds out that Machin is the man who stole his fiancée and then dumped her. He decides to get even by befriending Machin and then writing a character-assassinating book about him. Along the way, both men find out that they have a lot to learn about life and each other. When AIP gave Roger Corman a budget of $150,000 and the go-ahead to make a movie in Europe, he contacted R. Wright Campbell and asked him to take an unsold script that Campbell had written about a bullfighter and change the character to a race car driver. Campbell complied, thereby providing a juicy leading role for his brother, William. As actor "Robert Campbell," he also appears as Joe Machin's onscreen brother, Robert. In addition to the two Campbell brothers, Mark Damon and, in particular, Luana Anders give canny performances. As Stephen Children's secretary Henny, Ms. Anders makes every one of her scenes count, delivering her lines with quiet authority and an underlying sense of irony. British actor Patrick Magee is also on hand as a spiteful member of the gentry who has his own reasons for getting even with Joe Machin. It was shot on location in Monte Carlo, Belgium, France and England; Floyd Crosby's color cinematography at times seems like a beautiful travelogue of Europe. After filming on The Young Racers was completed, soundman Francis Coppola convinced Corman to finance a feature he wanted to direct in Dublin using cast members William Campbell, Luana Anders and Patrick Magee. The end result was Dementia 13.

The Young, the Evil and the Savage

"SLAVES TO THEIR OWN STRANGE DESIRES!"

(July 1968) Widescreen (Cromoscope) and Color by Perfect. Produced by Lawrence Woolner and G. De Blasio (Virgilio De Blasi). Directed by Anthony Dawson (Antonio Margheriti). Written by Anthony Dawson, Frank Bottar (Franco Bottari) and John Simonelli (Giovanni Simonelli). Starring Mark Damon, Michael Rennie, Eleanora Brown, Sally Smith. DVD: Dark Sky (as Naked You Die) (2.35) 98 min.; Italian-language version with English subtitles; Extras: Italian theatrical trailer; Photo gallery.

There are dire goings-on at St. Hilda's College, an exclusive school for girls. A mysterious killer is dispatching the students and staff one by one. Is it the new gym instructor, the uptight French teacher, the handsome riding instructor, or the lecherous handyman? Or, perhaps, it is one of the pretty students? This early Giallo features the requisite elements of a black-gloved killer, beautiful female victims, lots of suspicious characters, and a twist ending. It is, however, less bloody than most Gialli and has only the briefest nudity, despite an original title that would suggest otherwise (Nude ... si muore/Naked You Die). This was yet another American International European pickup which suffered the usual indignities of cutting (to 82 minutes) and a ridiculous title change. Although the Gialli would really take off a year later following the release of Dario Argento's The Bird with the Crystal Plumage, this is a respectable and entertaining enough addition to the genre. The main title song "Nightmare" (sung by Rose Brennen) lives up to its name and will torture your mind long after the film has ended. Mario Bava reportedly had a hand in writing the film but his name does not appear in the credits.

Appendix 1: American International Television

The following films were purchased by AIP for television release. Excluded are the films distributed by AIP-TV that had been released theatrically by other companies.

Attack of the Mushroom People

(1963) TohoScope and Eastman Color. A Toho Co. Ltd. Production. Produced by Tomoyuki Tanaka. Directed by Ishiro Honda. Written by Masami Fukushima, Shinichi Hoshi, and Sakyo Komatsu. Starring Akira Kubo, Miki Yashiro, Kumi Mizuno, Kenji Sahara. DVD: Media Blasters (as *Matango*) (2.35) 89 min.; Extras: Japanese with English subtitles or English-language options; Audio commentary by Akira Kubo; Video interview with Teruyoshi Nakano; Audio interview with Masami Fukushima; Trailers.

A yacht with seven passengers is shipwrecked on a mysterious island where, years before, a team of radioactivity experts disappeared while conducting a scientific investigation. The log of the previous expedition's captain warns not to eat the mushrooms which grow in great abundance all over the island. The castaways soon discover the reason for the captain's warning when fungus-covered monstrosities begin to menace them. Released in Japan in 1963 as *Matango*, the movie showed up the following year in the U.S. as part of an AIP television package. Rechristened *Attack of the Mushroom People*, it became much beloved by the adolescent aficionados of Saturday afternoon horror programs. The film is a definite change of pace for Toho, whose fantasy films usually consisted of an over-sized monster destroying Tokyo. *Attack of the Mushroom People* is very slow-paced and often silly but it does have a very creepy atmosphere which is some compensation. The English-language option on the DVD is the original AIP dub.

The Aztec Mummy
Curse of the Aztec Mummy
The Robot vs. the Aztec Mummy

(1957) Black & White. Cinematografica Calderon Productions. Produced by William (Guillermo) Calderon Stell. Directed by Rafael Portillo. Written by Guillermo Calderon Stell and Alfredo Salazar. Starring Ramon Gay, Rosita Arenas, Crox Alverado, Luis Aceves Castenada. DVD: BCI Eclipse (*The Aztec Mummy Collection*) (1.33) 195 min.

In 1957, Mexico's Guillermo Calderon Stell made three movies back to back in two months time. All of them featured a monster known as the Aztec Mummy. In the first of these films, *La Momia Azteca/The Aztec Mummy*, Dr. Eduardo Almada (Ramon Gay) regresses his fiancée Flora (Rosita Arenas) via

The raggedy Popoca makes an appearance in *Curse of the Aztec Mummy*.

hypnosis to her former life as an Aztec priestess in ancient Mexico. He learns that she had a forbidden love affair with the Aztec warrior Popoca and that she was put to death because of this. Popoca was buried alive to watch over a sacred bracelet and breastplate which together hold the key to finding the hidden treasure of the Aztecs. A masked criminal known as "The Bat" wants to find the treasure but his plans are thwarted when the mummy awakens to retrieve the two artifacts which have been stolen from him.

The second film is *La Maldición de la Momia Azteca/The Curse of the Aztec Mummy*. It picks up where the previous film left off with "The Bat" unmasked as the nefarious Dr. Krupp (Luis Aceves Castenada). Krupp gains possession of the bracelet and breastplate by hypnotizing Flora again. A masked avenger known as "The Angel" attempts to interfere with Krupp's scheme but, once again, it is the Aztec Mummy who saves the day and carries Krupp off to almost certain death. The final film in the trilogy, *La Momia Azteca contra el Robot Humano/The Robot vs. the Aztec Mummy*, takes place five years later. Dr. Almada and Flora are now married but Dr. Krupp reappears to disrupt their happiness. Krupp is still obsessed with getting that damn treasure and this time he has built a robot to get the artifacts away from the Aztec Mummy. The Aztec Mummy films are obviously heavily influenced by the Universal series of the Forties which featured Lon Chaney Jr. as Kharis the living mummy. Compared to poor Popoca, Kharis is almost debonair. Popoca is little more than a rag, a bone, and a hank o' hair. And his appearance in each of the three films is limited to the final reel. As in the Universal films, the flashback to ancient times is repeated over and over again throughout the trilogy. The final Aztec Mummy movie has flashbacks from the two previous films which take up nearly half the total running time which is only 65 minutes. K. Gordon Murray produced English-language versions of the second and third installments in the series and these were picked up by American International for television distribution in 1965. The DVD box set is called *The Aztec Mummy Collection*. There are three discs, one for each title. *The Aztec Mummy* was never dubbed into English so it has only a Spanish-language track with English subtitles. The other two films are presented both in Spanish with English subtitles and in the AIP television versions dubbed into English.

Count Dracula

(1970) Eastman Color. A Towers of London Production. Produced by Harry Alan Towers. Directed by Jess Franco. Written by Peter Welbeck (a.k.a. Harry Alan Towers). Starring Christopher Lee, Herbert Lom, Klaus Kinski, Maria Rohm. DVD: Dark Sky (1.33) 97 min. Extras: Jess Franco featurette "Beloved Count," Christopher Lee reads *Dracula*, Soledad Miranda essay by Amy Brown, Poster and still galleries.

"Over fifty years ago Bram Stoker wrote the greatest of all horror stories. Now, for the first time, we retell exactly as he wrote one of the first—and still the best—tales of the macabre." With this encouraging, though somewhat awkwardly written, statement,

Christopher Lee, shown here with Soledad Miranda, greatly resembles Bram Stoker's description of *Count Dracula*.

Count Dracula begins. Despite this lofty claim, the Spanish-Italian-West German co-production is only marginally more faithful to the novel than the movie versions which preceded it. After years of complaining about the treatment of the Dracula character in the Hammer films, Christopher Lee still expresses great enthusiasm for this one. In his autobiography, following the usual harangue about Hammer, he states: "*Count Dracula* ... was a damn good try at doing the Count as Stoker meant him to be. It was made with the deepest of bows to the theatre manager who invented the character. In the whole vast Dracula industry it was virtually unique in that." His fondness for *Count Dracula* seems to stem more from his antagonism towards Hammer than it does from the merits of the film itself. Herein, Lee as Dracula is first presented as a white-haired older gentleman with a mustache. As such, he delivers an impassioned monologue which is mostly taken verbatim from the book. Later on, with dark hair (his youth revived by the drinking of blood), Lee is basically required to do exactly what he did in the Hammer series. The main differences from Hammer are that in *Count Dracula* the costumes and sets are less opulent and the direction of the film consists primarily of zooms in and out ... over and over again. Director Jess Franco has legions of fans for his enormous body of work, some of it good and some bad. This movie falls firmly in the latter category. The Spanish locales never for a minute suggest England or Transylvania. The action is confined for the most part to Castle Dracula and the asylum run by Dr. Seward (Paul Muller) and Professor Van Helsing (Herbert Lom). This asylum is where all the characters converge and the majority of the story is played out. The casting of Klaus Kinski as Renfield would seem to be an inspired one but, unfortunately, he has no dialogue and is required to do little more than look crazy ... not a stretch for Mr. Kinski. The rest of the cast, with the exception of Lom, give lackluster performances. The fascinating details of Stoker's novel are, for the most part, missing and the film has no atmosphere whatsoever.

An Evening of Edgar Allan Poe

(1970) Color. Produced and Directed by Ken Johnson. Adapted by David Welch and Ken Johnson. Starring Vincent Price. DVD: MGM (1.33) 53 min., Midnite Movies co-feature: *The Tomb of Ligeia*.

In one of their rare excursions into original programming for television, American International, in conjunction with Ken Johnson Productions, produced this one-hour special for TV syndication. The program is a one-man showcase for the esteemed talents of Vincent Price who was, by 1970, considered the premier interpreter of Edgar Allan Poe onscreen. The show consists of four acts: "The Tell-Tale Heart," "The Sphinx," "The Cask of Amontillado" and "The Pit and the Pendulum." In each, Price, dressed in appropriate attire, is alone on a single set and enacts the Poe short story. *An Evening with Edgar Allan*

Vincent Price stars in the sequence "The Pit and the Pendulum" from *An Evening of Edgar Allan Poe*.

Poe is invaluable as a record of Price's forte as a stage performer. It is basically a theatrical performance with a minimum of camera tricks involved. Each segment is a gem of characterization and dramatic power. The weakest entry is "The Sphinx" but this has less to do with Price's performance than it does with the source (one of Poe's more obscure tales). The program should have earned an Emmy for Price but it didn't even garner a nomination. Price's costumes were designed by his wife at that time, Mary Grant. Les Baxter provides the background music, which is totally original and not cribbed from his Poe film scores. Oddly, this music was available on LP and CD while the fine music he composed for the Roger Corman Poe features was not.

Hercules Against the Mongols

"Hercules the Mighty, Pitted Against the Ruthless Mongol Conqueror!"

(1964) Totalscope and Eastman Color. A Jonia Film Production. Produced by Jacopo Comin. Directed by Domenico Paolella. Written by Alessandro Ferrau, Luciano Martino and Domenico Paolella. Starring Mark Forest, Maria Grazia Spina, Ken Clark, Jose Greci. DVD: DigiView (1.33) 90 min., DVD co-feature: *Hercules and the Princess of Troy*.

Once again Maciste undergoes a name change to Hercules for the U.S. release of *Maciste contro i mongoli/Maciste Against the Mongols*. This time around, Hercules (Mark Forest) runs afoul of the three beefy, lunkheaded sons of Genghis Khan (Ken Clark, Nadir Baltimore, and Renato Rossini). When the mighty Khan dies, his evil sons renege on their father's promises of peace. They kidnap a Polish princess (Maria Grazia Spina) and attempt to get her to reveal the whereabouts of her kingdom's hidden treasure. Hercules lets himself be taken prisoner in order to set the princess free. Much of the convoluted plot is merely an excuse to show off the requisite feats of strength which are part and parcel of the Peplum genre ... including the ever-popular fight with a lion. Clark had starred in AIP's *Attack of the Giant Leeches* (1958) before embarking on a European film career. Baltimore and Rossini (also known as Red Ross or Howard Ross) starred as Samson and Maciste respectively in *Ercole, Sansone, Maciste e Ursus: gli invincibili/Hercules, Samson, Maciste, and Ursus; The Invincibles* (1964) which was known as *Samson and the Mighty Challenge* on this side of the Atlantic. The DigiView DVD of *Hercules Against the Mongols* is just what you would expect from a disc which offers two movies for a buck. The source is a pan-and-scan 16mm print which has variable color but decent sound quality.

Hercules and the Black Pirate

"The Unrelenting Fury of a Titan's Strength!"

(1964) Totalscope and Eastman Color. A Romana Film Production. Produced by Fortunato Misiano. Directed by Luigi Capuano. Written by Arpad De Riso. Starring Alan Steel, Rosalba Neri, Piero Lulli, Andrea Aureli. DVD: Retromedia (1.33) 89 min., Main feature: *Hercules the Avenger*.

This movie, also known as *Hercules and the Pirates*, finds our muscle-bound hero in 16th century Spain. Hercules (Alan Steel) comes to the aid of the governor's family when the youngest daughter is kidnapped by pirates and held for ransom. A fairly standard Peplum plot is given a novel twist because of the unusual setting but little else has changed. For once, Rosalba Neri is the heroine, instead of her usual role of archvillainess. The DVD is taken from a pan-and-scan television print but it does have some decent color. The film was given only a limited, regional theatrical release by AIP before being relegated to a television package. The original Italian title was *Sansone contro il corsaro nero/Samson and the Black Pirate*.

Hercules and the Masked Rider

(1964) Totalscope and Eastman Color. A Romana Film Production. Produced by Fortunato Misiano. Directed by Piero Pierotti. Written by Luciano Martino and Piero Pierotti. Starring Alan Steel, Mimmo Palmara, Jose Greci, Ettore Manni. DVD: DigiView (1.33) 86 min., DVD co-feature: *Hercules and the Tyrants of Babylon*.

The original Italian title was *Golia e il cavaliere mascherto/Goliath and the Masked Rider* and in all European versions, the name of the title character translates to Goliath. Whether called Goliath or Hercules, the character seems out of place in what appears to be 16th century Spain. He is also a supporting character in the storyline with the main focus being on the Masked Rider. Don Juan (Mimmo Palmara) returns home from fighting in Flanders to find that his beloved Dona Blanca (Jose Greci) is unwillingly betrothed to Don Romero (the ever villainous Arturo Dominici). Don Juan is banished and takes up with a band of gypsies led by the fiery Estrella (Pilar Cansino). Also in this gypsy band is the strongman Hercules (Alan Steel). Don Juan dons a crimson mask, gloves, and cape and becomes the Masked Rider, a Zorro type who fights against the oppression of Don Romero. A secondary love story concerns Balasco (Ettore Manni), a reluctant soldier in Don Romero's army, who falls in love with Estrella. It all turns out well in the end with Don Juan marrying Dona Blanca, Balasco marrying Estrella, and Hercules riding off into the sunset with a very queenie gypsy gentleman on the back of his horse (what?!). *Hercules and the Masked Rider* is interesting for a number of reasons. The setting is a change of pace from the standard sword-and-sandal movie, but the Hercules character seems like an afterthought and has little to do with the plot other than participate in a few brawls. For once it is nice to see Mimmo Palmara as the heroic lead. A handsome and extremely capable performer, he seems to have appeared in more European costume movies than any other actor, usually as the villain. The role played by Ettore Manni (another costume picture regular) at first appears to be a relatively minor one but midway his character moves to the forefront of the story and remains a focal point to the end. The DigiView bargain DVD of this title is of course a pan-and-scan TV print (the American International Television logo is at the beginning) but both the color and sound are acceptable. There are certainly far worse copies of public domain Euro-epics out there which cost more than the one dollar price tag on this one.

Hercules and the Tyrants of Babylon

"AGAINST THE THUNDERING ATTACK OF THE MIGHTY BABYLONIAN CAVALRY STANDS HERCULES ... HIS ONLY WEAPON HIS SUPERHUMAN STRENGTH!"

(1964) Totalscope and Eastman Color. A Romana Film Production. Produced by Fortunato Misiano. Directed by Domenico Paolella. Written by Luciano Martino. Starring Rock Stevens, Helga Line, Piero Lulli, Livio Lorenzon. DVD: DigiView (1.33) 87 min., DVD co-feature: *Hercules and the Masked Rider*.

Bodybuilder Rock Stevens (real name: Peter Lupus) went from *Muscle Beach Party* to ancient Babylon to play Hercules in this substandard sword-and-sandal movie. The rulers of Babylon and Assyria are both attempting to locate Esperia, queen of the Helledes. Reportedly she is among the numerous captive slaves in Babylon. Hercules, who is in love with Esperia, is also trying to ascertain her whereabouts. This film employs numerous poorly matched outtakes from the big-budget Biblical spectacle *Sodom and Gomorrah* (1962). Hidden in the caverns below Babylon, Hercules discovers a mechanism which has huge chains attached to the buildings of the city. When he turns a great wheel, the chains tighten and pull the city down. This enabled the producers to use footage from the finale scenes of *Sodom and*

Gomorrah which shows the destruction of the twin cities. In addition to playing Willy on the television series Mission Impossible, Lupus was one of the earliest celebrities to show his "willie" in a 1974 issue of Playgirl magazine. Although AIP picked up a number of European sword-and-sandal films for distribution by American International Television, only a handful were given a theatrical regional release. Hercules and the Tyrants of Babylon was one of these titles but the release was a meager one.

Mars Needs Women

(1967) Color. An Azalea Pictures Production. Produced by Larry Buchanan and Edwin Tobolowsky. Written and Directed by Larry Buchanan. Starring Tommy Kirk, Yvonne Craig, Warren Hammack, Cal Duggan. DVD: MGM (1.33) 82 min.

Texas-based filmmaker Larry Buchanan (1923–2004) began his association with American International Pictures in 1963 when they distributed his "adults only" interracial drama Free, White and 21. Jim Nicholson and Sam Arkoff were so pleased with the box office results that they signed Buchanan to direct color features for their American International Television division. Using such familiar stars as Tommy Kirk, John Agar, Aron Kincaid, and Paul Petersen, Buchanan cranked out a body of work unrivaled in cheapness even by AIP standards. The resultant eight movies consisted of five remakes of AIP Fifties films and three original stories. The remakes were of Invasion of the Saucer Men (as The Eye Creatures, 1965), It Conquered the World (as Zontar, the Thing from Venus, 1966), Day the World Ended (as In the Year 2889, 1967), The She-Creature (as Creature of Destruction, 1967), and Suicide Battalion (as Hell Raiders, 1968). The three original stories were Curse of the Swamp Creature (1966), It's Alive (1967) and the movie at hand, Mars Needs Women (1967). Filmed in Texas by Buchanan's Azalea Pictures, the movies were all shot in 16mm with budgets between $22,000 and $30,000 ... and it certainly shows. What sets Mars Needs Women apart from Buchanan's other sci-fi efforts is its unforgettable title and the fact that it doesn't have a cheesy monster. Instead we get five horny Martian guys (Tommy Kirk, Warren Hammack, Larry Tanner, Anthony Huston, Cal Duggan) dressed in skin diving outfits. These five come to Earth for twenty-four hours with the purpose of abducting five fertile girls to help repopulate their female-deficient planet. Yvonne Craig is a scientist who becomes the object of Kirk's affections. But the most interesting of the candidates is stripper Bubbles Cash, who gets to perform one of her routines before being whisked off to the waiting spaceship. The one positive aspect of this picture is Kirk. Generally cast in comedic parts, here he gives a decent performance in a serious role. Gluttons for punishment can get most of Buchanan's other AIP TV titles on DVD from Retromedia.

Terror in the Crypt

(1964) Black & White. A Mec Cinematografica/Hispamer Film Production. Produced by William Mulligan. Directed by Thomas Miller (a.k.a. Camillo Mastrocinque). Written by Robert Bohr (Tonino Valeri) and Julian Berry (Ernesto Gastaldi). Starring Christopher Lee, Audrey Amber (Adriana Ambesi), Ursula Davis. (Pier Anna Quaglia), Jose Campos. DVD: Retromedia (as Crypt of the Vampire) (1.85) 84 min.

After Roger Vadim's Blood and Roses (1960) and before Hammer's The Vampire Lovers (1970), there was La cripta e l'incubo/Crypt of the Vampire. This Italian-Spanish co-production is yet another screen adaptation of J. Sheridan LeFanu's classic vampire novella Carmilla. Count von Karnstein (Christopher Lee) believes that his daughter Laura (Audrey Amber) may be the reincarnation of an ancestor who was put to death for being a witch. When a beautiful girl named Lyuba (Ursula Davis) arrives at Karnstein Castle, the count fears she may become Laura's next victim. Only a few incidents from LeFanu's story remain and, at times, *Terror in the Crypt* seems to owe more to Mario Bava's *Black Sunday* than its literary source of inspiration. As with many Euro-horror films, the plot seldom makes sense but the movie is suffused with creepy atmosphere. *Terror in the Crypt* (on the DVD, this is the title that appears on screen) was picked up by AIP exclusively for television release and never received theatrical distribution in the United States. The Retromedia print is uncut (the film was usually edited on TV to fit a 90-minute time slot) and is decent quality, though certainly not pristine.

The Vampire

(1957) Black & White. A Cinematografica ABSA Production. Produced by Abel Salazar. Directed by Fernando Mendez. Written by Ramon Obon. Starring German Robles, Abel Salazar, Ariadna Welter, Carmen Montego.

The Vampire's Coffin

(1957) Black & White. A Cinematografica ABSA Production. Produced by Abel Salazar. Directed by Fernando Mendez. Written by Raul Zenteno and Ramon Obon. Starring German Robles, Abel Salazar, Ariadna Welter, Alicia Montoya. DVD: CasaNegra (*The Vampire Collection*) (1.33) 168 min.; Extras: Audio commentary by Robert Cotter, Photo essay "Fear ala Mexicana!," U.S. theatrical radio spots, Abel Salazar's obituary from *The Boston Globe*.

Marta/Martha (Ariadna Welter) arrives in the small Mexican town of Sierra Negra. She has been away from her family home, the Sycamores, for many years but has now come back because her beloved aunt is ailing. When she arrives at the Sycamores, Martha finds the house in ruins and her aunt already dead. A mysterious Hungarian gentleman, Mr. Duval (German Robles), appears and insists that Martha and her remaining family sell the house to him. Duval is actually the vampire Count Lavud, who is attempting to revive a blood-sucking brother who is buried in the crypt at the Sycamores. Producer Abel Salazar also plays the hero of the piece, Enrique/Henry. By Mexican horror standards *El Vampiro* (*The Vampire*) is a fairly sophisticated film, particularly when compared to the Aztec Mummy series. Although there is some speculation that this film influenced *Horror of Dracula* (a.k.a. *Dracula*), which was released the following year, it is doubtful that *The Vampire* was shown in England prior to the filming of the Hammer movie. Other than Count Lavud having pronounced fangs (previously referred to but not shown in vampire movies) there no other connection to the Hammer film. *The Vampire* far more readily recalls the Universal horror films of the Thirties and Forties with German Robles' performance clearly influenced by Bela Lugosi. Six months after the release of *The Vampire*, a sequel called *El Ataud del Vampiro* (*The Vampire's Coffin*) was in theatres, featuring the three main stars reprising their roles from the previous film. In this picture, a misguided doctor steals the coffin of Count Lavud and brings it to a hospital in order to perform experiments on its occupant. In this hospital, Henry (Salazar) is a doctor trying to help his patient Martha (Welter) recover from her dreadful ordeal with the vampire. Count Lavud (Robles) is, of course, revived and takes up residence in a nearby wax museum. Once again he sets his undead sights on Martha. The biggest surprise in *The Vampire's Coffin* is that mousey Martha is the star of an elaborate stage musical (with the fastest costume and scenery changes you've ever seen). The best thing about both films is striking German Robles who makes a very impressive vampire. The worst thing is Abel Salazar, who plays Henry far too broadly for laughs. CasaNegra's *The Vampire Collection* features both movies in Spanish with English subtitles or in the English language-dubbed versions (courtesy of K. Gordon Murray). Both *The Vampire* and *The Vampire's Coffin* showed up in AIP television packages in the mid-sixties. Around that same time they also had limited theatrical showings in the U.S. *The Vampire's Coffin* was double billed with *The Robot vs. the Aztec Mummy* in 1965 and *The Vampire* was released with *Curse of the Doll People* in 1968.

Voyage to the Prehistoric Planet

(1965) Pathecolor. Produced by George Edwards. Written and Directed by John Sebastian (a.k.a. Curtis Harrington). Starring Basil Rathbone, Faith Domergue, Marc Shannon, Christopher Brand. DVD: Alpha (1.33) 77 min.

When Roger Corman and AIP acquired the rights to the 1962 Russian space film *Planeta Burg/Planet of Storms*, who could have imagined that it would be stretched into three feature films? The first of these was *Voyage to the Prehistoric Planet* in which three spaceships embark on the first manned voyage to the planet Venus. One of them is destroyed when it is hit by a meteor. The second crashlands on Venus and the third manages to land safely as a rescue party. While exploring the planet, the astronauts discover a variety of animal life much like that on Earth in prehistoric times. Among these are hopping man-sized lizards, a brontosaurus, and a flying reptile. Cut into the Russian film is useless expository footage shot by AIP featuring Basil Rathbone and Faith Domergue. Apparently Rathbone only worked a half-day on the film before moving on to *Queen of Blood* (1966), the second film to incorporate effects footage from *Planeta Burg*. The writing and direction of *Voyage to the Prehistoric Planet* is credited to John Sebastian, actually a pseudonym for Curtis Harrington. In 1968, footage from *Planeta Burg* was again utilized for *Voyage to the Planet of Prehistoric Women* starring Mamie Van Doren and directed by Peter Bogdanovich using the name Derek Thomas. Of the three films, *Queen of Blood*, also directed by Harrington, is the most interesting. *Voyage to the Prehistoric Planet* is a fairly dull affair, despite some interesting visuals. There is also an annoying *Lost in Space*-type robot who does nothing to enliven the proceedings. Ronald Stein contributes a background score which reuses his themes from earlier films such as *Dinosaurus!* and *Attack of the 50 Foot Woman*. AIP originally planned to release *Voyage to the Prehistoric Planet* theatrically on a double bill with *Psycho-Circus* but instead it was relegated to one of their TV packages.

War Gods of Babylon

(1962) CinemaScope and Eastman Color. An Apo Film/Globe Films International Production. Produced by Aldo Pomilia. Directed by Silvio Amadio. Written by Gino De Santis, Luigi De Simone, Sergio Spina. Starring Howard Duff, Jackie Lane, Luciano Marin, Giancarlo Sbragia. DVD: Retromedia (2.35) 82 min., DVD co-feature: *War Goddess*.

Over the years, TV viewers became accustomed to seeing many of the sixties Euro-epics in terrible pan-and-scan prints with washed-out color. Although many of the films were not particularly good, this is no way to see any movie and be able to judge it fairly. Fortunately the advent of DVD has caused some interested parties to restore a growing number of these films to their original theatrical presentations. *War Gods of Babylon* is one such title to benefit from this type of restoration. Never given a U.S. theatrical release, it was distributed as part of an AIP television package in 1964 and quickly forgotten. The movie's one claim to fame is the unusual casting of Howard Duff in the lead. Duff was best known at the time for the 1957 TV series *Mr. Adams and Eve* in which he co-starred with his then-wife Ida Lupino. Known in Europe as *La sette folgori di Assur/The Seventh Thunderbolt of Assur*, *War Gods of Babylon* features Duff as Sardanapale, the king of Nineveh and conqueror of Babylon. He places his brother Shamash (Luciano Marin) on the throne of Babylon but conflict arises between the brothers when Sardanapale falls in love with Shamash's betrothed, Myrrha (Jackie Lane). The climax of the film comes when a tremendous flood destroys the city of Nineveh. Although a fairly mediocre entry in the Euro-epic genre, *War Gods of Babylon* does have excellent production values and some impressive special effects. These can now be better appreciated in the fine widescreen restoration from Retromedia.

Yongary: Monster from the Deep

(1967) Widescreen and Color. Produced by Cha Tae-jin. Directed by Kim Ki-duk. Written by Seo Yoon-seong and Kim Ki-duk. Starring Oh Young-il, Nam Ching-im, Kang Moon, Lee Kwang-ho. DVD: MGM/Fox (2.35) 80 min., Midnite Movies co-feature: *Konga*.

From the deep what? Certainly not the ocean. South Korea's answer to Godzilla makes even the worst of the Japanese monster movies look like masterpieces by comparison. After much nonsense involving a Korean observation spacecraft, earthquakes begin to ravage Korea. As the quakes move closer to Seoul, it is discovered that they are being caused by an enormous prehistoric reptile who is immediately identified as Yongary.

Like his Japanese counterpart, Yongary breathes fire. Unlike his Japanese counterpart, you can clearly see the pipe in his mouth every time he does so. While most of the populace of Seoul flees in panic, a number of people stay behind to gorge themselves on Korean barbeque and dance drunkenly at the disco. After stomping on numerous miniature buildings, Yongary decides to stop for dinner at an oil refinery where he guzzles huge amounts of fuel oil and gasoline. This seems particularly horrifying in light of today's gas prices. A mischievous brat named Icho (Lee Kwang-ho) turns his "Itching Light Ray" on Yongary and the monster does a dance to a rock 'n' roll tune by composer Chun Jung-kun, who supplies the film's tedious background score. After Yongary's dance routine, the military fires missiles at the creature to no effect. A young scientist discovers that Yongary reacts badly to ammonia so they drop an ammonia powder on him from a helicopter. As the poor monster falls in the water writhing in pain he suddenly begins to bleed profusely from his rectum (I kid you not). Observing this, the cast members laugh and laugh and laugh until one of them soberly observes: "I wonder if he really meant to hurt us?" The original Korean title is *Daeguesu Yonggary/The Great Monster Yonggary*. After only being seen here in 16mm pan-and-scan television prints, the Midnite Movie version goes back to the original elements, resulting in a pristine 2.35 color transfer.

Appendix 2:
The Unfilmed AIP

Through the years, American International often announced future productions which would never see the light of day. There are many instances in which projects were announced that were not made or were eventually released under a different title (see Appendix 4 for title changes).

March 20, 1955, address to North Central Allied Exhibitors at their annual convention: James Nicholson announces *One Mile Below*, *Jungle Queen*, and *Johnny Big Gun* as forthcoming productions.

January 1956: England's *The Daily Film Renter* runs a front page article entitled "17 American Features in Anglo's Biggest Deal." It goes on to say that Nat Cohen, managing director of Anglo Amalgamated, has made an agreement with the American Releasing Corporation for 17 new features. Among these titles are *Day of the Beast*, *Girls of Hangtown*, *The Shotgunner*, *Teen Terror*, *Hell's Canyon*, *High School Girl*, *Queen of Hell's Acres*, *Johnny Big Gun*, *The Ant Man*, *The Invisible Monster*, *Hell Raiders*, and *Jet Fighter*. Although no films were produced using these titles, AIP and Anglo Amalgamated had a longstanding distribution deal which lasted over the next two decades.

Film Daily 1956: Advertisement for the newly rechristened American International Pictures lists *Johnny Big Gun*, *Jet Fighter*, *Hell Raiders*, *Ghost of Hell's Canyon*, *The Nth Man*, and *Wolf-Girl* among its future pictures.

Boxoffice October 20, 1956: 1957 combo releases will include *Motorcycle Girls/Underwater Girl* (April), *Rock N Roll Girl/The Juvenile Delinquent* (May), *Jet Fighter/Hell Raiders* (June), *The Nth Man/Last Woman on Earth* (July), *Teenage Revolt/Dragstrip Girl* (September), *Island of Prehistoric Women/Gorilla Girl* (November).

Variety November 1956: AIP will produce 14 to 20 pictures in the next 12 months. Among those are listed *Rock 'n' Roll Kid*, *The Juvenile Delinquent*, *The Nth Man*, *Hell Raiders*, and *Jet Squadron*.

Boxoffice March 2, 1957: AIP has a number of combinations planned for 1957 release which included: *I Was a Teenage Werewolf/Attack of the Saucer Men*, *Girls Reform School/Motorcycle Girl*, *The Cat Girl/Colossus*, *Jet Squadron/Hell Raiders*, *Last Woman on Earth/The Black Terror*, *Girl from 2,000,000 A.D./Island of Prehistoric Women*.

Film Daily April 1957: Alex Gordon's Golden State Productions will produce four more films for AIP in the next five months: *Motorcycle Girls*, *Jet Squadron*, *Battle Front* and *Hell's Canyon*.

In the fall of 1957, AIP sent out an elaborate foldout brochure to exhibitors to promote the release of their *I Was a Teenage Frankenstein/Blood of Dracula* combination. In addition to showing all the AIP films currently in release, it states: "Here are some more big ones coming your way from American International." Listed are the following double features: *The Viking Women/The Astounding She-Monster*, *Jet Attack/Hell Raiders*, *Hot Rod Rock/High School Hell Cats*, *The Fantastic Puppet People/Girl from 5,000 A.D.*

A March 1958 trade ad "introducing anamorphic SUPERAMA" lists the forthcoming double features: *The Fantastic Puppet People/The Girl from 5,000,000 A.D., How to Make a Monster/The Colossal Beast, Submarine X-2/Ram-Jet, The Spider/Beast Without a Body.*

Boxoffice October 20, 1958: *She*—to be shot in Australia with Roger Corman producing and directing. *Eve and the Dragon*—to be shot in South America with Stanley Shpetner producing from his own screenplay. *Take Me to Your Leader*—combination of animated cartoon and live action. *Tank Destroyer*—written, produced, and directed by Burt Topper. *Machine Gun Lady*—written and produced by Stanley Shpetner. *The Dragracers*—a Lou Rusoff production in color. *Insect Woman*—to be produced and directed by Roger Corman.

Boxoffice April 13, 1959: *Bombs Away, Blood Hill, Jules Verne's In the Year 2998, The Last Days of Rome,* and *The Barbarians.*

Boxoffice May 11, 1959: *Medusa, The Haunted House of Usher, Sheba and the Gladiator, The Girl on Death Row, Colossus and the Golden Horde, Take Me to Your Leader, Bombs Away, Foxhole,* and *Eve and the Dragon.*

A June 1959 trade advertisement lists *Colossus and the Golden Horde* as a November 1959 release, *Take Me to Your Leader* (in Cinemascope and color) as a January 1960 release, and *The Mysterious House of Usher* as a February 1960 release.

Boxoffice July 27, 1959: *Aladdin and the Giant*—to be produced in London. *In the Year 2889*—to be produced in Japan. *David and Goliath*—to be produced in Italy and several other European countries in early 1960.

Boxoffice April 18, 1960: *Male and Female, Gateway to Gaza, The Talking Dog,* and *Ali Baba and the 7 Wonders of the World* (in Technirama 70 and Technicolor for Thanksgiving).

Boxoffice May 2, 1960: *The Rough and the Smooth.*

Boxoffice November 14, 1960: *Fright*, a horror film "created for adult patronage" to be released in March 1961.

Boxoffice June 5, 1961: *When the Sleeper Wakes, X,* and *The Haunted Village.*

Boxoffice July 3, 1961: *Black Mutiny, The 7th Wonder of Sinbad, When the Sleeper Wakes, Conjure Wife,* and a color and scope remake of *Metropolis.*

Boxoffice August 28, 1961: *Alabab [sic] and the Seven Miracles of the World* (an animated feature to be made in Japan for release Christmas of 1963), *Witch Wife, The Haunted Village, X, The Sea Fighters.*

A 1962 AIP exhibitors manual includes *The Iron Mask, Warriors Three, The Seafighters, The Maid and the Martian, Survival, The Haunted Village, When the Sleeper Wakes.*

Boxoffice March 26, 1962: *The Adventures of Marco Polo, Wild Cargo, Goliath and the Golden City.*

Film Daily June 8, 1962: *The Seafighters, The Haunted Village, The Children, Anzio Express, Goliath and the Warriors of Genghis Khan, The Mutineers.*

Boxoffice August 27, 1962: *Genghis Khan, The Pit, Schizo, War of the Planets, The Great Deluge, Costa Brava, The Seafighters, The Children, Anzio Express.*

Hollywood Reporter October 4, 1962: A $2 million budget has been given to *War of the Planets* which will begin filming in Hollywood in March 1963. It will be personally produced by James Nicholson from an original script by Harlan Ellison with special effects by Projects Unlimited. The color film is set to star Vincent Price and Boris Karloff.

Hollywood Reporter February 4, 1963: *A Question of Consent, Miracle of the Vikings, Nightmare, Under 21.*

Hollywood Reporter June 7, 1963: *It's Alive, Muscle Beach, Under 21, War of the Planets, Something in the Walls, Genghis Khan, When the Sleeper Wakes, Sins of Babylon,* and *The Magnificent Leonardi.*

Hollywood Reporter October 18, 1963: *The Life and Art of Michaelangelo,* a one-hour TV documentary with Vincent Price as narrator and star, to be filmed in Rome.

Hollywood Reporter December 9, 1963: *Twelve Guns East, House of Terror, Captive City, Warlords of Space, Goliath and the Island of Vampires, The Gold Bug, It's a Wonderful Life, Rumble, Graveside Story, It's Alive, When the Sleeper Wakes, Moon Trap, The Hot Rod Set, Color*

Out of Space, City on the Sea, Genghis Khan, and *She.*

Film Daily March 4, 1964: Annette Funicello will star in *Fireball 500, Robinhood Jones,* and *The Jet Breed.*

A 1964 10th Anniversary trade ad for AIP has ads for both *The Maid and the Martian* and *Pajama Party.* The first lists Tommy Kirk and Annette Funicello as "[a] pair of American's most popular young stars involved in a series of terrifying experiences with unwelcome visitors from outer space." *Pajama Party* is described as "[a] rollicking, nerve-tingling new AIP dramatic innovation in which a pair of teenaged pretties host a pajama party in a haunted palace."

Film Daily June 16, 1964: *The Maid and the Martian, The Warlords of Space, Operation Warhead, Scarlet Friday* ("a terror production starring Boris Karloff and Christopher Lee"), *2145 A.D.—When the Sleeper Wakes, City in the Sea, Malibu Madness, Colour Out of Space, Genghis Khan, The Haunted Planet, 7 Footprints to Satan, Pajama Party,* and *Jet Set.*

Boxoffice June 14, 1964: *Rumble,* a teenage drama starring Frankie Avalon and Annette Funicello.

An AIP publicity announcement from Spring 1965 lists the following titles for release through 1966: *Planet of Terror, Bang! You're Dead, Frankenstein Meets the Giant Devil Fish, Mondo Taboo* (a documentary sequel to *Taboos of the World,* also to be narrated by Vincent Price), *Pajama Party in a Haunted House, Robinhood Jones* (a costume spoof directed by William Asher and starring Vincent Price, Frankie Avalon, Susan Hart, and Annette Funicello), *Girl in the Glass Bikini, Sergeant Deadhead Goes to Mars, Dr. Goldfoot for President, 2066 A.D.—When the Sleeper Wakes, Cruise Party, The Big Chase* (a silent comedy with Buster Keaton), and *Jet Set Party.*

Boxoffice November 29, 1965: *Bikini Party in a Haunted House, The Girl in the Glass Bikini, Dr. Goldfoot and the S-Bomb, Invasion of the Night Things,* and *File 777.*

Boxoffice February 7, 1966: *Land of Prehistoric Women* in color for December release.

Boxoffice May 9, 1966: *Jules Verne's Rocket to the Moon, Malibu 500, It* (based on a Richard Matheson short story), *Being, Girl in the Glass Castle, 2067 A.D.—When the Sleeper Wakes, The Golem, Dr. Goldfoot and the Love Bombs,* and *All the Wild Angels.*

Boxoffice May 22, 1966: *Those Fantastic Flying Fools, The Gold Bug,* and *The Be-Ins.*

Film Daily June 16, 1966: *Rebel 500, Guns of Anzio* (starring Richard Widmark), and *Sex and the Teenager* (to be released by Trans-American).

Boxoffice June 20, 1966: *Circus of Blood* (with Christopher Lee and Leo Genn) and *Voyage to a Prehistoric Planet* (with Basil Rathbone and Faith Domergue) are listed as a "horror combination for December"

Film Daily September 14, 1966: *The End,* about "a completely automated society 2,000 years hence" to be written by Charles Griffith and produced and directed by Roger Corman.

Boxoffice December 12, 1966: *The Black Jacket Girls, The Island of Amazons, The End, Sunset Strip, House of Dolls, The Hatfields and the McCoys, The Puppet Masters,* and *2267 A.D.—When the Sleeper Wakes.*

Boxoffice January 22, 1968: *Hell's Racers, The Wild Eye, Acapulco Gold, The Reincarnation, Hawaiian Beach Bum, The Gold Bug, The Marquis de Sade, The Day It All Happened Baby,* and *The Hatfields and the McCoys.*

Boxoffice February 5, 1968: *Dante's Inferno* to be filmed in Hamburg, Germany, from a script by Gary Russoff.

Boxoffice April 1, 1968: *Justine,* based on the book by the Marquis de Sade, to be filmed back to back with *The Marquis de Sade* with the total cost for both films at $5,000,000.

Boxoffice August 4, 1968: *The Late Boy Wonder, The Adultress, Public Parts and Private Places, Venus Examined, Implosion, Lay Me Down to Sleep, Sand Bum, The Lonely Hearts Killers, Dunwich,* and *Lola.*

Boxoffice November 3, 1969: *The Venus Machine, Virginity Jones, When the Sleeper Wakes,* and *Christmas with Grandma.*

Boxoffice May 4, 1970: *Wife Swappers, Legion of the Damned, Unchained, The Cannibals, Crunch!, The Promise, The Busy Bodies, Triangle, Savage Season,* and *Bunny and Claude.*

Boxoffice July 20, 1970: *I Shot Down the Red Baron—I Think* (directed and starring Cliff Robertson), *Beach Bum*, and *de Sade '71*.

The AIP 1971 release schedule included: *G.O.O.—Genetic Octopodular Ooze, Bloody Judge, Dracula #1, Wild Arctic, Baby Bride, Bodies Busy, The Switchers, Barracuda 2000, Dr. Phibes, Beach Bum,* and *Gingerbread House*.

Boxoffice January 4, 1971: *A Tale of Two Cities, Les Miserables, The House of the Seven Gables,* and *The Scarlet Letter*.

Boxoffice July 5, 1971: *The Year of the Cannibals, Gingerbread House, Carry Nation, Barracuda 2000 A.D., The House of the Seven Gables,* and *Camille*.

Boxoffice July 12, 1971: *Barracuda 2000 A.D.* has now become *Doomsday 2000 A.D.* and is scheduled to begin filming (from a James Whiton script) in Autumn for a 1972 release.

Cinefantastique Spring 1972: *Elmer, House of the Seven Gables, Return to Wuthering Heights, Waldo*.

Boxoffice October 13, 1975: *Carmela, Diamond Mercenaries, Vampirella,* and *Claws*.

Boxoffice November 17, 1975: AIP signs a deal to co-produce seven films with Hanna-Barbera. The first three titles announced are *Cerebus 1* ("an electronic espionage story"), *Lupezoids* ("a science fiction project set in the year 2000"), and *Dante's Trip* ("based on *Dante's Inferno* but developed as a contemporary love story").

Boxoffice April 9, 1979: After the merger with Filmways, Samuel Arkoff intended to produce a film version of Harold Robbin's *Dreams Die First*.

Focus on the Projects

The following is a closer look at the development of some of AIP's unrealized projects:

Aladdin and the Giant was first announced in July of 1959 as a co-production with Anglo Amalgamated to be produced by Herman Cohen. It was slated to start filming in Jamaica in March 1960. By November 1959, the location had been changed to Majorca with interiors to be filmed at both Merton Park and Shepperton Studios in London.

AIP's proposed film version of H.G. Wells' *When the Sleeper Wakes* was first announced in June 1961. It next appeared in AIP's 1962 exhibitors manual. In September 1963, *The Sleeper Wakes* was listed in *Hollywood Reporter* as a British co-production to star Vincent Price. A 1964 trade ad for AIP's 10th Anniversary lists *2165 A.D.—When the Sleeper Wakes* in color and scope starring Price and Martha Hyer. Shortly thereafter, the title was changed to *2145 A.D.—When the Sleeper Wakes*. In early 1965 it was announced as *2066 A.D.—When the Sleeper Wakes*. By May 1966 *2067 A.D. When the Sleeper Wakes* was "to be made in London using a profusion of special effects." At this point, the Wells story actually seemed as if it might finally be produced. Filming was set to begin October 1966 in Panavision and color with Harry Alan Towers as producer and Don Sharp writing and directing. In June 1966 it was announced that the production, now titled *2267 A.D.—When the Sleeper Wakes*, would be moved to Prague. Budgetary concerns put the title in limbo once again until the project was turned over to Louis M. Heyward in 1968. Shelley Stark wrote a new script and Heyward was impressed enough to pass it on to director Michael Reeves. Reeves' sudden death jettisoned this attempt to make the movie. In 1970, producer-director George Pal came onto the project and he commissioned a new script to be written by Richard Matheson. AIP and Pal eventually disagreed over the approach to the concept and once again the project was shelved. In January 1972, James Nicholson announced he would establish his own production company and his first picture would be *When the Sleeper Wakes*.

Genghis Khan was first announced in August 1961 as a multi-million dollar roadshow production to be filmed in Hollywood and abroad. In December 1963 Jacques Tourneur was announced as director. The 70mm Technirama production was set to begin filming in Italy and Spain in summer of 1964 with a budget of $4,500,000. By July 1964, plans for the filming had changed dras-

Appendix 2: The Unfilmed AIP   189

tically. It was decided that the story would be scaled down to a more romantic treatment because of the surfeit of spectaculars already in release ... and to cut costs. Also it would not be roadshown. James Nicholson was supposed to leave for Italy on July 31, 1964, to get the production started.

It's Alive was originally announced in July 1963 to star Peter Lorre, Elsa Lanchester and Harvey Lembeck. This was supposed to be the first in a series of films in which Lorre and Lanchester would be teamed as "lovers." In February 1964, Nicholson and Arkoff announced their intention to go into television production with *Beach Party*, a series based on the movie, and *It's Alive*. The feature version of the latter would be released to theatres within a year and the TV series would follow.

One unusual project announced in May 1966 was an untitled "high camp hillbilly comedy" budgeted at $1,250,000. By July 1966 the project had been given the title *The Hatfields and the McCoys*. AIP's 1966–67 publicity brochure stated that "the hilariously explosive tale of those fightin', fussin', families and their frantic, fun-filled feud" would be coming in 1967. It was to be filmed in color and Panavision starring Frankie Avalon, Annette Funicello, and Fabian. The title continued to be mentioned in publicity blurbs throughout the years and, in 1970, Ted Flicker was set to write and direct the picture.

Sunset Strip, "a drama of the long haired, teen-age kooks" written by Robert Kaufman, was first announced in September 1966 (and several times thereafter). Eventually AIP opted to release Sam Katzman's film *Riot on Sunset Strip* instead. That March 1967 release was written by Orville Hampton and directed by Arthur Dreifuss. In addition to Aldo Ray and Tim Rooney (son of Mickey), there is a mem-

The Hatfields and the McCoys is one of many AIP projects that were never made.

orable star turn by Mimsy Farmer in what is arguably AIP's most over-the-top "youth protest" movie. Why isn't this out on DVD?

Camille was first announced in July 1971 as part of AIP's plan to film stories "in a classic vein." According to a September 1971 *Boxoffice* article, filming was set to commence in England the following month with Mia Farrow in the title role. A May 1972 announcement by Arkoff stated that *Camille* would now begin filming in October with "two very exciting international stars."

Mimsy Farmer rocks in *Riot on Sunset Strip*.

Appendix 3: Prepackaged Features

American International Pictures were pioneers in the distribution of prepackaged double features. Below is a list of some of these double bill programs.

1956

January
Day the World Ended/The Phantom from 10,000 Leagues
  "The TOP Shock Show of ALL TIME!"

June
Female Jungle/The Oklahoma Woman

July
Girls in Prison/Hot Rod Girl
  "Double Sock ... Rock ... and Thrill Show!"

It Conquered the World/The She-Creature
  "The TWIN-TERROR SHOW That Tops Them All!"

October
Shake, Rattle and Rock/Runaway Daughters
  "Twin Bop Rock 'n' Sock Show"

1957

January
Naked Paradise/Flesh and the Spur
  "Together in One GIANT Action-Packed Program!"

March
Voodoo Woman/The Undead
  "The screen's new HIGH in VIOLENT, SHRIEKING TERROR!"

April
Rock All Night/Dragstrip Girl
  "Slap Happy, Speed-Crazy Youth!"

June
I Was a Teenage Werewolf/Invasion of the Saucer Men
  "We DARE You to See the Most Amazing Pictures of Our Time!"

August
Reform School Girl/Rock Around the World
  "Rockin' ... Rioting Teenage Fury!"

White Huntress/Naked Africa
  "Double! Dynamite! Action! Thrills!"

September
The Amazing Colossal Man/Cat Girl

October
Motorcycle Gang/Sorority Girl
  "Uncensored!"

November
I Was a Teenage Frankenstein/Blood of Dracula
  "FIENDISH! FRENZIED! BLOOD-CHILLING! Nothing Like This in All the History of Horror!"

December
Viking Women and the Sea Serpent/The Astounding She-Monster
  "Double SPECTACLE-TERROR! Fabulous! Fantastic! Terrifying!"

1958

February
Jet Attack/Suicide Battalion
  "THUNDERING DOUBLE-ACTION ... from Heaven to Hell and Back!"

192 *Appendix 3: Prepackaged Features*

March
Dragstrip Riot/The Cool and the Crazy
    "TWIN ROCK 'N RIOT SHOW!"

May
Machine-Gun Kelly/The Bonnie Parker Story

June
High School Hellcats/Hot Rod Gang
    "THE TRUTH ABOUT HIGH SCHOOL SORORITIES!"

July
Attack of the Puppet People/War of the Colossal Beast
    "INCREDIBLY FANTASTIC!
    YOU WON'T BELIEVE YOUR EYES!"

Hell Squad/Tank Battalion
    "RAGING INFERNO OF WAR!
    WHERE KIDS LEARNED TO KILL OR BE KILLED!"

How to Make a Monster/Teenage Caveman

August
Night of the Blood Beast/She Gods of Shark Reef
    "FROM TOWERING WILD ADVENTURE ... TO
    THE DEPTHS OF HELLISH HORROR!"

Screaming Skull/Terror from the Year 5000
    "TWIN GHOST STORIES ... TO
    HAUNT YOU FOREVER!"

October
The Spider/The Brain Eaters

1959

February
Submarine Seahawk/Paratroop Command
    "THE BIGGEST WAR SPECTACLES
    OF THE YEAR!"

March
Roadracers/Daddy-O
    "THE BIG 2 ... ROARING!
    ROCKETING! RELENTLESS!"

Tank Commandos/Operation Dames

April
Horrors of the Black Museum/The Headless Ghost

July
Diary of a High School Bride/Ghost of Dragstrip Hollow

October
A Bucket of Blood/The Giant Leeches

1962

August
The Brain That Wouldn't Die/Invasion of the Star Creatures

1963

September
The Terror/Dementia 13
    "ENTER THE DOMAIN OF THE DAMNED
    AND THE DEMENTED!"

1964

February
Samson and the Slave Queen/Goliath and the Sins of Babylon
    "ALL NEW SAMSON VS. GOLIATH
    NEVER SEEN!"

September
The Last Man on Earth/Unearthly Stranger

1965

March
The Lost World of Sinbad/War of the Zombies
    "NEW HIGHS IN ADVENTURE ... IT'S THE
    DOUBLE SHOCK SHOW OF THE YEAR!"

November
Die Monster Die!/Planet of the Vampires
    "FANTASTIC ... FRIGHTENING! TWO UNEARTHLY,
    SPINE TINGLING ADVENTURES!"

1966

March
Queen of Blood/Blood Bath
    "A NEW HIGH IN
    BLOOD CHILLING HORROR!"

July
Frankenstein Conquers the World/Tarzan and the Valley of Gold

Appendix 3: Prepackaged Features   193

1970

May
Horror House/The Crimson Cult
"TWICE THE TERROR ... TEN TIMES THE SHOCK!"

1972

May
Blood from the Mummy's Tomb/Night of the Blood Monster
"TWO HIDEOUS TALES OF TORTURE AND TERROR!"

AIP re-released many of their films in multi-picture combinations:

1961

Chills Unlimited: *How to Make a Monster, Invasion of the Saucer Men, Terror from the Year 5000, The Brain Eaters*

Thrills Unlimited: *Motorcycle Gang, Hot Rod Gang, Dragstrip Girl, Roadracers*

Action Unlimited: *Submarine Seahawk, Paratroop Command, Suicide Battalion, Tank Battalion*

Shocks Unlimited: *Girls in Prison, The Cool and the Crazy, Runaway Daughters, Reform School Girl*

1967

Mondodrama: *Taboos of the World, Ecco, Macabro*

Rollorama: *Rock All Night, Shake Rattle and Rock, Rock Around the World, Dragstrip Riot*

Horror and Thrill Show: *Blood of Dracula, It Conquered the World, Night of the Blood Beast, The Headless Ghost*

Beach-niks, Surfers, Ho-dads, and Gremmies: *Beach Party, Muscle Beach Party, Bikini Beach, Pajama Party, How to Stuff a Wild Bikini*

1971

Fonda Festival: *The Wild Angels, Spirits of the Dead, The Trip*

Big 3 Cycle Rider Spectacular: *The Wild Angels, The Glory Stompers, Hells Angels on Wheels*

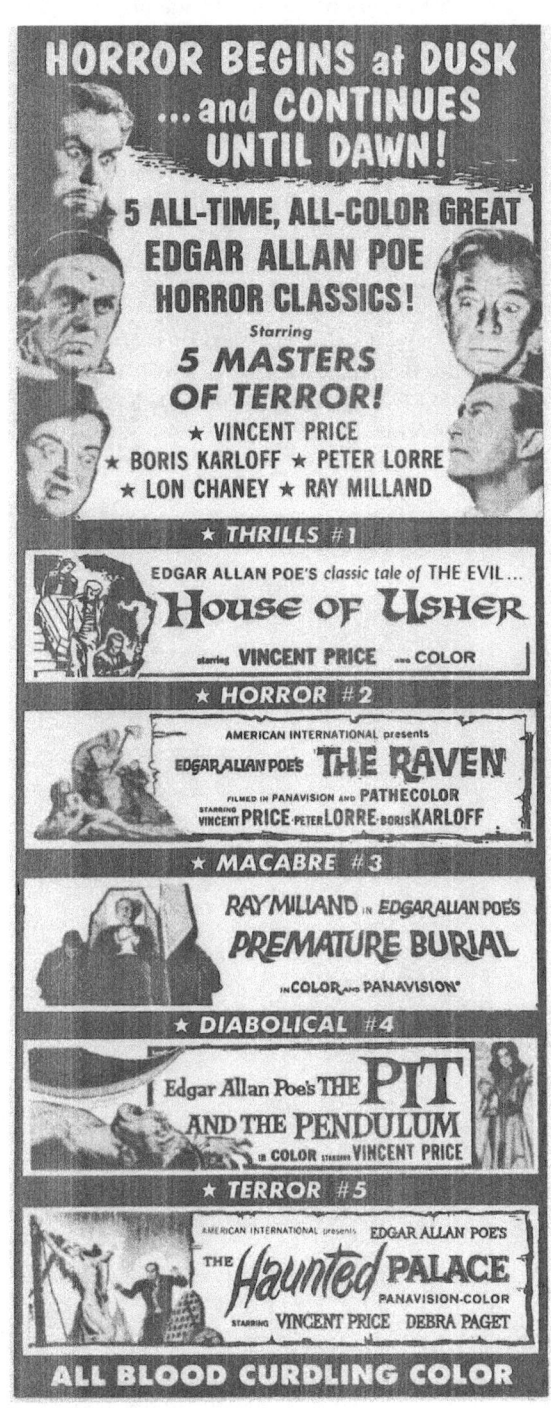

An example of one of AIP's multi-feature packages.

Appendix 3: Prepackaged Features

5 Orgies of Evil: *Comedy of Terrors, Masque of the Red Death, War-Gods of the Deep, Tomb of Ligeia, Tales of Terror*

5 Masters of Terror: *House of Usher, The Raven, Premature Burial, Pit and the Pendulum, The Haunted Palace*
"Horror Begins at Dusk ... and Continues Until Dawn!"

The Pot Show: *The Trip, Psych-Out, Maryjane, Riot on Sunset Strip, Hallucination Generation*
"5 Flicks That Will Blow Your Mind Now Together for the First Time"

Vincent Price's Festival of Horror: *Cry of the Banshee, Scream and Scream Again, The Haunted Palace, House of 1000 Dolls*
"Four Masterpieces of Horror from the Screen's Noble Savage!"

Blood-A-Rama: *Queen of Blood, Blood Bath, Blood of Dracula, A Bucket of Blood*
"New Highs of BLOOD CHILLING HORROR"

Ghoul-A-Rama: *The Oblong Box, The Conqueror Worm, The Crimson Cult*
"4 GREAT SHOWS ON ONE PROGRAM!"

There were also a number of combinations where theatre owners could select any four films from a list of thirty-three AIP horror features and package them for showing under any of the following headings:

Screaming Meemies	Marathon of Fright
Doomsday	13th Jinx
Black Cat	Wake of the Zombies
Fright Night	Banshee

Appendix 4: Title Changes

The Abominable Dr. Phibes: The Curse of Doctor Phibe, Dr. Phibes

The Amazing Colossal Man: Colossus, The Nth Man

Angel Unchained: Unchained

The Astounding She-Monster: The Naked Invader

Attack of the Puppet People: The Fantastic Puppet People

Bang! Bang! You're Dead!: Bang! You're Dead, I Spy You Spy We All Spy, Epitaph for a Spy

The Bat People: It Lives By Night

The Beast with a Million Eyes: The Unseen

Bikini Beach: Bikini Beach Party

Blast Off!: Those Fantastic Flying Fools, P.T. Barnum's Rocket to the Moon, Jules Verne's Rocket to the Moon

The Bonnie Parker Story: Machine Gun Lady

Born Wild: The Young Animals

The Brain Eaters: Battle of the Brain Eaters, Keepers of the Earth, The Keepers

The Brain That Wouldn't Die: The Head That Wouldn't Die

Bunny O'Hare: Bunny and Claude, Bunny

Burn Witch Burn: Conjure Wife, Witch Wife, Night of the Eagle

Cat Girl: Wolf Girl

Cervantes: The Young Rebel

The Comedy of Terrors: The Graveside Story

Conquered City: Captive City

The Crimson Cult: Curse of the Crimson Altar, The Reincarnation

Cult of the Damned: Angel, Angel Down We Go

De Sade: The Marquis de Sade

Devil's Angels: Hell Riders

The Devil's Widow: Tam Lin, The Legend of Tam Lin

Diary of a High School Bride: High School Bride

Die Monster Die: House at the End of the World, Color Out of Space

The Dirty Game: File 777

Dr. Goldfoot and the Girl Bombs: Dr. Goldfoot and the Love Bombs, Dr. Goldfoot and the S-Bomb

The Dunwich Horror: Dunwich

Earth vs the Spider: The Spider, The Black Terror

The Evil Eye: Schizo, The Girl Who Knew Too Much

Flesh and the Spur: Dead Man's Gun

Frankenstein Conquers the World: Frankenstein Meets the Giant Devil Fish, Frankenstein vs. Baragon

The Ghost in the Invisible Bikini: Girl in the Glass Bikini, Pajama Party in a Haunted House, Bikini Party in a Haunted House

Ghost of Dragstrip Hollow: The Haunted Hot Rod

Goliath and the Barbarians: Colossus and the Golden Horde, The Barbarians, Terror of the Barbarians

Goliath and the Dragon: Goliath's Revenge, The Vengeance of Hercules

Goliath and the Sins of Babylon: Sins of Babylon, Maciste the Greatest Hero in the World

Goliath and the Vampires: Goliath and the Island of Vampires, Maciste Against the Vampire

196 *Appendix 4: Title Changes*

The title **Hell Riders** was eventually changed to *Devil's Angels*.

Guns of the Black Witch: Black Mutiny
The Haunted Palace: The Haunted Village
Hell Squad: Hell Raiders
Horror House: The Haunted House of Horror, The Dark
Hot Rod Gang: Hot Rod Rock
House of Fright: Jekyll's Inferno, The Two Faces of Dr. Jekyll
House of 1,000 Dolls: House of Dolls, Sax Rohmer's House of Dolls
House of Usher: The Fall of the House of Usher, The Mysterious House of Usher, The Haunted House of Usher
Invasion of the Saucer Men: Attack of the Saucer Men
Island of the Damned: Trapped, Who Can Kill a Child?
J.D.'s Revenge: The Reincarnation of J.D. Walker
Jet Attack: Jet Squadron, Jet Fighter
Live a Little, Steal a Lot: Murph the Surf
Madam Kitty: Salon Kitty
Madhouse: The Revenge of Dr. Death
Marco Polo: The Adventures of Marco Polo
A Matter of Time: Carmela
The Mind Benders: The Pit
Mondo Teeno: Teenage Rebellion, Sex and the Teenager
Motorcycle Gang: Motorcycle Girl, Motorcycle Girls
Muscle Beach Party: Muscle Beach
Night of the Blood Beast: The Creature from Galaxy 27
Night of the Blood Monster: The Bloody Judge, Throne of Fire
Old Dracula: Vampira
Operation Bikini: The Seafighters
Operation Snafu: Operation Warhead
Pajama Party: The Maid and the Martian
Panic in Year Zero!: End of the World, Survival
Planet of the Vampires: Planet of Terror, Terror in Space
Prisoner of the Iron Mask: The Iron Mask
Portrait of a Sinner: The Rough and the Smooth

Psych-Out: The Love Children
Psycho Circus: Circus of Blood, Circus of Fear
Rape Squad: Act of Vengeance
Reform School Girls: Girls Reform School
Rock All Night: Rock 'n' Roll Kid
Rock Around the World: The Tommy Steele Story
Samson and the 7 Miracles of the World: Goliath and the Warriors of Genghis Khan, Goliath and the Golden City, Maciste at the Court of the Grand Khan
Schizoid: Lizard in a Woman's Skin
Shake, Rattle and Rock: Shake, Rattle, and Roll
Sign of the Gladiator: Sheba and the Gladiator, The Last Days of Rome, The Sign of Rome
Sorority Girl: Confessions of a Sorority Girl
Submarine Seahawk: Submarine X-2
Suicide Battalion: Battle Front
The Swappers: Wife Swappers
Taboos of the World: Taboo
Tank Commandos: Tank Destroyer
Teenage Caveman: Prehistoric World
Terror from the Year 5000: The Girl from 5,000,000 A.D., The Girl from 2,000,000 A.D.
Terror in the Crypt: Crypt of the Vampire
They Came from Within: Shivers, The Parasite Murders
The Time Travelers: Time Trap
The Tomb of Ligeia: Ligeia, The House at the End of the World
The Undead: The Trance of Diana Love
Under Age: Under 21
Up in the Cellar: The Late Boy Wonder
Viking Women and the Sea Serpent: The Viking Women
Voodoo Woman: Black Voodoo

Voyage to the Planet of Prehistoric Women: Gill Women, Land of Prehistoric Women
War Goddess: The Amazons
War-Gods of the Deep: City Under the Sea, City in the Sea
War of the Colossal Beast: The Colossal Beast, Revenge of the Colossal Man
Warriors Five: Warriors Three
White Huntress: Jungle Queen
White Slave Ship: The Mutineers
Who Slew Auntie Roo?: Whoever Slew Auntie Roo?, Gingerbread House, Christmas with Grandma
Why Must I Die?: I Was on Death Row, Death Row
The Wild Angels: All the Fallen Angels
The Wild Pack: The Sandpit Generals
The Year of the Cannibals: The Cannibals

Trans American Films

Trans American Films, a division of American International Pictures, released the following titles:

1966: *Hallucination Generation, Macabro*
1967: *It's a Bikini World, Mondo-Teeno*
1968: *Trans Euro Express*
1969: *Succubus*
1970: *The Cycle Savages, Fearless Frank, I Am a Groupie, Madigan's Millions, The Swappers, Witchcraft '70*
1971: *Dagmar's Hot Pants*
1976: *They Came From Within*
1977: *Madam Kitty*
1979: *The Stud*

Appendix 5: AIP Comic Book and Paperback Novel Tie-Ins

Paperbacks

At the Earth's Core: Edgar Rice Burroughs. Ace, 1976.
Bloody Mama: Robert Thom. Paperback Library, 1970.
A Bullet for Pretty Boy: Michael Avallone. Fawcett, 1970.
Circus of Horrors: Tom Owen. Panther Books (England), February 1960.
Comedy of Terrors: Elsie Lee. Lancer Books, 1964.
Conjure Wife (*Burn Witch Burn*): Fritz Leiber. Berkley Medallion, April 1962.
Dressed to Kill: Brian De Palma and Campbell Black. Bantam Books, July 1980.
Dr. Phibes (*The Abominable Dr. Phibes*): William Goldstein. Fontana Books, 1971.
Dr. Phibes Rises Again: William Goldstein. Fontana Books, 1971.
Empire of the Ants: Lindsay West. Ace, 1977.
End of the World (*Panic in Year Zero!*): Dean Owen. Ace, 1962.
The Incredible Melting Man: Phil Smith. New English Library (England), February 1978.
Konga: Dean Owen. Monarch Movie Book, August 1960.
The Land That Time Forgot: Edgar Rice Burroughs. Ace, 1975.
The Late Boy Wonder (*Up in the Cellar*): Angus Hall. Ace, 1970.
Love at First Bite: Robert Kaufman. Fotonovel Publications, 1979.
Madhouse (*Devilday*): Angus Hall. Award Books, 1974.
Masque of the Red Death, The: Elsie Lee. Lancer Books, 1964.
Master of the World: Jules Verne. Ace, 1961.
The Mind Benders: James Kennaway. Pan Books (England), 1963.
The People That Time Forgot: Edgar Rice Burroughs. Ace, 1977.
The Pit and the Pendulum: Lee Sheridan. Lancer Books, 1961.
Premature Burial: Max Hallan Danne. Lancer Books, 1962.
The Raven: Eunice Sudak. Lancer Books, 1963.
Reptilicus: Dean Owen. Monarch Movie Book, June 1961.
Scream and Scream Again (*The Disoriented Man*): Peter Saxon. Paperback Library, February 1970.
Tales of Terror: Eunice Sudak. Lancer Books, 1962.
The Vampire Lovers (*Carmilla*): J. Sheridan le Fanu. Fontana Books (England), 1970.
Witchfinder General (*Conqueror Worm*): Ronald Bassett. Macmillan (England), April 1968.
X (*X, the Man with the X-Ray Eyes*): Eunice Sudak. Lancer Books, 1963.

Comic Books

Beach Blanket Bingo: Dell, 1965.
Die, Monster, Die!: Dell #12-175-603, March 1966.

The Island of Dr. Moreau: Marvel Movie Special #1, 1977.
Konga: Charlton, 1960.
The Land That Time Forgot: Marvel Movie Premier #1, September 1975.
Masque of the Red Death: Dell #12-490-410, August-October 1964.
Master of the World: Dell #1157, 1961.
Meteor: Marvel Comics Super Special #14, Fall/October 1979.
Operation Bikini: Dell # 12-597-310, 1963.
The Raven: Dell #12-680-309, 1963.
Reptilicus: Charlton, August 1961.
Ski Party: Dell #12-743-511, September-November 1965.
Tales of Terror: Dell #12-793-302, 1962.
Tomb of Ligeia: Dell #12-830-506, April-June 1965.
War-Gods of the Deep: Dell #12-900-509, July-September 1965.
X, The Man With the X-Ray Eyes: Gold Key #10083-309, 1963.

Bibliography

Books

Aaronson, Charles S., ed. *1970 International Motion Picture Almanac*. New York: Quigley, 1969.

Arkoff, Samuel Z., with Richard Trubo. *Flying Through Hollywood by theSeat of My Pants*. New York: Birch Lane, 1992.

Benton, Mike. *The Illustrated History of Horror Comics*. Dallas, TX: Taylor, 1991.

Butler, Ivan. *Horror in the Cinema*. London: A. Zwemmer, 1970.

Corman, Roger, with Jim Jerome. *How I Made a Hundred Movies in Hollywood and Never Lost a Dime*. New York: Random House, 1990.

Everman, Welch. *Cult Horror Films*. New York: Citadel, 1993.

Gertner, Richard, ed. *1980 International Motion Picture Almanac*. New York: Quigley, 1980.

Gray, Beverly. *Roger Corman*. Los Angeles: Renaissance, 2000.

Heffernan, Kevin. *Ghouls, Gimmicks, and Gold: Horror Films and the American Movie Business, 1953–1968*. Durham, NC, and London: Duke University Press, 2004.

Howarth, Troy. *The Haunted World of Mario Bava*. Surrey, England: Fab, 2002.

Lee, Christopher. *Tall, Dark and Gruesome*. Baltimore, MD: Midnite Marquee, 1999.

Lloyd, Ann, and David Robinson, eds. *There's Something Going on Out There*. London: Orbis, 1982.

McGee, Mark Thomas. *Fast and Furious: The Story of American International Pictures*. Jefferson, NC: McFarland, 1984. [McFarland published a revised edition of this book in 1996 under the title *Faster and Furiouser: The Revised and Fattened Fable of American International Pictures*.]

_____. *Roger Corman: The Best of the Cheap Acts*. Jefferson, NC: McFarland, 1988.

Muller, Eddie, and Daniel Faris. *That's Sexploitation!!* London: Titan, 1997.

Naha, Ed. *The Films of Roger Corman*. New York: Arco, 1982.

Piselli, Carlos, and Riccardo Morrocchi, eds. *Cultish Shocking Horrors*. Firenze, Italy: Glittering Images, 2002.

Porges, Irwin. *Edgar Rice Burroughs: The Man Who Created Tarzan*. Provo, Utah: Brigham Young University Press, 1975.

Stidworthy, David. *High on the Hogs: A Biker Filmography*. Jefferson, NC: McFarland, 2003.

Weaver, Tom. *Eye on Science Fiction*. Jefferson, NC: McFarland, 2003.

Williams, Lucy Chase. *The Complete Films of Vincent Price*. New York: Citadel, 1995.

Worth, D. Earl. *Sleaze Creatures*. Key West, FL: Fantasma, 1995.

Periodical Articles

Bean, Robin. "Muscles and Mayhem." *Films and Filming*. Vol. 10, no. 9 (June 1964): 14–18.

"Blood Pudding." *Time*. September 1, 1961, p. 50.

"Fallen Angels." *Newsweek*. August 15, 1966, pp. 84–85.

Koetting, Christopher. "The AIP X Films." *Filmfax*. No. 56 (May-June 1996): 59–72.

Nashawaty, Chris. "Sam Arkoff." *Entertainment Weekly*. January 2, 2002, p. 41.

Price, Vincent. "Mean, Moody and Magnificent." *Films and Filming*. Vol. 11, no. 6 (March 1965): 5–8.

Index

Abby 9
The Abominable Dr. Phibes 9, 10
Ackerman, Forrest J 117, 156
Adam, Ken 109
Adams, Nick 54, 71
Addams, Dawn 89
Adler, Jay 136
Adrian, Iris 66
Agar, John 17, 18, 102, 181
Ai, Kyoko 51
Airport 111
Akins, Claude 153
Aladdin and the Giant 188
Alakazam the Great 25
Alien 125
Allen, Nancy 61, 62
Allen, Woody 165
Allredge, Michael 96
Alonso, Chelo 77, 78, 142
Alverado, Crox 175
Amadio, Silvio 183
Amati, Edmondo 137
The Amazing Colossal Man 10, 11, 18, 64, 138, 164
The Amazing Transparent Man 11, 12
The Amazons see *War Goddess*
Amber, Audrey (Adriana Ambesi) 181
Amicus 15, 16, 91, 97, 105, 109, 137
The Amityville Horror 12, 13
Amsterdam, Morey 107
Anders, Luana 48, 49, 118, 119, 124, 125, 131, 157, 172
Anders, Merry 155
Anders, Richard 84
Anderson, Asbjorn 131, 132
Anderson, Donna 43, 44
Anderson, Suzy 25, 165
Ando, Hideo 165
Andre, Gaby 79
Andrews, Harry 7, 170
Angel, Heather 126
Angel, Angel Down We Go 169
Angel Unchained 13

Angeli, Fabrizio 145
The Angry Red Planet 13, 14, 102, 128, 156
Ankrum, Morris 172
Anne of the Thousand Days 46
Anson, Jay 12
Antonelli, Laura 57
Antonini, Gabiele 136
Apache Woman 3, 14, 15, 68
Aranda, Angel 125
Archerd, Army 168
Ardamaglia, Francesco 79
Ardisson, Giorgio 65
Arenas, Rosita 175
Argento, Dario 173
Arikawa, Shinichi 76
Arkoff, Samuel Z. 3, 4, 5, 7, 8, 9, 15, 20, 21, 22, 40, 41, 50, 51, 56, 61, 62, 63, 67, 68, 73, 79, 88, 91, 93, 96, 100, 115, 116, 121, 122, 124, 126, 131, 132, 136, 151, 152, 160, 166, 168, 169, 170, 181, 189, 190
Armageddon 113
Armitage, George 72, 73
Armstrong, Michael 87
Armstrong, Richard 38
Ashcroft, Ronnie 15
Asher, Jane 110
Asher, William 20, 21, 22, 25, 67, 93, 115, 116
Ashley, John 60, 61, 84, 92, 114, 115, 148, 149
Askew, Larry 13
Assonitis, Ovidio 149, 153
The Astounding She Monster 15
At the Earth's Core 15
Atkins, Eileen 52
Atlas 35
Atragon 16, 77
Attack of the Crab Monsters 48, 158
Attack of the 50 Ft. Woman 129, 131, 138, 158, 183
Attack of the Giant Leeches 8, 16, 17, 131, 179

Attack of the Mushroom People 175
Attack of the Puppet People 17, 18, 64
Aubrey, Richard 162
Aumont, Tina 109
Aureli, Andrea 179
Avalon, Frankie 5, 20, 21, 22, 23, 24, 56, 67, 68, 87, 93, 115, 116, 120, 121, 122, 143, 155, 189
Avery, Margaret 83
Ayers, Robert 37
The Aztec Mummy 175, 176, 177

Baccala, Donna 63
Backus, Jim 121
The Bad Seed 114
Baer, John 117
Bakalyan, Richard 31, 42, 43, 122, 123
Baker, Chet 160
Baker, Rick 97, 147, 155
Baker, Roy Ward 58, 159, 160
Baker, Stanley 137
Baker, Tom 41
Ball, Bob 99
The Ballad of Tam Lin see *The Devil's Widow*
Baltimore, Nadir 179
Banas, Bob 46
Banks, Linda 46
Banno, Yoshimitsu 76
Bardot, Brigitte 145, 146
Barfod, Bent 102
Barger, Sonny 84, 85
Baron Blood 18, 19
Barr, Patrick 91
Barr, Tim 111
Barresi, Paul 169
Barron, Keith 105
Barron, Robert 151
Barrymore, John Drew 165
The Bat People 19
Bates, Ralph 44, 52, 58
Battle Beyond the Sun 19, 20
Bava, Mario 18, 19, 25, 26, 57, 65, 66, 125, 173, 182

204 Index

Baxley, Gary 100
Baxt, George 36, 37, 39
Baxter, Les 19, 26, 41, 46, 65, 66, 77, 79, 111, 179
Beach Blanket Bingo 20
Beach Party 20, 21, 121, 189
Beacham, Stephanie 52, 53, 54
The Beast with a Million Eyes 3, 4, 21, 47
The Beatles 73
Beaumont, Charles 36, 82, 109, 110, 126
Beck, Jim 122
Becket 110
Beginning of the End 11, 65
Begley, Ed 63, 168
Bell, Rodney 124
Belli, Melvin 168
Bender, Russ 74, 99, 115, 148, 162, 164
Bengell, Anna 125
Benjamin, Richard 106, 107
Bennet, Julie 165
Bennet, Spencer G. 147
Bennett, Charles 163
Bennett, Jill 103
Bentley, John 147, 166
Bercovitch, Reuben 71
Berger, Helmut 59, 60, 108, 109
Berger, Senta 50, 51
Bergman, Ingmar 110
Bergner, Elisabeth 45
Berle, Milton 85
Berlinger, Warren 155
Bernds, Edward L. 86, 131
Bernstein, Morey 140
Berry, Julian (Ernesto Gastaldi) 181
Beswick, Martine 58
Bettoia, Franca 105
Bevilacqua, Alberto 25
Bewitched 21
Bey, Marki 148
Beyond the Door 9
Bianchi, Eleanora 79
Biancoli, Oreste 65, 136
Bickford, John 21
Biddlewood, Clement 145
Bikini Beach 22, 23, 24, 25
Billy Jack 32
Billy Jack Goes to Washington 32
Birch, Paul 21, 47, 68
The Bird with the Crystal Plumage 173
The Birds 21, 38
Birth of a Nation 75
Bishop, Larry 13, 136, 168
Bishop, Wes 38, 154, 155
Bissell, Whit 94, 95, 96
The Bitch 65
Bixby, Jerome 117

Black Caesar 25
The Black Cat (1934) 11
Black Mama, White Mama 40
Black Sabbath 25, 26
Black Sunday 26, 27, 124, 182
Blacula 27
Blaine, Jerry 29
Blair, Janet 36, 37
Blaisdell, Paul 21, 47, 74, 98, 99, 101, 140, 162
Blanc, Erica 116
Blast-Off 27, 28
Blees, Robert 58, 72, 166
Bloch, Richard 62
Block, Irving 160, 161
The Blockbusters 134
Blood and Roses 181
Blood from the Mummy's Tomb 28
Blood of Dracula 29, 88
Blood of the Vampire 81
The Bloody Judge see *Night of the Blood Monster*
Bloody Mama 29, 30, 31, 33, 55, 155
Bloom, John 98
Blossom, Roberts 49, 50
Boccardoa, Deli 153
Bogarde, Dirk 113
Bohr, Robert (Tonino Valeri) 181
Bolkan, Florinda 137
Bonanza 96
Bond, Derek 81
Bonnie and Clyde 30, 33, 108
The Bonnie Parker Story 31, 108, 123
Bono, Sonny 37, 38
Books, Ray 91
The Born Losers 31, 32, 85
Bottar, Frank (Franco Bottari) 173
Boulanger, Daniel 145
Bowie, David 87
Boxcar Bertha 32, 33, 55, 56
Bradford, Marshall 66
Bradley, Al (Alfonso Brescia) 149
Bradley, Leslie 151
Bradshaw, Booker 40
Brady, Scott 120
The Brain Eaters 33
The Brain That Wouldn't Die 33, 34, 100
Brame, Bill 46
Brand, Christopher 183
Brandenburg, Otto 102
Brando, Marlon 100
Brandy, Howard 28
Brass, Tinto 108
Braun, Zev 106
Breakston, George 166
Brennen, Rose 173
Bridges, Alicia 107

Bridges, Lloyd 14, 15
Brighton, Bruce 33
Brignone, Guido 141
Brinegar, Paul 92
Brodrick, Susan 58
Brolin, James 12, 13
Bronson, Charles 107, 108, 110, 111
Brontë, Emily 170
Brown, Chelsea 155
Brown, Eleanora 173
Brown, James 25, 143
Brown, John Moulder 92
Brown, Peter 38, 70
The Brute and the Beast 34
Bryan, Dr. William Joseph 48
Bryant, Michael 113
Buchanan, Larry 74, 181
A Bucket of Blood 34, 35
Bucktown 35, 36
Burden, Hugh 28
Burge, Stuart 102
Burman, Tom 70
Burn Witch Burn 36, 37
Burnett, Carol 103
Burroughs, Edgar Rice 16, 105, 123
Burton, Richard 159
Burton, Robert 94
Burton, Tim 157
Bushman, Francis X. 74
Buxton, Frank 165
Byrnes, Edward 131

Cabaret 108
Cabot, Bruce 77
Cabot, Susan 107, 108, 143, 144, 161
Cahn, Edward L. 60, 74, 98, 102, 114, 135, 136, 139, 140, 148, 162
Caine, Michael 61
Calder-Marshall, Anna 7, 170
Caligula 108
Callard, Kay 37
Cambridge, Godfrey 72
Camille 190
Caminneci, Pier A. 147
Camp on Blood Island 81
Campanella, Joseph 112
Campbell, Choker 139
Campbell, R. Wright (aka Bob Campbell) 68, 84, 107, 109, 151, 152, 172, 173
Campbell, William 148, 172, 173
Campo, Wally 83, 151
Campogalliani, Carlo 77
Campos, Jose 181
Canale, Giana Maria 80
Cansino, Pilar 180
Cantafora, Antonio 18

Capuano, Luigi 179
Carabatsos, Steve 153
Carbone, Anthony 34, 125
Carey, Philip 155
Carlisle, Bruce 66
Carlton, Rex 33
Carpentieri, Luigi 136
Carpi, Tito 153
Carr, Paul 19
Carradine, David 32
Carradine, John 33, 67, 140
Carras, Anthony 120
Carrera, Barbara 100
Carreras, Michael 28, 89, 160
Carroll, Brandon 83
Carson, John David 64
Carter, Terry 9, 70
Carthage in Flames 79
Casanova, Tony 54
The Case of the Scorpion's Tail 148
Casey, Bernie 32
Cash, Bubbles 181
Cass, Henry 81
Castelnuovo, Nino 34
Castenada, Luis Aceves 175, 176
Castillo, Gloria 98, 99, 131, 135, 136
Castle of Bloody Lust 148
Cat Girl 37
Cater, James 59
Cawthorn, James 105
Chakiris, George 168
Chambers, John 100
Chandler, Patti 24
Chanel, Helene 136
Chaney, Lon 82
Chang, Wah 111
Chapman, Marguerite 11
Charles, Tommy 139
Chase, Stephen 45
Chastity 37, 38
Checchi, Andrea 26
Cher 38
Chinatown 128, 157
Ching-nim, Nam 184
ChiPs 38
Christian, Roger 21
Christopher, Jordon 169
Chrome and Hot Leather 38
Cipriani, Stelvio 19
Circus of Fear see *Psycho-Circus*
Circus of Horrors 39, 40, 128
City Under the Sea see *War-Gods of the Deep*
Clark, Dane 134
Clark, Dick 126, 136, 168
Clark, Fred 155
Clark, Jim 109
Clark, Ken 16, 17, 179
Clarke, Gary 92
Clarke, Robert 15

Claudelle Inglish 155
Claydon, George 52
Clemens, Brian 57, 58
Clements, John 113
Coates, Phyllis 74, 94
Coco, James 169
Coelho, Susie 119
Coffy 40, 70, 72
Cohen, Herman 4, 5, 29, 82, 87, 88, 92, 94, 95, 96, 104, 188
Cohen, Larry 25, 83, 84
Cohen, Nat 88, 185
Colbert, Nicholas 19
Colchart, Thomas 19
Cole, Albert 97, 98
Cole, Dona 21
Cole, George 159
Coll, Julio 128
Colley, Don Pedro 148
Collier, Marian 133
Collins, Joan 52, 64, 65
Come Back to the Five and Dime Jimmy Dean 38
The Comedy of Terrors 40, 41, 130
Comin, Jacopo 179
Conklin, Chester 21
Conners, Chuck 88
Conners, Touch (Mike) 47, 68, 139, 148, 162
Connery, Sean 111, 112
Connor, Kevin 16, 105, 123
Conqueror Worm 41, 42, 118
Conrad, Jess 104
Conrad, Michael 138
Constantine and the Cross 165
Contino, Dick 46, 47
Conway, Gary 92, 93, 94, 95, 161
Conway, Russ 138
Conway, Tom 136, 140, 162
The Cool and the Crazy 8, 42, 43
Cooney, Ray 81
Coppola, Francis Ford 19, 20, 48, 154, 173
Coquilon, John 46, 170
Corbucci, Enzo 66
Corbucci, Sergio 79
Cord, Bill 140, 141
Corff, Robert 72, 73
Corman, Gene 16, 17, 117, 143
Corman, Roger 3, 4, 5, 14, 15, 16, 17, 19, 20, 21, 30, 31, 32, 33, 34, 35, 40, 47, 48, 51, 54, 63, 64, 66, 72, 73, 81, 82, 90, 91, 100, 101, 107, 108, 109, 110, 117, 118, 124, 125, 126, 129, 134, 137, 140, 141, 143, 144, 150, 151, 154, 157, 158, 160, 161, 167, 171, 172, 173, 178, 183
Corney, Norma 52
Cornwell, Judy 7, 166

Corrington, John William 32
Corrington, Joyce H. 32
Cort, Bud 72, 73
Cortesa, Valentina 66
Coscia, Marcello 26, 59
Cottafavi, Vittorio 79
Cotton, Joseph 9, 18, 19
Count Dracula 177, 178
Count Yorga Vampire 43, 44, 133
Countess Dracula 52
Country Joe and the Fish 73
Court, Hazel 104, 126, 129
Cousin, Pascal 145
Crabtree, Arthur 87
Craig, Ed 121
Craig, Yvonne 143, 181
Crain, William 27
Crawford, Broderick 79
Crawford, Joan 104
Creature of Destruction 181
The Crimson Cult 44, 45, 87
Cristophe, Francoise 65
Crosby, Bing 28
Crosby, Floyd 41, 68, 91, 135, 173
Crothers, Scatman 72
Crowley, Kathleen 67
Crudo, Aldo 149
Crudup, Carl 101
Crutchley, Rosalie 166
Cry of the Banshee 45, 46
Crypt of the Vampire see *Terror in the Crypt*
Culley, Zara 148
Cummings, Bob 20, 21
Cunningham, June 87
Curnow, Graham 87
Curse of Frankenstein 94, 95
Curse of the Aztec Mummy 175, 176
Curse of the Crimson Alter see *The Crimson Cult*
Curse of the Doll People 182
Curse of the Swamp Creature 181
Curtis, Dan 55
Cushing, Peter 16, 59, 109, 137, 159
Cycle Savages 46
The Cyclops 11, 165

Daddy "O" 46, 47
Dallamano, Massimo 59
Dalton, Abby 134, 160, 161
Dalton, Timothy 170
Daly, Tyne 13
The Damned 108, 109
Damon, Mark 25, 90, 91, 124, 172, 173
Danforth, Jim 79
Danieli, Emma 105
Danning, Sybil 112

Danova, Cesare 153
Dante, Michael 121
Danton, Ray 48
Dark, John 15, 105, 123
Dark Shadows 55
Darren, James 160
Darwell, Jane 75
Daughter of Dr. Jekyll 11
Davenport, Nigel 100
Davies, Rupert 41, 119
Davis, Ursula (Pier Anna Quaglia) 181
Dawson, Anthony (Antonio Margheriti) 173
Day of the Animals 141
Day the World Ended 3, 4, 8, 47, 48, 74, 104, 152, 181
Dean, James 54
De Angeles, Nato 52
Dearden, Basil 113
Death Line see *Raw Meat*
Deathmaster 48
DeBenning, Burr 96
De Blasio, G. (Virgilio De Blasi) 173
De Concini, Ennio 26, 66, 108
Dee, Sandra 63, 64
Deep Impact 113
De Felice, Lionello 79
De Feo, Francesco 141
De Kova, Frank 108, 151
De La Roche, Serge 162
De Laurentiis, Dino 80, 147, 155
Delon, Alan 145, 146
De Los Arcos, Luis 128
De Los Rios, Waldo 92
De Luca, Lorella 141
De Martino, Ferruccio 165
Dementia 13 8, 48, 49, 173
Demme, Jonathan 97
The Demon Planet see *Planet of the Vampires*
De Niro, Robert 30
Denning, Richard 47, 74
De Palma, Brian 7, 61, 62, 142, 143
De Paola, Alessio 37
DePego, Gerry 170
Deranged 48, 49
Derevitsky, Alexander 79
De Riso, Arpad 149
De Rita, Massimo 26, 65, 66, 162, 165
Dern, Bruce 30, 46, 97, 98, 126, 157, 167, 168
De Rouen, Reed 81
De Sabata, Eliana 66
De Sade 50, 51
De Santis, Gino 183
De Simone, Luigi 183
Destroy All Monsters 16, 51, 52, 77

The Devil Rides Out 37
Devil-Ship Pirates 55
The Devil Within Her 52
The Devil's 8 55
The Devil's Widow 52, 53, 54
Devlin, Don 121
Devon, Richard 108, 158, 160
Dexter, Maury 85, 113
Diary of a High School Bride 54
Dicken, Roger 105, 123
Dickerson, Beach 64, 134, 137, 152, 157
Dickinson, Angie 61
Dickson, Brenda 48
Die, Monster, Die 54, 55
Die Screaming Marianne 91
Dierkes, John 172
Differing, Anton 39, 105
Di Leo, Fernando 34
Dillinger 55, 56
Dillion, Robert 22, 115, 171
Di Masi, Francesco 80
Dinehart, Mason Alan, Jr. 133
Dinosaurus! 183
Di Paolo, Dante 66
Disney, Walt 121
Dobson, James 102
Dr. Goldfoot and the Bikini Machine 56, 57
Dr. Goldfoot and the Girl Bombs 57
Dr. Jekyll and Sister Hyde 44, 57, 58
Dr. No 163
Dr. Phibes Rises Again 58, 59
Domergue, Faith 183
Dominici, Arturo 26, 142, 180
Domino, Fats 139
Donaggio, Pino 62
Donahue, Troy 27, 28
Donati, Ermanno 136
Donlevy, Brian 93
Doqui, Robert 40
Doria, Enzo 153
Dorian Gray 59, 60
D'Orsi, Umberto 145
Douglas, John M. 34
Douglas, Sarah 123
Dow, R.A. 146
Downs, Cathy 10, 11, 124, 139, 140
Dracula A.D. 1972 54
Dracula Prince of Darkness 37
Dragonwyck 11, 157
Dragoti, Stanley 106
Dragstrip Girl 7, 60, 61, 114
Dreifuss, Arthur 189
Dressed to Kill 7, 61, 62
Dreyfuss, Richard 55
Dubov, Paul 139
Duff, Howard 183

Dufour, Val 158
Duggan, Cal 181
Dukes, David 169
Dullea, Keir 50, 51
Dumbrille, Douglass 139
Dumont, Margaret 139
Dunas, Ronald S. 9
Dunaway, Faye 31
Duncan, Kenne 15
Duncan, Pamela 158
Dunlap, Pamela 30
Dunn, Michael 115
The Dunwich Horror 63, 64
Duperey, Anny 145
Durant, Don 140, 141
Durning, Charles 143
D'Urville, Martin 25
Dwyer, Hilary 7, 41, 45, 119, 120, 170
Dynasty 65, 143
Dysart, Richard 112

Earth vs. the Flying Saucers 75
Earth vs. the Spider 8, 64, 69, 102
Eastwood, Clint 159
Easy Rider 167
Eddy, Duane 137
Eden, Mark 44
Edwards, George 72, 129, 183
Ekberg, Anita 141, 142
Eller, Harry 128
Ellerbe, Harry 90
Elliott, Sam 72
Elliott, William 40
Ellison, Bob 35
Elmes, Gary 170
Elvira 92
Emmet, Michael 16, 117
Empire of the Ants 64, 65
Endfield, Cy 50, 51
Endrigo, Sergio 34
English, Marla 135, 139, 140, 162
Erik the Conqueror 65
Estrada, Erik 38
Evans, Linda 20
Eve and the Handyman 121
An Evening with Edgar Allan Poe 178, 179
Evers, Herb (Jason) 33
The Evil Eye 65, 66
Ewing, Bill 48
The Exorcist 9, 12, 52, 141
The Eye Creatures 74, 181

Fabian 57, 67, 68, 87, 155, 189
Fahey, Myrna 90, 91
Fair, Jody 74
Fairman, Paul 98
The Fantastic Puppet People see *Attack of the Puppet People*
Farmer, Mimsy 190

Farmer, Suzan 54, 55
Farretta, Donato 151
Farrow, Mia 190
The Fast and the Furious 3, 66, 67, 68
Fehmiu, Bekim 108, 109
Feitshans, Buzz 55, 70
Felisatti, Massimo 116
Fellini, Federico 145, 146
Female Jungle 67
Fennell, Albert 36, 57
Ferrau, Arturo 179
Ferrer, Mel 118
Ferris, Paul 41, 42
Fiander, Lewis 59
Fiedler, John 48
Field, Sally Anne 87
Filer, Tom 21
Fine, Harry 159
Finley, Bill 142, 143
Fire Maidens from Outer Space 156
Fireball 500 67, 68
First Man into Space 97
Fisher, Michael 136
Fisher, Terence 89
Fiskin, Jeffrey Alladin 13
Five Easy Pieces 21
Five Guns West 3, 68, 69
Fleischer, Richard 65
Flicker, Ted 189
Fonda, Henry 111, 112, 153
Fonda, Jane 145
Fonda, Peter 145, 157, 158, 167, 168
Fondato, Marcello 25
The Food of the Gods 69, 70, 147
Ford, John 11
Ford, Ross 131
Forest, Mark 79, 179
Forest, Michael 161
Forever Amber 11
Forte, Vincent G. 18
Foster, Jody 106
Foster, Preston 155
Foster, Ronald 54
Fowler, Gene, Jr. 95, 96
Foxy Brown 40, 70, 71, 72, 141
Franchel, Dr. Emil 88
Francis, Derek 157
Francisci, Pietro 77
Franco, Jess 118, 147, 148, 160, 177, 178
Franco and Ciccio 57
Frank, Joanna 136
Frank, T.C. 31
Franken, Steve 156
Frankenstein Conquers the World 71
Franklin, Pamela 69
Franks, Chloe 167
Fraser, Sally 64, 100, 133, 164

Frazetta, Frank 124
Freda, Riccardo 136
Free, White and 21 181
Freeman, Dave 27
Freeman, Joel 106
Friday Foster 70, 71, 72
Frobe, Gert 27, 28
Frogs 72, 146
Frost, Alan 33
Frost, Lee 38, 155
Fry, Christopher 141
Fuchs, Gianni 79
Fuest, Robert 9, 58, 59, 170
Fujiki, Yu 76
Fujiyam, Yoko 16
Fukushima, Masami 175
Fulci, Lucio 34, 137
Fuller, Lance 14, 74, 75, 135, 136, 139, 162
Funicello, Annette 5, 20, 21, 22, 23, 24, 57, 67, 68, 93, 94, 115, 116, 121, 122, 143, 155, 189
Furnival, Robert 102
Fusco, Maria Pia 108

Galbo, Cristina 92
Galli, Ida 165
Ganley, Gail 29
Gardner, Ava 52, 53
Garland, Beverly 81, 100, 101
Garland, Richard 122, 158
Garrani, Ivo 26
Gas-s-s-s 72, 73
Gates, Tudor 159
Gavlin, Fredric 83
Gay, Ramon 175
Gaye, Lisa 139
Gaye, Marvin 38
Geisinger, Elliot 12
Gelfman, Samuel W. 96
Gemma, Giuliano 79
Genghis Khan 188, 189
Genn, Leo 118, 127, 128, 137
Gentilomo, Giacomo 80
Gerber, Ludwig 140, 141
Gerson, Jeanne 140, 141
Gessner, Nicholas 106
The Ghost in the Invisible Bikini 57, 73, 74
Ghost of Dragstrip Hollow 74, 98, 99
The Giant Claw 132
The Giant Leeches see *Attack of the Giant Leeches*
Gianviti, Roberto 70, 137
Gielgud, John 102
Giftos, Elaine 72, 73
Gilbert, Helen 74, 75
Gilchrist, Connie 107, 108
Giles, Sandra 46, 47
Gillen, Jeff 49

Gillespie, Dana 123
Gilliam, Terry 46
Gindes, Mark 106
Gingold, Hermione 28
Girdler, William 9, 141
The Girl Who Knew Too Much see *The Evil Eye*
Girls in Prison 8, 74
Girotti, Massimo 18
Glasser, Albert 161
Glindemann, Ib 102
Glory, Vittorio Musy 141
The Glory Stompers 75, 76
Glover, Julian 7
God Forgives ... I Don't 34
Godfrey, Derek 103
Godzilla vs. the Smog Monster 76
Godzilla vs. the Thing 76, 77
Gogol, Nikolai 26
Goldblatt, Harold 113
Golden Ivory see *White Huntress*
Goldman, Lawrence L. 160
Goldstein, William 9
Goliath and the Barbarians 77, 78
Goliath and the Dragon 79
Goliath and the Sins of Babylon 79
Goliath and the Vampires 79, 80, 81
Gone with the Wind 103
Gonzalez, Arturo 92
Gordon, Alex 3, 60, 61, 74, 102, 114, 115, 135, 136, 139, 147, 162
Gordon, Bert I. 10, 11, 17, 18, 64, 65, 69, 70, 147, 164, 165
Gordon, Claire 104
Gordon, Dorothy 91
Gordon, Keith 61
Gordon, Leo 16, 154
Gore, Leslie 143
Gorgo 104
The Gorgon 37
Gori, Lallo 34
Gorog, Laslo 64
Gorshin, Frank 60, 88, 98, 136
Gortner, Marjoe 69, 70
Gossett, Lou 101
Gothard, Michael 137, 166, 167
Gough, Michael 44, 87, 88, 104
Grant, Cy 16
Grant, Mary 179
Graves, Peter 100
Greci, Jose 79, 179, 180
Green, Joseph 33
Green, Pat 54, 157
Greene, Angela 117
Greenwood, Jack 82, 87
Grier, Pam 35, 36, 40, 70, 72, 137, 141, 148
Grier, Roosevelt (Rosey) 154, 155
Griffith, Charles B. 11, 34, 81, 101, 134, 158, 167

Griffith, D.W. 75
Griffith, Hugh 9, 46, 59, 166
Griffith, James 11
Grizzly 141
Grizzly Adams 38
Grove, R.L. 48
Guccione, Bob 108
Guerrini, Mino 66
Gumby 68
Gunslinger 68, 81, 158
Gurney, Robert, Jr. 98, 131
Gurney, Sharon 130
Guthrie, Lester D. 11

Hagen, Jean 122
Hagen, Ross 113
Haggerty, Dan 38
Hagopian, Berj 99
Haisman, Mervyn 44
Hall, Anthony Michael 35
Hall, Frank 15
Haller, Daniel 41, 54, 63, 91, 110, 126, 130, 163
Halsey, Brett 86, 147
Hama, Mia 165
Hamilton, George 106, 107
Hamilton, Joe 102
Hammack, Warren 181
Hammer 5, 28, 37, 44, 52, 54, 55, 57, 81, 88, 89, 90, 91, 94, 95, 105, 126, 128, 159, 160, 178, 181, 182
Hampton, Orville 71, 102, 189
The Hand 81
Hands of the Ripper 52
Hanley, Jenny 54
Hanna, Mark 10, 11, 81, 158
Hannibal 165
Hannibal, Mark 149
Hanson, Curtis Lee 63
Harman, David 134
Harrington, Curtis 118, 119, 129, 183
Harris, Julius W. 25, 83, 84
Harris, Robert H. 92, 93
Harrison, Richard 111
Harrison, Sandra 29
Hart, Susan 7, 8, 56, 73, 121, 163
Hartford, James 57
Hartley, Mariette 132, 133
Harvey, Marilyn 15
The Hatfields and the McCoys 189
Hatti, Hilo 149
Hatton, Raymond 98, 139
The Haunted House of Horror see *Horror House*
The Haunted Palace 82
Hawthorne, Nathaniel 170
Haworth, Jill 87
Hayden, Linda 109
Hayden, Nora 13, 14

Hayers, Sidney 36, 39
Hayes, Allison 81, 158
Hayes, Nora 134
Haynes, Michael Allen 38
Haze, Jonathan 14, 68, 81, 99, 100, 101, 134, 152, 154, 161, 172
The Head That Wouldn't Die see *The Brain That Wouldn't Die*
The Headless Ghost 82, 83
Healey, Myron 96, 97
Hedren, Tippi 38
Heffley, Wayne 147
Heinlein, Robert 33
Heinrich, Mimi 102, 131
Hell Raiders 181
Hell Riders (The Devil's Angels) 196
Hell Squad 83
Hell Up in Harlem 25, 83, 84
Hellman, Monte 154
Hellman, Oliver 153
Hello Dolly 19
Hell's Angels on Wheels 84, 85
Hell's Angels '69 85
Hell's Belles 85, 113
Help! 73
Helton, Percy 139
Hemric, Guy 24
Hemsley, Sherman 107
Henderson, Chuck 121
Henderson, Don 31
Hendry, Gloria 25, 83, 84
Henry, Mike 9
Hercules 77
Hercules Against the Mongols 179
Hercules and the Black Pirate 179
Hercules and the Masked Rider 180
Hercules and the Tyrants of Babylon 180, 181
Hercules in the Haunted World 65
Hercules Unchained 77
Herman, Norman 88
Herrmann, Bernard 143
Hershey, Barbara 32
Hessler, Gordon 45, 51, 115, 119, 120, 137
Heston, Charlton 102, 103, 106
Hewitt, David 155
Heyward, Louis M. "Deke" 9, 41, 44, 51, 57, 58, 73, 87, 115, 119, 121, 125, 137, 159, 163, 166, 170, 188
Heyward, Pat 166
Hickman, Dwayne 56, 93, 94, 143
High School Hellcats 86, 87, 115
Hill, Jack 33, 40, 70, 154
Hill, Jo Ann 151
Hill, Robert 141
Hilton, George 34
Hilton, Tony 81

Hingle, Pat 30
Hitchcock, Alfred 21, 48, 62, 90, 143
Hogan, Jack 31, 122, 123
Holbrook, Hal 168
Hole, William 74
Holloway, Sterling 139
Holm, Celeste 85
Holt, Seth 28
Honda, Ishiro 16, 51, 71, 76, 172, 175
Hoover, J. Edgar 56
Hopkins, Bo 153
Hopper, Dennis 76, 118, 119, 129, 157
Horror House 25, 87
Horror of Dracula 182
Horrors of the Black Museum 39, 74, 83, 87, 88, 92
Hoshi, Shinichi 175
Hoshi, Yuriko 76
Hot Rod Gang 74
Hot Rod Girl 88, 89
Houghland, Arnold 122
House of Fright 89, 90
House of Long Shadows 87
House of 1000 Dolls 90
House of Usher 5, 90, 91, 111, 115, 124
House of Wax 5, 128
House of Whipcord 91, 92
The House That Screamed 92
Hoven, Adrian 147, 148
How to Make a Monster 4, 8, 88, 92, 93
How to Stuff a Wild Bikini 93, 94
Howard, Sandy 100, 111
Howard, Trevor 112
Howell, Jean 66
Hoyt, John 17, 155, 172
Hua, Yueh 149
Hudson, John 138
Hudson, Vanda 39
Hudson, William 10, 138, 140
Hughes, Mary 22
Hull, Henry 110, 111
Hunnicutt, Gayle 168
Hunt, Ronald Leigh 81
Hunter, Bruce 19
Hunter, Tab 120, 163
Huntingdon, Lawrence 119
Huston, Anthony 181
Huston, John 50, 51, 152, 153
Hutch, Willie 71
Hutchison, Robert 72
Hyer, Martha 23, 90, 128, 188

I Don't Want to Be Born see *The Devil Within Her*
I Love Lucy 21

I Was a Teenage Frankenstein 5, 88, 92, 94, 95, 96
I Was a Teenage Werewolf 3, 5, 29, 88, 92, 95, 96
The Image 87
Imitation of Life 9
In the Year 2889 181
The Incredible Melting Man 96, 97
The Incredible Shrinking Man 11
The Incredible 2-Headed Transplant 76, 97, 98
Inescort, Freida 140
Infanti, Angelo 162, 163
Innocenzi, Carlo 77
Intolerance 75
The Invaders see *Erik the Conqueror*
Invasion of the Body Snatchers 64
Invasion of the Saucer Men 74, 98, 99, 136, 181
Invasion of the Star Creatures 34, 98, 99, 100
Ireland, John 66, 81
Irving, Penny 91
The Island of Dr. Moreau 100
The Island of Lost Souls 100
It Conquered the World 100, 101, 181
It Lives by Night see *The Bat People*
It's Alive 189
It's Alive (1967) 181
It's Alive (1974) 83
I've Lived Before 140
Ives, Burl 27, 28
Ivory, James 169

Jackson, Brad 160
Jackson, Freda 54, 55
Jackson, Sherry 113, 114
Jacoby, Scott 106
Jaffe, Sam 63
Jailbreakers 7
Jailhouse Rock 115
Jakob, Dennis 154
James, Elizabeth 31
Jameson, Jerry 19
Jameson, Joyce 41, 150
Jane Eyre 157
Jaws 153
J.D.'s Revenge 101, 102
The Jeffersons 107
Jeffrey, Peter 10, 59
Jeffries, Lionel 28, 166
Jekyll's Inferno see *House of Fright*
Jergens, Adele 11, 47, 74, 75, 135, 136
Jet Attack 102
Johns, Margo 104
Johnson, Arte 107
Johnson, Ben 55

Johnson, Candy 21, 121
Johnson, Ken 178
Johnson, Larry D. 148
Johnson, Richard 103
Johnson, Russell 134
Johnston, Alena 162, 163
Johnston, Margaret 36
Jones, Ceri 130
Jones, Christopher 168
Jones, Dick 42
Jones, Jennifer 169
Jones, Morgan 14
Jones-Moreland, Betsy 161
Jonson, Tom 33
Jordon, Nick (Aldo Canti) 149
Joseph, Jackie 148
Josephs, Wilfred 45
Journey to the Center of the Earth 163
Journey to the Seventh Planet 102
Jules, Maurice 138
Julius Caesar 102, 103, 104
Jung-kun, Chun 184

Kaiser, Burt 67
Kallis, Stanley 121, 133
Kandel, Aben 87, 88, 96, 104
Kantarian, Aram 118
Kanter, Jay 130
Karloff, Boris 24, 25, 26, 40, 44, 54, 55, 73, 82, 87, 129, 130, 154
Karr, Tom 49
Kasem, Casey 76, 97, 98
Katcher, Bruce 73
Katzman, Sam 189
Kaufman, Mark 106
Kaufman, Robert 56, 57, 143, 189
Kaufmann, Christine 115
Kawase, Hiroyuki 76
Kaye, Mary Ellen 135
Keaton, Buster 57, 93, 121
Keir, Andrew 28
Keith, Brian 112
Keith, Sheila 91
Kelljan, Bob 43, 84, 132, 138
Kelly, Patsy 74
Kelly, Tim 45, 148
Kemmer, Edward 64
Kemp, Valli 58, 59
Kendall, Suzy 127
Kennaway, James 113
Kennedy, Douglas 11, 31
Kenny, June 17, 18, 64, 144, 160
Kerr, John 124, 125
Kessler, Alice and Ellen 65
Key, Janet 52
Ki-duk, Kim 184
Kidder, Margot 12, 142, 143
Kieling, Wolfgang 90

Kilpatrick, Shirley 15
Kimbrough, Clint 30
Kimura, Toshie 76
Kincaid, Aron 57, 74, 181
King, Perry 169
King Dinosaur 11
King Kong (1976) 147, 155
King Kong vs. Godzilla 71
Kingsley, Martin 81
Kinski, Klaus 28, 128, 160, 177, 178
Kirk, Tommy 73, 74, 121, 181
Kiss Me Monster 148
Kitt, Eartha 72
Kneubuhl, John 138
Knight, Peter 44
Knight, Sandra 154
Kobayashi, Yukiko 51
Koenig, Laird 106
Koenig, Raymond 27, 137
Koizumi, Hiroshi 76
Komatsu, Sakyo 175
Konga 88, 104
Konopka, Magda 149
Kossoff, David 89
Kotto, Yaphet 72
Kovacs, Lazlo 84, 137
Kowalski, Bernard L. 16, 17, 117
Kozyr, Alexander 20
Kramarsky, David 21
Krisman, Nino 162
Kristen, Marta 20
Kruschen, Jack 13, 14, 131
Kubo, Akira 51, 172, 175
Kukla, Fran, and Ollie 131
Kwang-ho, Lee 184

Ladd, Alan, Jr. 52, 130
Ladd, Cheryl 38
Ladd, David 130
Ladd, Diane 167
Lagerfeld, Karl 148
Lain, Jewel 148
Lambert, Gavin 166
Lamont, Adele 33
Lamour, Dorothy 121
Lancaster, Burt 100
Lanchester, Elsa 121, 189
The Land That Time Forgot 105, 123
Landau, Martin 112
Landon, Michael 96, 97
Lane, G. Cornell 9
Lane, Jackie 183
Lane, Jocelyn 85
Langan, Glenn 10, 11, 164
Langtry, Kenneth 82, 88, 92, 94
Lansing, Robert 64
Lanza, Anthony N. 75, 76, 97
LaSalle, Richard 156
Lasko, Ed 121, 133

Lasser, Louise 165
The Last Man on Earth 105, 106
The Last Picture Show 55
Laugh In 107
Laughlin, Tom 31, 32
Laughton, Charles 100
Laverne and Shirley 73
Lavi, Daliah 27, 28
Lawrence, Joel 133
Lawrence, John 75, 76, 97
Lawrence, Maggie 151
Lawson, Linda 118, 119
Lawson, Richard 148
Leachman, Cloris 55
Lean, David 168
Lee, Bill 142
Lee, Christopher 44, 89, 103, 118, 119, 120, 127, 128, 130, 131, 137, 177, 178, 181
Lee, Cosette 49
Lee, Joanna 33
Lee, Margaret 59, 118, 129, 160
LeFanu, J. Sheridan 181, 182
The Legend of Hell House 7
Legrand, Michel 170
Leiber, Fritz 37
Leicester, William 105
Leigh, Janet 48
Leith, Virginia 33
Lembeck, Harvey 57, 68, 74, 116, 121, 139, 189
Lemoine, Michel 147
Leon, Valerie 28
Leone, Alfredo 18
Leone, Sergio 141
Lester, Mark 166, 167
Lester, Richard 73
Levine, Joseph E. 77
Levison, Ken 109
Lewis, Fiona 58, 59
Lewis, Jack 11
Lewis, Louise 29
Libel 89
Lieberman, Leo 143
The Life and Times of Judge Roy Bean 55
Life with Father 115
Liljedaul, Marie 59, 60
Lime, Yvonne 86, 96
Lincoln, Henry 44
Line, Helga 180
Lippert, Robert L. 105
Litel, John 135, 136
The Little Girl Who Lives Down the Lane 106
The Little Shop of Horrors (1960) 34, 148
Litto, George 61
Lizard in a Woman's Skin see Schizoid
Lloyd, James 31, 32

Loder, Kataherine 70
Lom, Herbert 59, 115, 177, 178
London, Barbara 38
Longo, Malisa 149
Loren, Donna 155
Loren, Sophia 165
Lorenson, Livio 77, 79, 180
Lorre, Peter 40, 116, 129, 130, 140, 150, 189
The Lost World (1960) 163
The Lost World of Sinbad 165
Love at First Bite 106, 107
Lovecraft, H.P. 44, 54, 63, 82
The Loves of Count Iorga see Count Yorga, Vampire
The Lovin' Spoonful 165
Lowell, Mark and Jan 54, 86
Lucisano, Fulvio 57, 125
Luckwell, Bill 81
Lugosi, Bela 182
Lulli, Fulco 142
Lulli, Piero 179, 180
Lumley, Joanna 54
Lund, Art 25, 35
Lund, Jana 86
Lund, John 68
Lupino, Ida 69, 70, 183
Lupo, Michele 79
Lupus, Peter see Stevens, Rock
Lynch, Kenny 122
Lynde, Paul 20
Lynley, Carol 87
Lyon, Richard 82

Mabuchi, Kaoru 51, 71, 76
Macaulay, Charles 27
Machine Gun Kelly 107, 108
Maciste Against the Vampire see Goliath and the Vampires
Maciste in the Court of the Grand Khan see Samson and the 7 Miracles of the World
Maciste the Greatest Hero in the World see Goliath and the Sins of Babylon
Macready, George 133
Macready, Michael 43, 132, 133
Mad Dog Time 168
Madame Kitty 108, 109
Madden, Jimmie 133
Madden, Lee 13, 85
Madhouse 109
Mafei, Livio 34
Magee, Patrick 48, 110, 173
Mahoney, Jock 76
Maiuri, Dino 162
Majors, Lee 119
Make Room for Daddy 114
Malden, Karl 111, 112
Malfatti, Marina 116
Malle, Louis 145, 146

Malone, Dorothy 20, 21, 66, 68
Man Eater of Hydra 92
The Man from Planet X 11
Man from U.N.C.L.E. 152
Manasse, George 146
Manfred Mann 160
Mangini, Gino 77
Mangione, Giuseppe 141
The Manitou 141
Mankowitz, Wolf 89
Mann, Barry 168
Mann, Stanley 52, 111
Manni, Ettore 165, 180
Mannix 48
Mansfield, Jayne 67
Manson, Charles 133
Marandi, Evi 125
March, Joseph Moncure 169
Marchal, Georges 141, 142
Marcus, Peter (Gerry Levy) 87
Margheriti, Antonio see Dawson, Anthony
Marin, Luciano 183
Marinuzzi, Gino, Jr. 126
Mark, Michael 17
Mark of the Devil 87
Markham, Barbara 91
Marks, Arthur 35, 71, 101
Marks, Walter 169
Marlowe, Scott 42, 96
Marly, Florence 129
Mars Needs Women 181
Marsh, Mae 75
Marshall, Darrah 151
Marshall, Don 155
Marshall, Penny 137
Marshall, Tony 96
Marshall, William 9, 27, 137
Martin, Al 98
Martin, Bill 144
Martin, Skip 128
Martino, Luciano 179, 180
Martino, Sergio 148
Martinson, Leslie 88
Marvin, Lee 134
Maryjane 114
Mask of Satan see Black Sunday
Maslansky, Paul 130, 148
Mason, Buddy 99
Mason, D'Urville 141
Mason, Pamela 168
The Masque of the Red Death 109, 110
Massacre Time see The Brute and the Beast
Massey, Anna 51
Massie, Paul 89
Master of the World 6, 110, 111
Matango see Attack of the Mushroom People
Matheson, Richard 36, 40, 50,

51, 90, 105, 106, 110, 124, 129, 150, 188
Maude, Mary 92
Mauer, Norman 13
Max, Jerome 153
Maxwell, Frank 82
Maxwell, Len 165
Maxwell, Paul 147
McAndrew, Marianne 19
McBain, Diane 113, 114, 155
McCann, Henry 74
McClure, Doug 16, 105, 123
McCormack, Patty 113, 114
McCowan, George 72
McCrea, Jody 20, 76, 121
McDonald, Michael 35
McDowall, Roddy 52, 53, 54
McEnery, John 105
McGee, Vonetta 27
McGillvray, David 91
McGreevey, John 88
McMullen, R.G. 85
McNair, Barbara 160
McShane, Ian 52, 53
Mean Streets 33
Meeker, Ralph 69, 70
Melchior, Ib 13, 102, 125, 131, 155, 156
Melvin Purvis G-Man 55
Mendez, Fernando 182
Merchant, Ishmail 169
Mercier, Michele 25, 26
Meredith, Judy 129
Merrifield, David 141
Merrow, Jane 87
Meteor 111, 112, 113
Meyer, Eve 121
Meyer, Richard C. 128
Meyer, Russ 19, 121
Michelle, Anne 91
Mikashi, Tatsuya 165
Milius, John 55
Milland, Ray 72, 122, 126, 154, 155, 171, 172
Miller, Arnold L. 41
Miller, Dick 11, 14, 34, 35, 81, 101, 108, 134, 143, 144, 154, 157, 158, 172
Miller, Kenny 17
Miller, Thomas (Camillo Mastrocinque) 181
The Million Eyes of Su-Muru 90
Milner, Dan 4, 124
Milner, Jack 4, 124
Milton, Ernest 37
The Mind Benders 113
Minelli, Liza 32
Mini-Skirt Mob 85, 113, 114
Miraglia, Emilio P. 116, 117
Miranda, Isa 59
Miranda, Soledad 128, 177

The Misadventures of Merlin Jones 121
Misiano, Fortunato 179, 180, 181
Missile to the Moon 156
Mission Impossible 181
Mr. Adams and Eve 183
Mitchell, Cameron 65
Mitchell, Don 138
Mitchell, Laurie 17
Mitchell, Steve 147
Mizuno, Kumi 71, 175
Moessinger, David 46
Moffa, Paolo 80
Mohr, Gerald 13, 14
Molla, Jose 137
Monlaur, Yvonne 39
Monroe, Marilyn 67
Monster from the Ocean Floor 66
Monster of Terror see *Die Monster Die*
Montego, Carmen 182
Montell, Lisa 140, 141
Montgomery, Elizabeth 93
Montoya, Alice 182
Moon, Kang 184
Moorcock, Michael 105
Moore, Juanita 9
Morand, Leonard 129
Morell, Andre 103
Morris, Barboura 34, 35, 51, 64, 108, 134, 143, 144, 152, 157, 172
Morris, Chester 139, 140
Morrison, Greg 109
Morton, John 122
Moss, Stewart 19
Motorcycle Gang 8, 61, 114, 115
Mower, Patrick 45
Moxey, John 127
Muir, Gavin 118
Muller, Paul 178
Mulligan, William 181
Munro, Caroline 10, 16, 52, 58
The Munsters 98
Murders in the Rue Morgue 115
Murphy, Bridey 140, 158
Murphy, Jimmy 122
Murphy, Michael 43
Murray, Jan 155
Murray, K. Gordon 177, 182
Muscle Beach Party 115, 116, 180
My Darling Clementine 11

Naar, Joseph T. 12, 138
Nader, George 90, 143
Nader, Mike 68, 143
Nakamuru, Tadao 165
Nakamuru, Tetsu 172
Naked Africa 166
Naked Paradise 141

The Naked You Die see *The Young, the Evil and the Savage*
Nason, Richard W. 5
Neame, Ronald 111, 112
Neibel, David 38
Nelson, Edwin (Ed) 33, 34, 99, 117, 134, 152
Nelson, Lori 47, 88, 89
Neri, Rosalba 179
Nero, Franco 34
Neumann, Dorothy 74, 153, 154, 158
Newlands, Anthony 127
Ney, Richard 126
Neyland, Anne 114, 115
Nicholas, Denise 27
Nicholls, Anthony 36
Nicholson, Jack 12, 84, 85, 96, 126, 127, 129, 153, 154, 157
Nicholson, James H. 3, 4, 5, 6, 7, 8, 20, 21, 22, 40, 50, 56, 57, 63, 67, 68, 73, 79, 88, 91, 93, 96, 98, 100, 110, 115, 120, 121, 124, 126, 132, 139, 151, 152, 166, 168, 170, 181, 188, 189
Nicol, Alex 30, 138, 139
Nicolai, Bruno 118
Nicolosi, Roberto 26, 27, 65, 66
Niebo Zowiet see *Battle Beyond the Sun*
The Night Evelyn Came Out of the Grave 116, 117
Night of the Blood Beast 17, 117, 118
Night of the Blood Monster 28, 118
Night of the Demon 37
Night of the Eagle see *Burn Witch Burn*
Night of the Living Dead 106
Night Tide 49, 118, 119
Nimoy, Leonard 33
Niven, David 107
Noel, Chris 76
The Norseman 119
North, Edmund H. 111
North, Virginia 21, 129
Not of This Earth 21, 129
Novarese, Vittorio Nino 66

Oates, Warren 55
The Oblong Box 119, 120
Obon, Ramon 182
O'Brien, Willis 71
Odium, John 66
Ogawa, Ei 172
Ogilvy, Ian 41, 87, 170
The Oklahoma Woman 68
Old Dracula 107
Olivier, Laurence 166
O'Mara, Kate 159

212   Index

The Omega Man 106
The Omen 12
One Million B.C. 152
One Million Years B.C. 105
O'Neill, Barboura see Morris, Barboura
Operation Bikini 120, 121
Operation Dames 121
Orgolini, Harold 111
Ormsby, Alan 49
Orr, Pat 49
Osborn, David 166
Ottosen, Carl 102, 131
Owen, Beverly 98

Pace, Ronald 164
Paget, Debra 82, 139, 150
Pajama Party 121
Pal, George 111, 188
Palance, Jack 38
Pallonttini, Riccardo 34
Palmara, Mimmo 79, 142, 180
Palmer, Edward 19
Palmer, Lili 50, 92, 115
Paluzzi, Luciana 115, 116
Panic in Year Zero 122
Paolella, Domenico 179, 180
Papazian, Robert A. 40
Paratroop Command 122, 123
Parkin, Dean 164
Parkyn, Leslie 36, 39
Parrish 155
Parrish, Julie 67, 68
Parvin, Theodore 111
Pataki, Michael 19
Patterson, Melody 46
Patton, Bart 48
Pearcy, Patricia 146, 147
Pee-Wee's Playhouse 27
Penafiel, Luis Verna 92
Penhaligon, Susan 105
The People That Time Forgot 105, 123, 124
Perkins, Millie 168
Perreau, Gigi 42
Perry, Ed 19
Perry, Roger 43, 132, 133
Persson, Essy 45
Persson, Gene 64
Peters, Donald 30
Peters, Scott 17
Peterson, Paul 181
Pettyjohn, Angelique 85
Peyton Place 155
The Phantom from 10,000 Leagues 4, 11, 66, 124
The Phantom Planet 8
Phillips, Michelle 55
Piazzi, Achille 79
Piccolo, Marco 79
Pickett, Bobby "Boris" 38

Pierce, Charles B. 119
Pierotti, Piero 65, 165, 180
Pierreux, Jacqueline 26
Pink, Sidney 13, 14, 102, 128, 131, 132
The Pit and the Pendulum 49, 124, 125, 172
Pitt, Ingrid 159
Pittorru, Fabio 116
Place, Lou 46
Plan 9 from Outer Space 100
Planet of Blood see Queen of Blood
Planet of the Apes 100
Planet of the Vampires 125, 126, 129
Planeta Burg 129, 183
The Platters 134
Pleasence, Donald 39, 52, 130
Poe, Edgar Allan 5, 41, 45, 73, 82, 90, 91, 109, 110, 115, 124, 126, 129, 144, 145, 150, 154, 157, 163, 171, 179
Pollard, Michael J. 168
Pollard, Snub 66
Pomilia, Aldo 183
Portillo, Rafael 175
The Poseidon Adventure 111, 112
Powell, Arla 19
Prehistoric World see Teenage Caveman
The Premature Burial 126, 172
Premis, Barry 32
Prendes, Luis 128
Presley, Elvis 60, 115
Pressman, Edward R. 142
Price, Dennis 28, 87, 160
Price, Stanley 52
Price, Vincent 5, 6, 9, 10, 21, 24, 40, 41, 45, 56, 57, 58, 82, 90, 91, 105, 109, 110, 111, 119, 120, 124, 125, 126, 128, 129, 130, 137, 150, 157, 163, 178, 179, 188
Priest, Pat 97, 98
Pringle, Joan 101
Prosperi, Franco 66
Provine, Dorothy 31
Pryor, Richard 168
Psych-Out 126, 127
Psycho 48, 49
Psycho-Circus 127, 128, 183
Pupa, Piccola 74
The Puppet Masters 33
Pyne, Natasha 109
Pyro 128, 129

Q the Winged Serpent 83
Quarry, Robert 43, 44, 48, 58, 59, 109, 132, 133, 148
Queen of Blood 129, 183
Quinn, Dermot 166

Rabin, Jack 161
Rafkin, Alan 143
Raksin, David 119
Ramrus, Al 100
Randone, Salvo 145
Rasputin the Mad Monk 37
Rasulala, Thalmus 27, 35, 72
Rathbone, Basil 40, 74, 129, 150, 183
The Raven 40, 41, 129, 130, 154
Raw Meat 130, 131
Ray, Aldo 13, 189
Ray, Anita 139
Ray, Frankie 99
Rea, Mabel 147
Rebar, Alex 96, 97
Rebecca 157
The Red Queen Kills 7 Times 117
Redlin, William 155
Reed, Dolores 99
Reefer Madness 42
Reeves, Michael 41, 42, 119, 120.188
Reeves, Steve 77, 78, 79
Reform School Girl 8, 131
Reid, Beryl 59
Reid, Milton 59, 123
Relph, Michael 113
Remberg, Erika 39
Rennie, Michael 173
Reptilicus 102, 128, 131, 132
The Return of Count Yorga 132, 133
Revill, Clive 82
Reynaud, Janine 147, 148
Rhoden, Elmer C., Jr. 42, 46
Richardson, John 26
Richardson, Ralph 166
Rickles, Don 23, 115, 116, 121, 171
Rigg, Diana 103
Riot on Sunset Strip 189, 190
Roadracers 8, 133
Roarke, Adam 72, 84, 85, 127, 136
Robards, Jason 102, 103, 115
Robbins, Harold 109
Robertson, Dale 55
Robertson-Justice, James 145
Robinson, Chris 46, 54
Robles, German 182
Robot Monster 100
The Robot vs. the Aztec Mummy 175, 176, 183
Rock All Night 134, 135
Roeg, Nicholas 110
Rogers, Charles "Buddy" 86
Rohm, Maria 59, 90, 118, 160, 177
Roman, Leticia 66

Rome Against Rome see War of the Zombies
Rooney, Mickey 93, 189
Rooney, Tim 189
Rose, David 82
Rose, Louisa 143
Rose, Mickey 165
Rosemary's Baby 52
Rosenbaum, Henry 63
Rosenberg, Max J. 16, 96, 97, 105, 109, 123, 137
Rosenberg, Stewart 12
Ross, Rosalind 136
Rossi, Giorgio Carlo 149
Rossi-Stuart, Giacomo 105, 116
Rossini, Renato (Red Ross, Howard Ross) 179
Ruffo, Eleonora 79, 80
Run, Angel, Run 38
Runaway Daughters 8, 135, 136
Rush, Richard 84, 126, 136, 155
Rusoff, Lou 4, 14, 20, 37, 47, 60, 74, 100, 101, 114, 120, 122, 124, 135, 139, 147, 148
Russell, Jane 32
Russell, Ray 126, 171
Ryan's Daughter 168

Sachs, William 96, 97
Sadoff, Fred 48
Sahara, Kenji 16, 51, 172, 175
Saint James, Susan 106, 107
Saland, Ronald 12
Salazar, Abel 182
Salazar, Alfredo 175
Salkow, Sidney 105
Salkowitz, Sy 155
Salmi, Albert 64
Salon Kitty see *Madame Kitty*
Salt, Jennifer 143
Salvi, Emimmo 77
Samson, Edward 66
Samson and the Mighty Challenge 179
Samson and the 7 Miracles of the World 136
Sandor, Steve 85
Sands, Anita 54
Sanford, Isabel 107
Sangster, Jimmy 166
Saperstein, Henry G. 71, 165
Sapphire 89
Sarafian, Richard C. 42
Sargent, Richard (Dick) 21
Sarno, Antonio 116
Sartarelli, Marcello 165
Sasdy, Peter 52
The Savage Seven 136, 137
Savoy, Teresa Ann 108
Saxon, John 66, 129
Saxon, Peter 137

Sbragia, Giancarlo 183
Scardamaglia, Elio 79
Scardamaglia, Francesco 79
Scardino, Don 146, 147
Scharf, Sabrina 84, 85
Schell, Maria 118
Schick, Elliot 148
Schizoid 137
Schmidt, Kendall 41, 42, 44, 126
Schwartz, Bernard 35
Scorsese, Martin 32, 33, 53
Scott, Alex 10
Scott, Gordon 80, 136
Scott, Lizabeth 46
Scott, Peter Graham 82
Scott, Ridley 125
Scream and Scream Again 137, 138
Scream Blacula Scream 138
The Screaming Skull 8, 54, 138, 139
The Search for Bridey Murphy 140
Sebastian, John see Harrington, Curtis
Sekizawa, Shinichi 16
Serandrei, Mario 26
Sergeant Deadhead 93
Sernas, Jacques 80, 141, 142
Serrador, Narciso, Ibanez 92
The Seven Minutes 19
The Seventh Seal 110
77 Sunset Strip 131
Sewell, George 87
Sewell, Vernon 44
Shake, Rattle and Rock 8, 139
Shaner, John Herman 100
Shannin, Mark 183
Shaughnessy, Alfred 37
Shaw, Lou 19
Shawlee, Joan 168
Shawn, Dick 106, 107
Shay, John 133
She 105
The She-Creature 8, 11, 74, 139, 140, 152, 181
She Gods of Shark Reef 140, 141
Shear, Barry 168
Sheba Baby 70, 141
Sheen, Martin 106
Sheldon, David 141
Shelley, Barbara 37
Shepard, Jan 16
Shepherd, Elizabeth 157
Sheptner, Stan 31, 122, 123
Sherman, Bobby 168
Sherman, Gary 130
Shibamoto, Toshio 76
Shindig 57
The Shining 12
Shire, Talia 73
Sidney, Suzanne 86, 115
Sign of the Gladiator 136, 141, 142

Siloksky, Ronald 63
Sim, Gerald 58, 59
Simms, Jay 122
Simon, Melvin 106
Simonelli, John (Giovanni) 173
Sinatra, Nancy 20, 74, 167, 168
Sirk, Douglas 9, 68
Sisters 61, 142, 143
Six, Eva 120
Ski Party 143
Slate, Jeremy 31, 85, 113
Slesar, Henry 115
Smith, Alexis 106
Smith, Herbert 37
Smith, John 88, 89
Smith, Madeline 54
Smith, Maurice 46
Smith, Rainbeaux 97
Smith, Sally 173
Smith, Will 106
Smith, William 38
Smyrner, Anne 90, 102, 131, 132
Snell, Peter 102
Sodom and Gomorrah 180
Sohl, Jerry 54, 71
Solomon, Joe 38, 84
Some Like It Hot 143
Sommer, Elke 18
The Sonny and Cher Show 38
Sorel, Jean 137
Sorority Girl 7, 143, 144
Sottane, Liliane 82
South Pacific 17
Space Amoeba see *Yog—Monster from Space*
Spain, Fay 60, 61
Speed, Carol 9
The Spider see *Earth vs. the Spider*
Spier, William 52
Spina, Maria Grazia 179
Spina, Sergio 183
Spirits of the Dead 144, 145, 146
Squirm 146, 147
Stahl, C. Ray 166
Stamp, Terence 145, 146
Stanton, Harry Dean 55
Stanwyck, Barbara 38
A Star Is Born 13
Stark, Graham 28
Stark, Shelley 188
Starkes, Jaison 101
Steel, Alan 179, 180
Steele, Barbara 26, 44, 124
Steffen, Anthony 116
Steiger, Rod 12
Stein, Ronald 14, 82, 101, 102, 126, 129, 151, 183
Stein, Sandor 12
Steiner, John 108
Stell, William (Guillermo) Calderon 175

Steloff, Skip 100
Sten, Anna 135, 136
Stephan, Susan 166
The Sterile Cuckoo 32
Stern, Tom 85
Sterns, Michael 38
Stevens, Rock (Peter Lupus) 116, 180
Stewart, Andy 19
Stewart, Gregg 83
Stockwell, Dean 63, 126
Stoker, Austin 9
Stoker, Bram 28, 177, 178
Stoloff, Victor 141
Stone, Harold J. 171
Stone, James 68
Stoumen, Louis Clyde 121
Strasberg, Susan 126, 127, 157
Streisand, Barbra 13
Stresa, Nino 77
Strindberg, Anita 137
Strock, Herbert L. 29, 92, 94
Stroud, Don 12, 13, 30
The Stud 65
Sturgess, Olive 129
Style, Michael 159
Styner, Jerry 24
Submarine Seahawk 147
Subotsky, Milton 16, 105, 109, 137
Succubus 147, 148
Sugar Hill 148
Suicide Battalion 83, 148, 149, 181
Sullivan, Barry 125, 128
Sullivan, Jean 146
Summers, Jeremy 90
Sun, Sabine 162, 163
Sunset Strip 189
Super Stooges vs. the Wonder Women 149, 150
Sutherland, Donald 33
Swanson, Logan (Richard Matheson) 105
Swerdlaff, Arthur 133
Switzer, Carl 115, 116

Tafarel, Giuseppe 77
Tait, Don 38, 85
Takarada, Akira 76
Takashima, Tadao 16, 71
Tales of Terror 129, 150
Tanaka, Fumio 172
Tanaka, Tomoyuki 16, 51, 71, 76, 172, 175
Tani, Yoko 136
Taniguchi, Senkichi 165
Tank Commandos 151
Tanner, Larry 181
Tarlton, Alan 166
Taste the Blood of Dracula 52
Taurog, Norman 56

Taylor, Delores 32
Taylor, Don 100
Taylor, Jack 147
Taylor, Joan 14, 15, 74, 75
Taylor, Kent 124
Tayman, Robert 91
Tazaki, Jun 16
Tea and Sympathy 115
Teege, Joachim 28
Teenage Caveman 8, 118, 151, 152
Temple-Smith, John 100
Tenser, Tony 87
Tentacles 152, 153
Terrell, Steve 60, 61, 98, 114, 115, 136
The Terror 153, 154
Terror in the Crypt 8, 181, 182
Terror of the Barbarians see *Goliath and the Barbarians*
Terry-Thomas 28, 59
Tessari, Duccio 80, 136
Thayer, Lorna 21
Thellung, Francesco 141
Theodora, Slave Empress 79
The Thing with Two Heads 98, 154, 155
Thom, Robert 30, 168
Thomas, Danny 114
Thomas, Derek (Peter Bogdanovich) 183
Thomas, Peter 72
Thompson, Bertha 32
Thor, Larry 71
Thornton, Ralph 29, 88, 95
Those Fantastic Flying Fools see *Blast-Off*
Those Magnificent Men in Their Flying Machines 27
Three Faces of Fear see *Black Sabbath*
Three in the Attic 168
Thulin, Ingrid 108, 109
Thunder Alley 114, 155
Thunderball 163
Thyssen, Greta 102
Tierney, Lawrence 67
Tigon 41, 44, 87
Tilly, Kevin 123
Tilly, Patrick 170
The Time Machine 111
The Time Travelers 155, 156
Tobolowsky, Edwin 181
Todd, Richard 59
Toho 16, 51, 71, 76, 165, 172, 175
Tomb of Ligeia 157
Tomerlin, John 120
Tomlinson, David 163
Topper, Burt 54, 67, 83, 151, 155
Torn Curtain 90
Torres, Joan 27, 137

The Torture Chamber of Baron Blood see *Baron Blood*
Totter, Audrey 102
Tourneur, Jacques 40, 163, 164, 188
Towers, Harry Alan 27, 28, 59, 90, 118, 127, 128, 160, 177, 188
Towne, Robert 157
Townsend, Leo 20, 22, 67, 93
Tranche, Andre 137
Trans-American Films 46, 108, 147, 148, 160, 197
Travolta, John 169
Tremayne, Les 13, 14
The Trial of Billy Jack 32
Triesault, Ivan 11
The Trip 35, 157, 158
Trog 104
Tsuchiya, Yoshio 71, 172
Turley, Jack 64
Turman, Glynn 101
Turner, Joe 139
20 Million Miles to Earth 75
The Two Faces of Dr. Jekyll see *House of Fright*
Two Nights with Cleopatra 165
2001: A Space Odyssey 50

Ullman, Elwood 56, 73
Ulmer, Edgar G. 11
Ulus, Betty 126
The Undead 158, 159
Ure, Mary 113
Urquhart, Gordon 33
Urquhart, Robert 166
Usher, Gary 21

The Vampire 182, 183
The Vampire Lovers 133, 159, 160, 181
Vampirella 160
The Vampire's Coffin 182, 183
Van Ark, Joan 72
Van Cleef, Lee 100, 101
van der Vlis, Diane 171
Van Doren, Mamie 183
Van Dyke, Conny 85
Van Haren, Chuck 121
Vargas, Daniele 145
Vari, Giuseppe 165
Varno, Martin 117, 118
Varsi, Diane 30, 155, 168
Vaughn, Robert 103, 151, 152
Veitch, Anthony Scott 118
The Vengeance of Hercules see *Goliath and the Dragon*
Venus in Furs 160
Vereen, Ben 72, 73
Verne Jules 28, 110
VeSota, Bruno 33, 46, 66, 67, 81, 99, 100, 134, 158

Vickers, Yvette 16, 17, 131
Victor, Gloria 46, 99
Viking Women and the Sea Serpent 152, 160, 161
The Vikings 65
Village of the Giants 69
Villiers, James 28
Visconti, Luchino 109
Von Richtofen and Brown 73
Voodoo Woman 162
Voss, V.I. 162
Voyage to the Planet of Prehistoric Women 183
Voyage to the Prehistoric Planet 129, 183

Waddilove, Philip 41
Wait Until Dark 163
Wakabayshi, Akiko 165
Walcott, Gregory 102
Wald, Malvin 160
Walden, Ralph 30
Walk on the Wild Side 38
Walker, Pete 91
Walker, Robert, Jr. 136
Walley, Deborah 20, 57, 73, 74, 143
Walsh, Edward 132
Walters, Thorley 123
War Goddess 162, 163
War Gods of Babylon 183, 184
War Gods of the Deep 163, 164
War Italian Style 57
War of the Colossal Beast 11, 164, 165
War of the Gargantuas 71
War of the Zombies 165
Ward, Skip 133
Warner, Robert 49
Warren, Gene 111
Warwick, Gina 87
Waters, Ed 143
Waters, John 34, 43
Wattis, Richard 52
Wayne, Patrick 123
Webber, Peggy 138, 139
Webster, Mary 110
Weil, Cynthia 168
Weird Woman 37
Weis, Don 73, 121

Welbeck, Peter (Harry Alan Towers) 27, 90, 127, 177
Welch, David 178
Welch, Raquel 169
Welles, Mel 134, 158
Wellman, William, Jr. 31
Wells, Dolores 23
Wells, H.G. 64, 69, 100, 188
Welter, Ariadna 182
Wertham, Dr. Fredric 5
Westbrook, John 157
Wetherell, Virginia 44
Whalen, Michael 124
What's the Matter with Helen? 166
What's Up Tiger Lily? 165
When Dinosaurs Ruled the Earth 105
When the Sleeper Wakes 188
Where Eagles Dare 159
Whitaker, David 138
White, James Gordon 76, 85, 97, 98, 113, 155
White, Jesse 122
White Huntress 166
Whiton, James 9
Whittaker, David 163
Whittaker, Stephen 38
Who Slew Auntie Roo? 166, 167
Wicking, Christopher 28, 45, 115, 119, 137
The Wild Angels 167, 168
Wild in the Streets 168, 169
The Wild Party 169, 170
The Wild, Weird World of Dr. Goldfoot 57
Wildaker, Paul 132
Wilde, Cornel 119
Wilde, Oscar 59
Wilde, Wendy 54
Wilder, Yvonne 132
Willett, E. Hunter 126
Williams, Cindy 73
Williams, John 47
Williams, Rhoda 86
Williamson, Alister 120
Williamson, Fred 25, 35, 36, 83, 84
Willis, Marlene 17, 18
Willoughby, George 163

Wilson, Bryna 165
Wilson, Earl 20
Winchell, Walter 168
The Wind and the Lion 56
Winston, Stan 19
Winters, Shelley 30, 31, 152, 153, 166, 167, 168
Wintle, Julian 36, 39
Witchfinder General see *Conqueror Worm*
Witney, William 31, 42, 110, 122, 123
Wonder, Stevie 116
Wood, Ed 15
Wood, Natalie 112
Woolner, Lawrence 173
World Without End 156
Written on the Wind 68
Wuthering Heights 7, 170
Wyngarde, Peter 36, 37
Wynn, Keenan 23
Wynter, Mark 87

"X" the Man with the X-Ray Eyes 171, 172

Yamauchi, Akira 76
Yanni, Rossana 162
Yaru, Marina 145
Yashiro, Miki 175
Yates, George Worthing 17, 64, 164
Yog—Monster from Space 172
Yongary: Monster from the Deep 184
Yoon-seong, Seo 184
York, Michael 100
Young, Terence 162, 163
Young, Tony 38
The Young Racers 172, 173
The Young, the Evil and the Savage 173
Young-il, Oh 184

Zapponi, Bernardo 145, 146
Zenteno, Raul 182
Zontar the Thing from Venus 181
Zounds, Archibald, Jr. 79
Zulu 50

www.ingramcontent.com/pod-product-compliance
Lightning Source LLC
Chambersburg PA
CBHW060259240426
43661CB00060B/2842